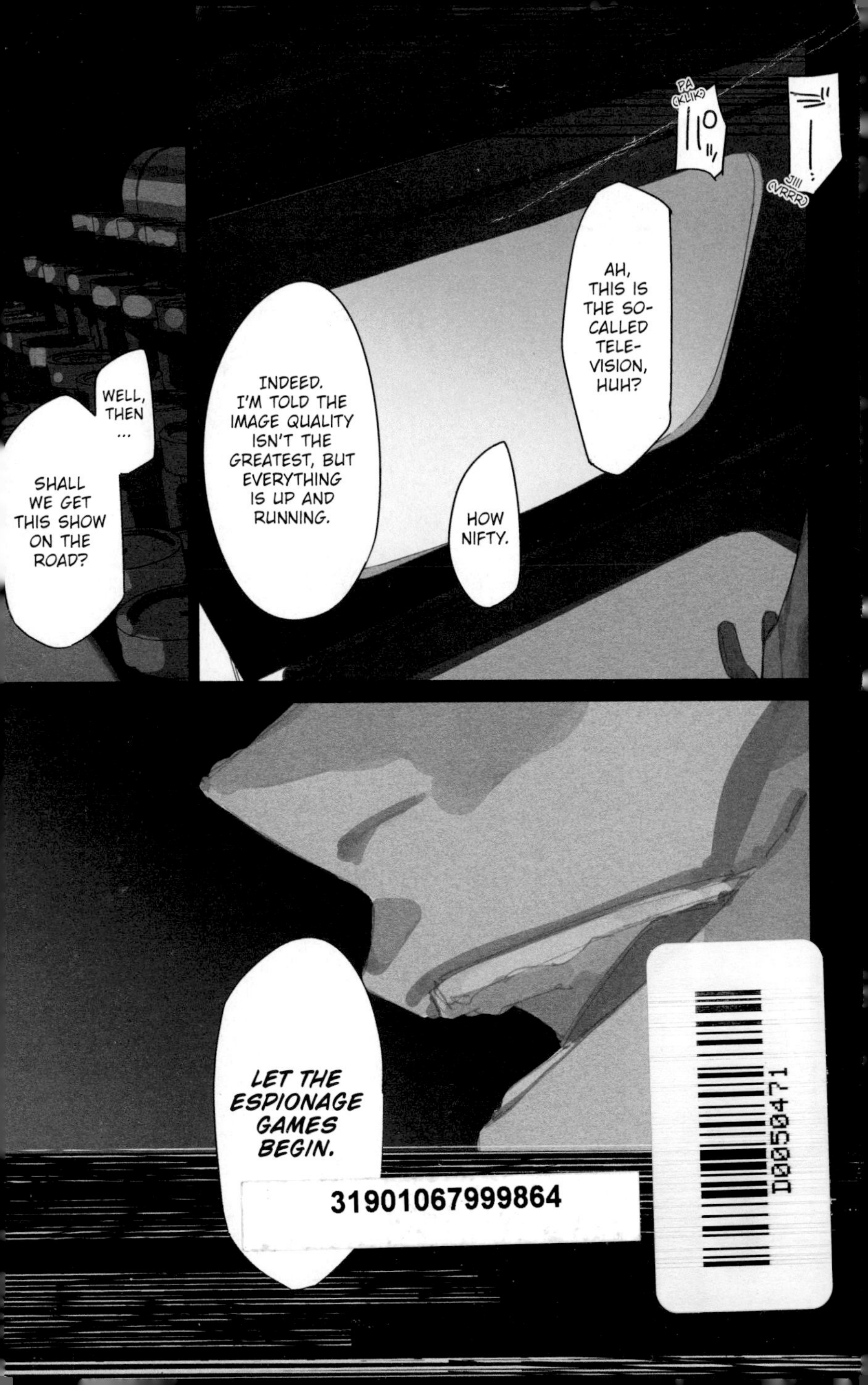
JIII (VRRR)
PA (KLIK)
AH, THIS IS THE SO-CALLED TELE-VISION, HUH?
INDEED. I'M TOLD THE IMAGE QUALITY ISN'T THE GREATEST, BUT EVERYTHING IS UP AND RUNNING.
HOW NIFTY.
WELL, THEN...
SHALL WE GET THIS SHOW ON THE ROAD?
LET THE ESPIONAGE GAMES BEGIN.

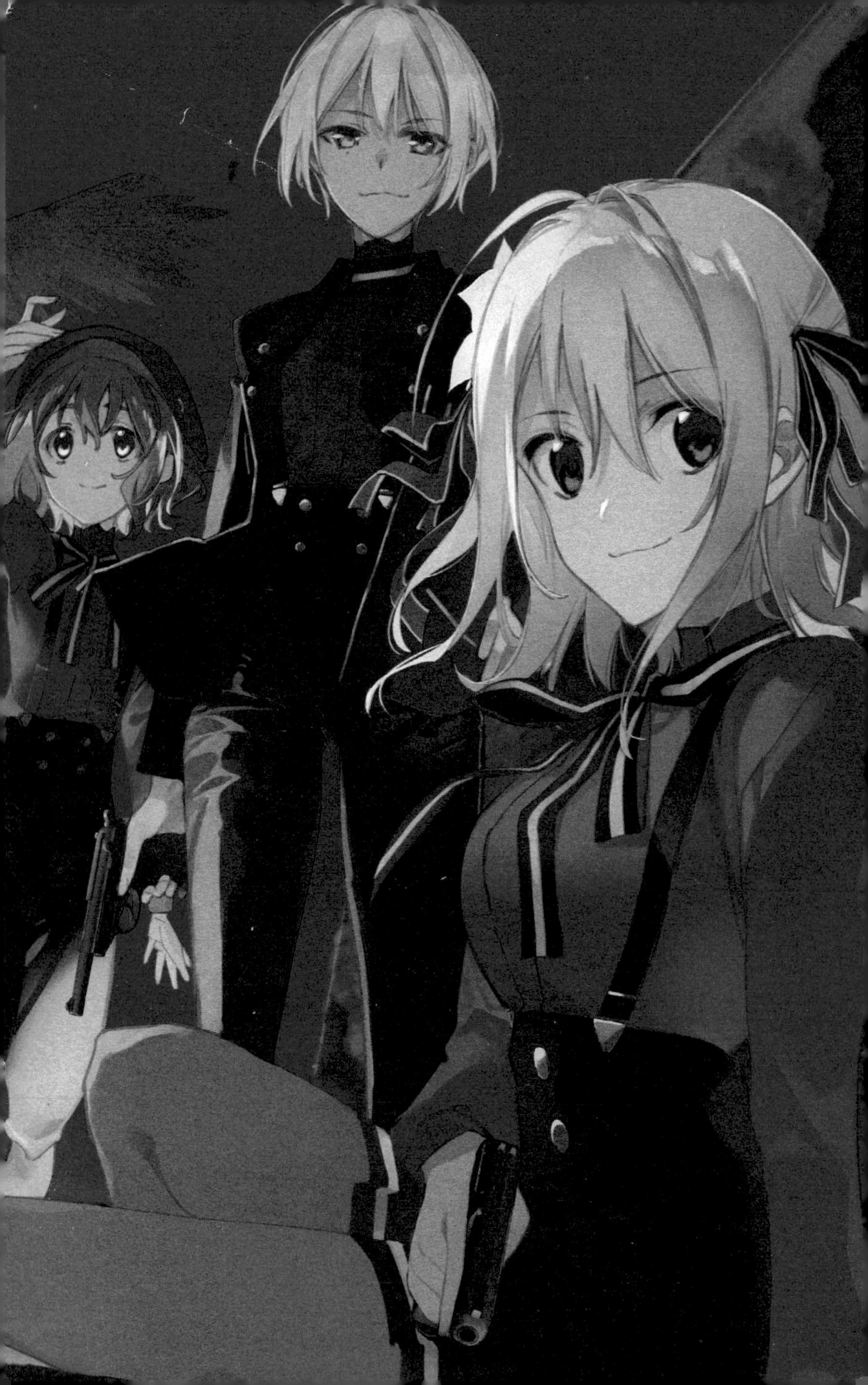

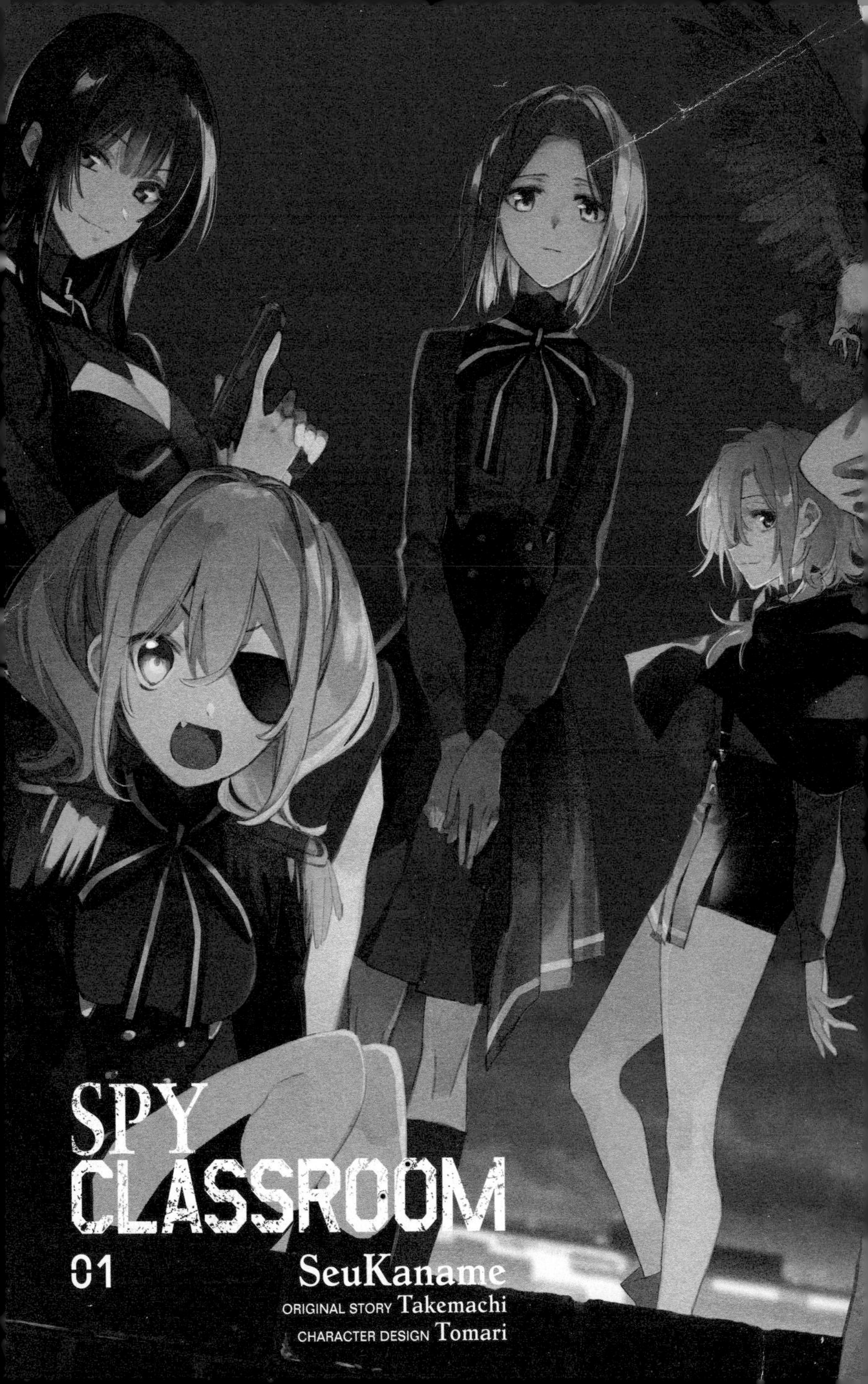

# SPY CLASSROOM

01

SeuKaname

ORIGINAL STORY Takemachi

CHARACTER DESIGN Tomari

# CONTENTS

SPY CLASSROOM
Specialized lessons for an Impossible Mission
Code name Flower Garden

# Chapter 1

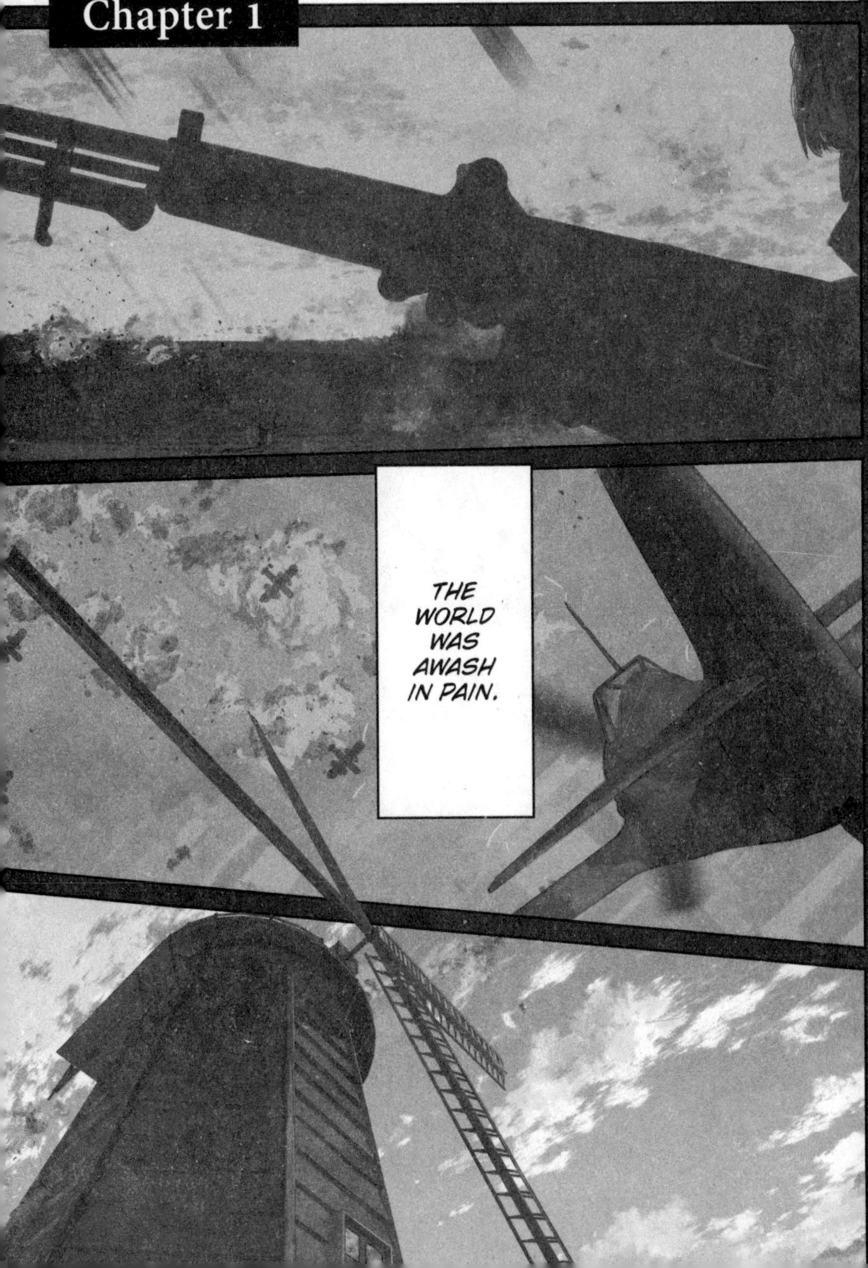
THE WORLD WAS AWASH IN PAIN.

THE LARGEST WAR IN HUMAN HISTORY, KNOWN AS THE GREAT WAR...

...HAD LEFT THE NATIONS OF THE WORLD SCARRED.

THE ADVANCED WEAPONRY OF THE NEW ERA HAD CLAIMED TOO MANY LIVES.

POLITICIANS CAME TO THE REALIZATION—

WAR WAS INEFFICIENT.

THAT MARKED THE END...

...OF THE ERA WHERE GUNS WERE WIELDED OUT IN THE OPEN.

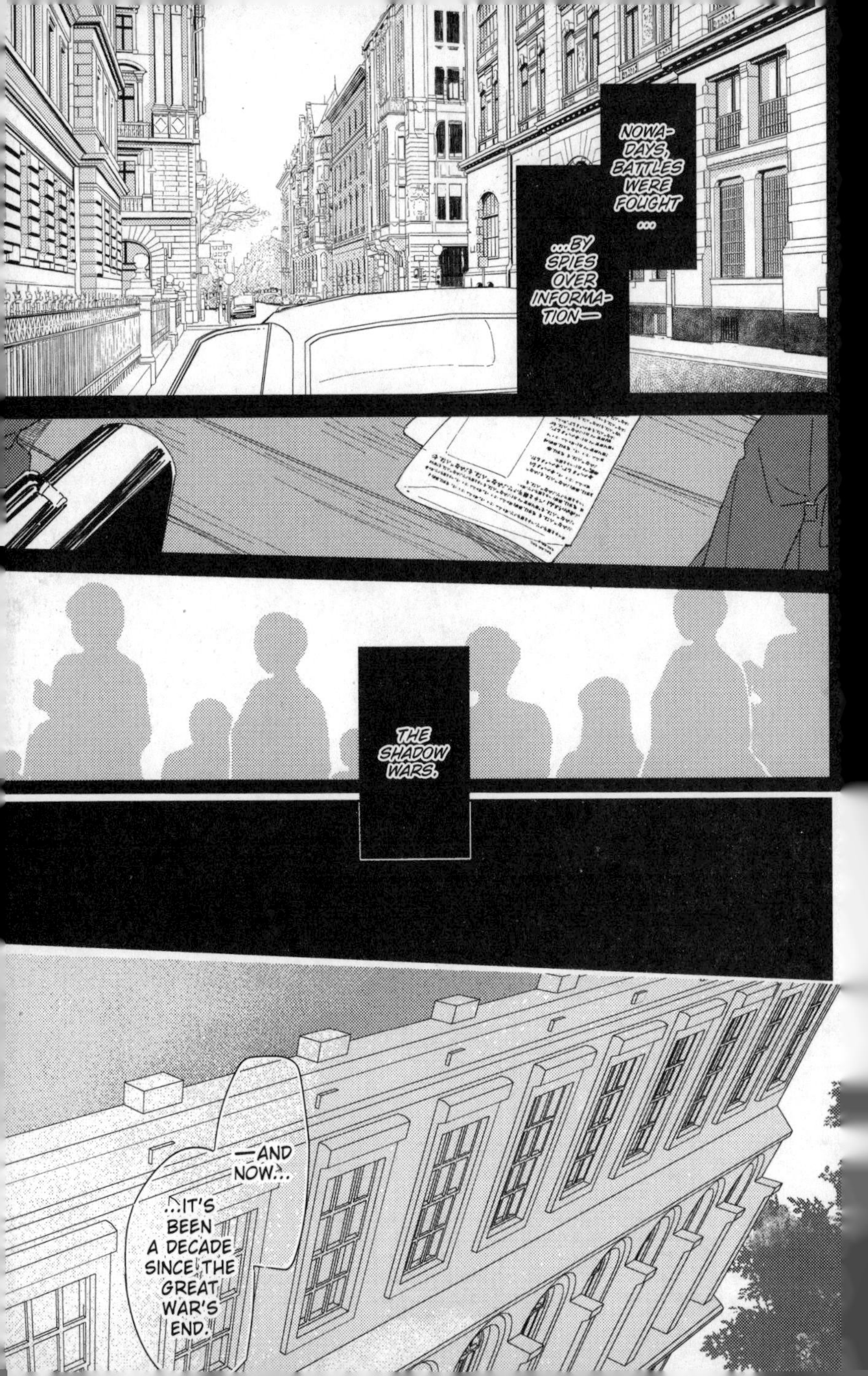
NOWA-DAYS, BATTLES WERE FOUGHT...
...BY SPIES OVER INFORMA-TION—
THE SHADOW WARS.
—AND NOW...
...IT'S BEEN A DECADE SINCE THE GREAT WAR'S END.

# Chapter 1 — Assembly

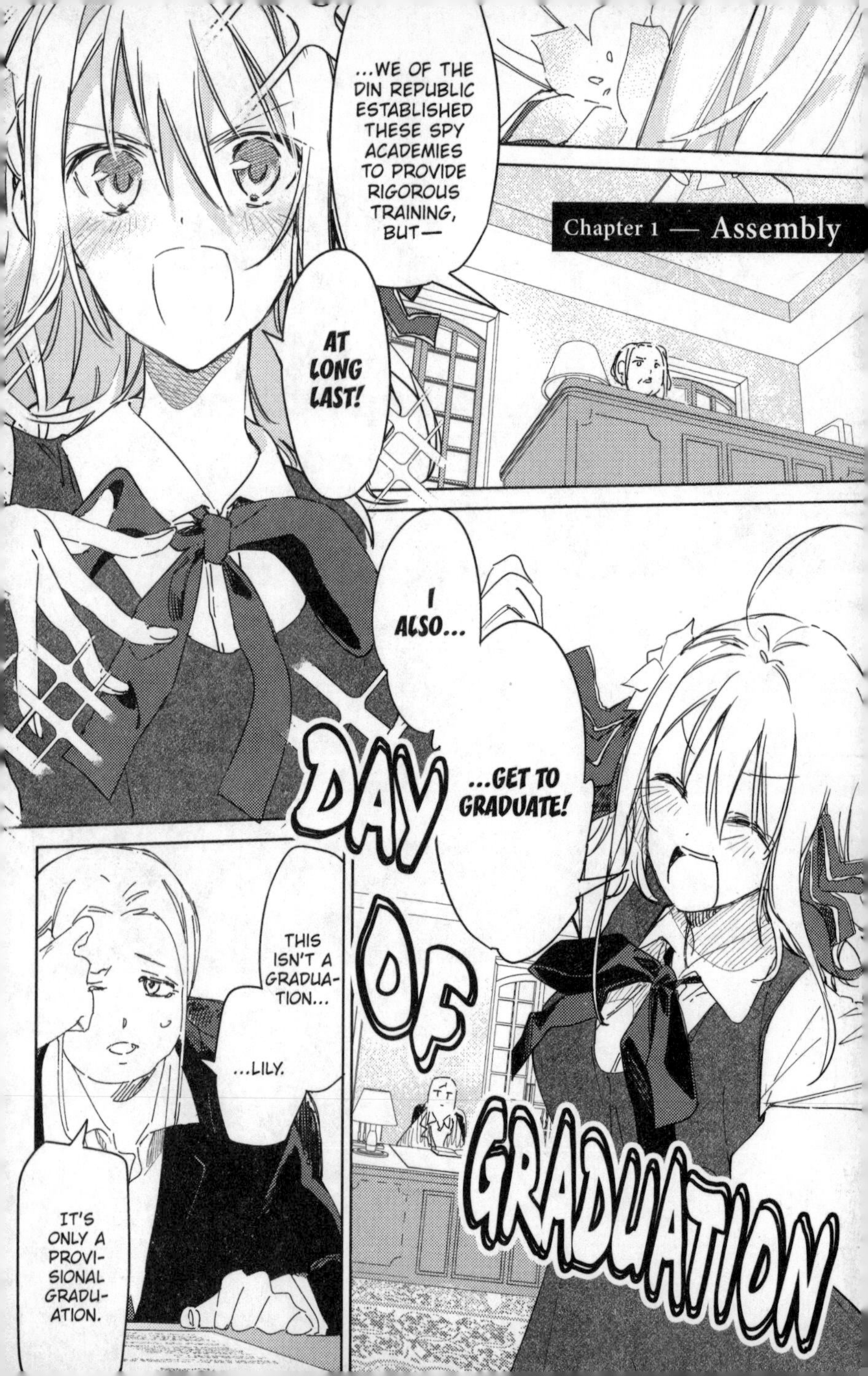
...WE OF THE DIN REPUBLIC ESTABLISHED THESE SPY ACADEMIES TO PROVIDE RIGOROUS TRAINING, BUT—
AT LONG LAST!
I ALSO...
...GET TO GRADUATE!
DAY OF GRADUATION
THIS ISN'T A GRADUATION...
...LILY.
IT'S ONLY A PROVISIONAL GRADUATION.

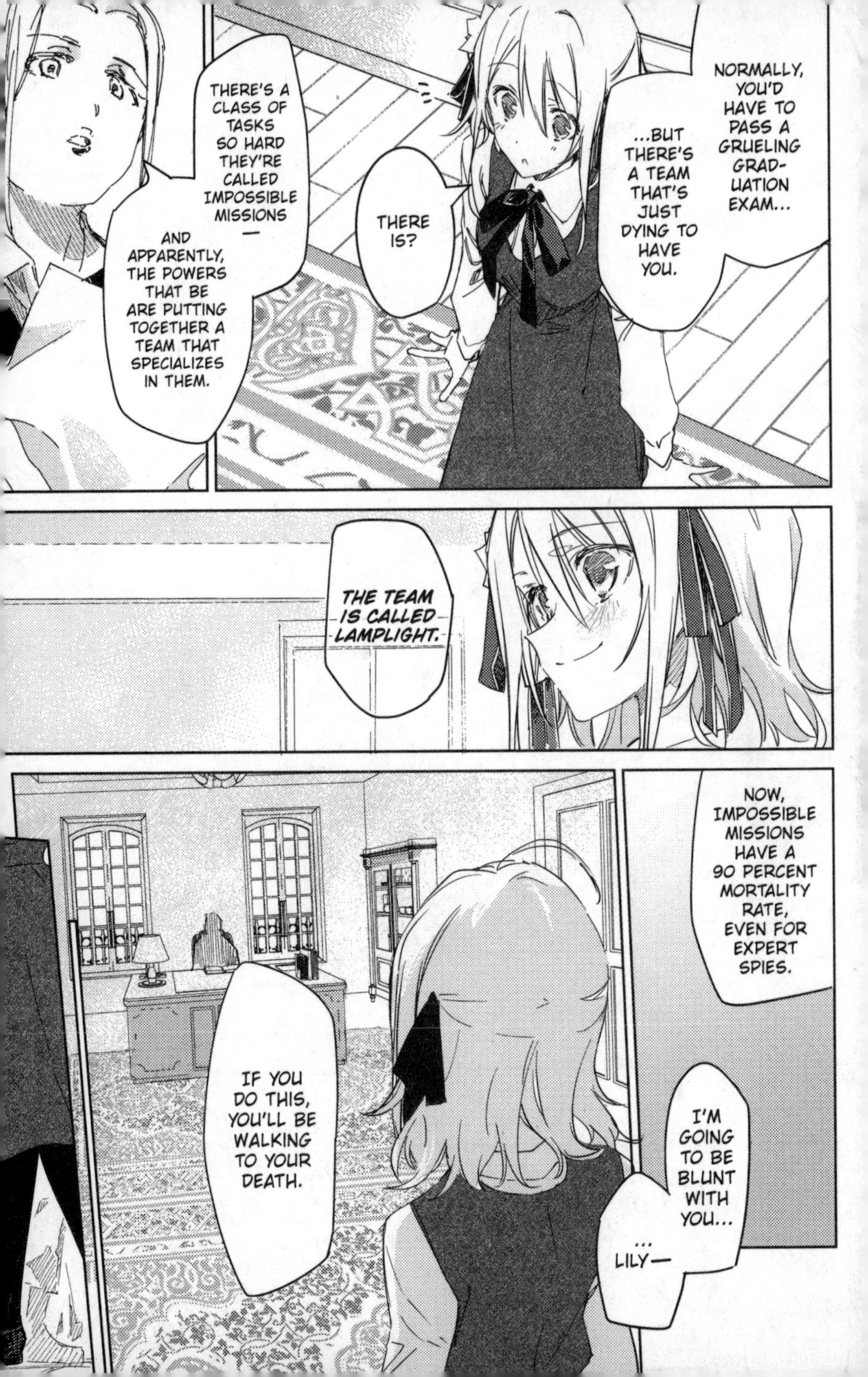
NORMALLY, YOU'D HAVE TO PASS A GRUELING GRAD-UATION EXAM...
...BUT THERE'S A TEAM THAT'S JUST DYING TO HAVE YOU.
THERE IS?
THERE'S A CLASS OF TASKS SO HARD THEY'RE CALLED IMPOSSIBLE MISSIONS—
AND APPARENTLY, THE POWERS THAT BE ARE PUTTING TOGETHER A TEAM THAT SPECIALIZES IN THEM.
THE TEAM IS CALLED LAMPLIGHT.
NOW, IMPOSSIBLE MISSIONS HAVE A 90 PERCENT MORTALITY RATE, EVEN FOR EXPERT SPIES.
I'M GOING TO BE BLUNT WITH YOU...
...LILY—
IF YOU DO THIS, YOU'LL BE WALKING TO YOUR DEATH.

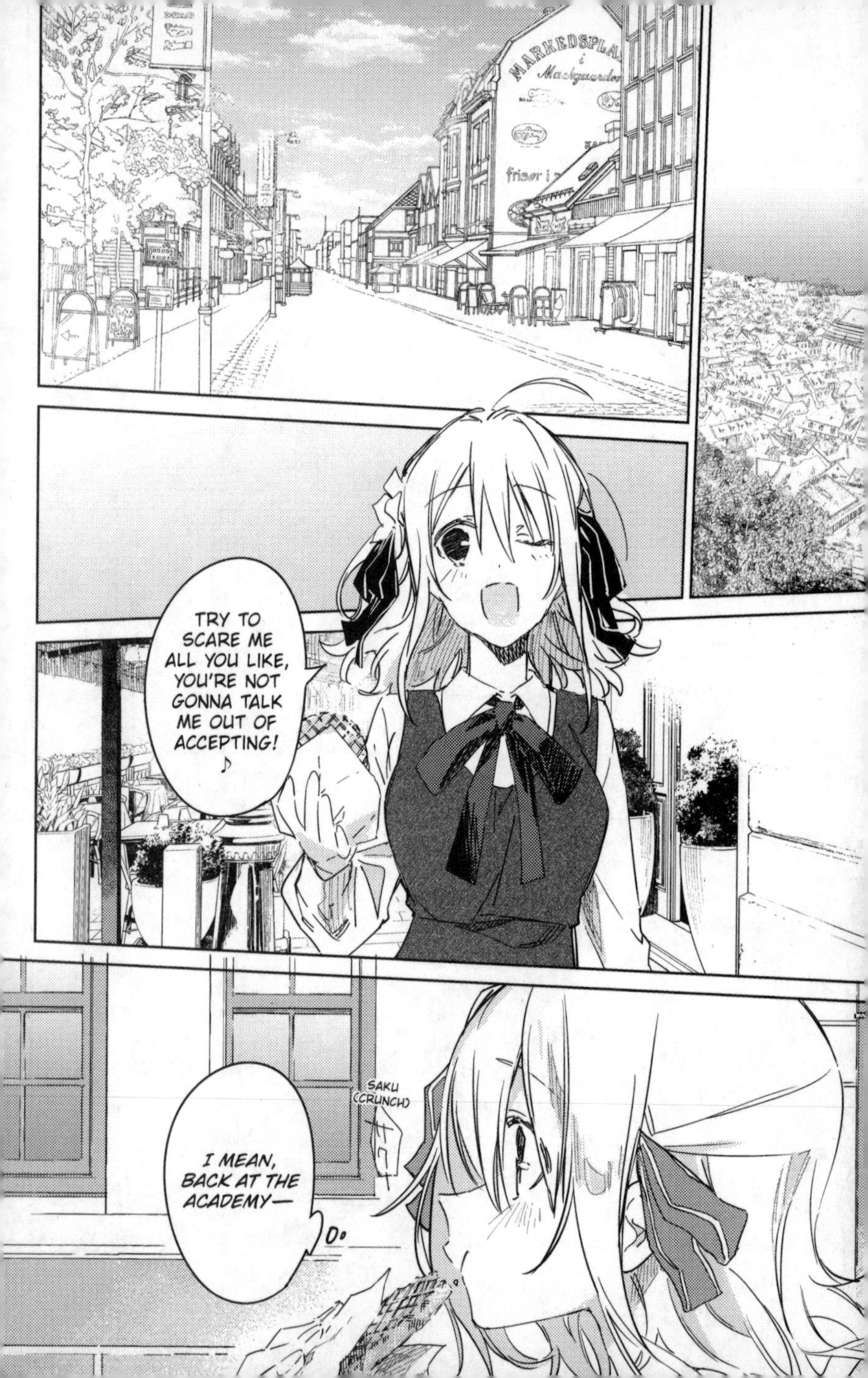
TRY TO SCARE ME ALL YOU LIKE, YOU'RE NOT GONNA TALK ME OUT OF ACCEPTING! ♪
SAKU (CRUNCH)
I MEAN, BACK AT THE ACADEMY—

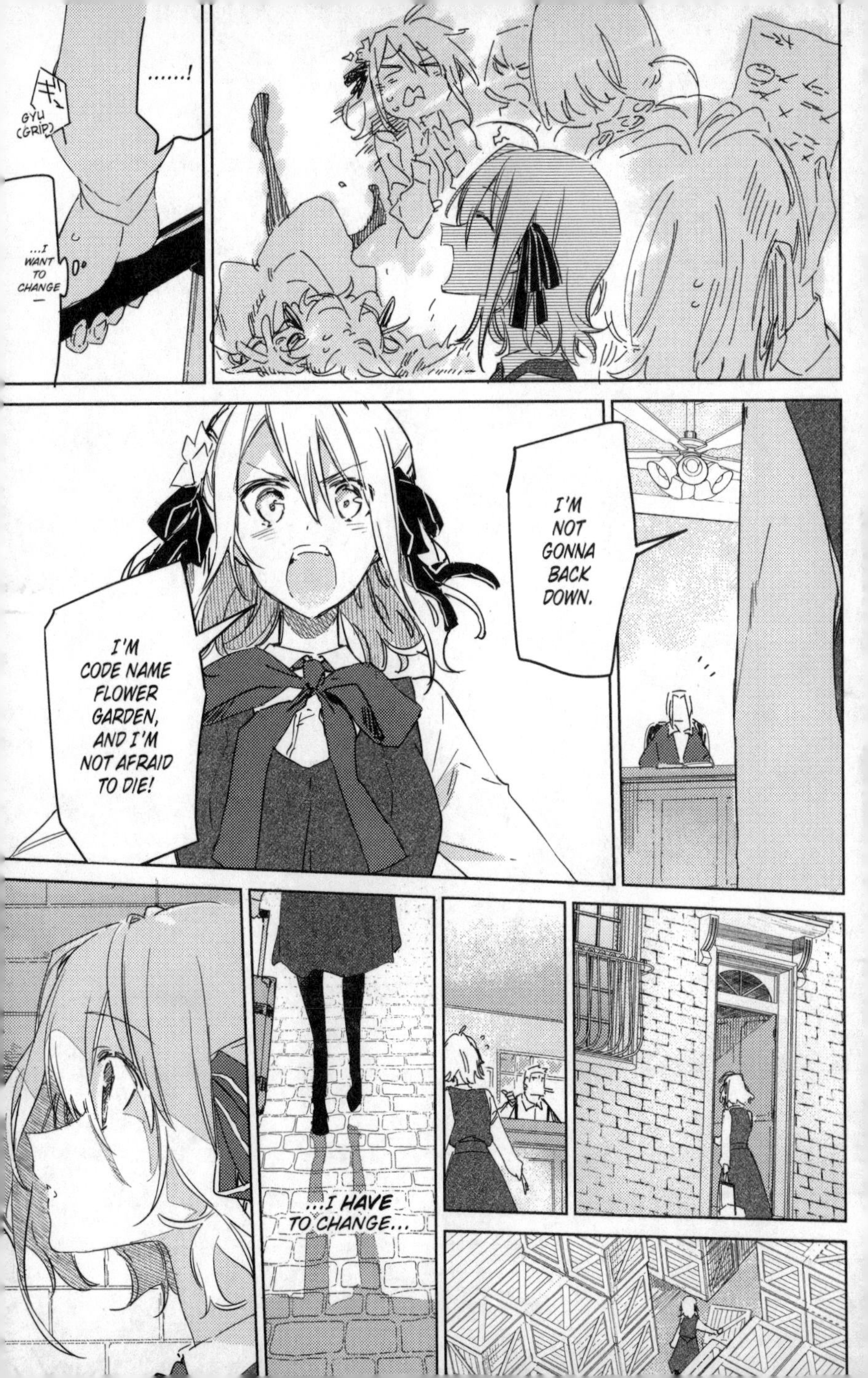
......!
GYU (GRIP)
...I WANT TO CHANGE—
I'M NOT GONNA BACK DOWN.
...
I'M CODE NAME FLOWER GARDEN, AND I'M NOT AFRAID TO DIE!
...I HAVE TO CHANGE...

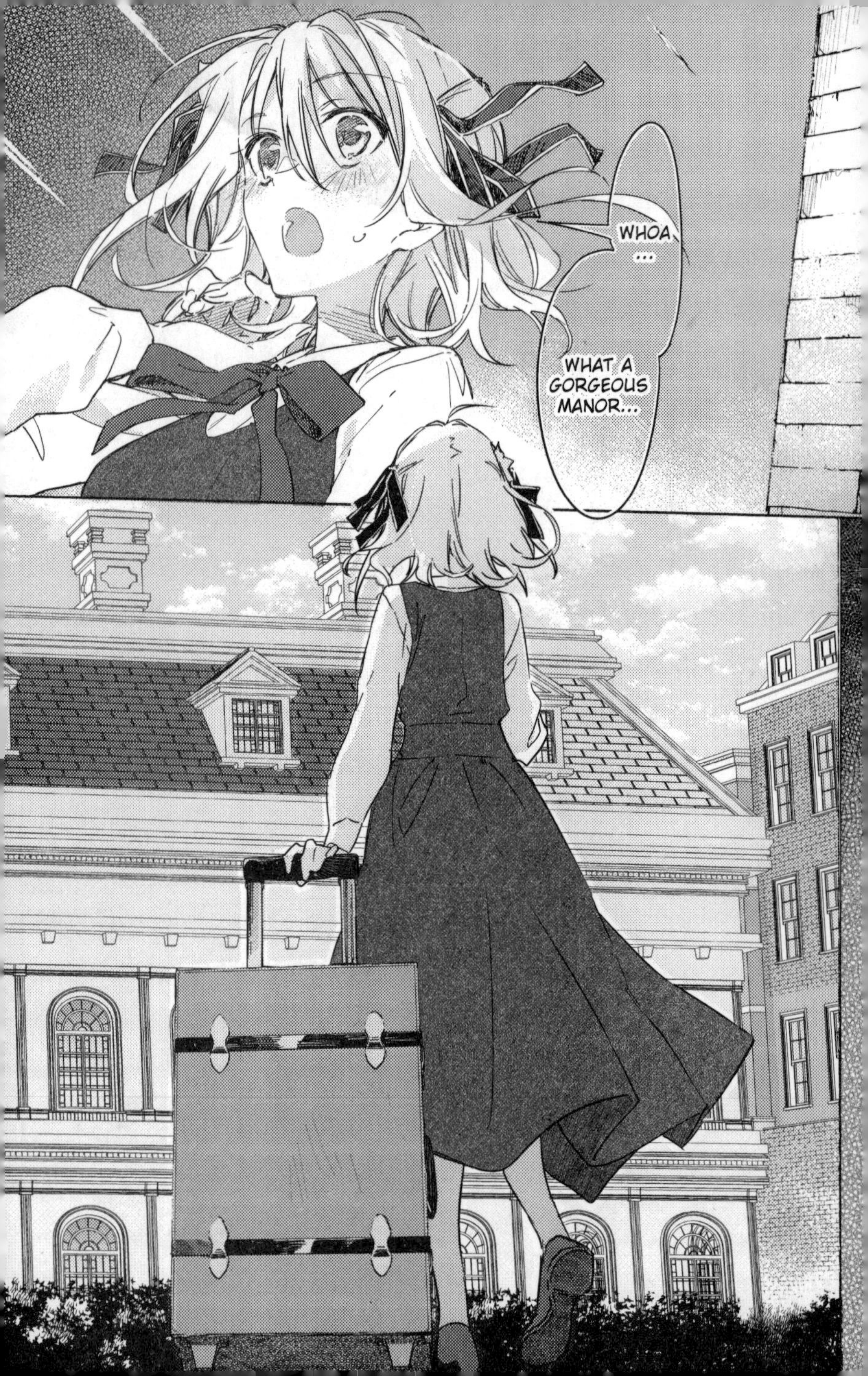
WHOA ...
WHAT A GORGEOUS MANOR...

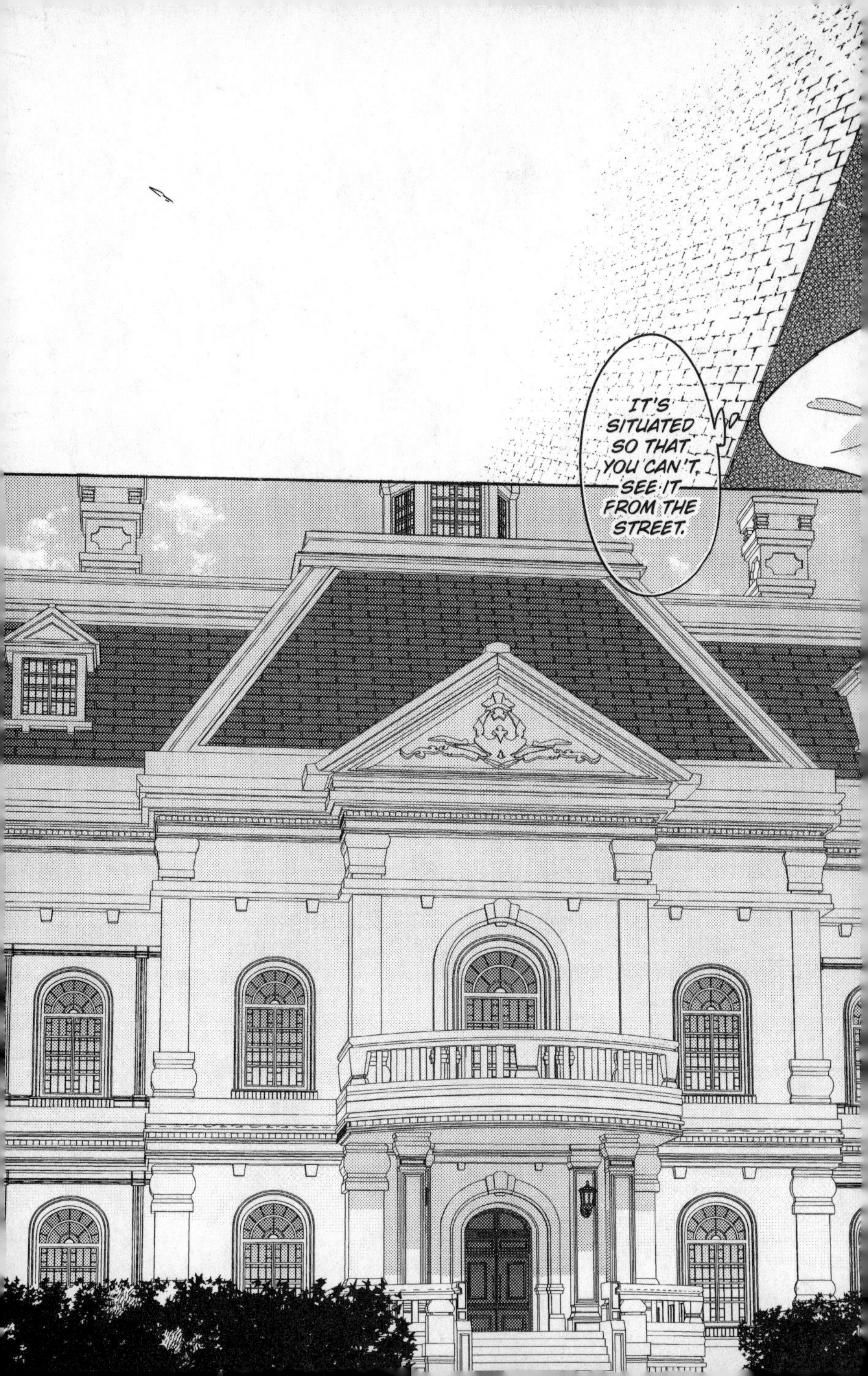
IT'S SITUATED SO THAT YOU CAN'T SEE IT FROM THE STREET.

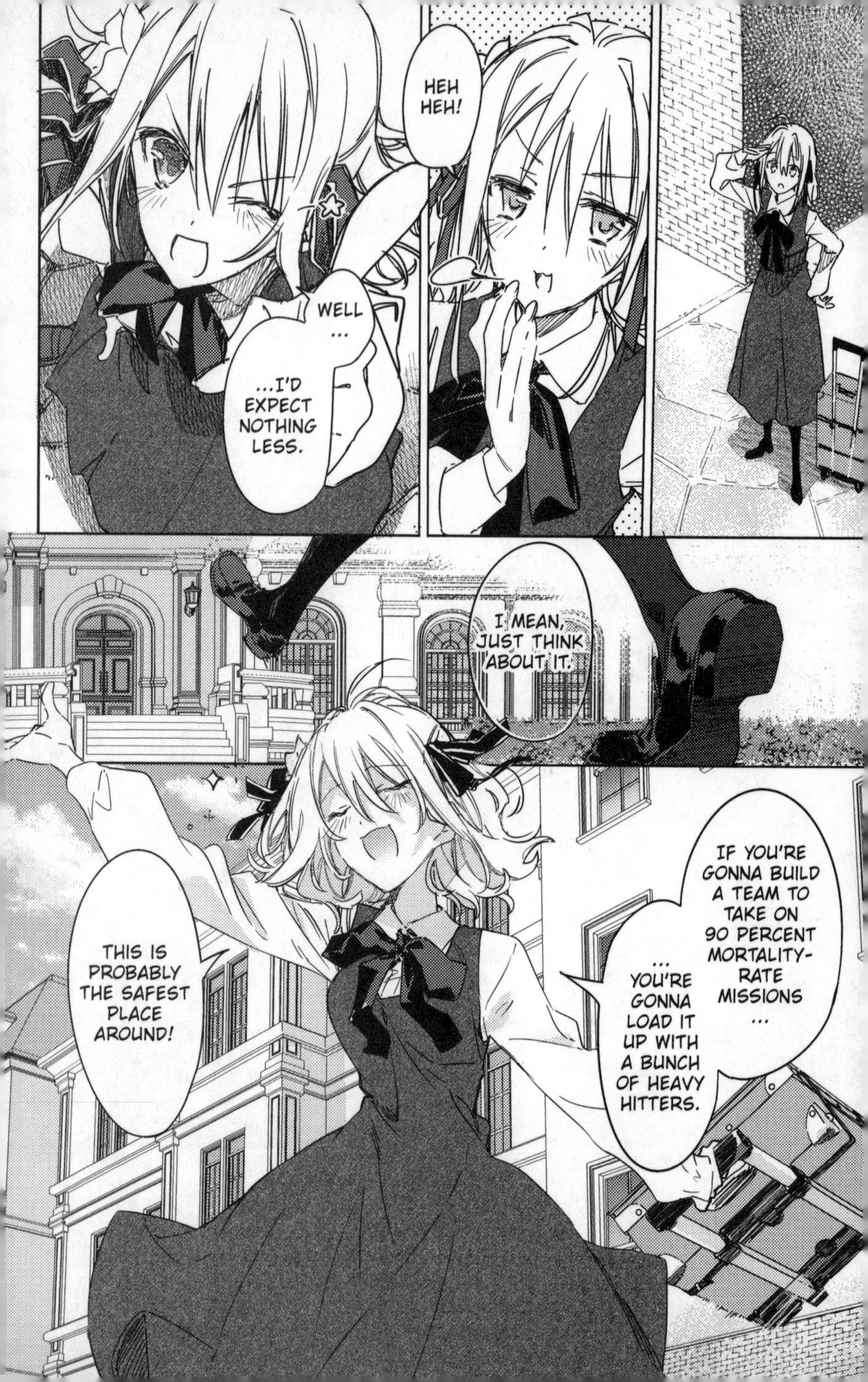
HEH HEH!
WELL ...
...I'D EXPECT NOTHING LESS.
I MEAN, JUST THINK ABOUT IT.
IF YOU'RE GONNA BUILD A TEAM TO TAKE ON 90 PERCENT MORTALITY-RATE MISSIONS ...
... YOU'RE GONNA LOAD IT UP WITH A BUNCH OF HEAVY HITTERS.
THIS IS PROBABLY THE SAFEST PLACE AROUND!

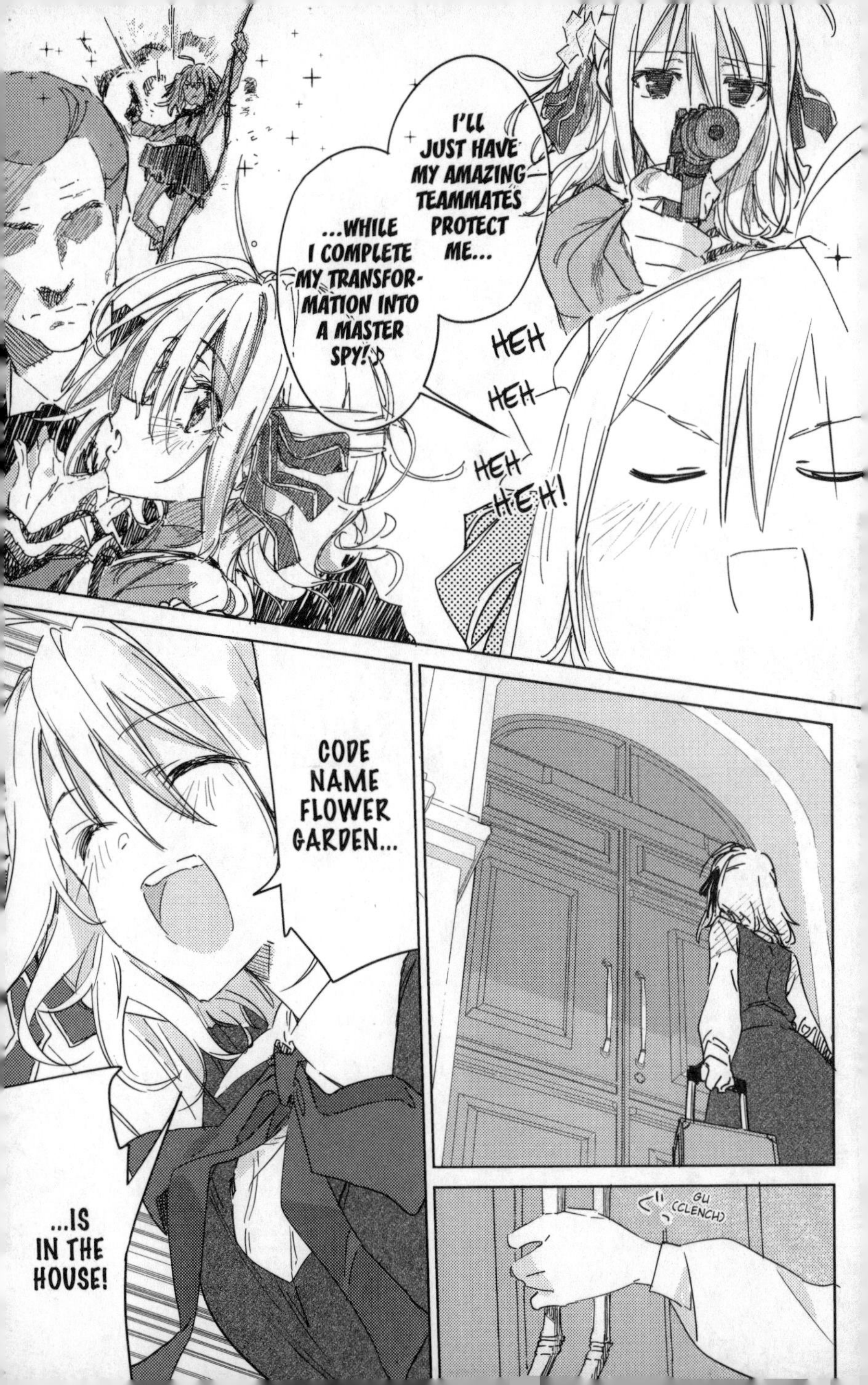
I'LL JUST HAVE MY AMAZING TEAMMATES PROTECT ME...
...WHILE I COMPLETE MY TRANSFORMATION INTO A MASTER SPY!♪
HEH HEH HEH HEH!
CODE NAME FLOWER GARDEN...
...IS IN THE HOUSE!
GU (CLENCH)

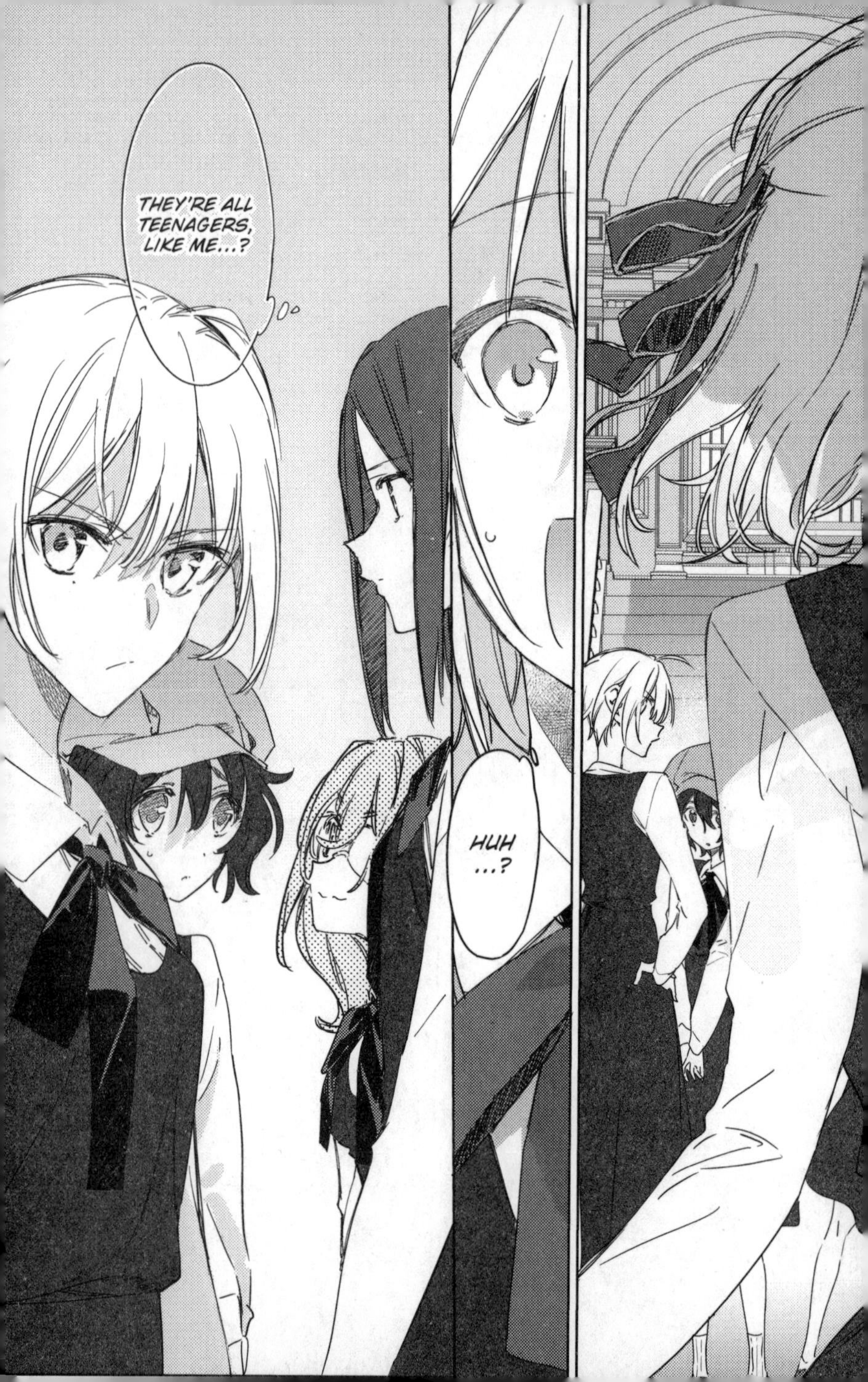
HUH ...?
THEY'RE ALL TEENAGERS, LIKE ME...?

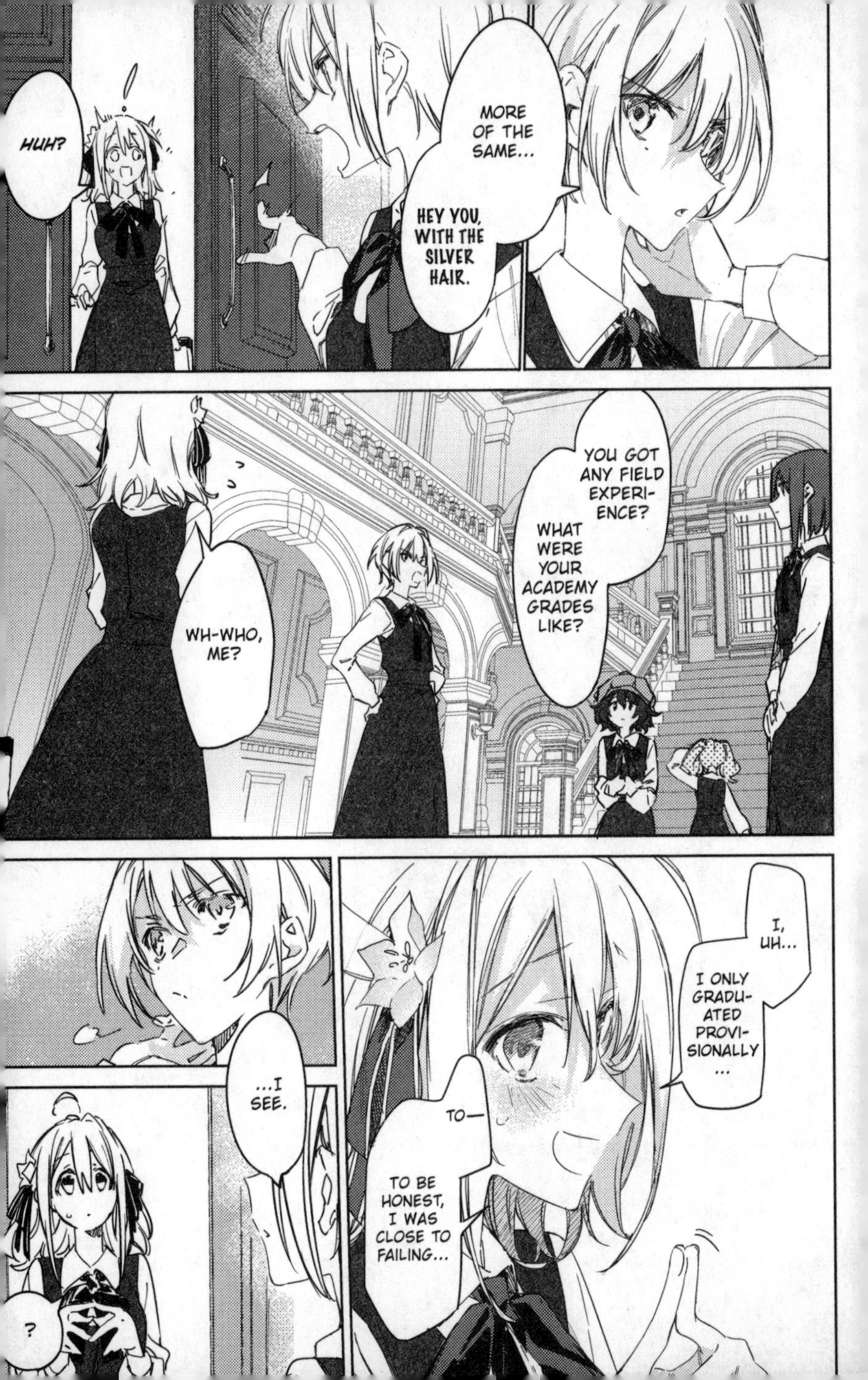
MORE OF THE SAME...
HEY YOU, WITH THE SILVER HAIR.
!
HUH?
YOU GOT ANY FIELD EXPERIENCE?
WHAT WERE YOUR ACADEMY GRADES LIKE?
WH-WHO, ME?
I, UH...
I ONLY GRADUATED PROVISIONALLY...
TO—
TO BE HONEST, I WAS CLOSE TO FAILING...
...I SEE.
?

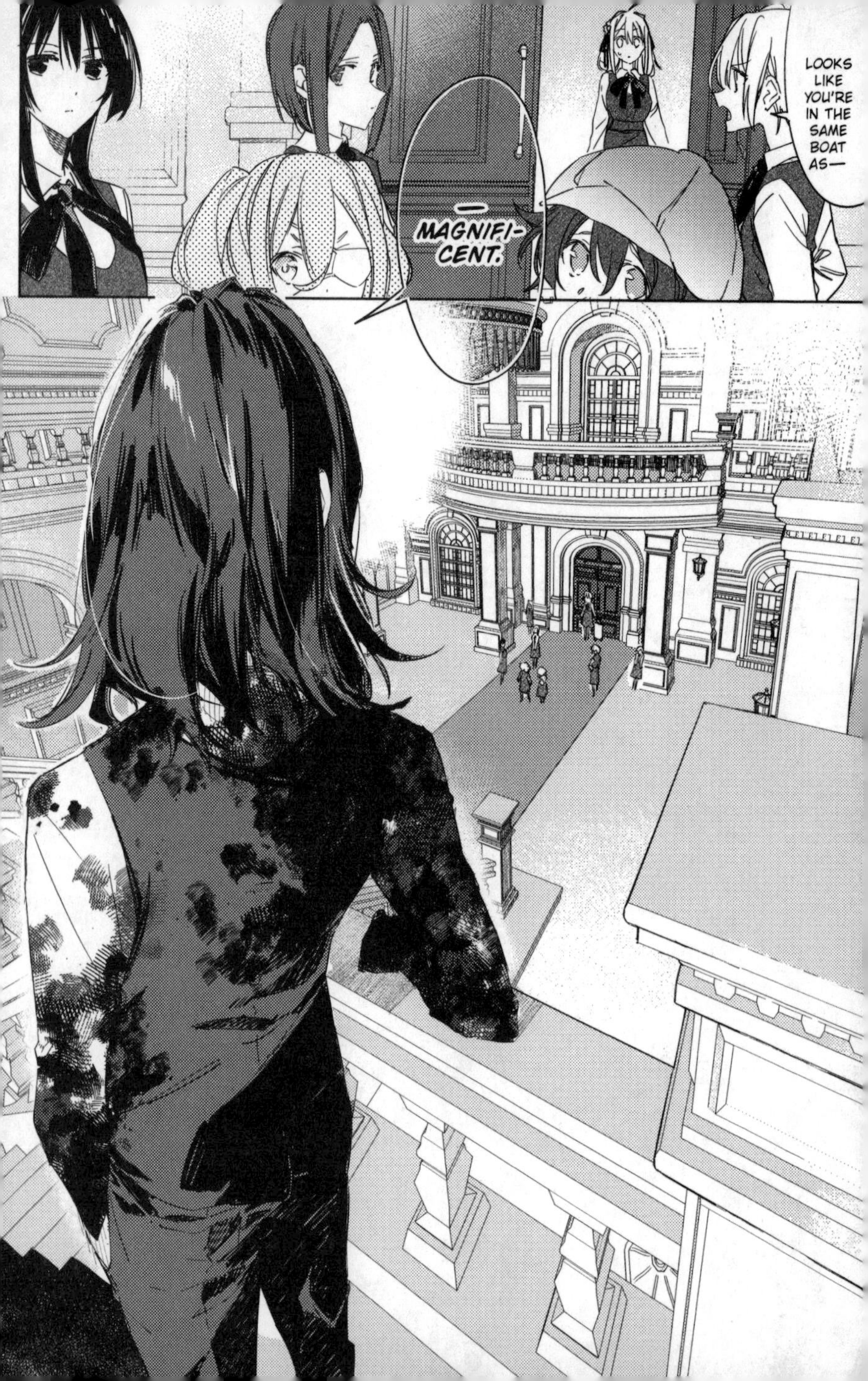
LOOKS LIKE YOU'RE IN THE SAME BOAT AS—
—MAGNIFICENT.

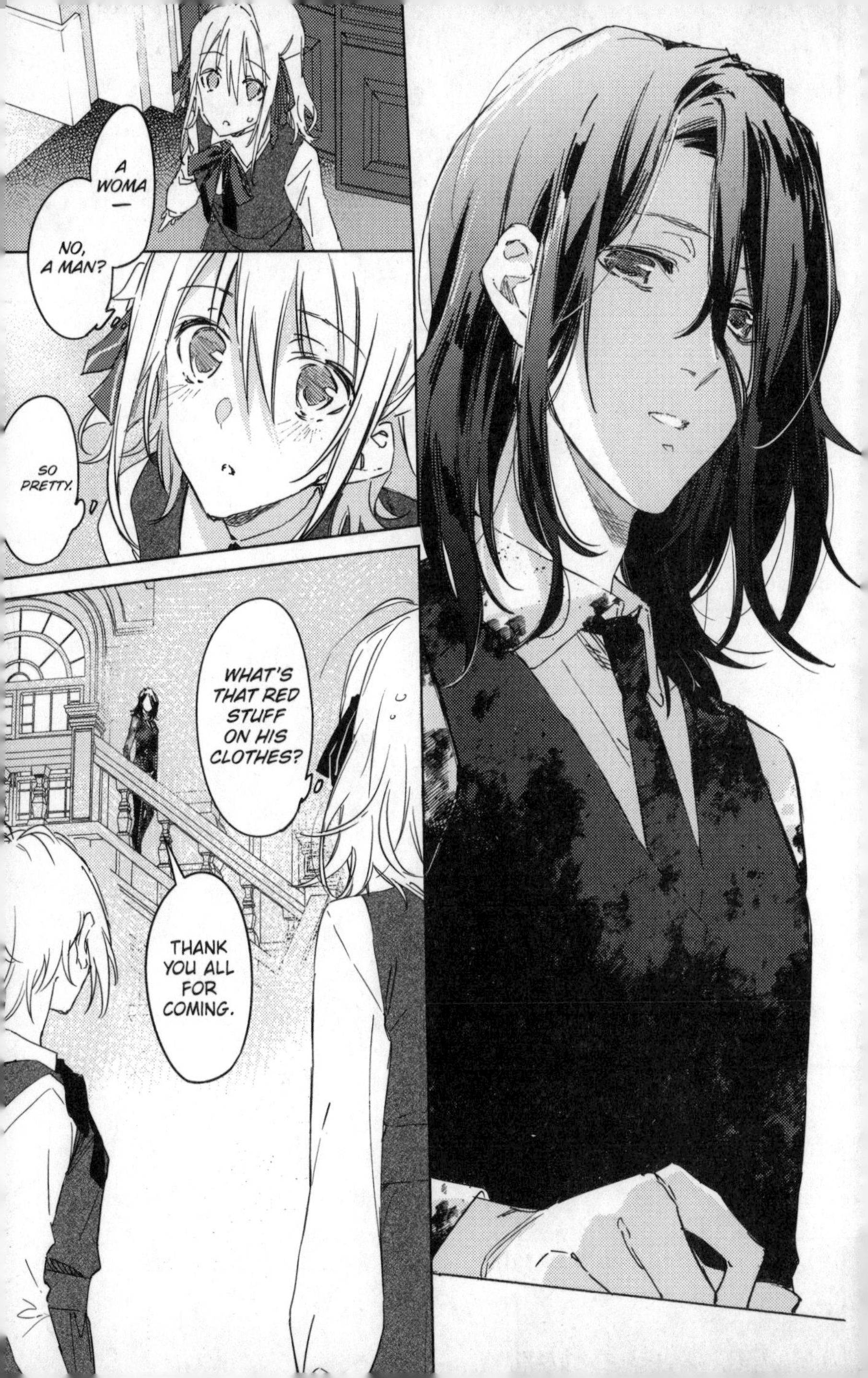
A WOMA—
NO, A MAN?
SO PRETTY.
WHAT'S THAT RED STUFF ON HIS CLOTHES?
THANK YOU ALL FOR COMING.

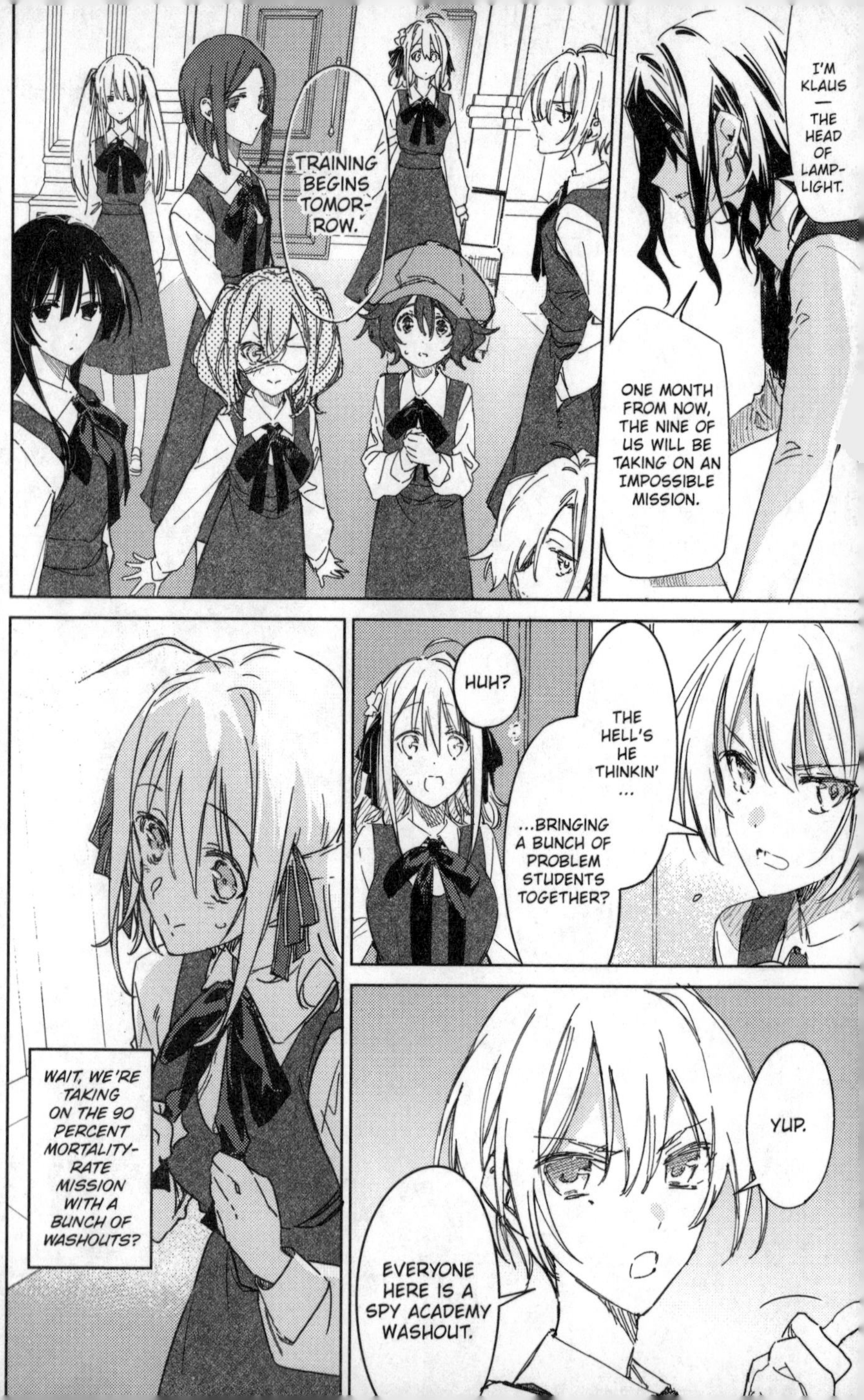
I'M KLAUS — THE HEAD OF LAMP-LIGHT.
ONE MONTH FROM NOW, THE NINE OF US WILL BE TAKING ON AN IMPOSSIBLE MISSION.
TRAINING BEGINS TOMOR-ROW.
THE HELL'S HE THINKIN' ...
...BRINGING A BUNCH OF PROBLEM STUDENTS TOGETHER?
HUH?
YUP.
EVERYONE HERE IS A SPY ACADEMY WASHOUT.
WAIT, WE'RE TAKING ON THE 90 PERCENT MORTALITY-RATE MISSION WITH A BUNCH OF WASHOUTS?

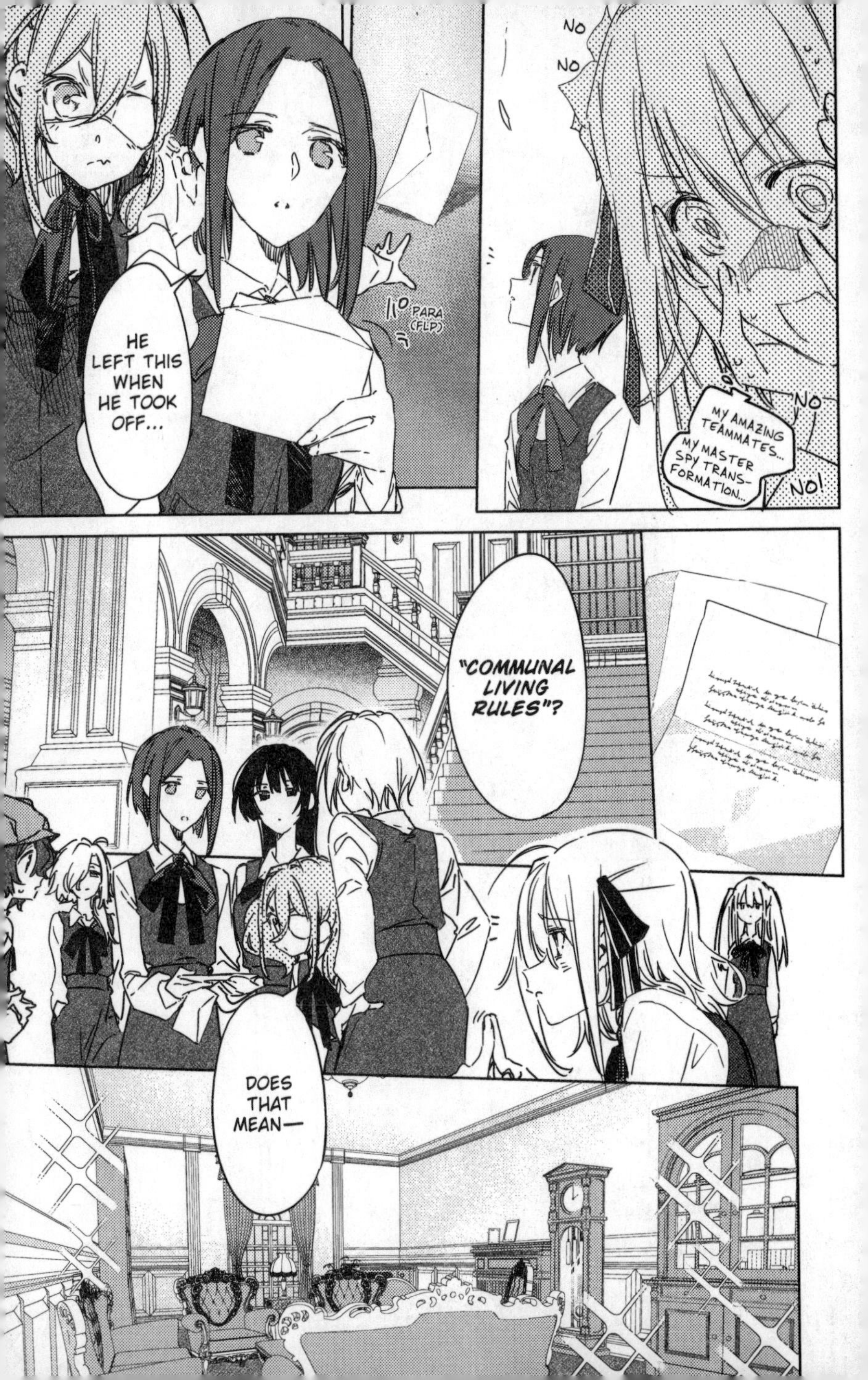
NO
NO
MY AMAZING TEAMMATES... MY MASTER SPY TRANS-FORMATION...
NO
NO!
PARA (FLIP)
HE LEFT THIS WHEN HE TOOK OFF...
"COMMUNAL LIVING RULES"?
DOES THAT MEAN—

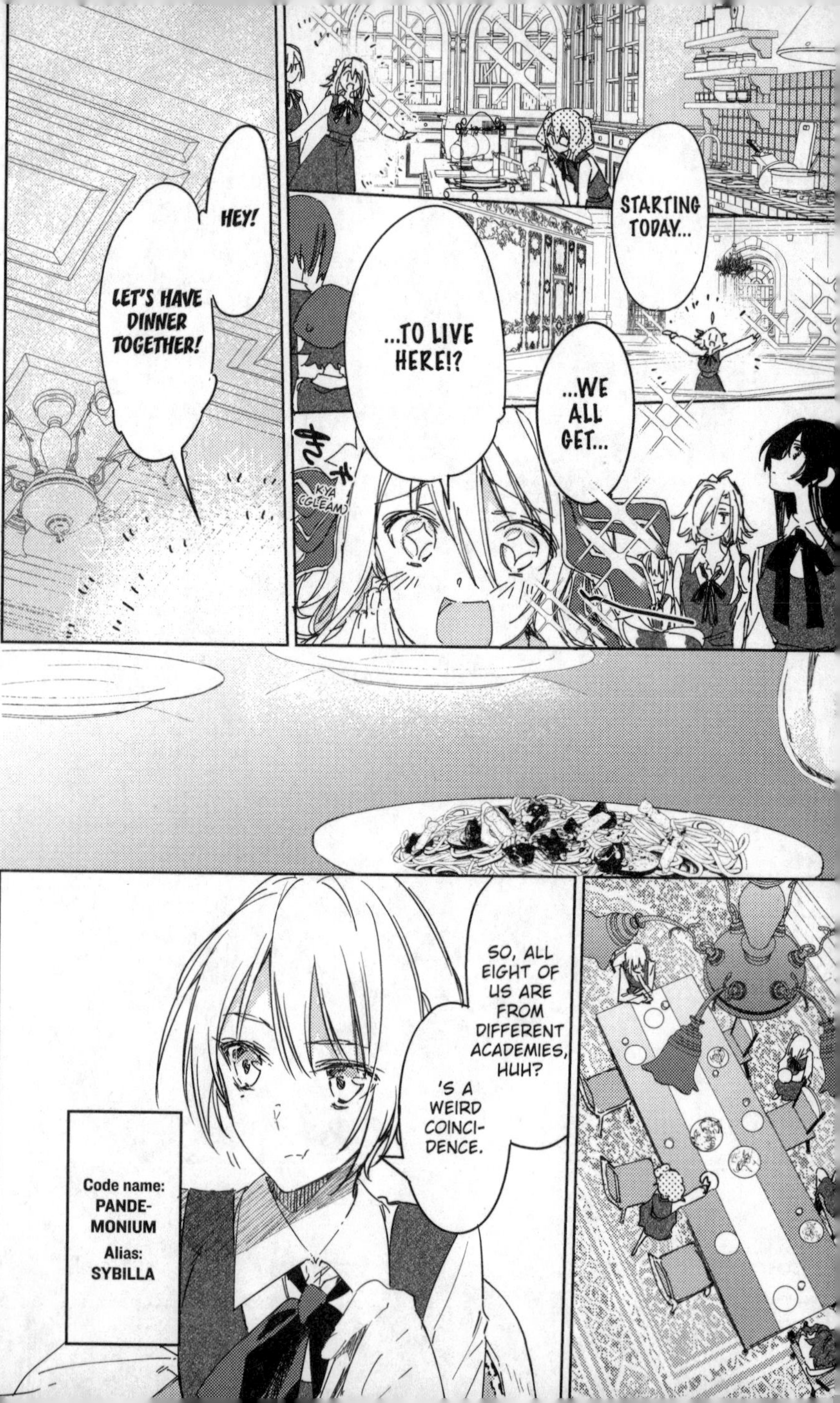
STARTING TODAY...
...WE ALL GET...
...TO LIVE HERE!?
KYA (GLEAM)
HEY!
LET'S HAVE DINNER TOGETHER!
SO, ALL EIGHT OF US ARE FROM DIFFERENT ACADEMIES, HUH?
'S A WEIRD COINCIDENCE.
Code name: PANDE-MONIUM
Alias: SYBILLA

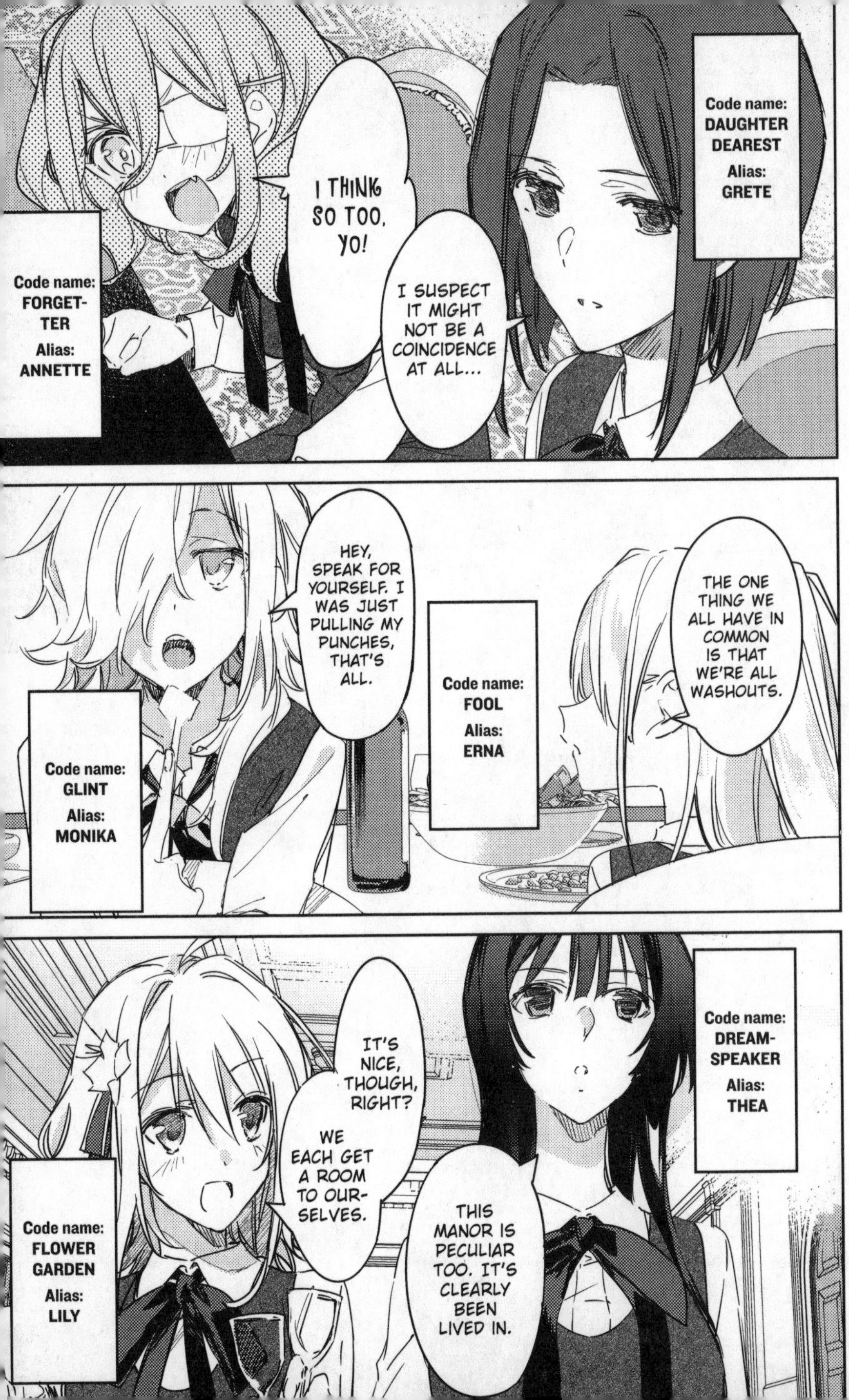
Code name: DAUGHTER DEAREST
Alias: GRETE
I SUSPECT IT MIGHT NOT BE A COINCIDENCE AT ALL...
I THINK SO TOO, YO!
Code name: FORGET-TER
Alias: ANNETTE
THE ONE THING WE ALL HAVE IN COMMON IS THAT WE'RE ALL WASHOUTS.
Code name: FOOL
Alias: ERNA
HEY, SPEAK FOR YOURSELF. I WAS JUST PULLING MY PUNCHES, THAT'S ALL.
Code name: GLINT
Alias: MONIKA
Code name: DREAM-SPEAKER
Alias: THEA
THIS MANOR IS PECULIAR TOO. IT'S CLEARLY BEEN LIVED IN.
IT'S NICE, THOUGH, RIGHT?
WE EACH GET A ROOM TO OUR-SELVES.
Code name: FLOWER GARDEN
Alias: LILY

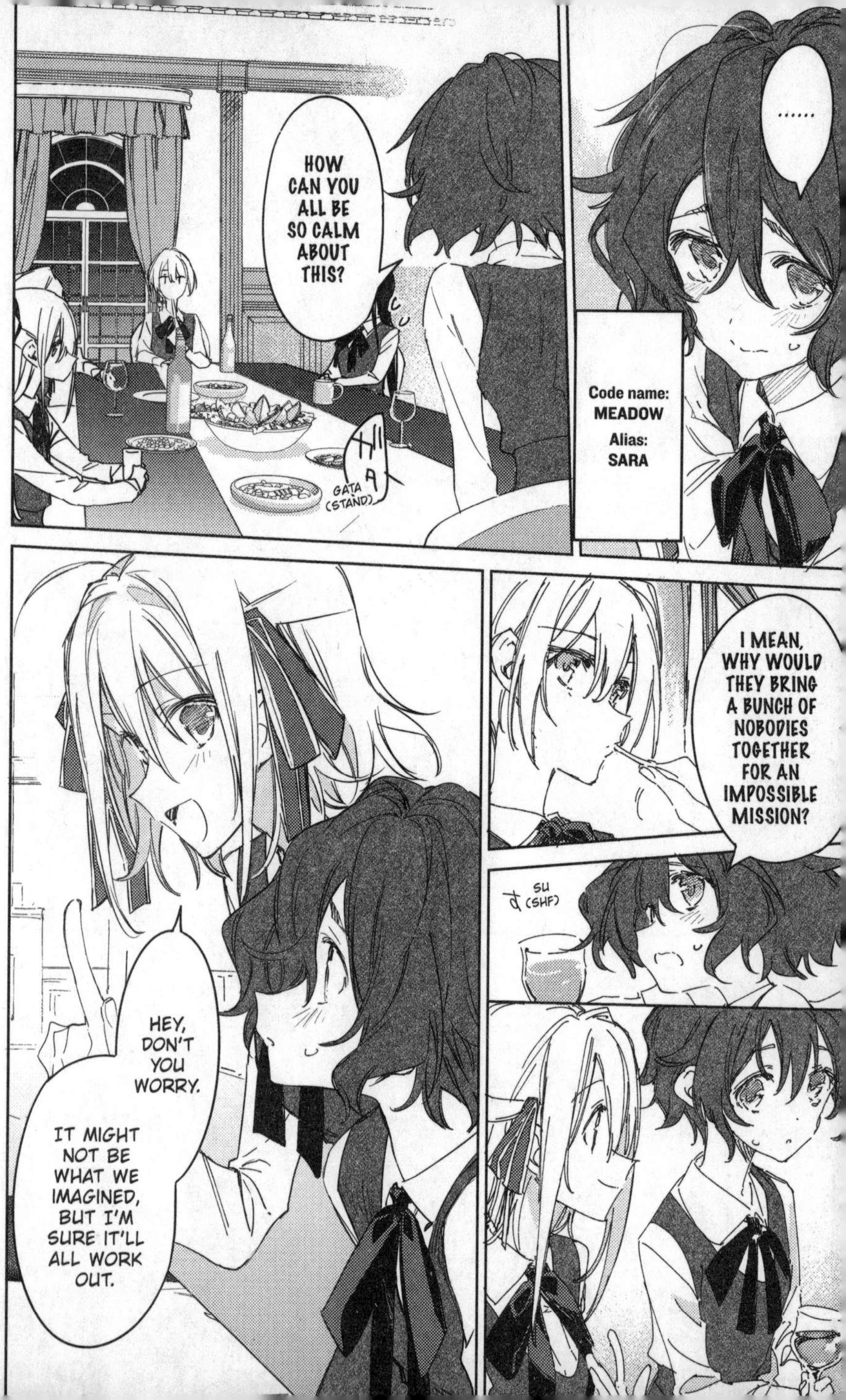
......
Code name: MEADOW
Alias: SARA
HOW CAN YOU ALL BE SO CALM ABOUT THIS?
GATA (STAND)
I MEAN, WHY WOULD THEY BRING A BUNCH OF NOBODIES TOGETHER FOR AN IMPOSSIBLE MISSION?
SU (SHF)
HEY, DON'T YOU WORRY.
IT MIGHT NOT BE WHAT WE IMAGINED, BUT I'M SURE IT'LL ALL WORK OUT.

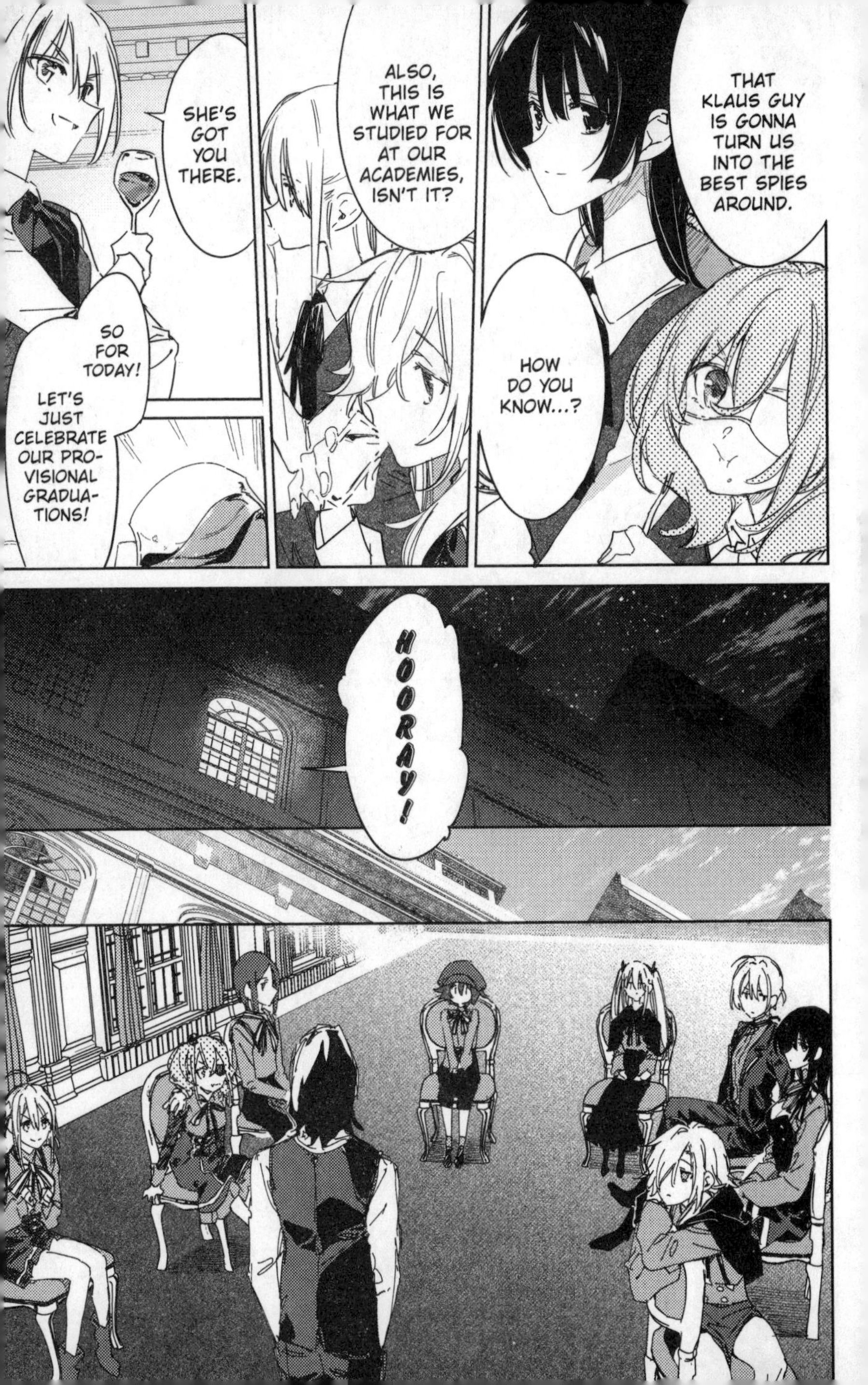
THAT KLAUS GUY IS GONNA TURN US INTO THE BEST SPIES AROUND.
HOW DO YOU KNOW...?
ALSO, THIS IS WHAT WE STUDIED FOR AT OUR ACADEMIES, ISN'T IT?
SHE'S GOT YOU THERE.
SO FOR TODAY!
LET'S JUST CELEBRATE OUR PRO-VISIONAL GRADUA-TIONS!
HOORAY!

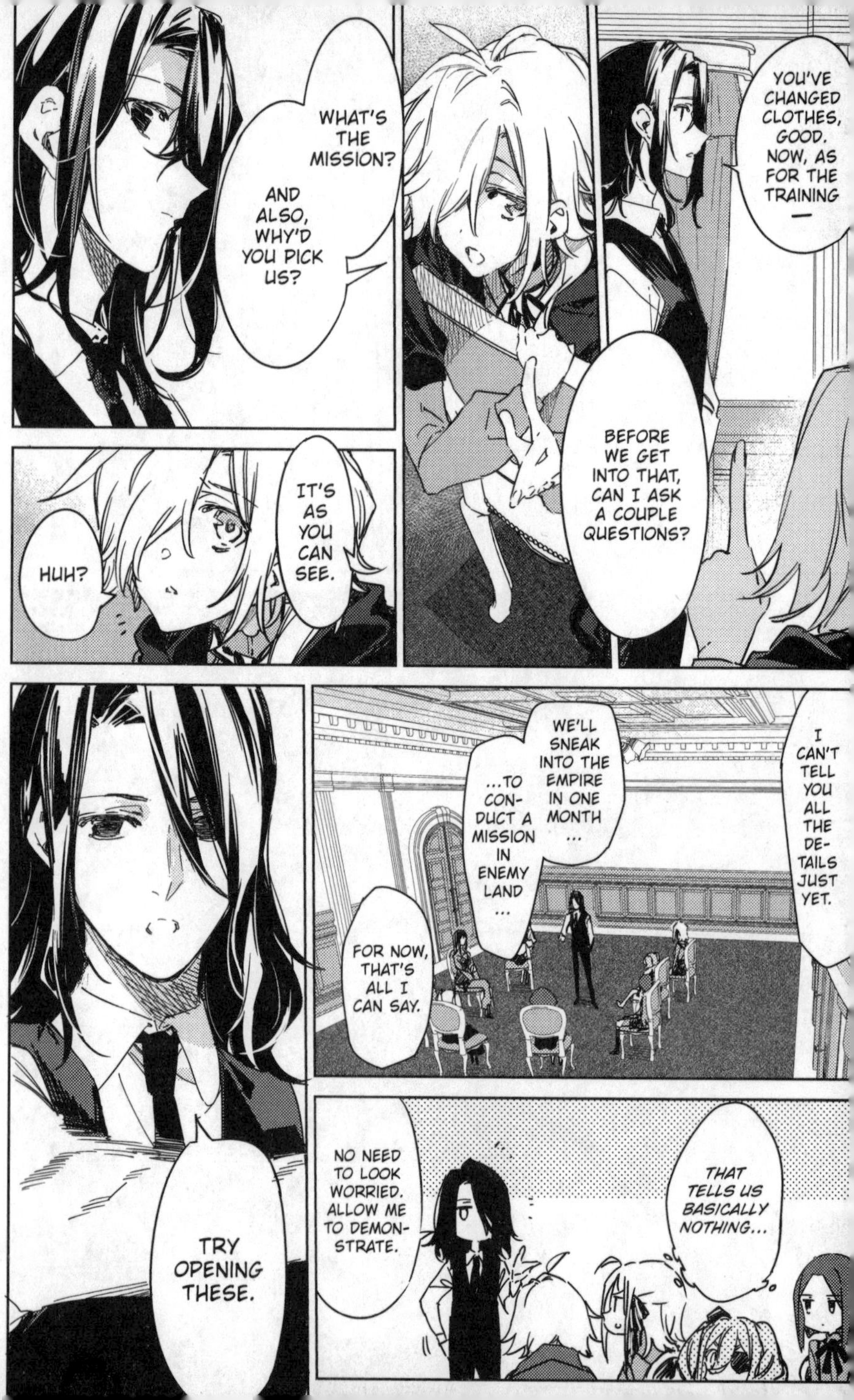
YOU'VE CHANGED CLOTHES, GOOD. NOW, AS FOR THE TRAINING—
BEFORE WE GET INTO THAT, CAN I ASK A COUPLE QUESTIONS?
WHAT'S THE MISSION?
AND ALSO, WHY'D YOU PICK US?
IT'S AS YOU CAN SEE.
HUH?
I CAN'T TELL YOU ALL THE DETAILS JUST YET.
WE'LL SNEAK INTO THE EMPIRE IN ONE MONTH...
...TO CONDUCT A MISSION IN ENEMY LAND...
FOR NOW, THAT'S ALL I CAN SAY.
THAT TELLS US BASICALLY NOTHING...
NO NEED TO LOOK WORRIED. ALLOW ME TO DEMONSTRATE.
TRY OPENING THESE.

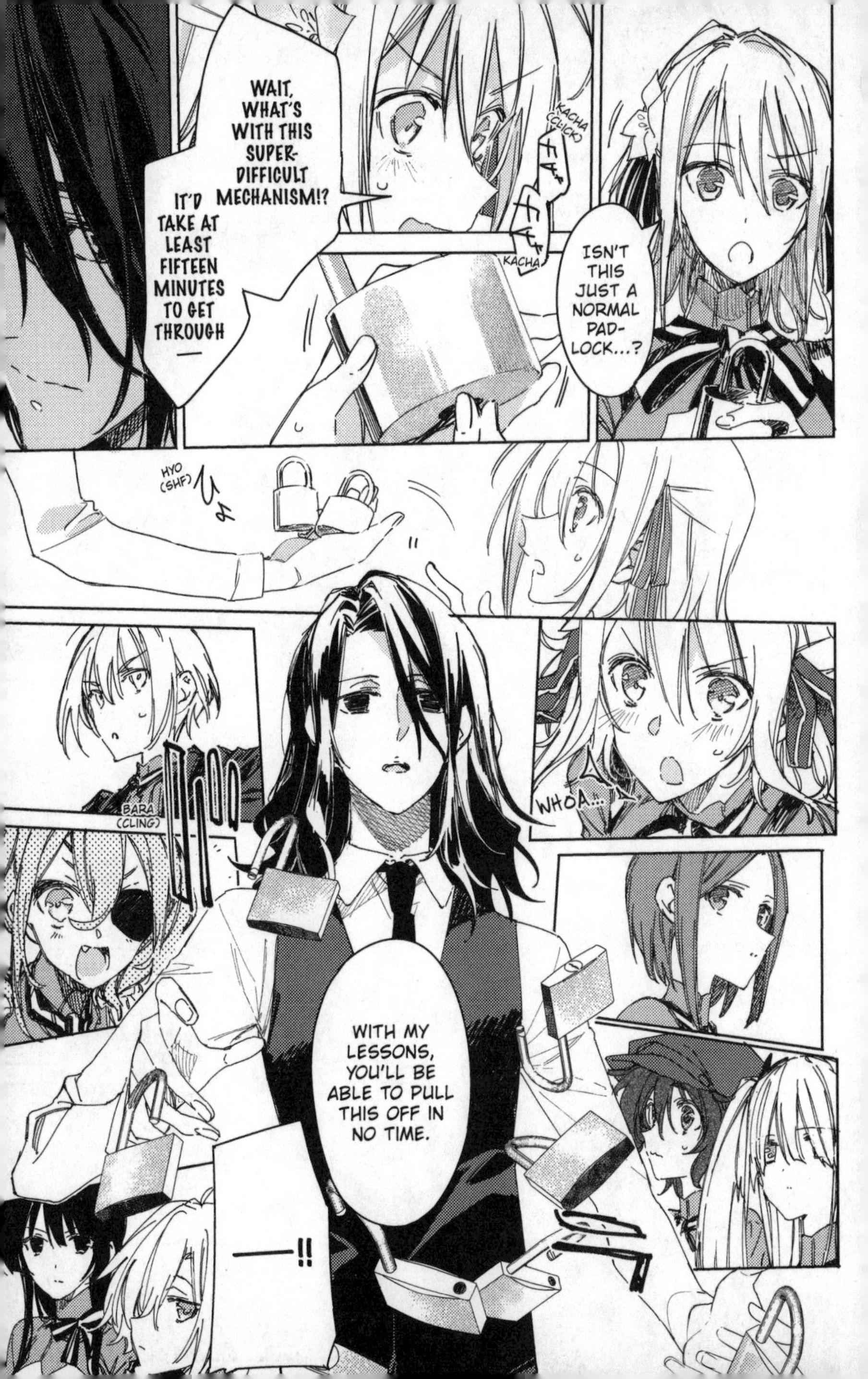
ISN'T THIS JUST A NORMAL PADLOCK...?
KACHA (CLICK)
KACHA
WAIT, WHAT'S WITH THIS SUPER-DIFFICULT MECHANISM!?
IT'D TAKE AT LEAST FIFTEEN MINUTES TO GET THROUGH—
HYO (SHF)
WHOA...
BARA (CLING)
WITH MY LESSONS, YOU'LL BE ABLE TO PULL THIS OFF IN NO TIME.
——!!

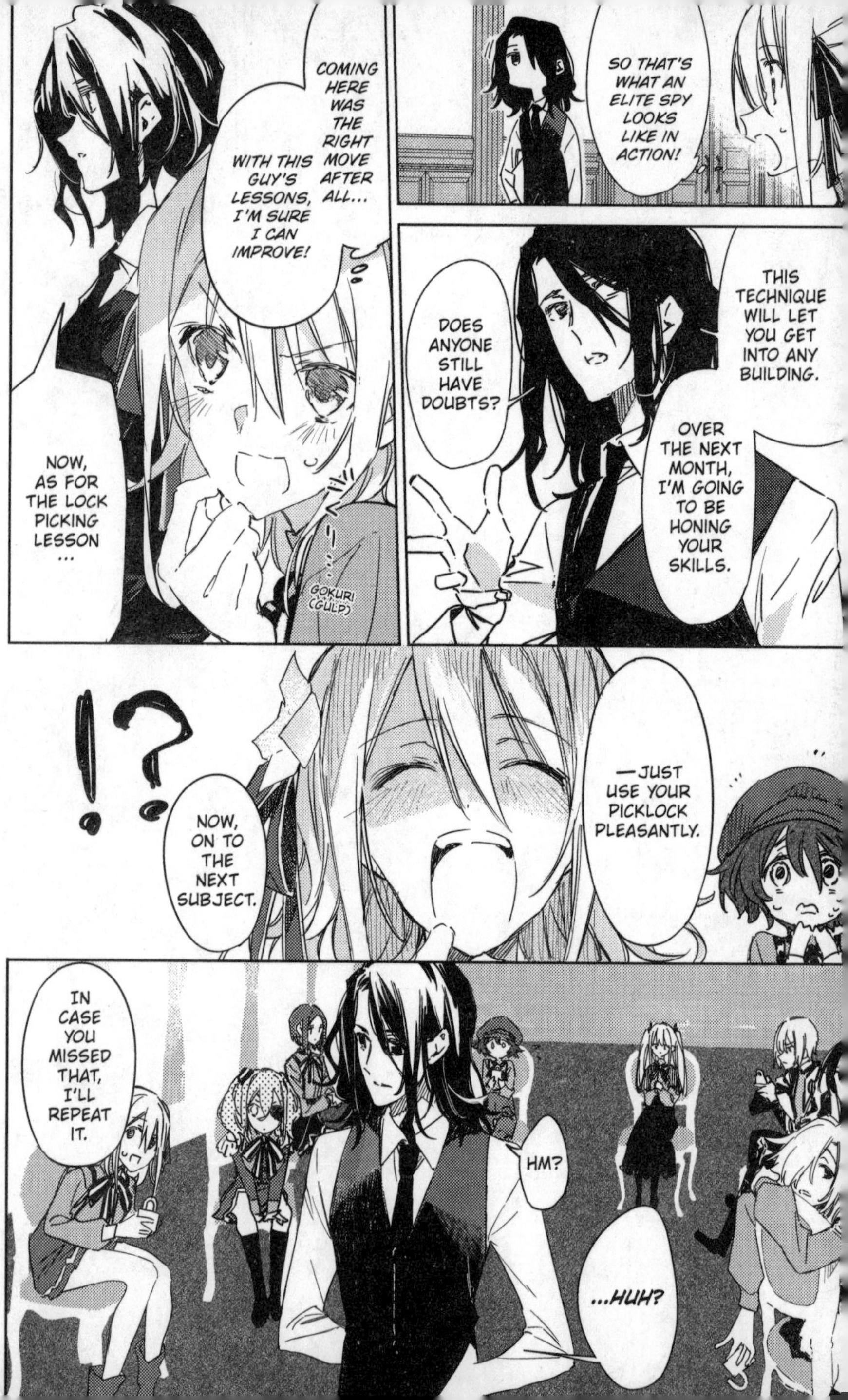
SO THAT'S WHAT AN ELITE SPY LOOKS LIKE IN ACTION!
THIS TECHNIQUE WILL LET YOU GET INTO ANY BUILDING.
OVER THE NEXT MONTH, I'M GOING TO BE HONING YOUR SKILLS.
DOES ANYONE STILL HAVE DOUBTS?
COMING HERE WAS THE RIGHT MOVE AFTER ALL...
WITH THIS GUY'S LESSONS, I'M SURE I CAN IMPROVE!
GOKURI (GULP)
NOW, AS FOR THE LOCK PICKING LESSON ...
—JUST USE YOUR PICKLOCK PLEASANTLY.
NOW, ON TO THE NEXT SUBJECT.
!?
HM?
...HUH?
IN CASE YOU MISSED THAT, I'LL REPEAT IT.

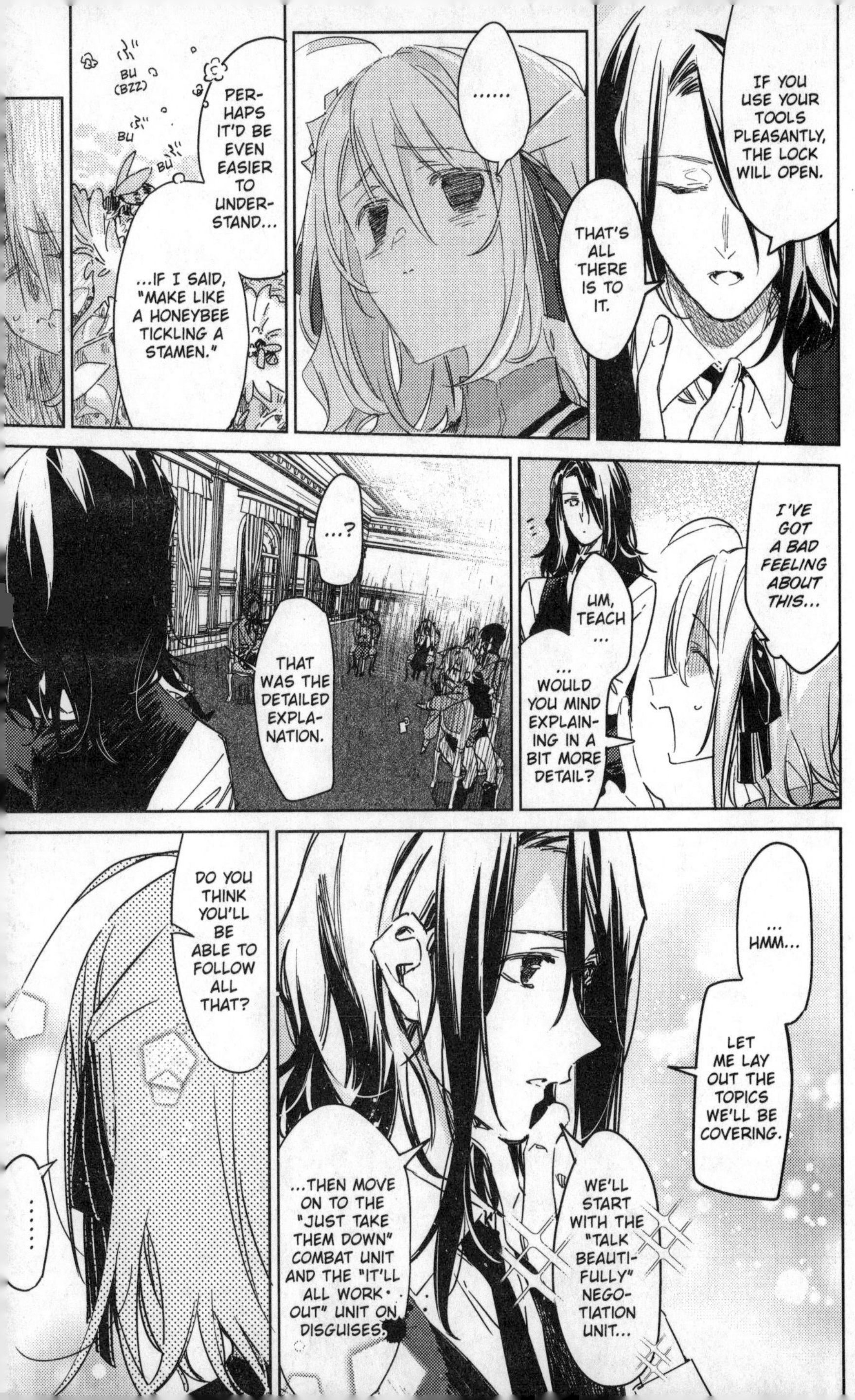
IF YOU USE YOUR TOOLS PLEASANTLY, THE LOCK WILL OPEN.
THAT'S ALL THERE IS TO IT.
......
BU (BZZ)
BU
BU
PER-HAPS IT'D BE EVEN EASIER TO UNDER-STAND...
...IF I SAID, "MAKE LIKE A HONEYBEE TICKLING A STAMEN."
I'VE GOT A BAD FEELING ABOUT THIS...
UM, TEACH...
...WOULD YOU MIND EXPLAIN-ING IN A BIT MORE DETAIL?
...?
THAT WAS THE DETAILED EXPLA-NATION.
...HMM...
LET ME LAY OUT THE TOPICS WE'LL BE COVERING.
WE'LL START WITH THE "TALK BEAUTI-FULLY" NEGO-TIATION UNIT...
...THEN MOVE ON TO THE "JUST TAKE THEM DOWN" COMBAT UNIT AND THE "IT'LL ALL WORK・OUT" UNIT ON DISGUISES.
DO YOU THINK YOU'LL BE ABLE TO FOLLOW ALL THAT?
......

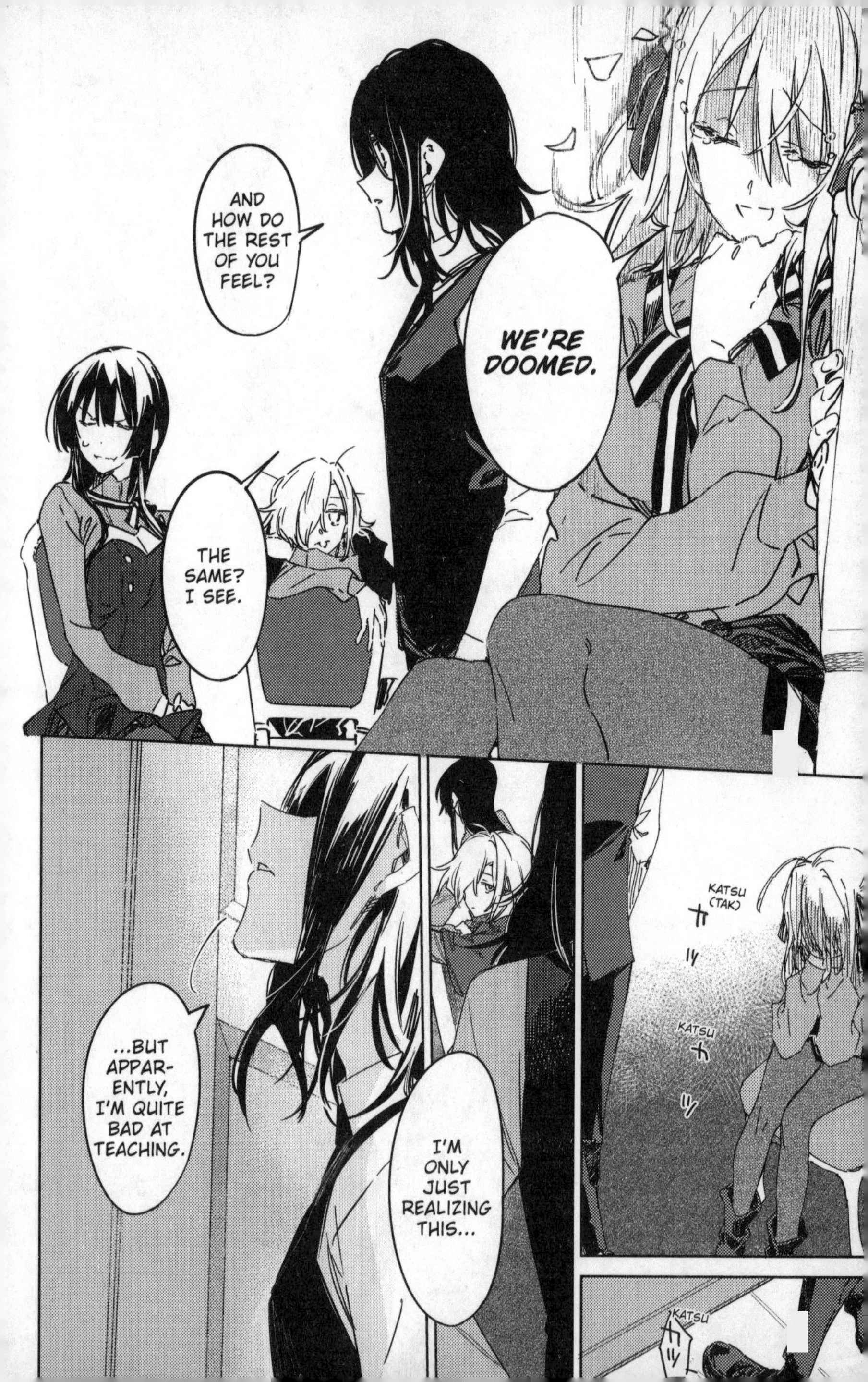
WE'RE DOOMED.
AND HOW DO THE REST OF YOU FEEL?
THE SAME? I SEE.
KATSU (TAK)
KATSU
KATSU
I'M ONLY JUST REALIZING THIS...
...BUT APPARENTLY, I'M QUITE BAD AT TEACHING.

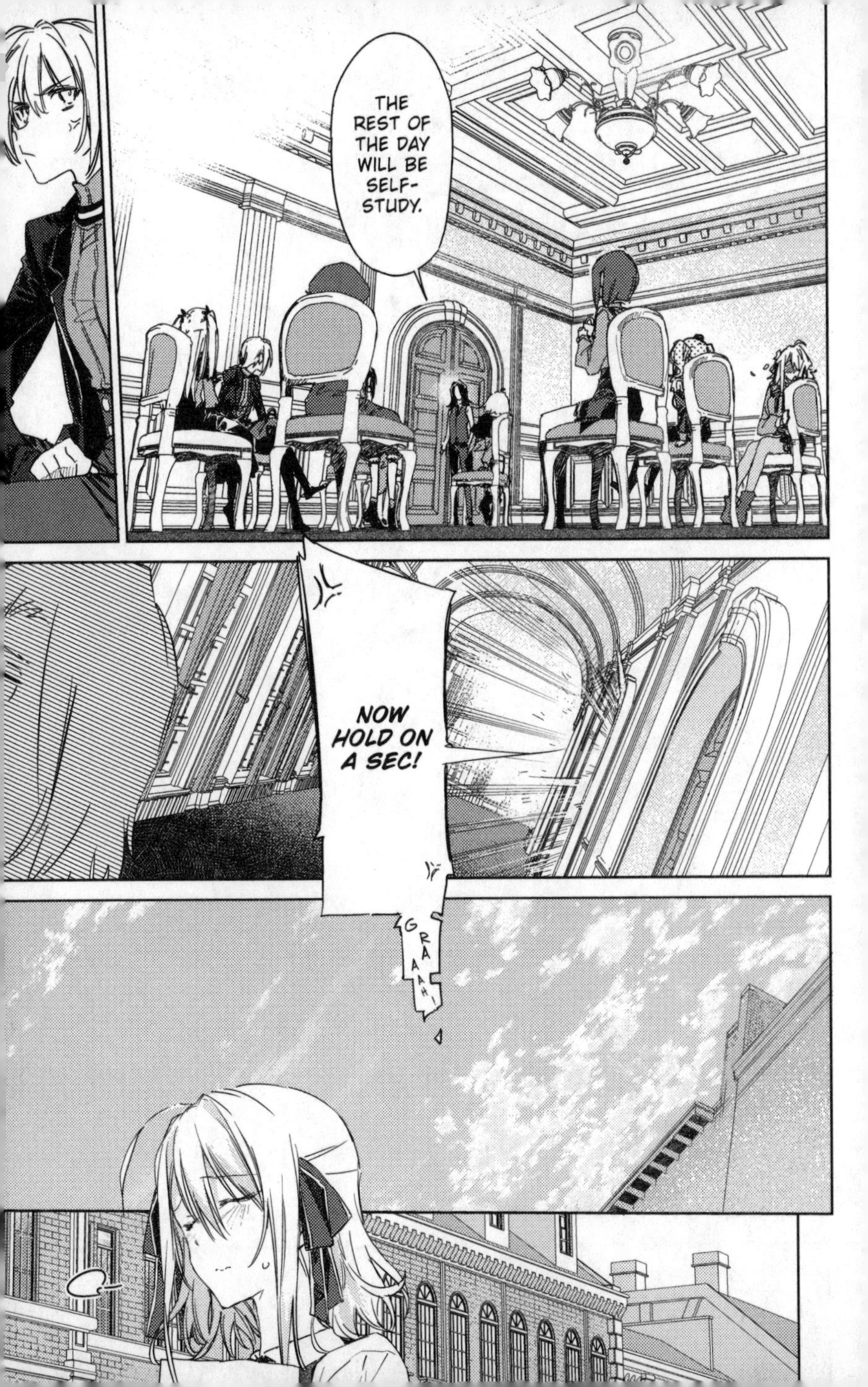
THE REST OF THE DAY WILL BE SELF-STUDY.
NOW HOLD ON A SEC!
GRAAAH!

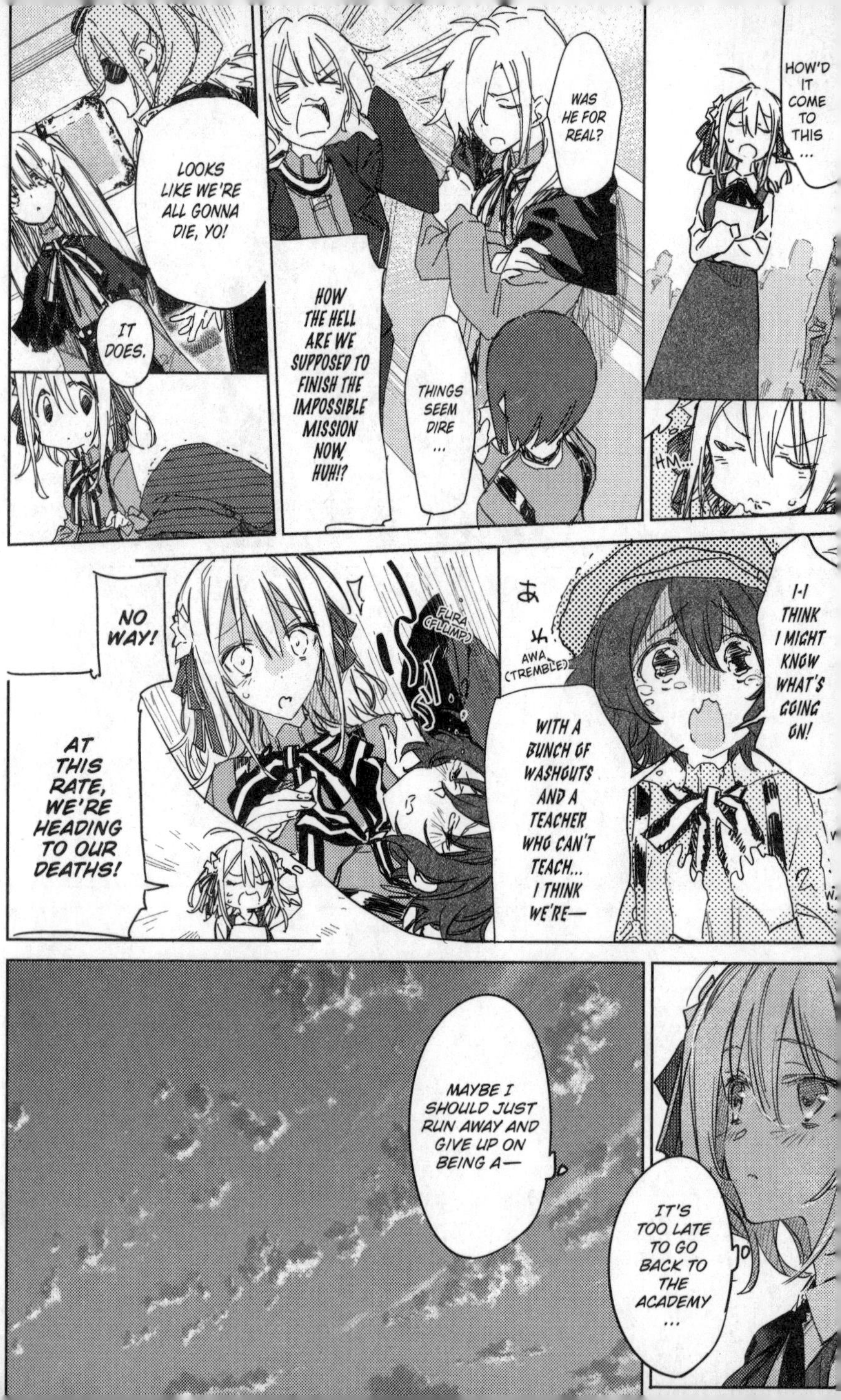
HOW'D IT COME TO THIS...
HM...
WAS HE FOR REAL?
HOW THE HELL ARE WE SUPPOSED TO FINISH THE IMPOSSIBLE MISSION NOW, HUH!?
THINGS SEEM DIRE...
LOOKS LIKE WE'RE ALL GONNA DIE, YO!
IT DOES.
I-I THINK I MIGHT KNOW WHAT'S GOING ON!
あわ
AWA (TREMBLE)
WITH A BUNCH OF WASHOUTS AND A TEACHER WHO CAN'T TEACH... I THINK WE'RE—
FURA (FLUMP)
NO WAY!
AT THIS RATE, WE'RE HEADING TO OUR DEATHS!
IT'S TOO LATE TO GO BACK TO THE ACADEMY...
MAYBE I SHOULD JUST RUN AWAY AND GIVE UP ON BEING A—

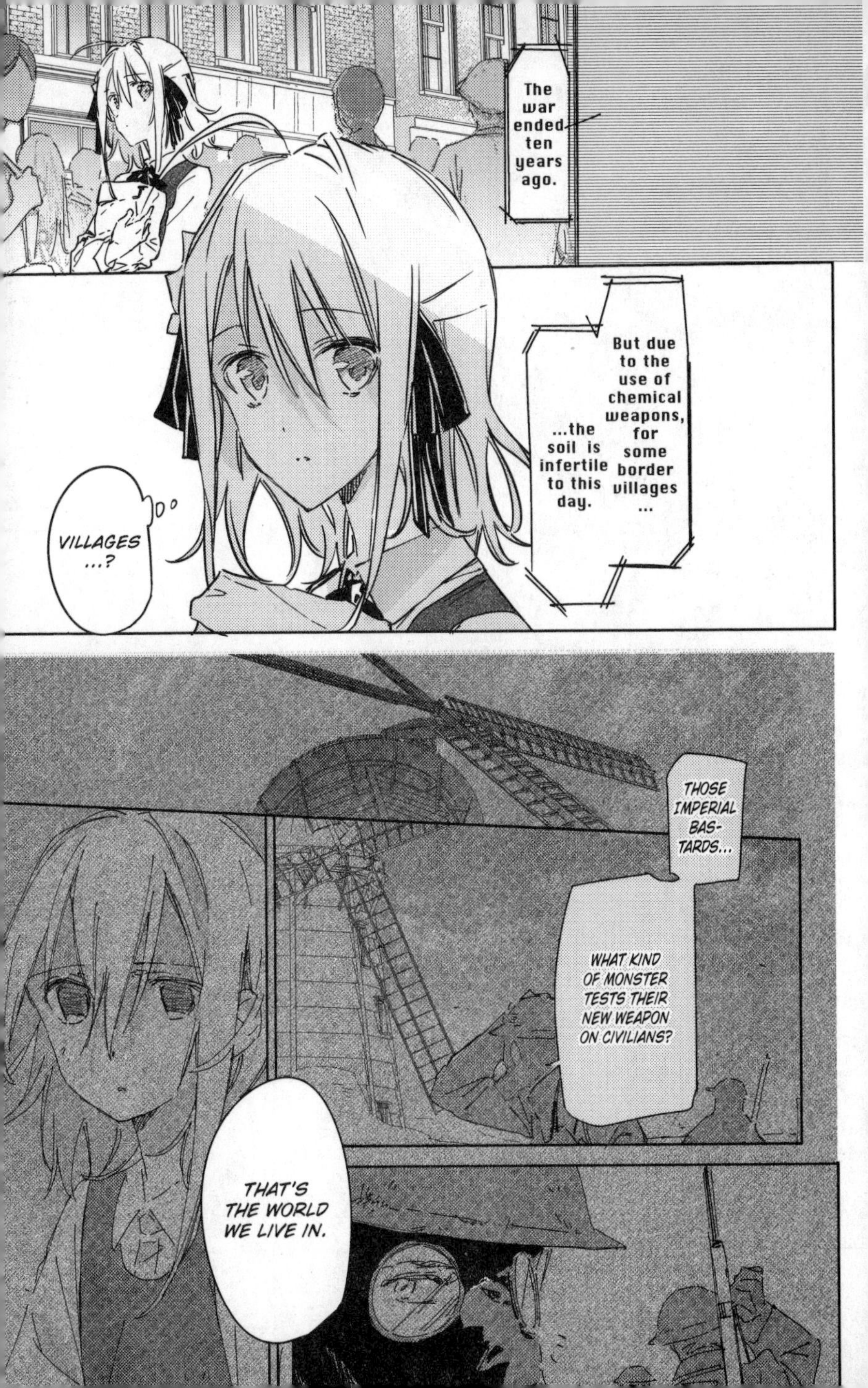
The war ended ten years ago.
But due to the use of chemical weapons, for some border villages...
...the soil is infertile to this day.
VILLAGES...?
THOSE IMPERIAL BAS-TARDS...
WHAT KIND OF MONSTER TESTS THEIR NEW WEAPON ON CIVILIANS?
THAT'S THE WORLD WE LIVE IN.

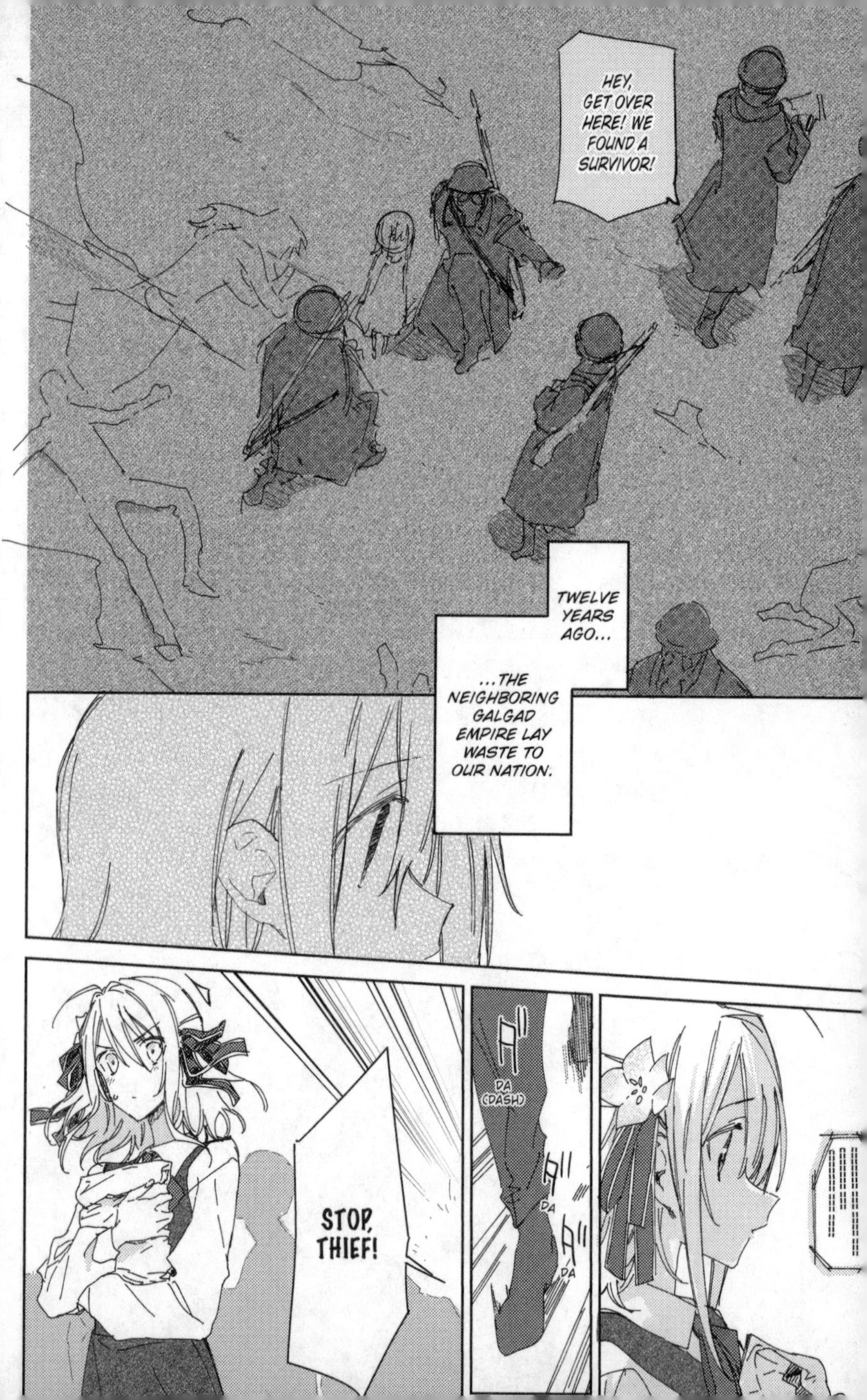
HEY, GET OVER HERE! WE FOUND A SURVIVOR!
TWELVE YEARS AGO...
...THE NEIGHBORING GALGAD EMPIRE LAY WASTE TO OUR NATION.
DA (DASH)
DA
DA
STOP, THIEF!

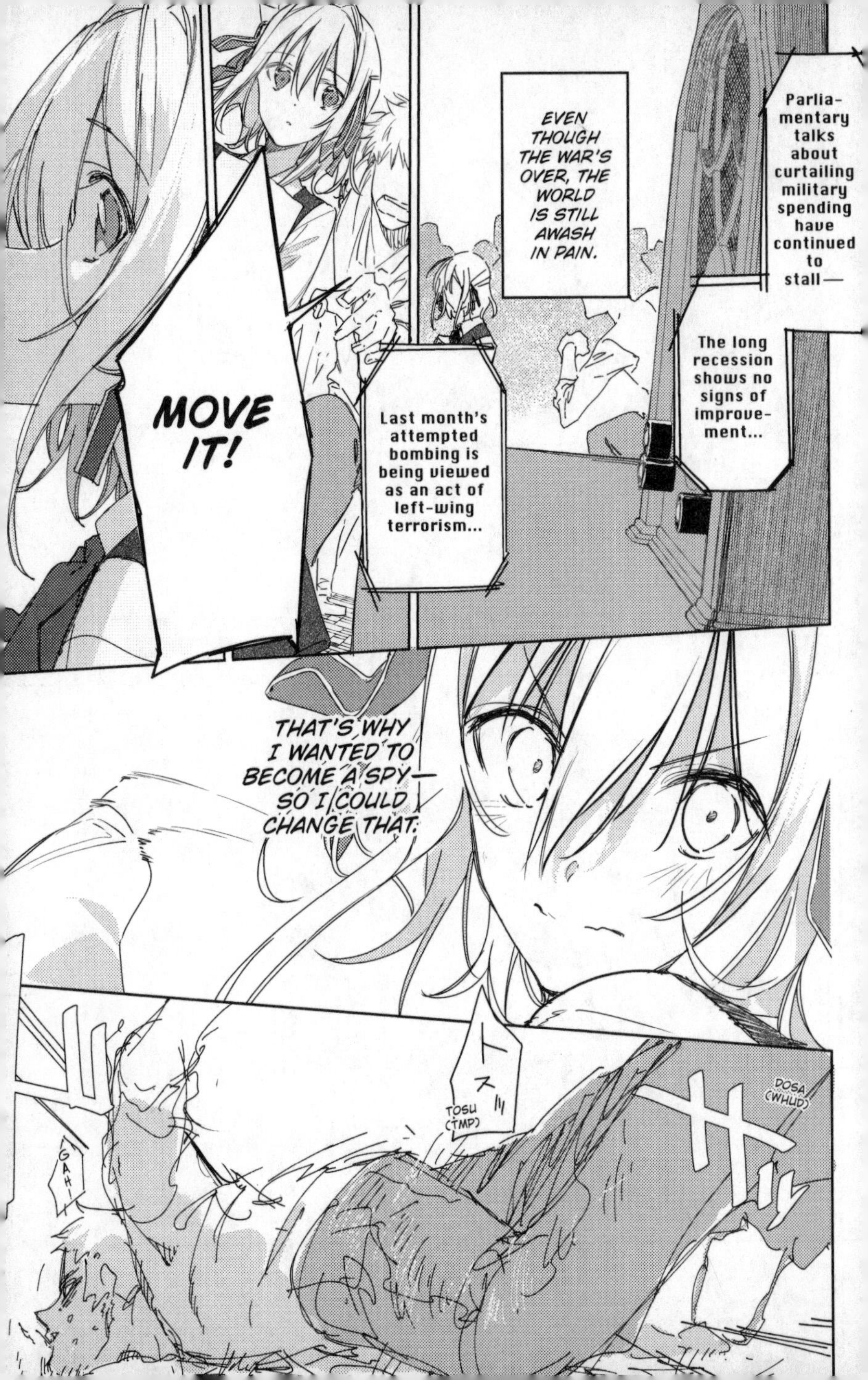
Parliamentary talks about curtailing military spending have continued to stall—
The long recession shows no signs of improvement...
EVEN THOUGH THE WAR'S OVER, THE WORLD IS STILL AWASH IN PAIN.
Last month's attempted bombing is being viewed as an act of left-wing terrorism...
MOVE IT!
THAT'S WHY I WANTED TO BECOME A SPY—SO I COULD CHANGE THAT.
DOSA (WHUD)
TOSU (TMP)
GAH!

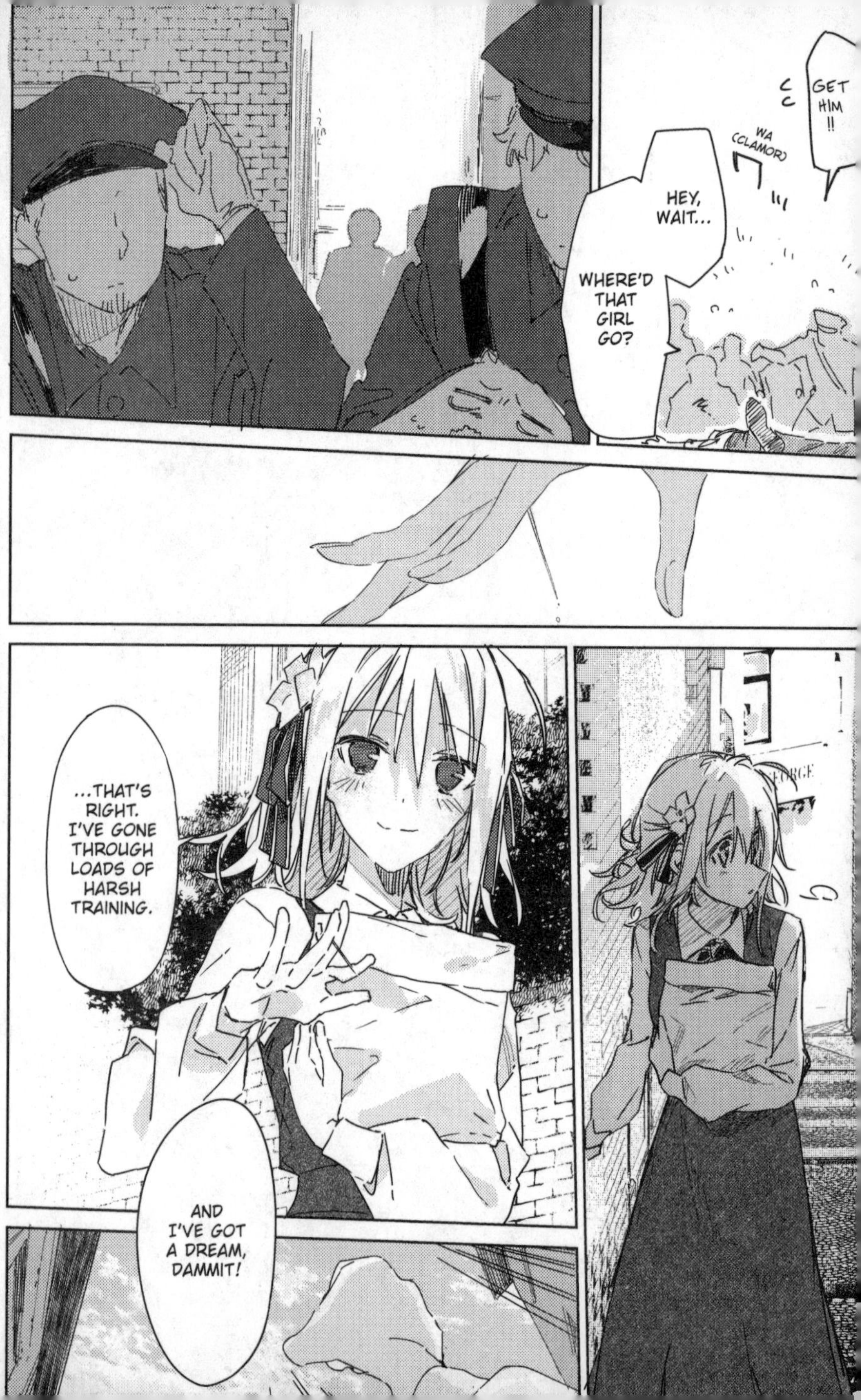
GET HIM!!
WA (CLAMOR)
HEY, WAIT...
WHERE'D THAT GIRL GO?
...THAT'S RIGHT. I'VE GONE THROUGH LOADS OF HARSH TRAINING.
AND I'VE GOT A DREAM, DAMMIT!

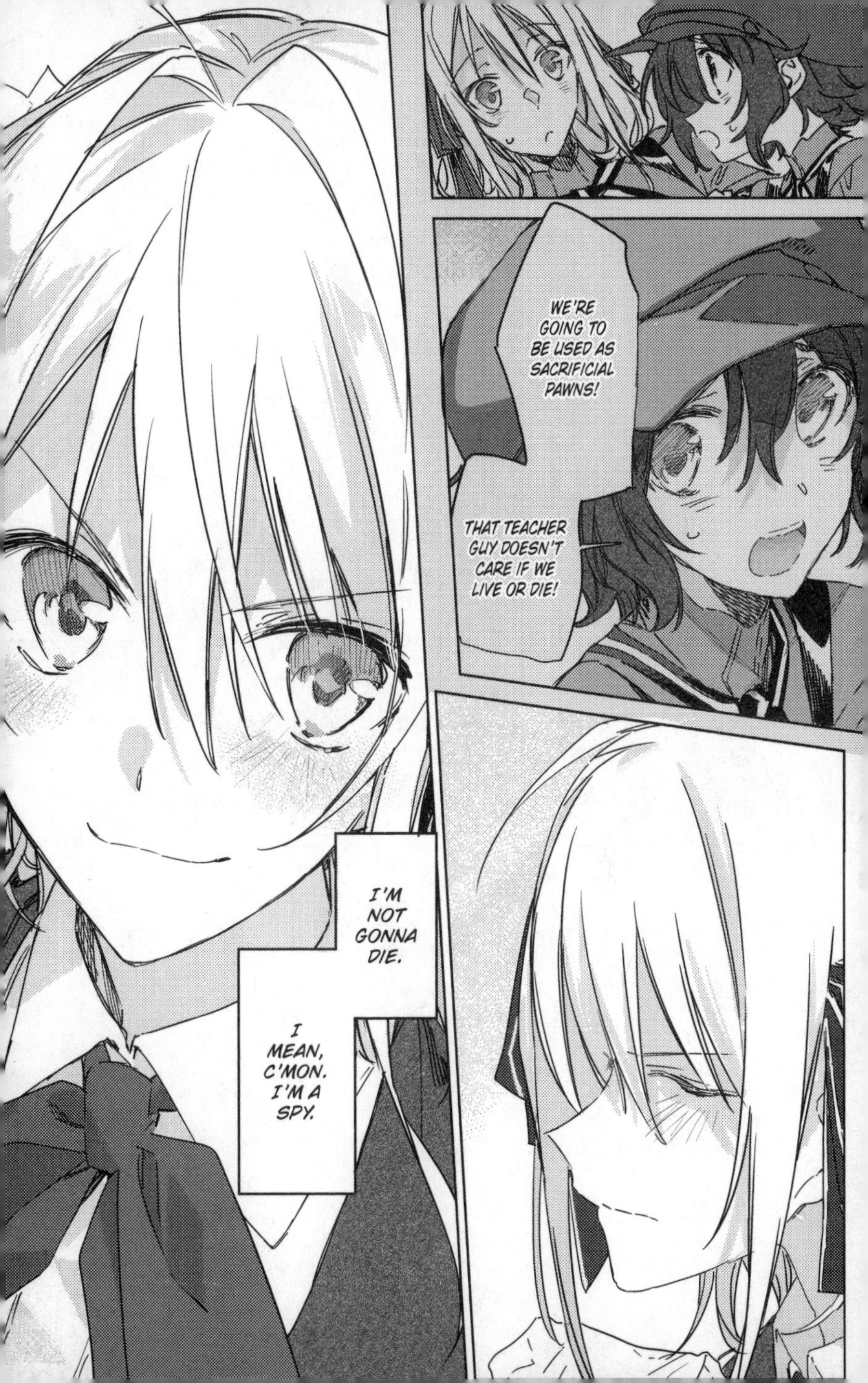
WE'RE GOING TO BE USED AS SACRIFICIAL PAWNS!
THAT TEACHER GUY DOESN'T CARE IF WE LIVE OR DIE!
I'M NOT GONNA DIE.
I MEAN, C'MON. I'M A SPY.

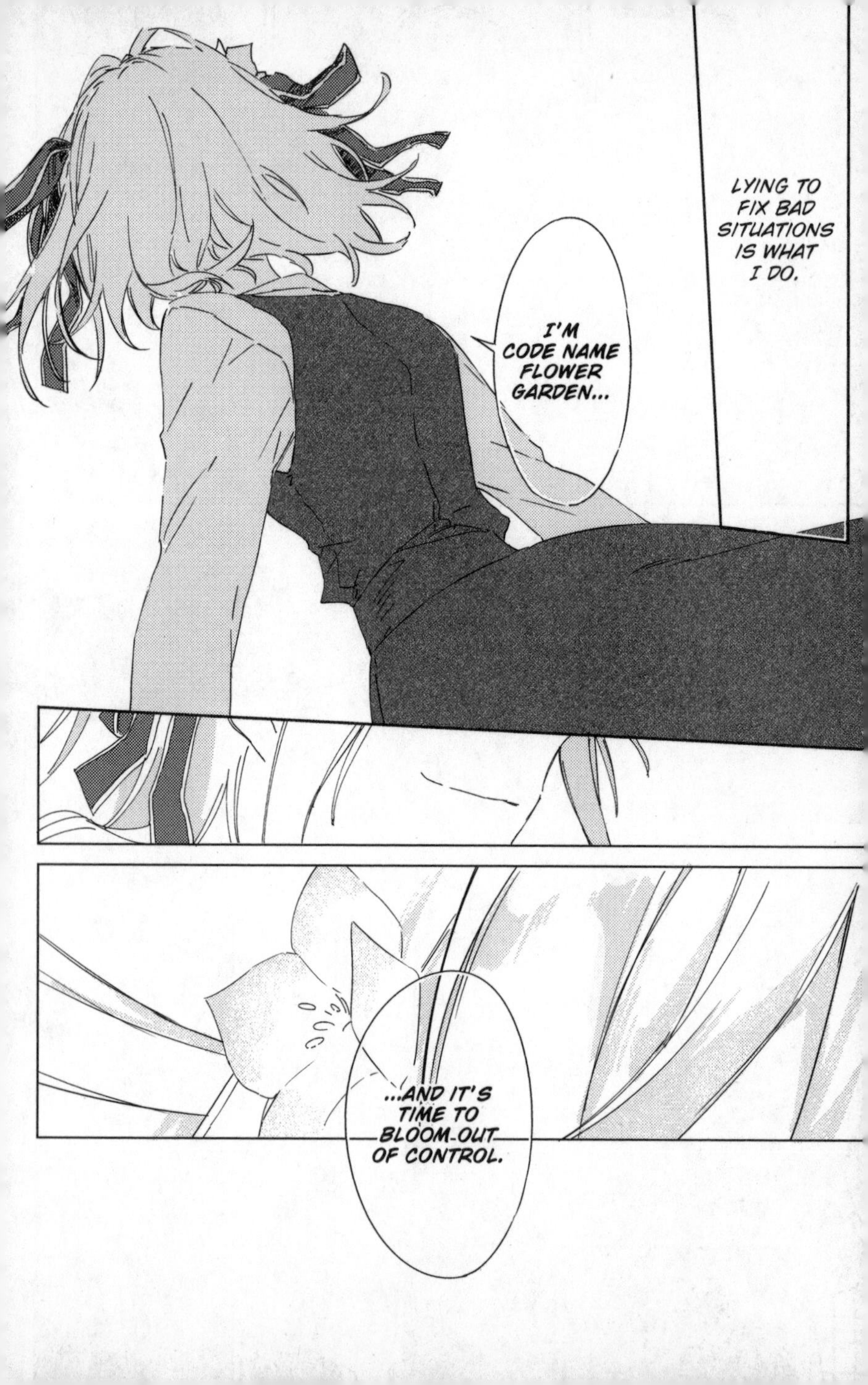
LYING TO FIX BAD SITUATIONS IS WHAT I DO.
I'M CODE NAME FLOWER GARDEN...
...AND IT'S TIME TO BLOOM OUT OF CONTROL.

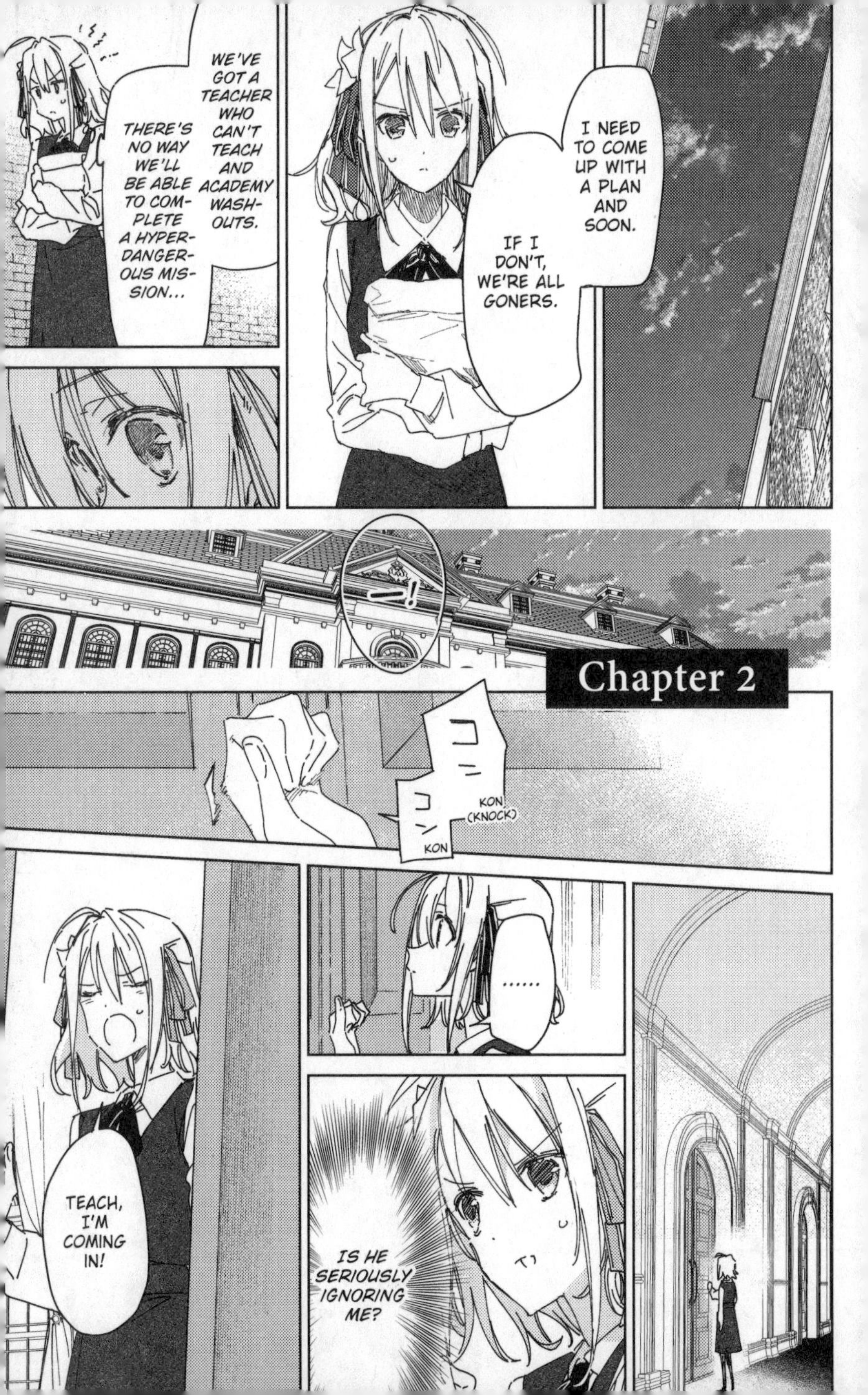
I NEED TO COME UP WITH A PLAN AND SOON.
IF I DON'T, WE'RE ALL GONERS.
WE'VE GOT A TEACHER WHO CAN'T TEACH AND ACADEMY WASH-OUTS.
THERE'S NO WAY WE'LL BE ABLE TO COMPLETE A HYPER-DANGEROUS MISSION...
Chapter 2
KON (KNOCK)
KON
......
IS HE SERIOUSLY IGNORING ME?
TEACH, I'M COMING IN!

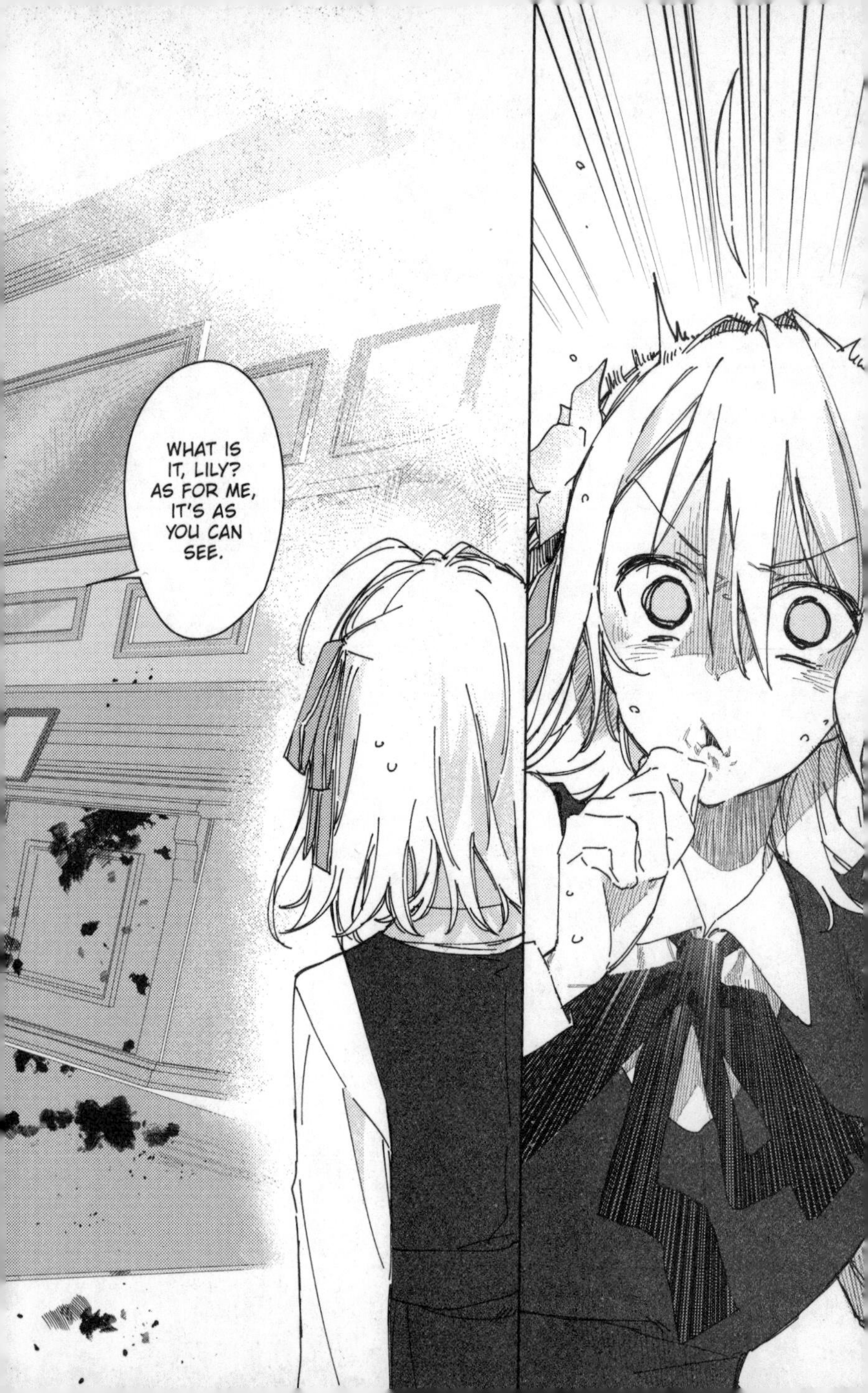
WHAT IS IT, LILY? AS FOR ME, IT'S AS YOU CAN SEE.

## Chapter 2 — Coercion

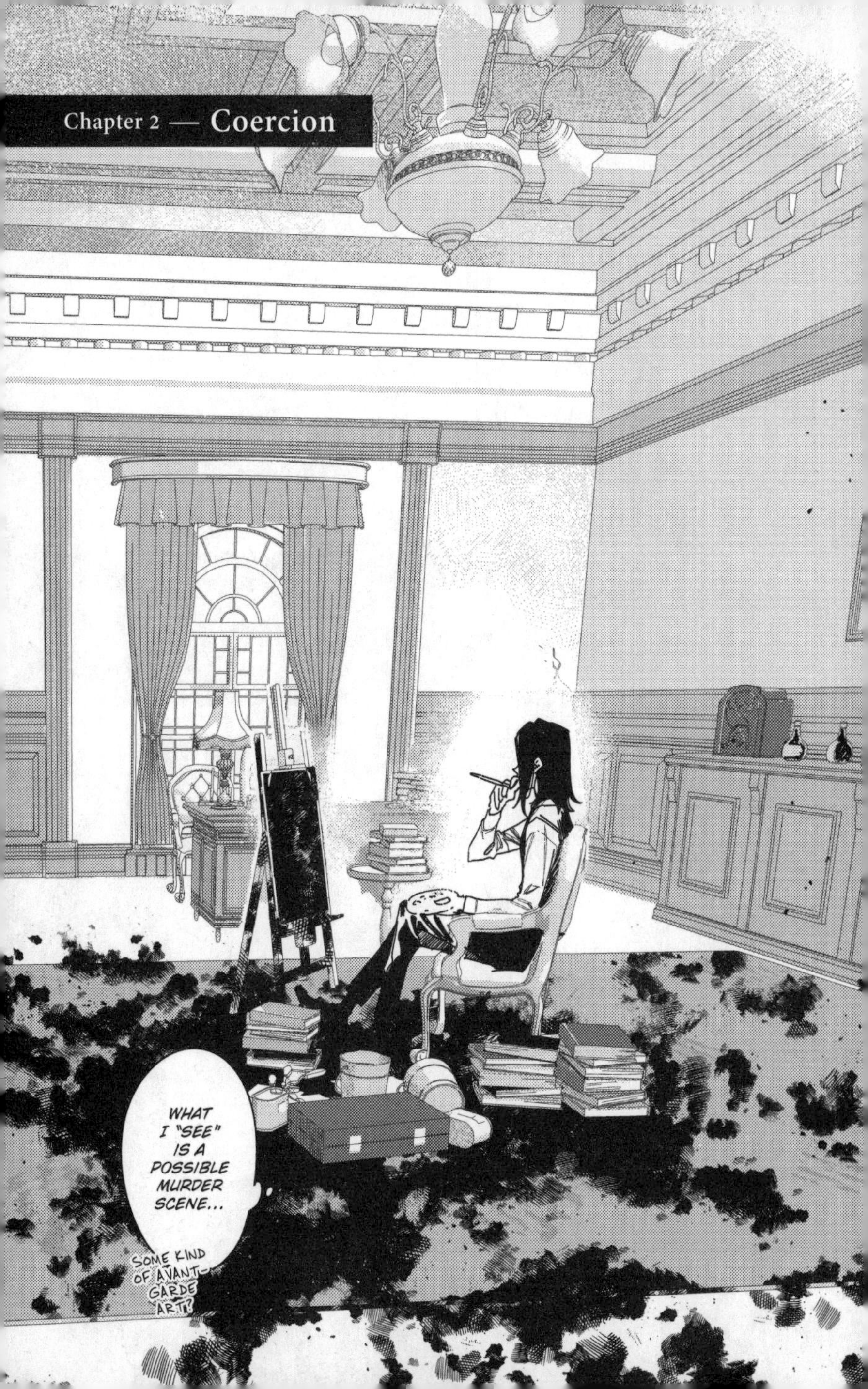
WHAT I "SEE" IS A POSSIBLE MURDER SCENE...
SOME KIND OF AVANT-GARDE ART?

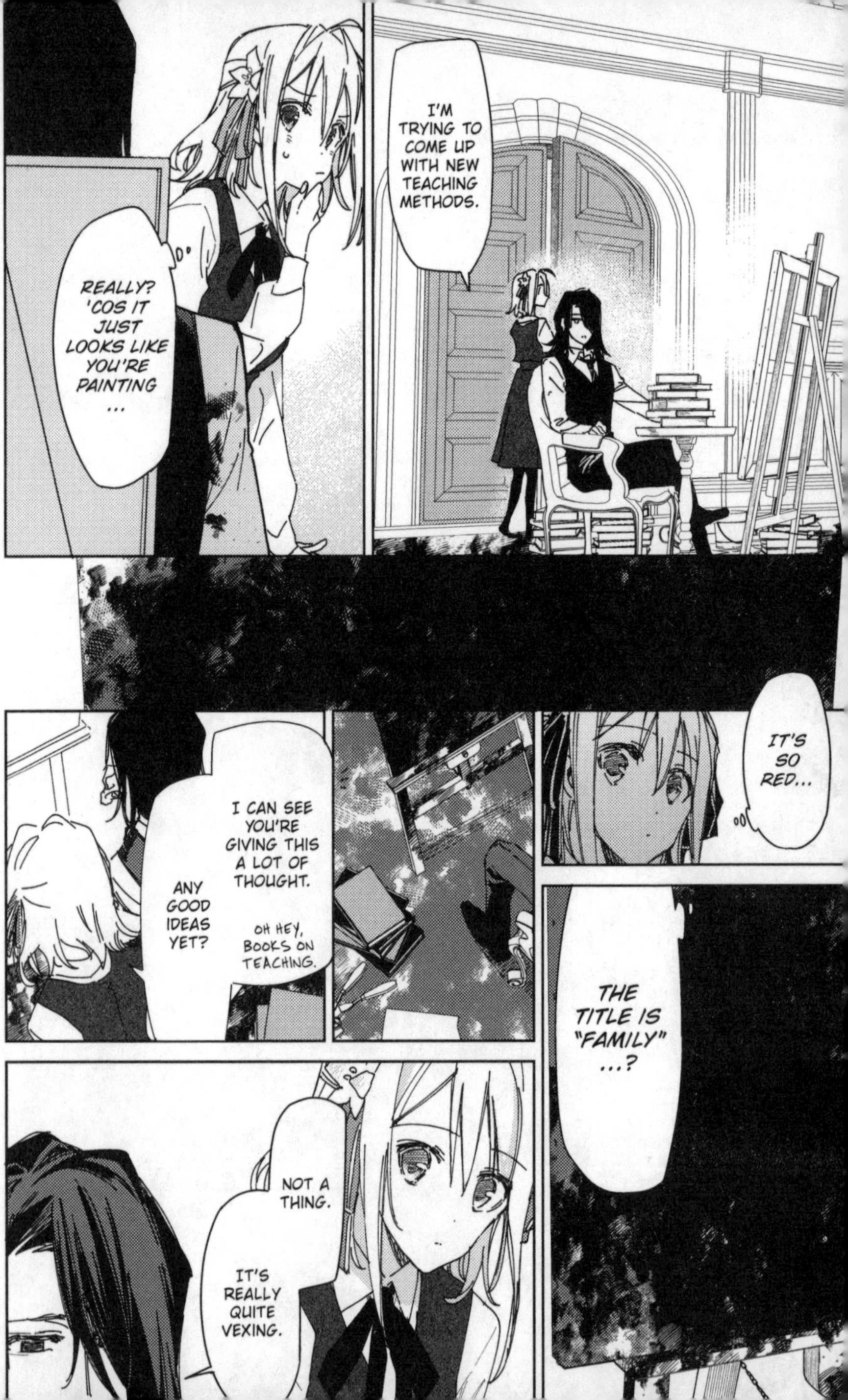
I'M TRYING TO COME UP WITH NEW TEACHING METHODS.
REALLY? 'COS IT JUST LOOKS LIKE YOU'RE PAINTING ...
IT'S SO RED...
I CAN SEE YOU'RE GIVING THIS A LOT OF THOUGHT.
OH HEY, BOOKS ON TEACHING.
ANY GOOD IDEAS YET?
THE TITLE IS "FAMILY" ...?
NOT A THING.
IT'S REALLY QUITE VEXING.

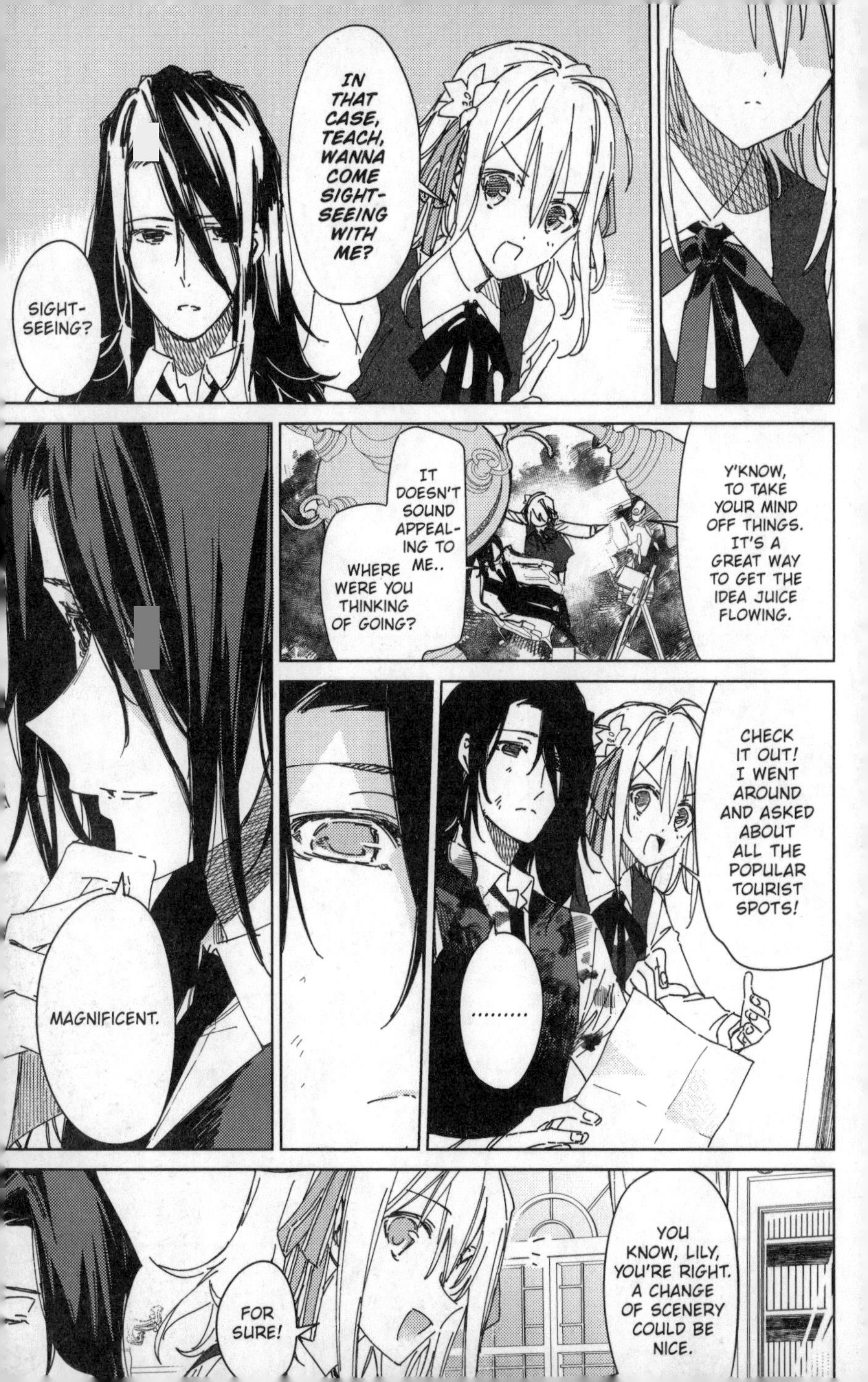
IN THAT CASE, TEACH, WANNA COME SIGHT-SEEING WITH ME?
SIGHT-SEEING?
Y'KNOW, TO TAKE YOUR MIND OFF THINGS. IT'S A GREAT WAY TO GET THE IDEA JUICE FLOWING.
IT DOESN'T SOUND APPEALING TO ME.. WHERE WERE YOU THINKING OF GOING?
CHECK IT OUT! I WENT AROUND AND ASKED ABOUT ALL THE POPULAR TOURIST SPOTS!
.........
MAGNIFICENT.
YOU KNOW, LILY, YOU'RE RIGHT. A CHANGE OF SCENERY COULD BE NICE.
FOR SURE!

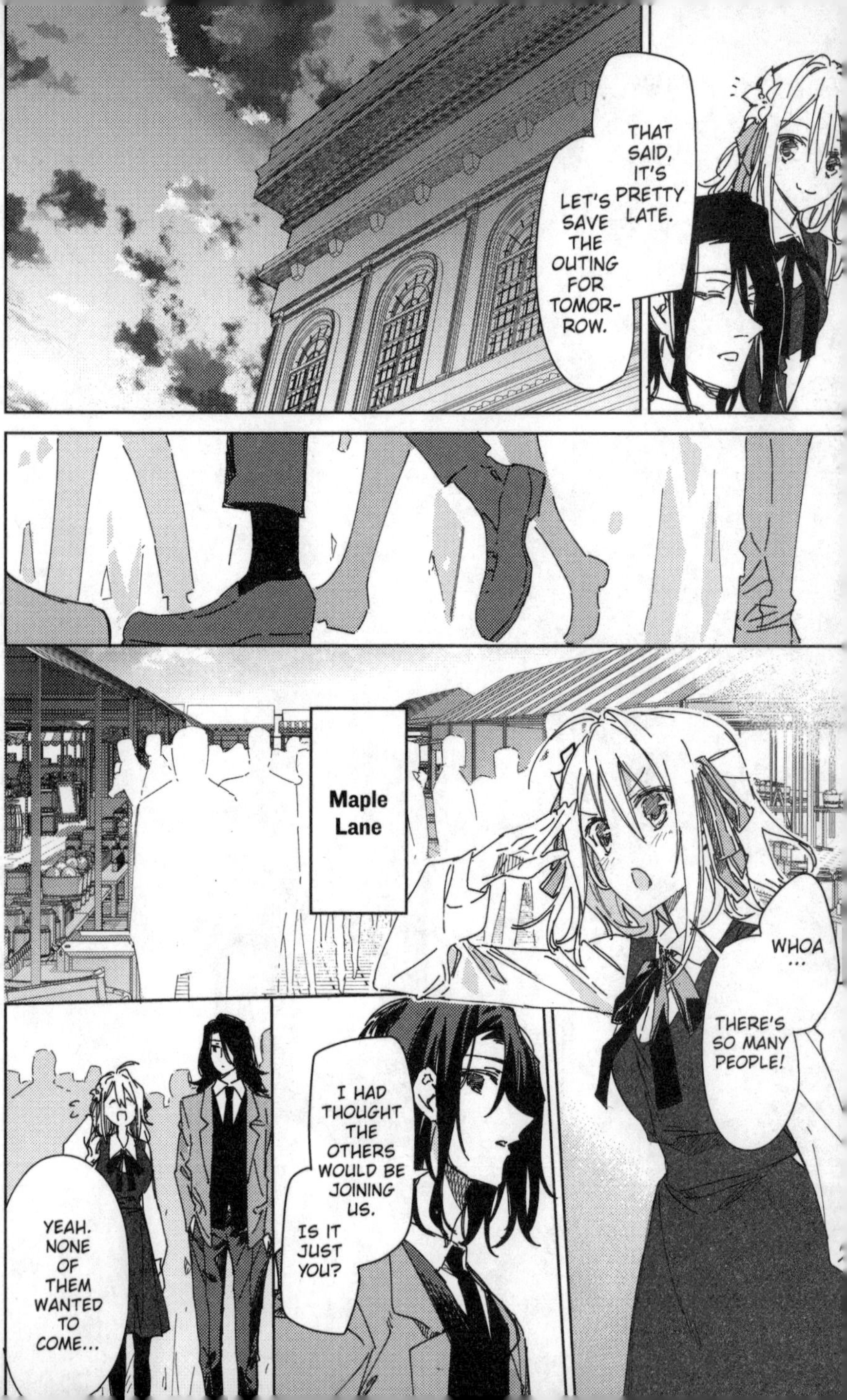

THAT SAID, IT'S PRETTY LATE.
LET'S SAVE THE OUTING FOR TOMOR-ROW.
Maple Lane
WHOA...
THERE'S SO MANY PEOPLE!
I HAD THOUGHT THE OTHERS WOULD BE JOINING US.
IS IT JUST YOU?
YEAH. NONE OF THEM WANTED TO COME...

IN THAT CASE, WE SHOULD BRING SOMETHING BACK FOR THEM.

HM... SOMETHING CANNED MAYBE?

YEAH! WHAT DO YOU THINK THEY'D LIKE?

OOH, SOUNDS TASTY— WAIT, HEY!

SARDINES PACKED IN OIL GO WONDER-FULLY WITH PASTA.

WE HAVE ADVAN-CES IN VACUUM-SEALING TECHNOL-OGY TO THANK.

THEY'VE STARTED SELLING A LOT OF HIGH-GRADE IMPORTS THAT WAY THESE PAST FEW YEARS.

HUH?

HOW'D YOU KNOW WHAT KIND OF FOODS I LIKE?

ALL I HAD TO DO WAS PICK ONE THAT SUITED YOUR TASTES.

I MEMO-RIZED A LIST OF EVERY GOOD OUR NATION IMPORTS.

YOU WERE ABLE TO GET THROUGH THAT EXPLANA-TION JUST FINE!

I JUST DID.

SHOULD I NOT HAVE BEEN?

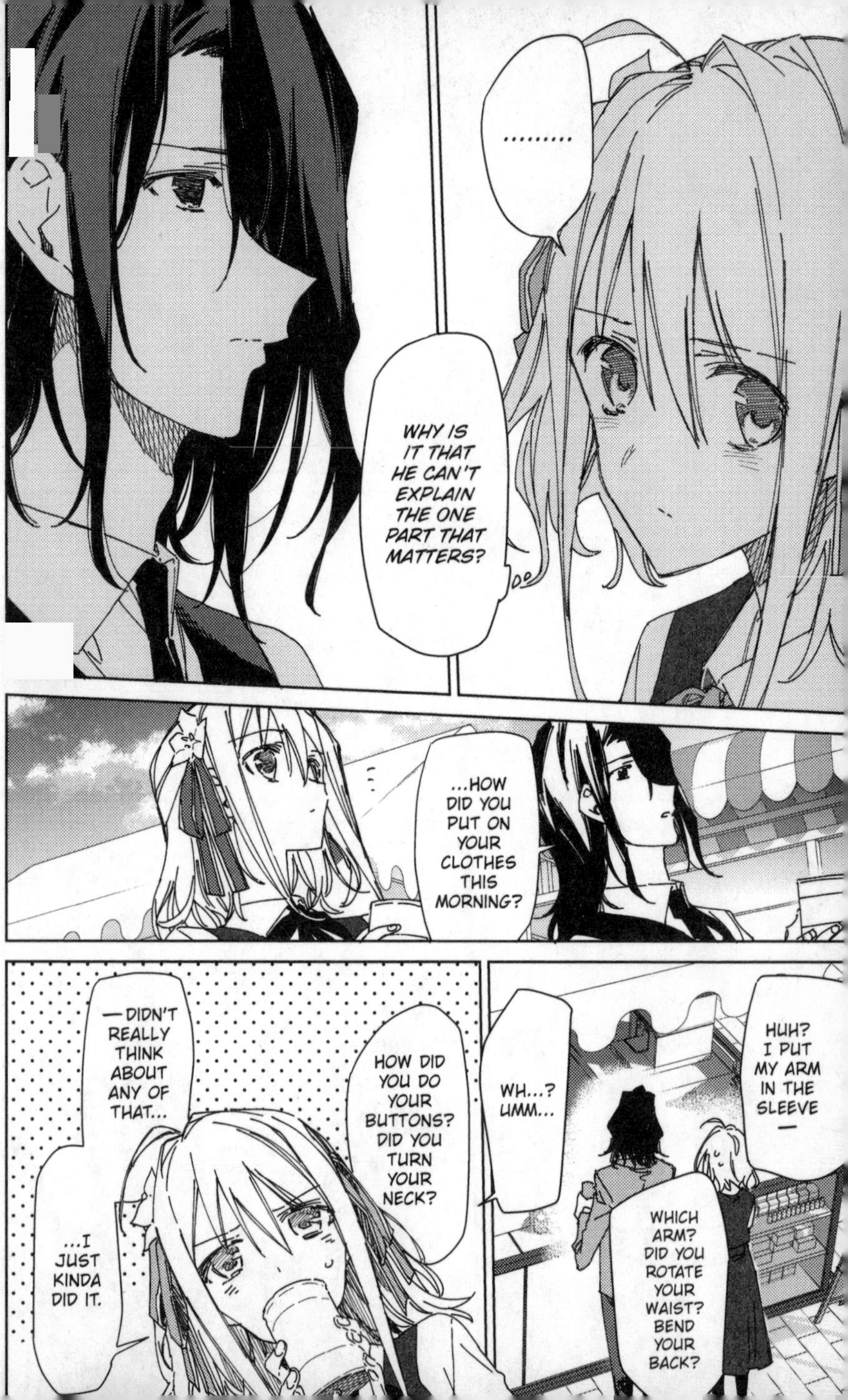
..........
WHY IS IT THAT HE CAN'T EXPLAIN THE ONE PART THAT MATTERS?
...HOW DID YOU PUT ON YOUR CLOTHES THIS MORNING?
HUH? I PUT MY ARM IN THE SLEEVE —
WHICH ARM? DID YOU ROTATE YOUR WAIST? BEND YOUR BACK?
WH...? UMM...
HOW DID YOU DO YOUR BUTTONS? DID YOU TURN YOUR NECK?
—DIDN'T REALLY THINK ABOUT ANY OF THAT...
...I JUST KINDA DID IT.

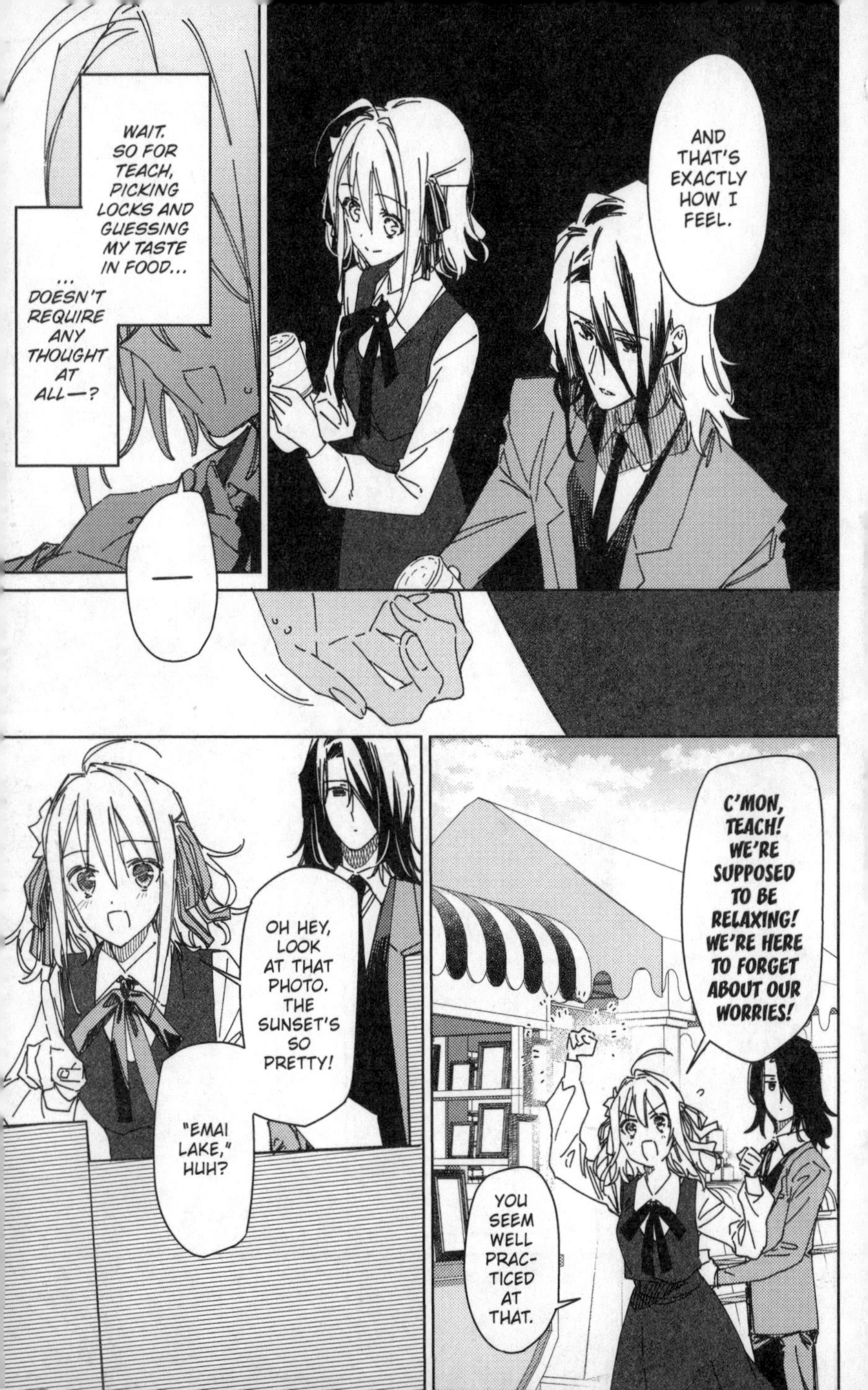
AND THAT'S EXACTLY HOW I FEEL.
WAIT. SO FOR TEACH, PICKING LOCKS AND GUESSING MY TASTE IN FOOD... ...DOESN'T REQUIRE ANY THOUGHT AT ALL—?
—
C'MON, TEACH! WE'RE SUPPOSED TO BE RELAXING! WE'RE HERE TO FORGET ABOUT OUR WORRIES!
YOU SEEM WELL PRAC-TICED AT THAT.
OH HEY, LOOK AT THAT PHOTO. THE SUNSET'S SO PRETTY!
"EMAI LAKE," HUH?

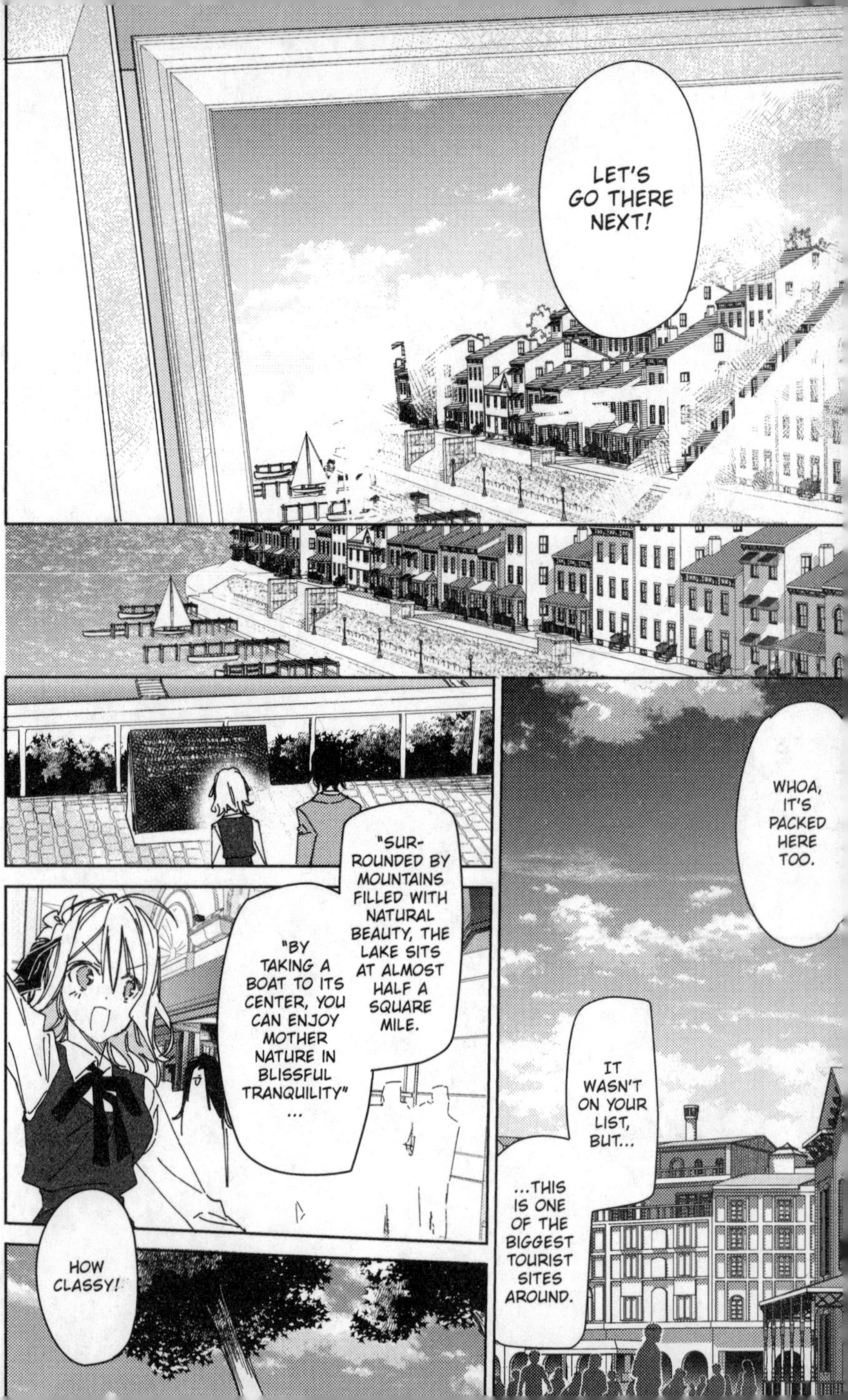
LET'S GO THERE NEXT!
WHOA, IT'S PACKED HERE TOO.
IT WASN'T ON YOUR LIST, BUT...
...THIS IS ONE OF THE BIGGEST TOURIST SITES AROUND.
"SUR-ROUNDED BY MOUNTAINS FILLED WITH NATURAL BEAUTY, THE LAKE SITS AT ALMOST HALF A SQUARE MILE.
"BY TAKING A BOAT TO ITS CENTER, YOU CAN ENJOY MOTHER NATURE IN BLISSFUL TRANQUILITY" ...
HOW CLASSY!

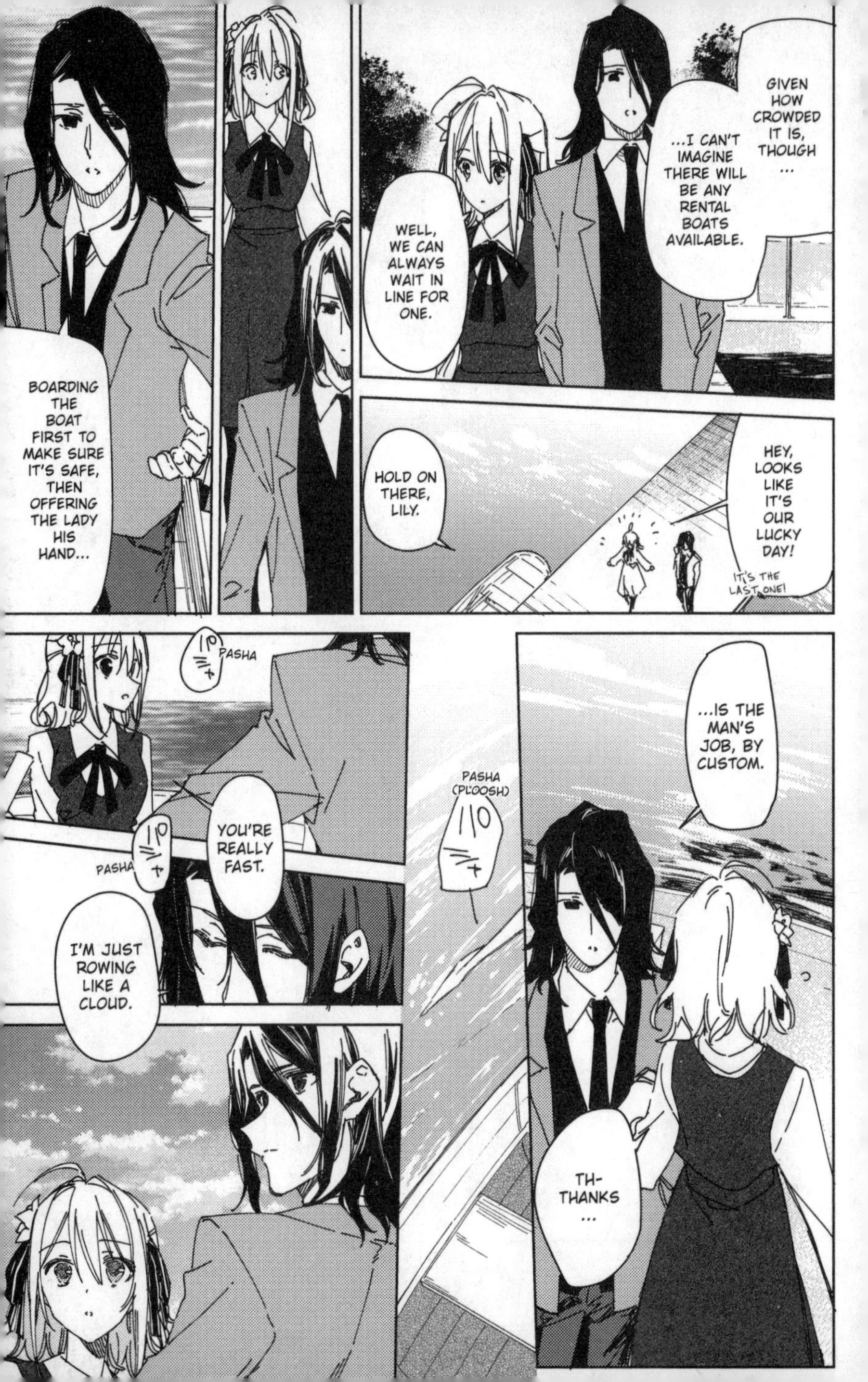
GIVEN HOW CROWDED IT IS, THOUGH ...
...I CAN'T IMAGINE THERE WILL BE ANY RENTAL BOATS AVAILABLE.
WELL, WE CAN ALWAYS WAIT IN LINE FOR ONE.
HEY, LOOKS LIKE IT'S OUR LUCKY DAY!
IT'S THE LAST ONE!
HOLD ON THERE, LILY.
BOARDING THE BOAT FIRST TO MAKE SURE IT'S SAFE, THEN OFFERING THE LADY HIS HAND...
...IS THE MAN'S JOB, BY CUSTOM.
PASHA (PLOOSH)
TH- THANKS ...
PASHA
YOU'RE REALLY FAST.
PASHA
I'M JUST ROWING LIKE A CLOUD.

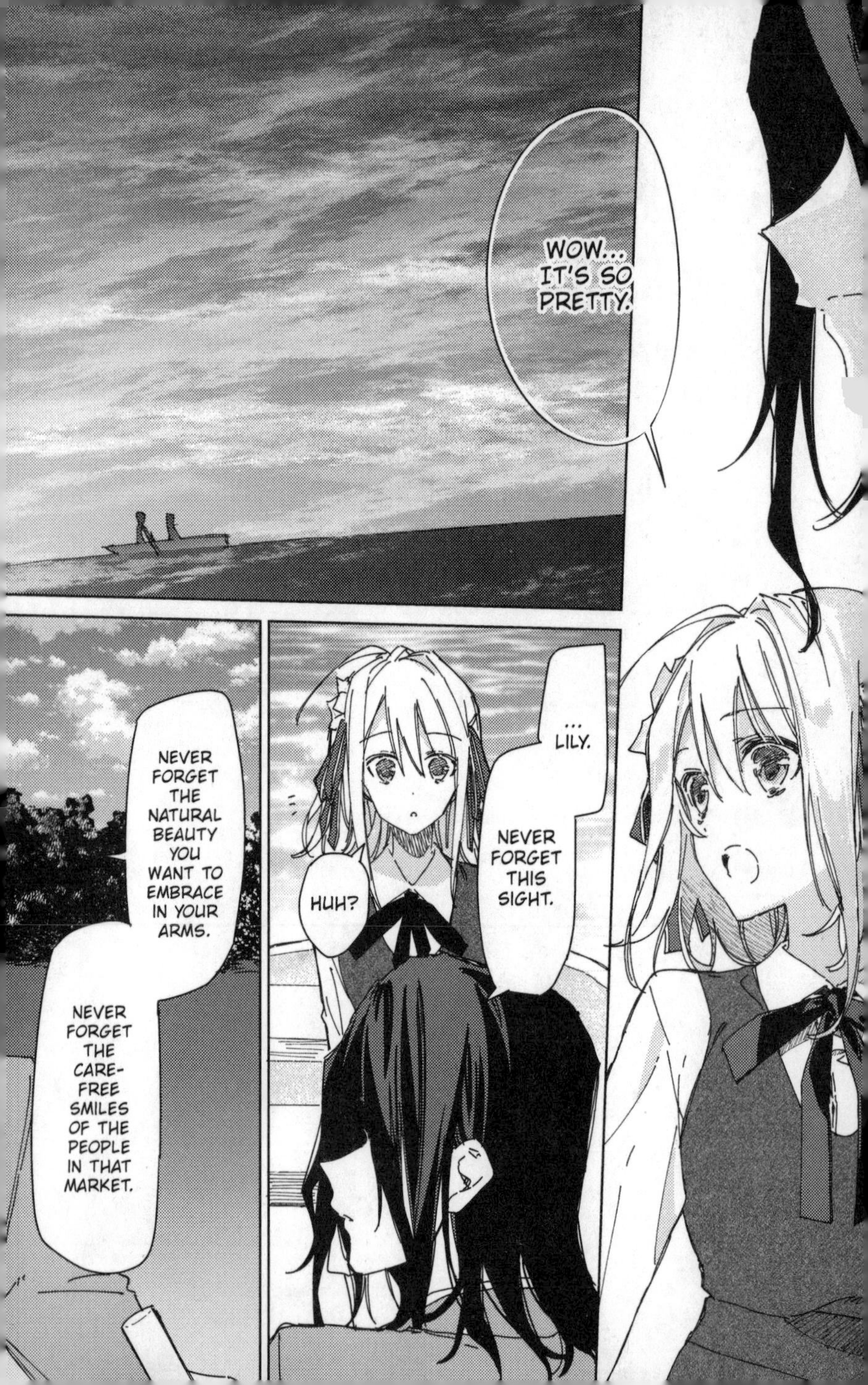
WOW... IT'S SO PRETTY.
...LILY.
NEVER FORGET THIS SIGHT.
HUH?
NEVER FORGET THE NATURAL BEAUTY YOU WANT TO EMBRACE IN YOUR ARMS.
NEVER FORGET THE CARE-FREE SMILES OF THE PEOPLE IN THAT MARKET.

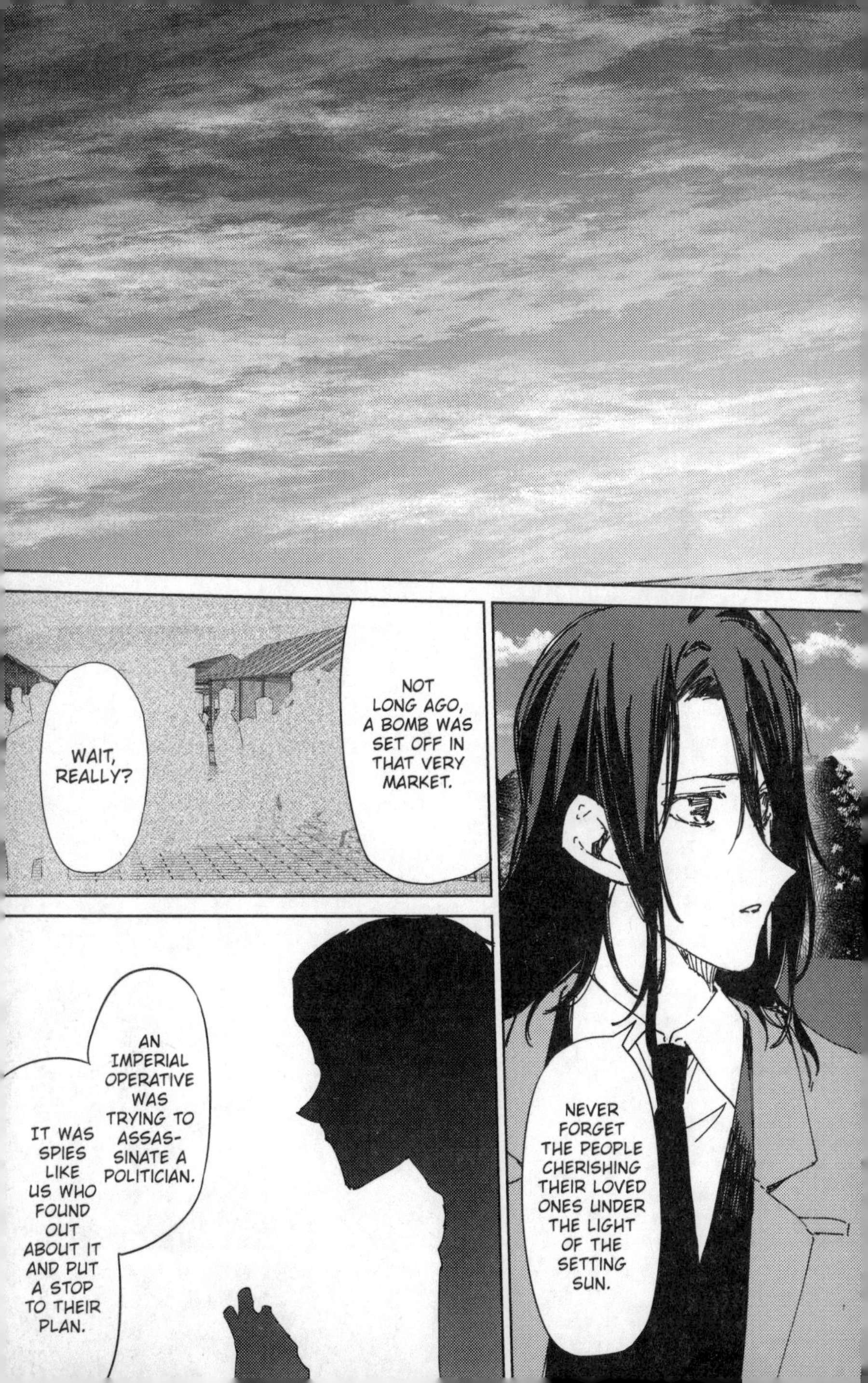
NEVER FORGET THE PEOPLE CHERISHING THEIR LOVED ONES UNDER THE LIGHT OF THE SETTING SUN.
NOT LONG AGO, A BOMB WAS SET OFF IN THAT VERY MARKET.
WAIT, REALLY?
AN IMPERIAL OPERATIVE WAS TRYING TO ASSAS-SINATE A POLITICIAN.
IT WAS SPIES LIKE US WHO FOUND OUT ABOUT IT AND PUT A STOP TO THEIR PLAN.

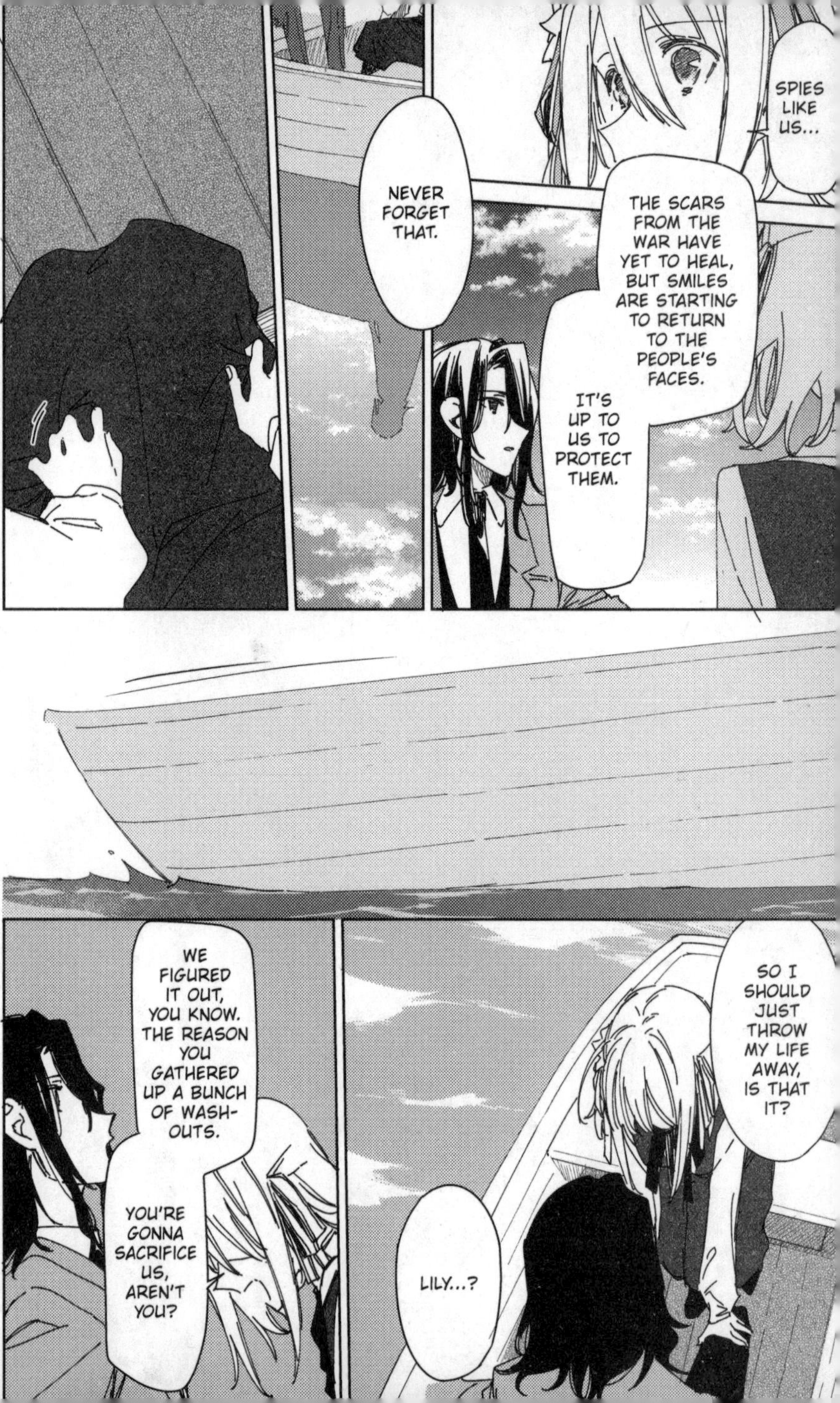
SPIES LIKE US...
THE SCARS FROM THE WAR HAVE YET TO HEAL, BUT SMILES ARE STARTING TO RETURN TO THE PEOPLE'S FACES.
IT'S UP TO US TO PROTECT THEM.
NEVER FORGET THAT.
SO I SHOULD JUST THROW MY LIFE AWAY, IS THAT IT?
LILY...?
WE FIGURED IT OUT, YOU KNOW. THE REASON YOU GATHERED UP A BUNCH OF WASH-OUTS.
YOU'RE GONNA SACRIFICE US, AREN'T YOU?

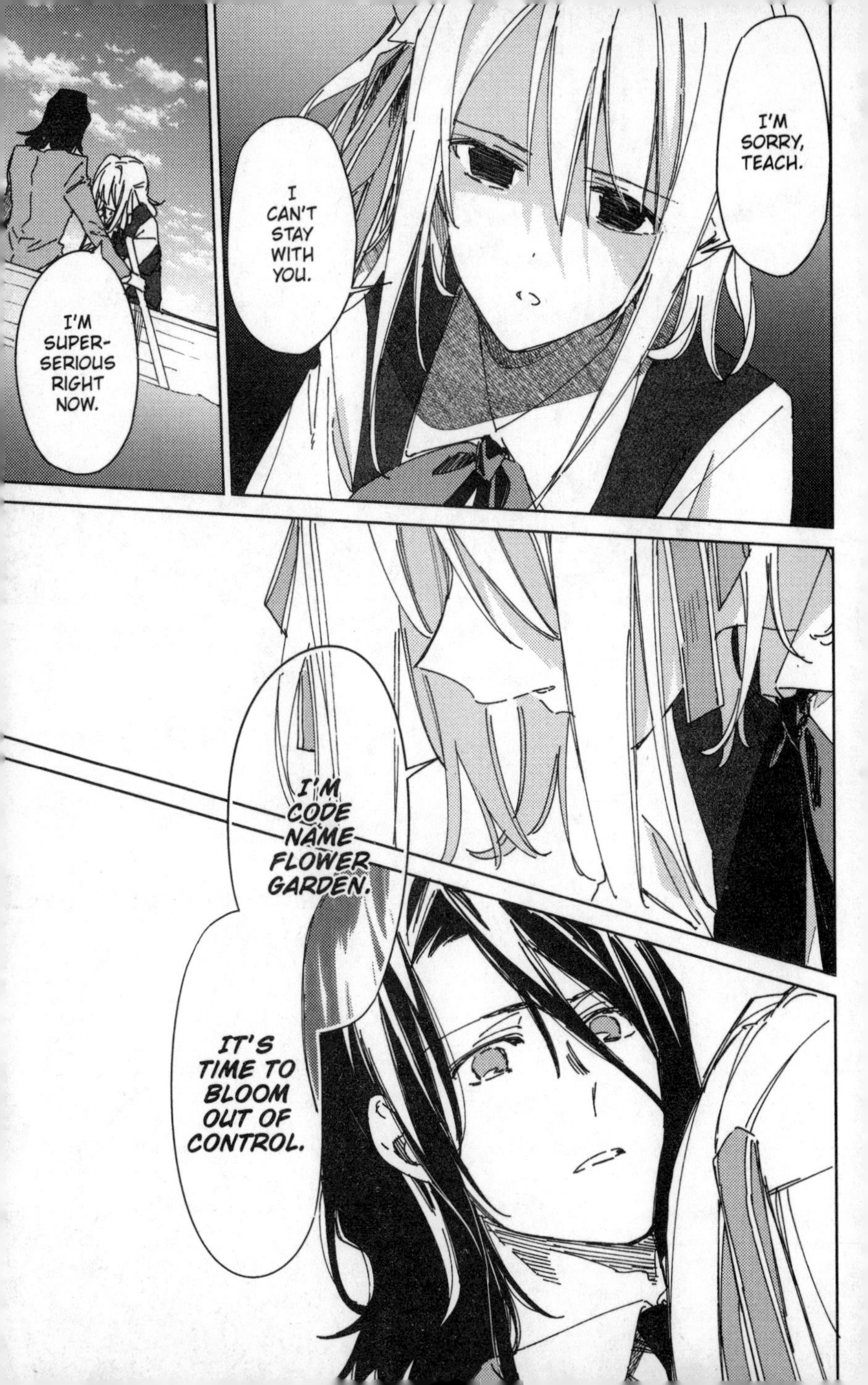
I'M SORRY, TEACH.
I CAN'T STAY WITH YOU.
I'M SUPER-SERIOUS RIGHT NOW.
I'M CODE NAME FLOWER GARDEN.
IT'S TIME TO BLOOM OUT OF CONTROL.

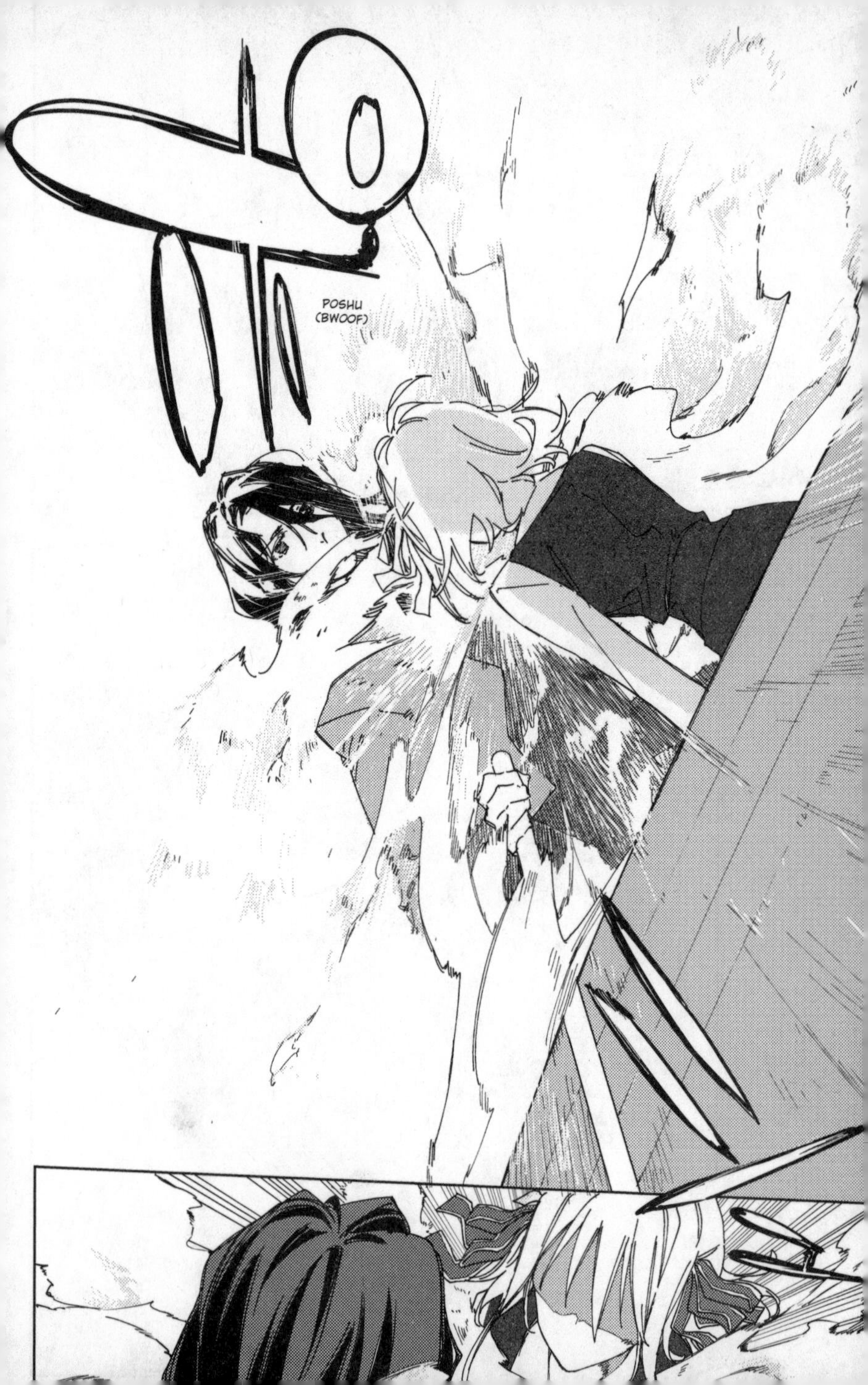
POSHU
(BWOOF)

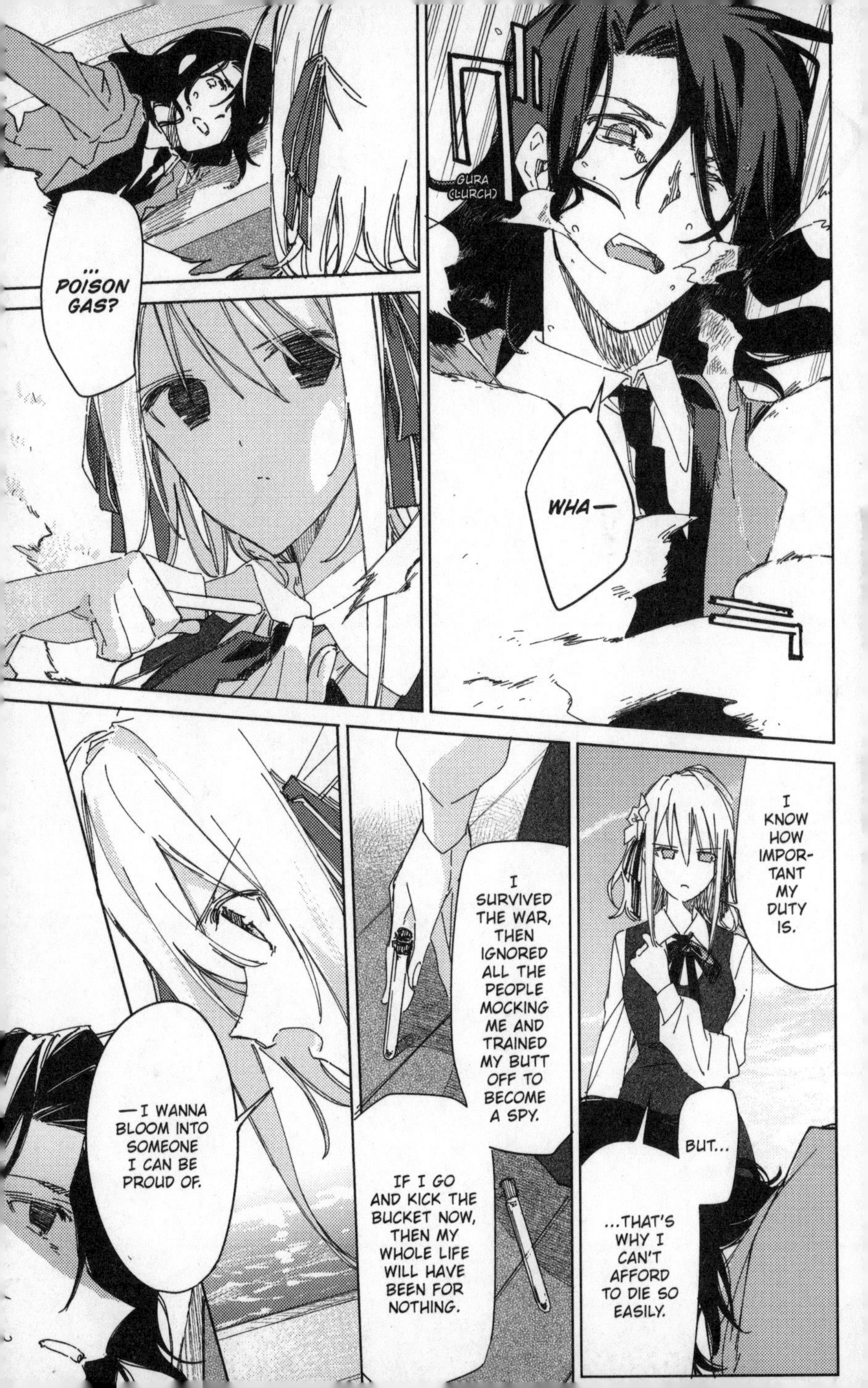
GURA (LURCH)
WHA—
... POISON GAS?
I KNOW HOW IMPORTANT MY DUTY IS.
BUT...
...THAT'S WHY I CAN'T AFFORD TO DIE SO EASILY.
I SURVIVED THE WAR, THEN IGNORED ALL THE PEOPLE MOCKING ME AND TRAINED MY BUTT OFF TO BECOME A SPY.
IF I GO AND KICK THE BUCKET NOW, THEN MY WHOLE LIFE WILL HAVE BEEN FOR NOTHING.
—I WANNA BLOOM INTO SOMEONE I CAN BE PROUD OF.

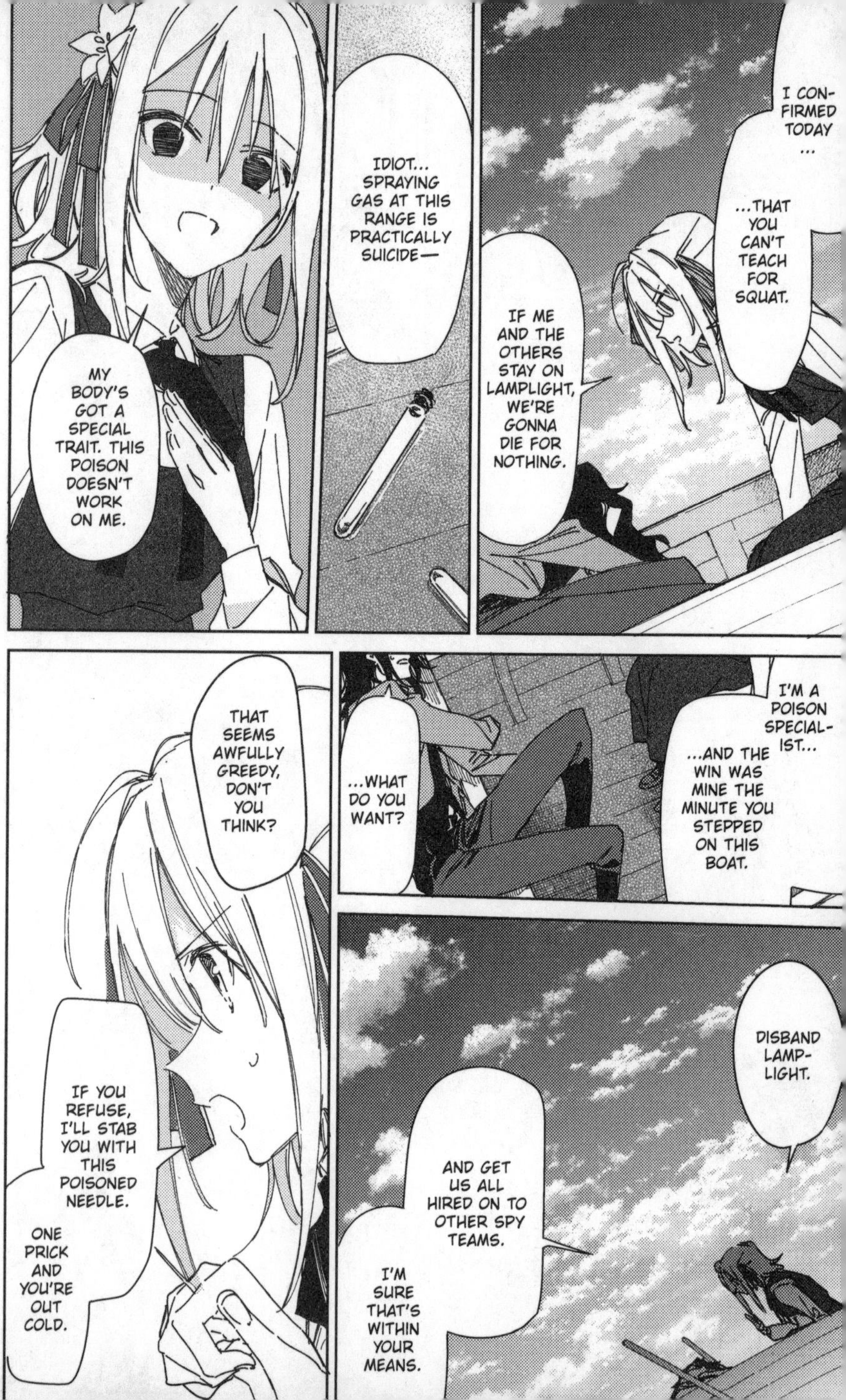
I CONFIRMED TODAY...
...THAT YOU CAN'T TEACH FOR SQUAT.
IF ME AND THE OTHERS STAY ON LAMPLIGHT, WE'RE GONNA DIE FOR NOTHING.
IDIOT... SPRAYING GAS AT THIS RANGE IS PRACTICALLY SUICIDE—
MY BODY'S GOT A SPECIAL TRAIT. THIS POISON DOESN'T WORK ON ME.
I'M A POISON SPECIALIST...
...AND THE WIN WAS MINE THE MINUTE YOU STEPPED ON THIS BOAT.
...WHAT DO YOU WANT?
DISBAND LAMPLIGHT.
AND GET US ALL HIRED ON TO OTHER SPY TEAMS.
I'M SURE THAT'S WITHIN YOUR MEANS.
THAT SEEMS AWFULLY GREEDY, DON'T YOU THINK?
IF YOU REFUSE, I'LL STAB YOU WITH THIS POISONED NEEDLE.
ONE PRICK AND YOU'RE OUT COLD.

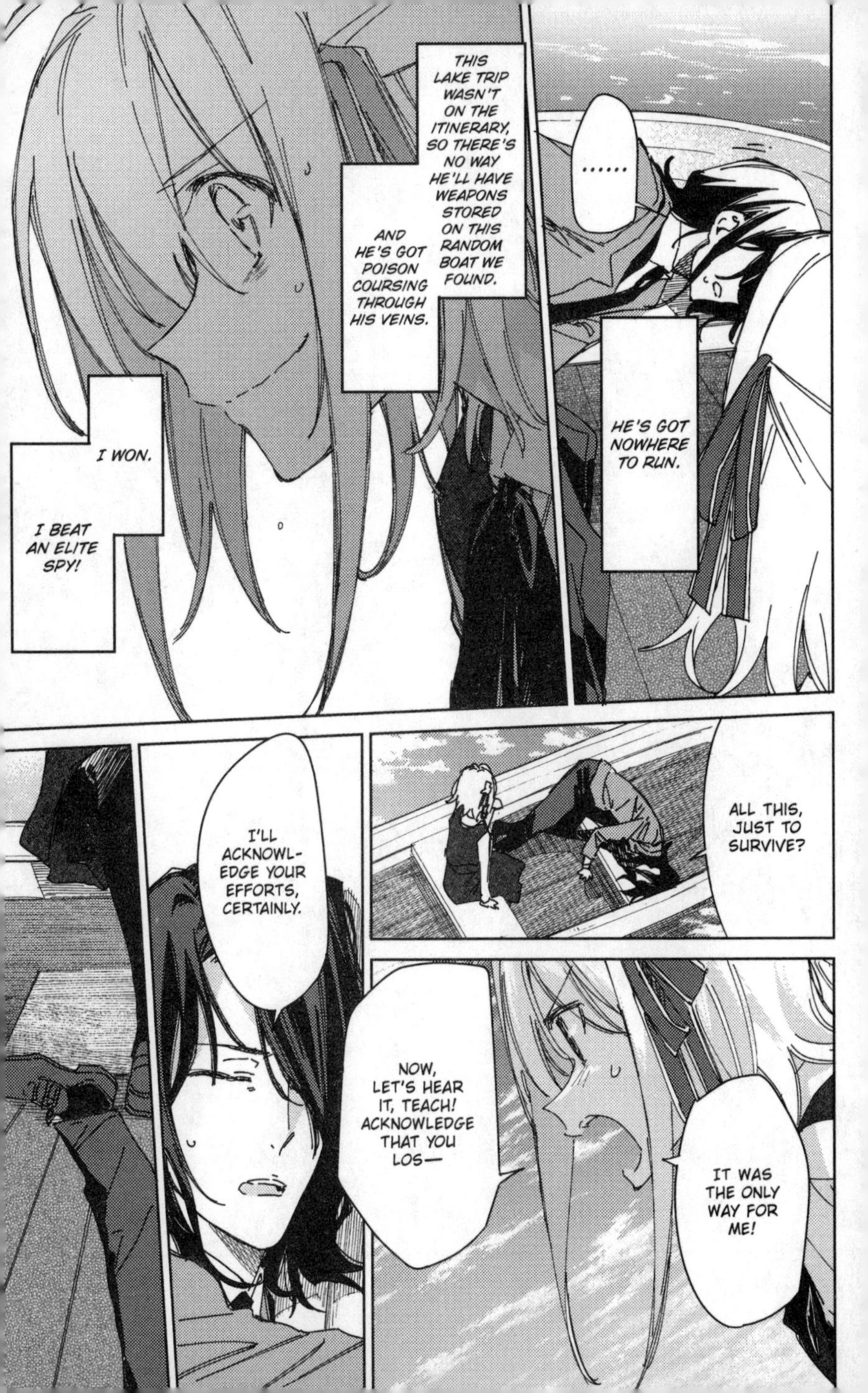
......
HE'S GOT NOWHERE TO RUN.
THIS LAKE TRIP WASN'T ON THE ITINERARY, SO THERE'S NO WAY HE'LL HAVE WEAPONS STORED ON THIS RANDOM BOAT WE FOUND.
AND HE'S GOT POISON COURSING THROUGH HIS VEINS.
I WON.
I BEAT AN ELITE SPY!
ALL THIS, JUST TO SURVIVE?
IT WAS THE ONLY WAY FOR ME!
NOW, LET'S HEAR IT, TEACH! ACKNOWLEDGE THAT YOU LOS—
I'LL ACKNOWL-EDGE YOUR EFFORTS, CERTAINLY.

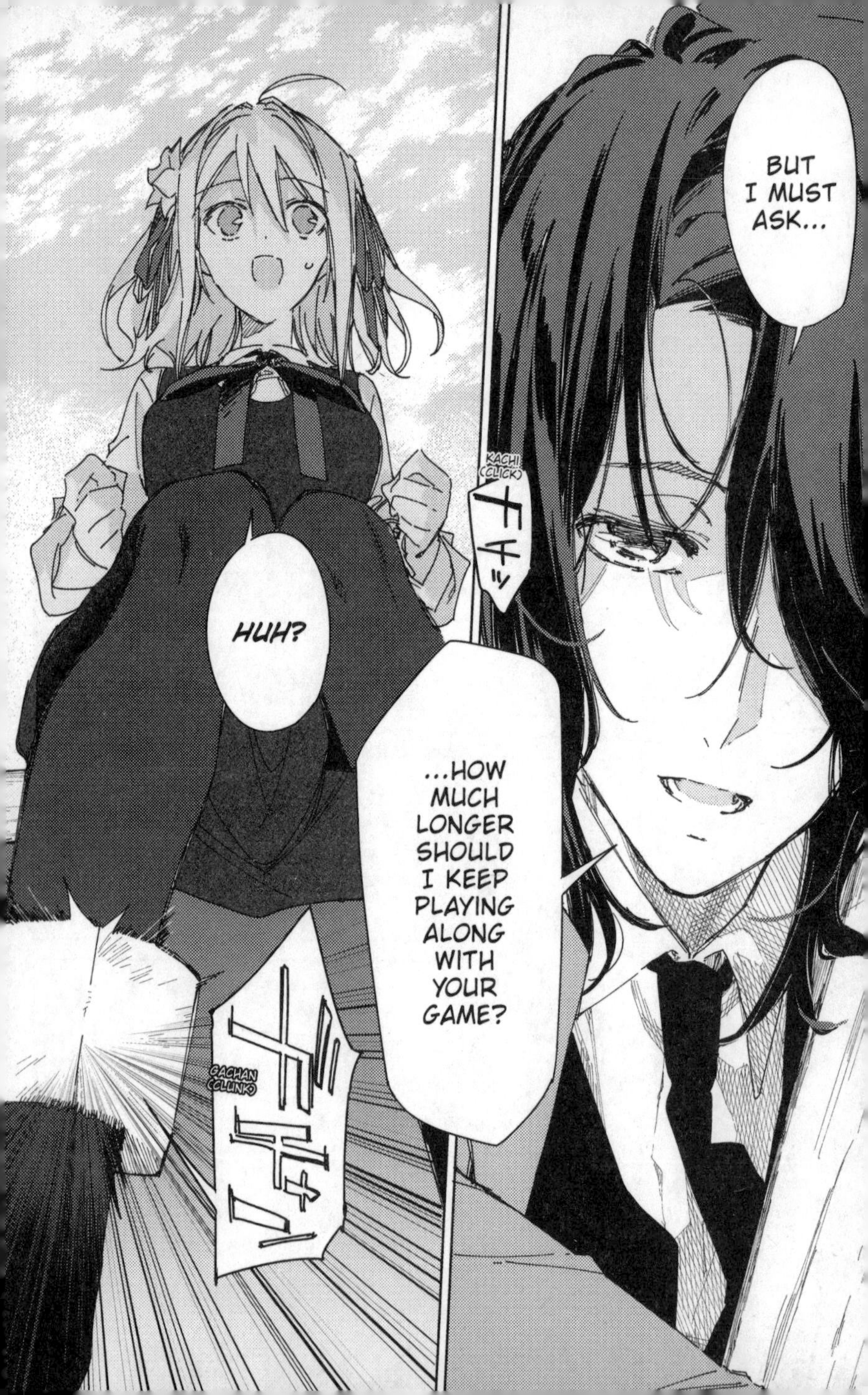
BUT I MUST ASK...
KACHI (CLICK)
...HOW MUCH LONGER SHOULD I KEEP PLAYING ALONG WITH YOUR GAME?
HUH?
GACHAN (CLUNK)

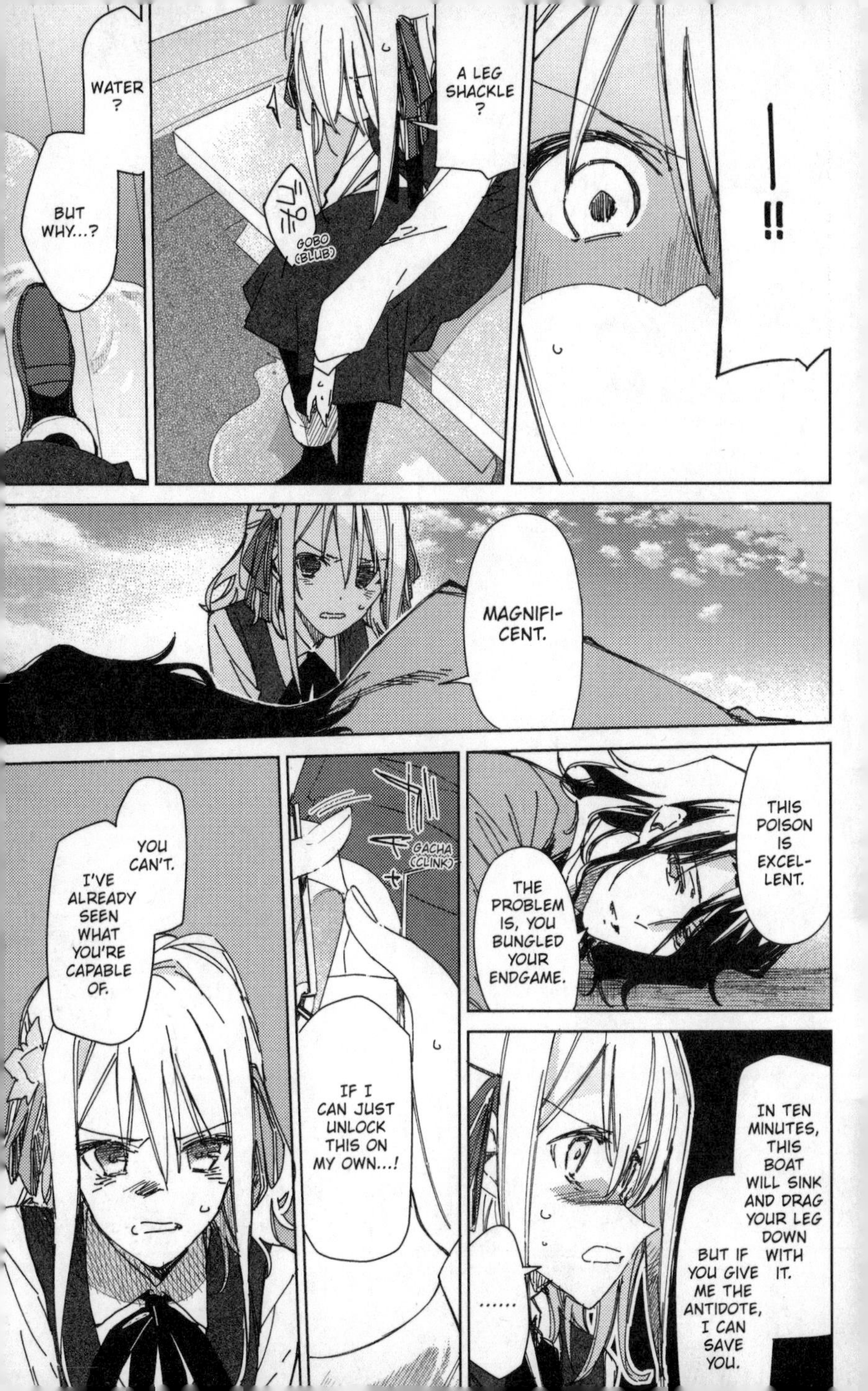
—!!
A LEG SHACKLE?
GOBO (BLUB)
WATER?
BUT WHY...?
MAGNIFI-CENT.
THIS POISON IS EXCEL-LENT.
THE PROBLEM IS, YOU BUNGLED YOUR ENDGAME.
IN TEN MINUTES, THIS BOAT WILL SINK AND DRAG YOUR LEG DOWN WITH IT.
BUT IF YOU GIVE ME THE ANTIDOTE, I CAN SAVE YOU.
......
GACHA (CLINK)
IF I CAN JUST UNLOCK THIS ON MY OWN...!
YOU CAN'T.
I'VE ALREADY SEEN WHAT YOU'RE CAPABLE OF.

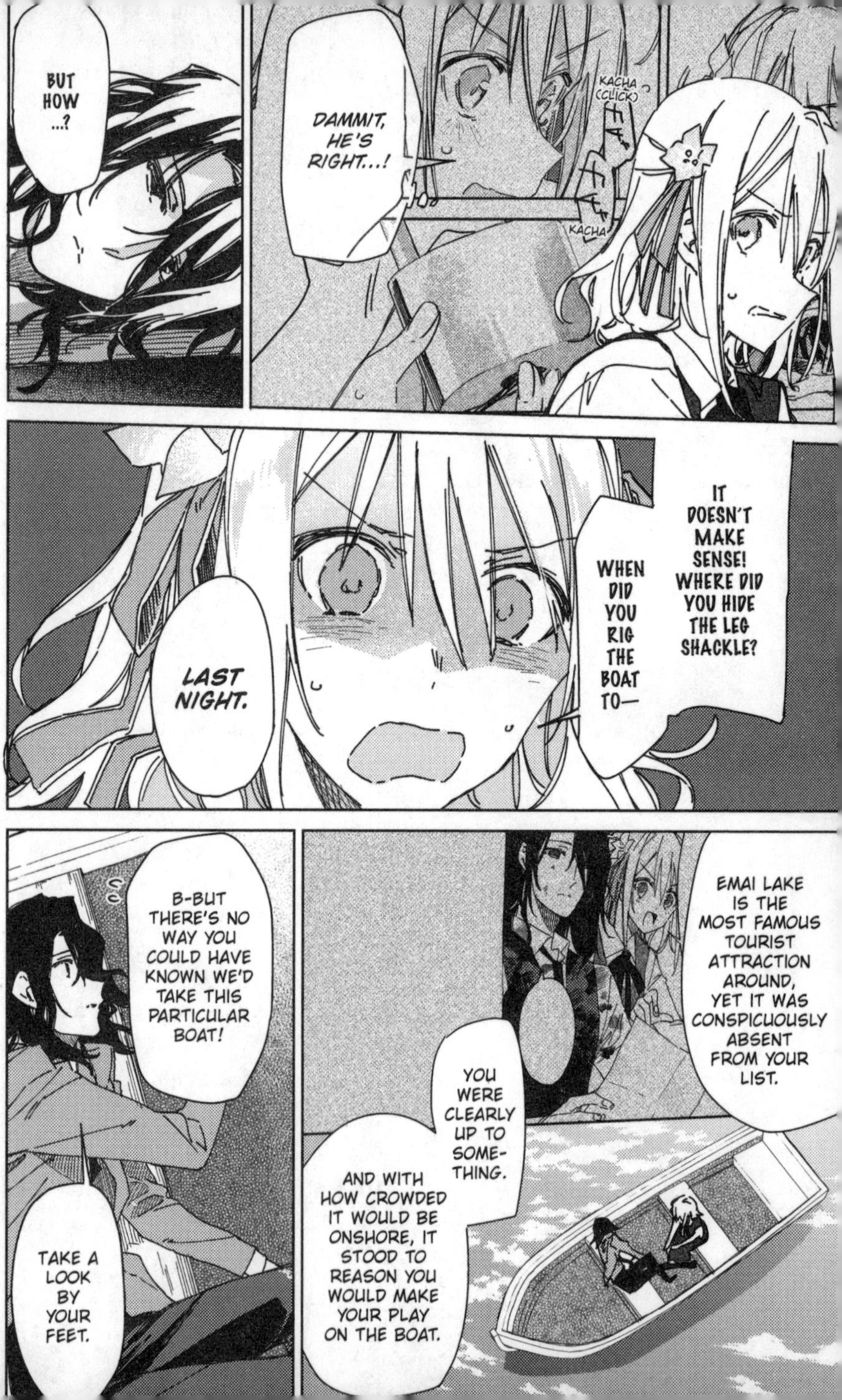
KACHA (CLICK)
KACHA
DAMMIT, HE'S RIGHT...!
BUT HOW...?
IT DOESN'T MAKE SENSE! WHERE DID YOU HIDE THE LEG SHACKLE?
WHEN DID YOU RIG THE BOAT TO—
LAST NIGHT.
EMAI LAKE IS THE MOST FAMOUS TOURIST ATTRACTION AROUND, YET IT WAS CONSPICUOUSLY ABSENT FROM YOUR LIST.
YOU WERE CLEARLY UP TO SOME-THING.
AND WITH HOW CROWDED IT WOULD BE ONSHORE, IT STOOD TO REASON YOU WOULD MAKE YOUR PLAY ON THE BOAT.
B-BUT THERE'S NO WAY YOU COULD HAVE KNOWN WE'D TAKE THIS PARTICULAR BOAT!
TAKE A LOOK BY YOUR FEET.

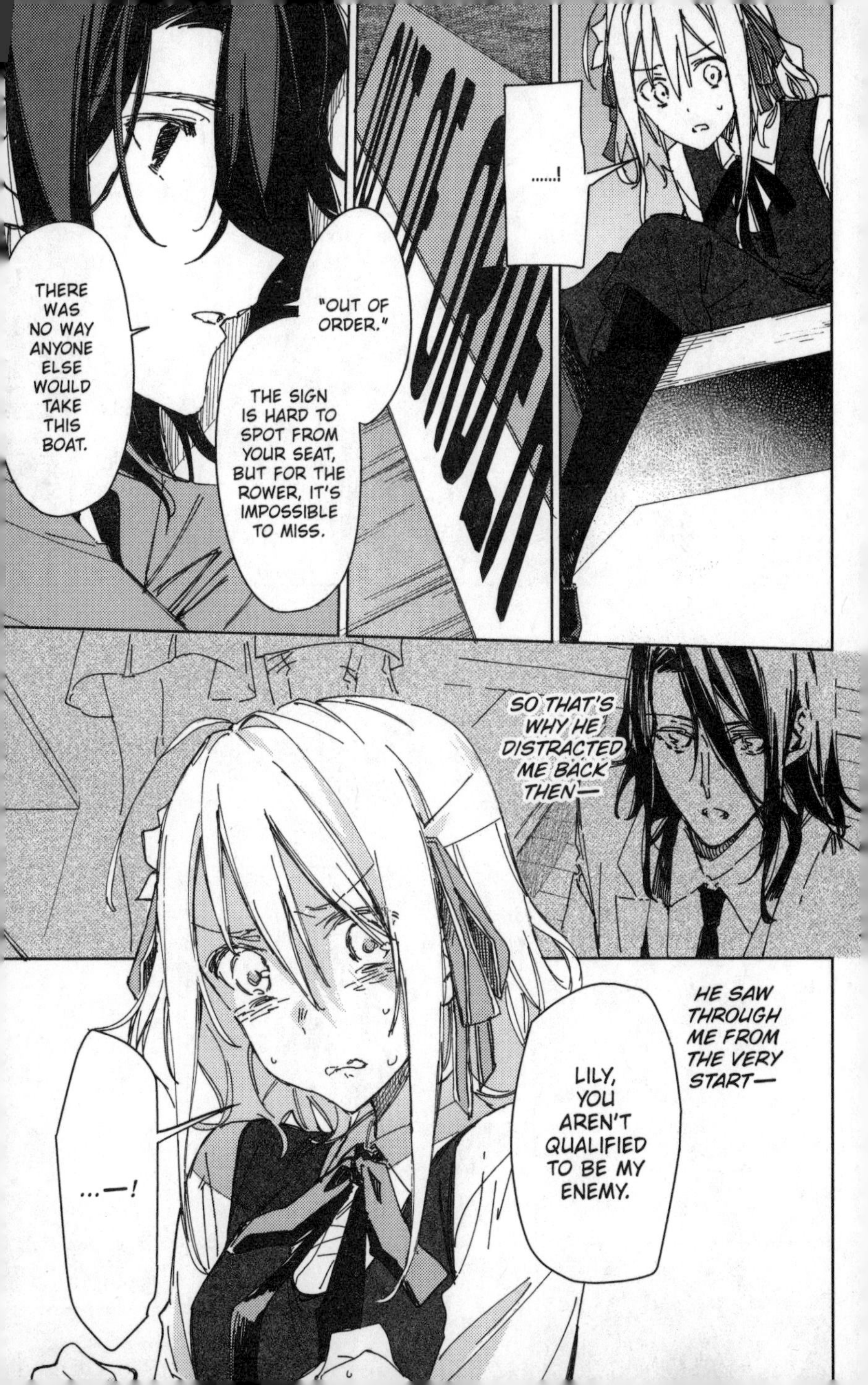
......!
"OUT OF ORDER."
THE SIGN IS HARD TO SPOT FROM YOUR SEAT, BUT FOR THE ROWER, IT'S IMPOSSIBLE TO MISS.
THERE WAS NO WAY ANYONE ELSE WOULD TAKE THIS BOAT.
SO THAT'S WHY HE DISTRACTED ME BACK THEN—
HE SAW THROUGH ME FROM THE VERY START—
LILY, YOU AREN'T QUALIFIED TO BE MY ENEMY.
...—!

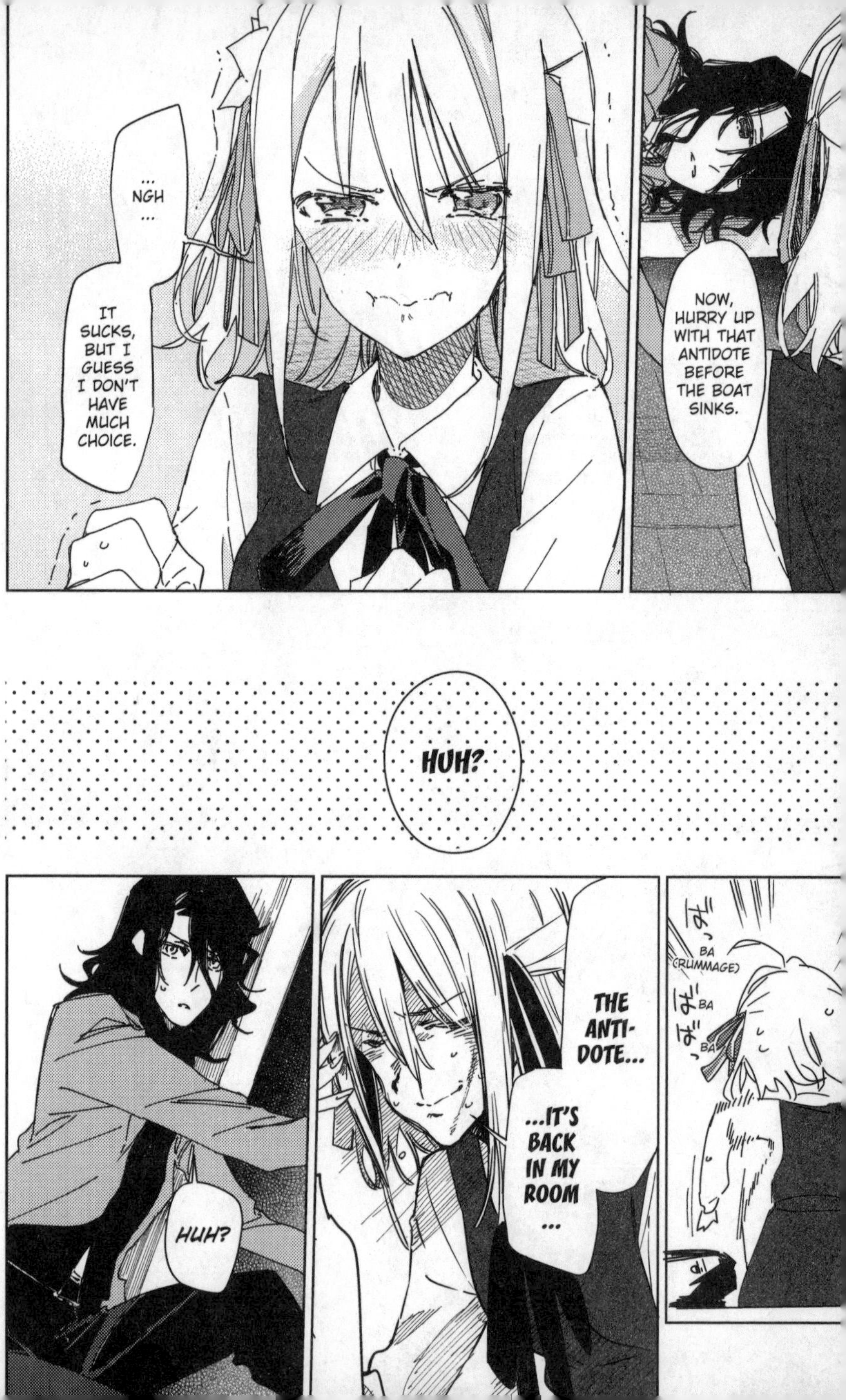
NOW, HURRY UP WITH THAT ANTIDOTE BEFORE THE BOAT SINKS.
...NGH...
IT SUCKS, BUT I GUESS I DON'T HAVE MUCH CHOICE.
HUH?
ばっ BA (RUMMAGE) ばBA ばっBA
THE ANTI-DOTE...
...IT'S BACK IN MY ROOM...
HUH?

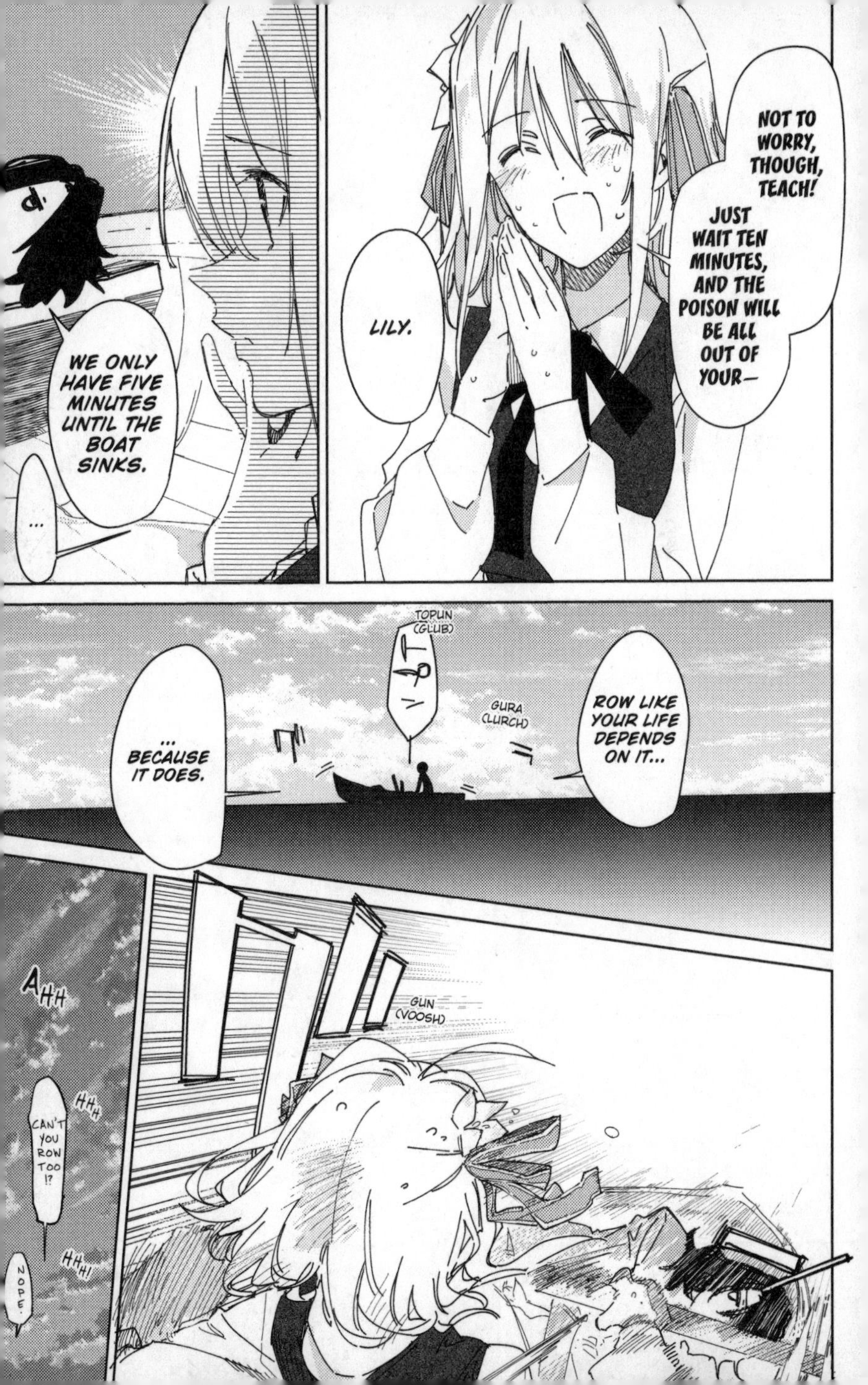
NOT TO WORRY, THOUGH, TEACH!
JUST WAIT TEN MINUTES, AND THE POISON WILL BE ALL OUT OF YOUR—
LILY.
WE ONLY HAVE FIVE MINUTES UNTIL THE BOAT SINKS.
...
TOPUN (GLUB)
ROW LIKE YOUR LIFE DEPENDS ON IT...
GURA (LURCH)
... BECAUSE IT DOES.
GUN (VOOSH)
AHHHHHHH!
CAN'T YOU ROW TOO!?
NOPE.

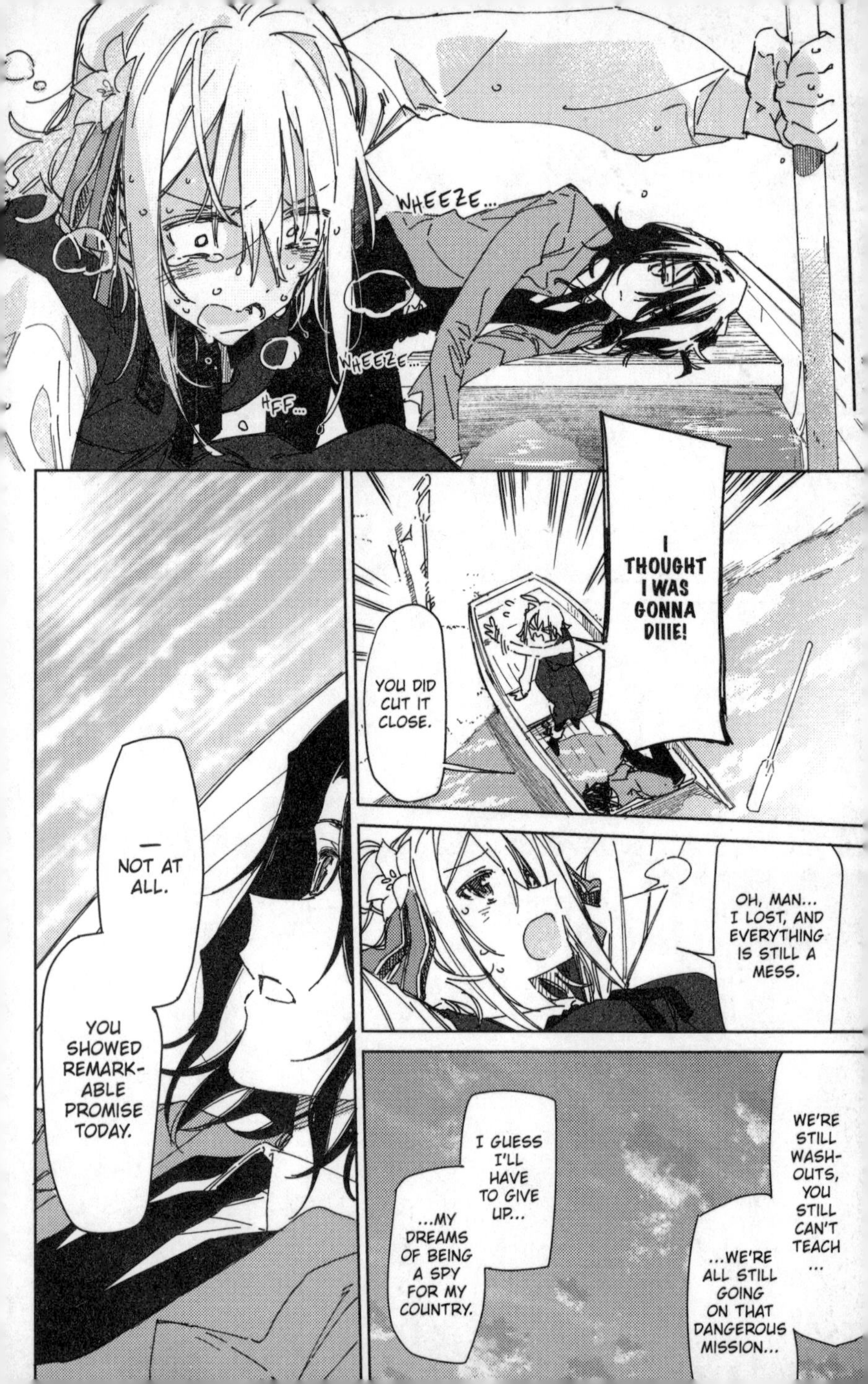
WHEEZE...
WHEEZE...
HFF...
I THOUGHT I WAS GONNA DIIIE!
YOU DID CUT IT CLOSE.
OH, MAN... I LOST, AND EVERYTHING IS STILL A MESS.
WE'RE STILL WASH-OUTS, YOU STILL CAN'T TEACH...
...WE'RE ALL STILL GOING ON THAT DANGEROUS MISSION...
I GUESS I'LL HAVE TO GIVE UP...
...MY DREAMS OF BEING A SPY FOR MY COUNTRY.
— NOT AT ALL.
YOU SHOWED REMARKABLE-ABLE PROMISE TODAY.

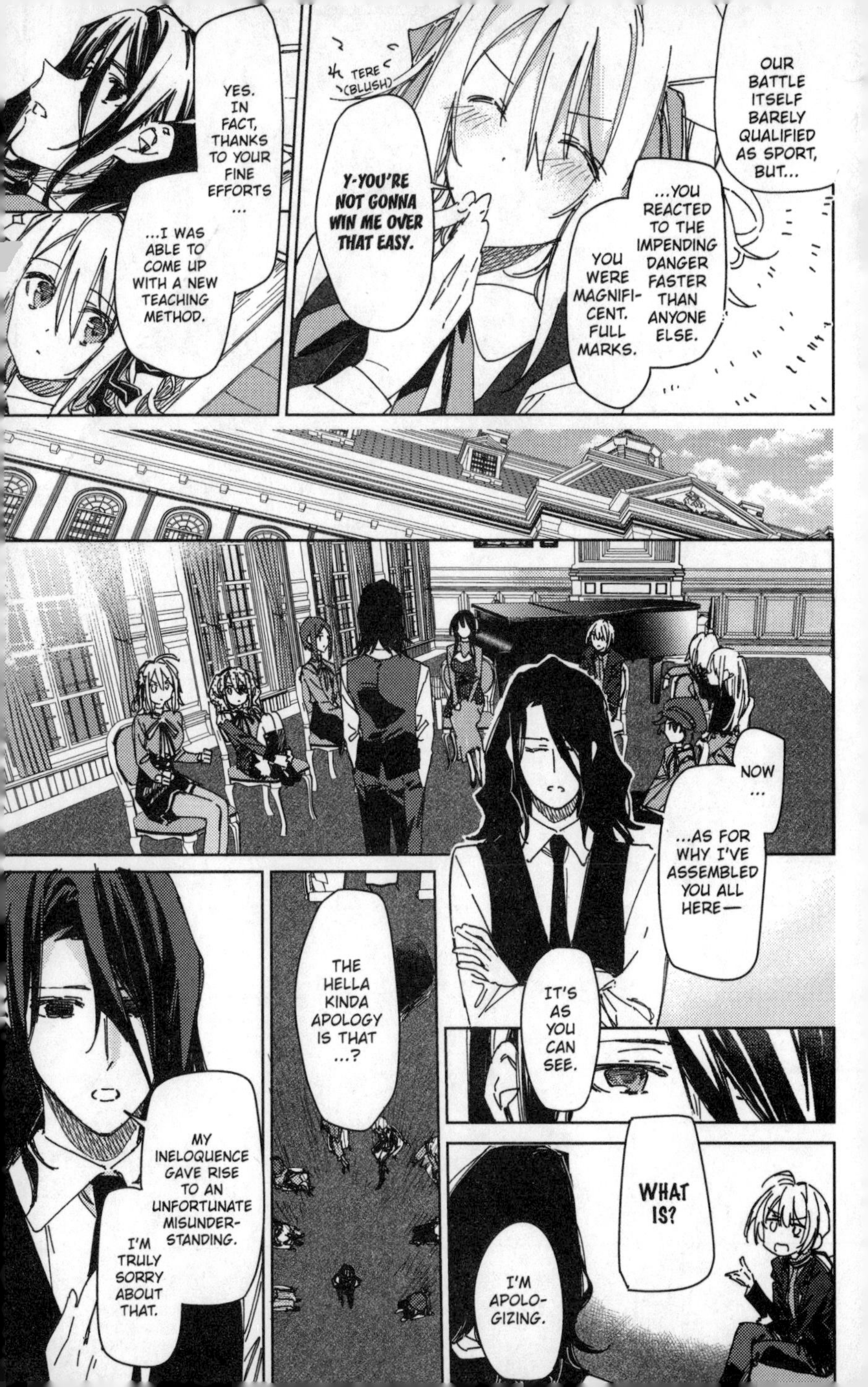
OUR BATTLE ITSELF BARELY QUALIFIED AS SPORT, BUT...
...YOU REACTED TO THE IMPENDING DANGER FASTER THAN ANYONE ELSE.
YOU WERE MAGNIFICENT. FULL MARKS.
TERE (BLUSH)
Y-YOU'RE NOT GONNA WIN ME OVER THAT EASY.
YES. IN FACT, THANKS TO YOUR FINE EFFORTS...
...I WAS ABLE TO COME UP WITH A NEW TEACHING METHOD.
NOW...
...AS FOR WHY I'VE ASSEMBLED YOU ALL HERE—
IT'S AS YOU CAN SEE.
WHAT IS?
I'M APOLOGIZING.
THE HELLA KINDA APOLOGY IS THAT...?
MY INELOQUENCE GAVE RISE TO AN UNFORTUNATE MISUNDERSTANDING.
I'M TRULY SORRY ABOUT THAT.

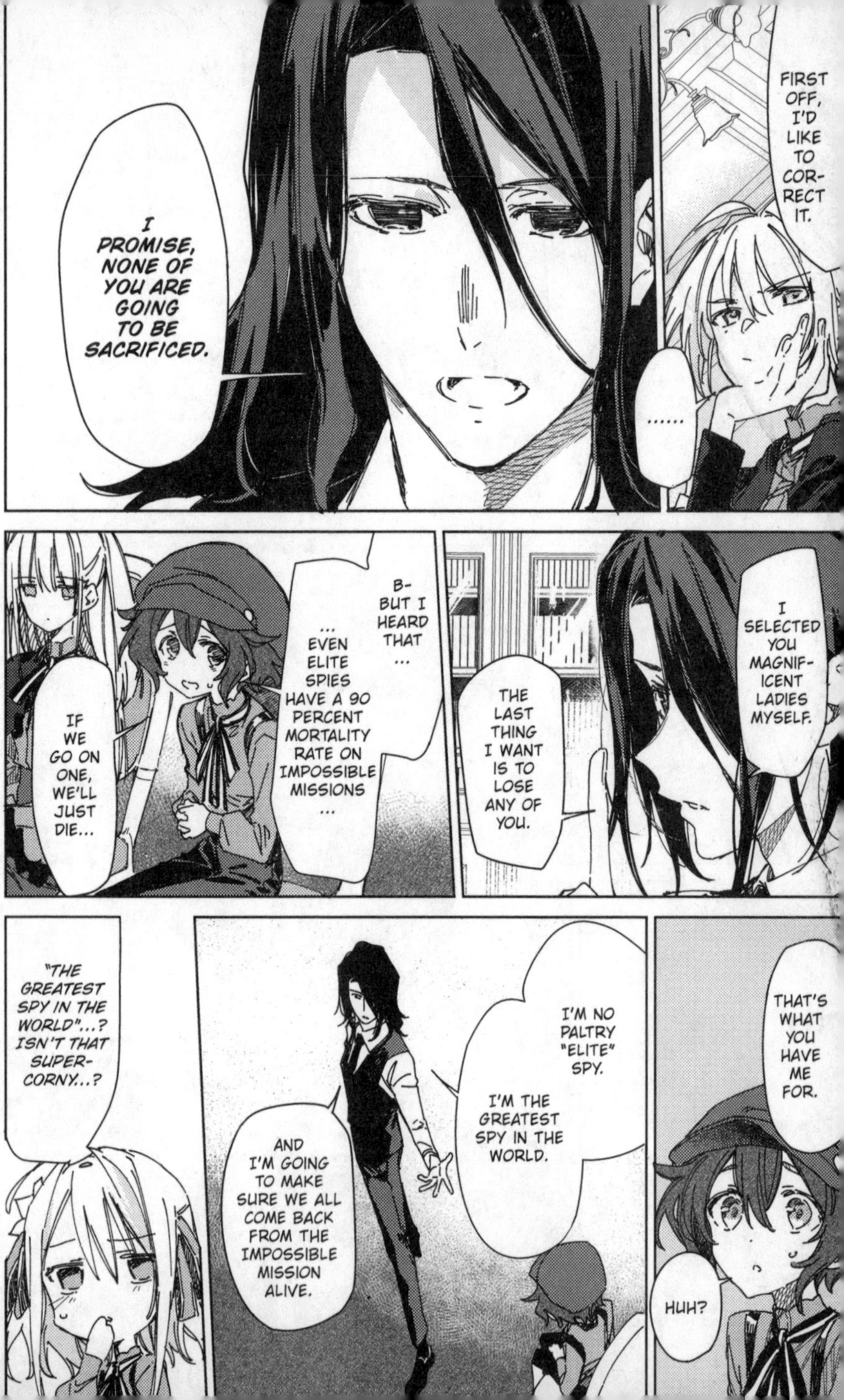
FIRST OFF, I'D LIKE TO COR-RECT IT.
......
I PROMISE, NONE OF YOU ARE GOING TO BE SACRIFICED.
I SELECTED YOU MAGNIF-ICENT LADIES MYSELF.
THE LAST THING I WANT IS TO LOSE ANY OF YOU.
B- BUT I HEARD THAT ...
... EVEN ELITE SPIES HAVE A 90 PERCENT MORTALITY RATE ON IMPOSSIBLE MISSIONS ...
IF WE GO ON ONE, WE'LL JUST DIE...
THAT'S WHAT YOU HAVE ME FOR.
HUH?
I'M NO PALTRY "ELITE" SPY.
I'M THE GREATEST SPY IN THE WORLD.
AND I'M GOING TO MAKE SURE WE ALL COME BACK FROM THE IMPOSSIBLE MISSION ALIVE.
"THE GREATEST SPY IN THE WORLD"...? ISN'T THAT SUPER-CORNY...?

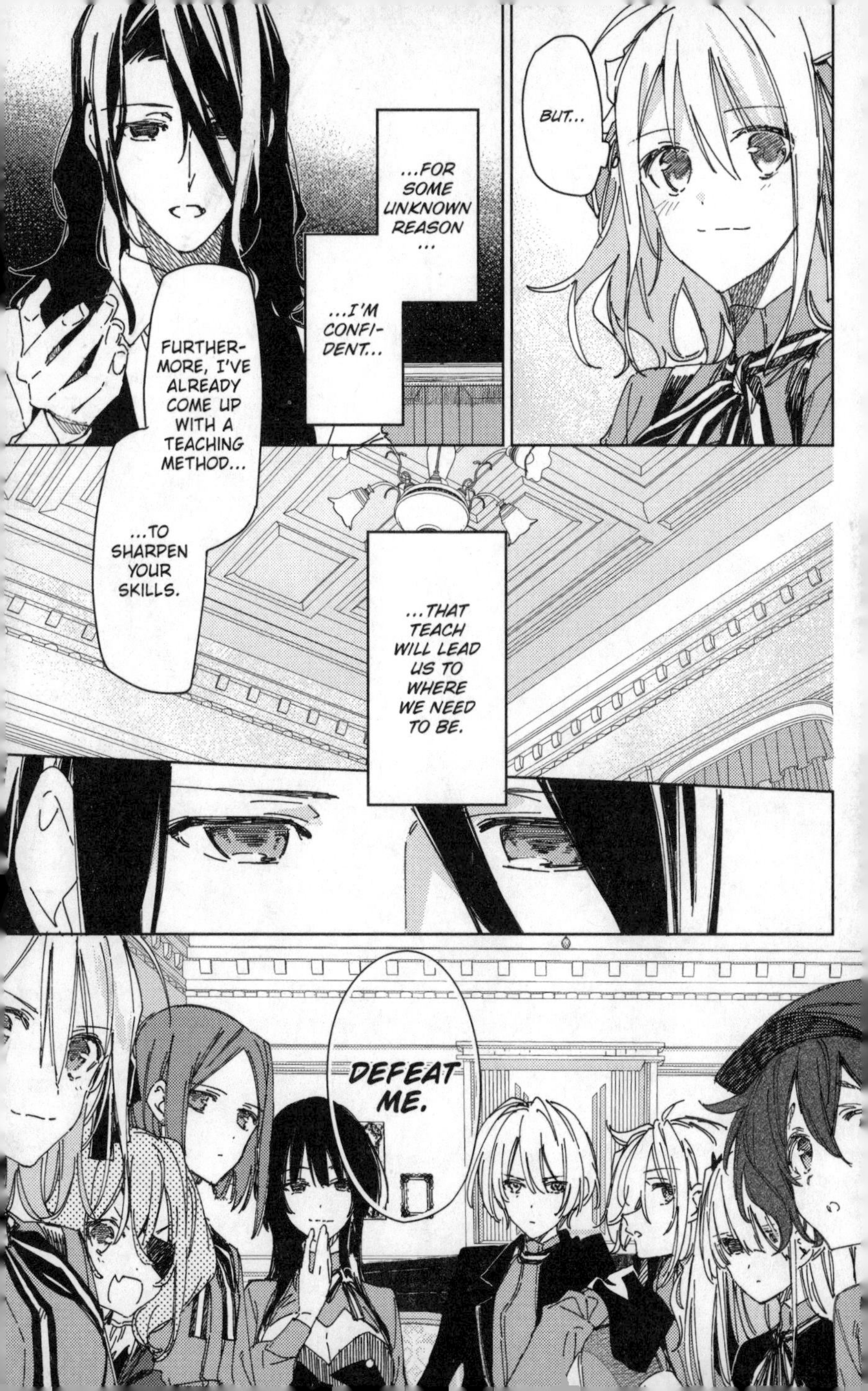
BUT...
...FOR SOME UNKNOWN REASON ...
...I'M CONFI-DENT...
FURTHER-MORE, I'VE ALREADY COME UP WITH A TEACHING METHOD...
...TO SHARPEN YOUR SKILLS.
...THAT TEACH WILL LEAD US TO WHERE WE NEED TO BE.
DEFEAT ME.

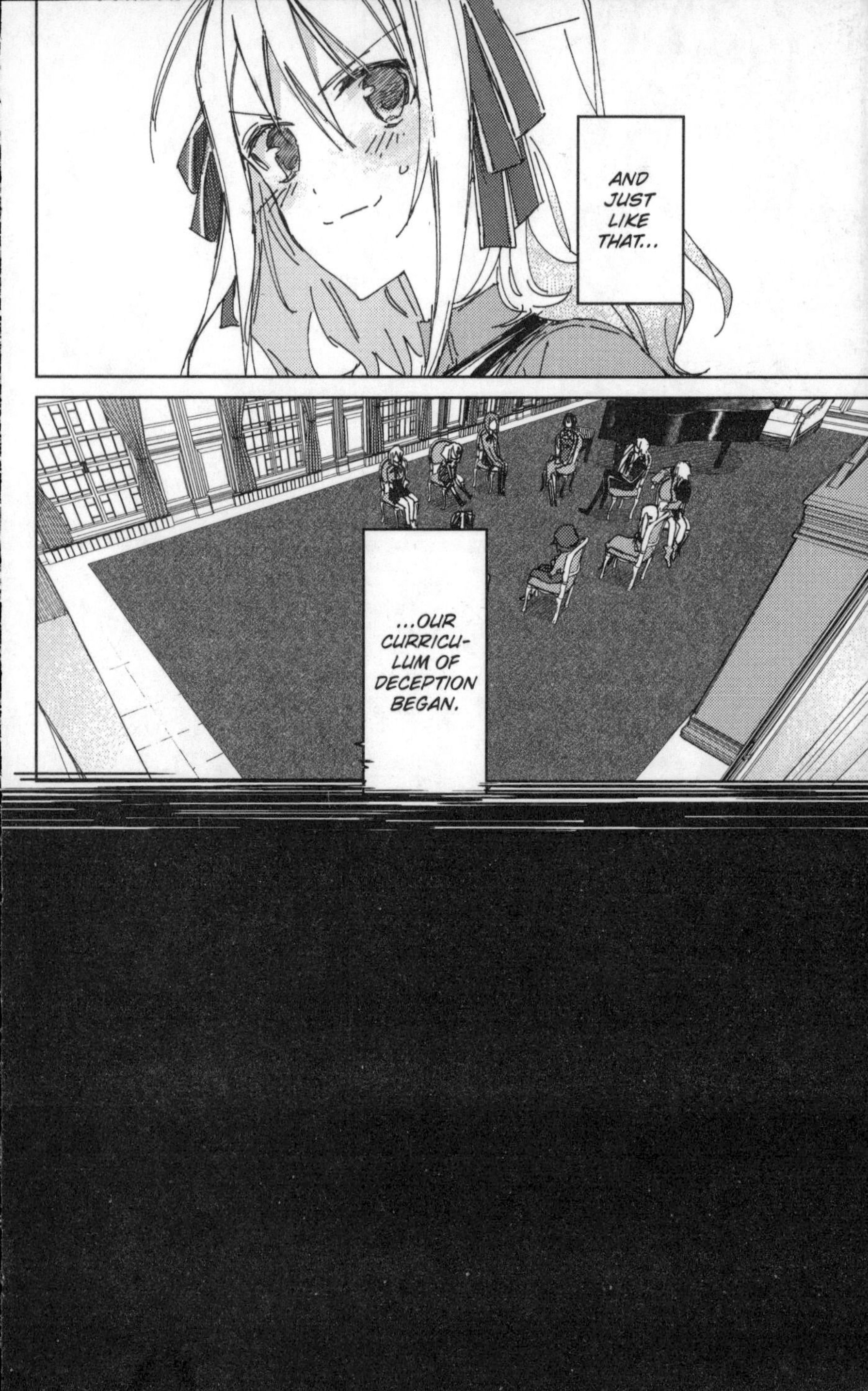
AND JUST LIKE THAT...
...OUR CURRICULUM OF DECEPTION BEGAN.

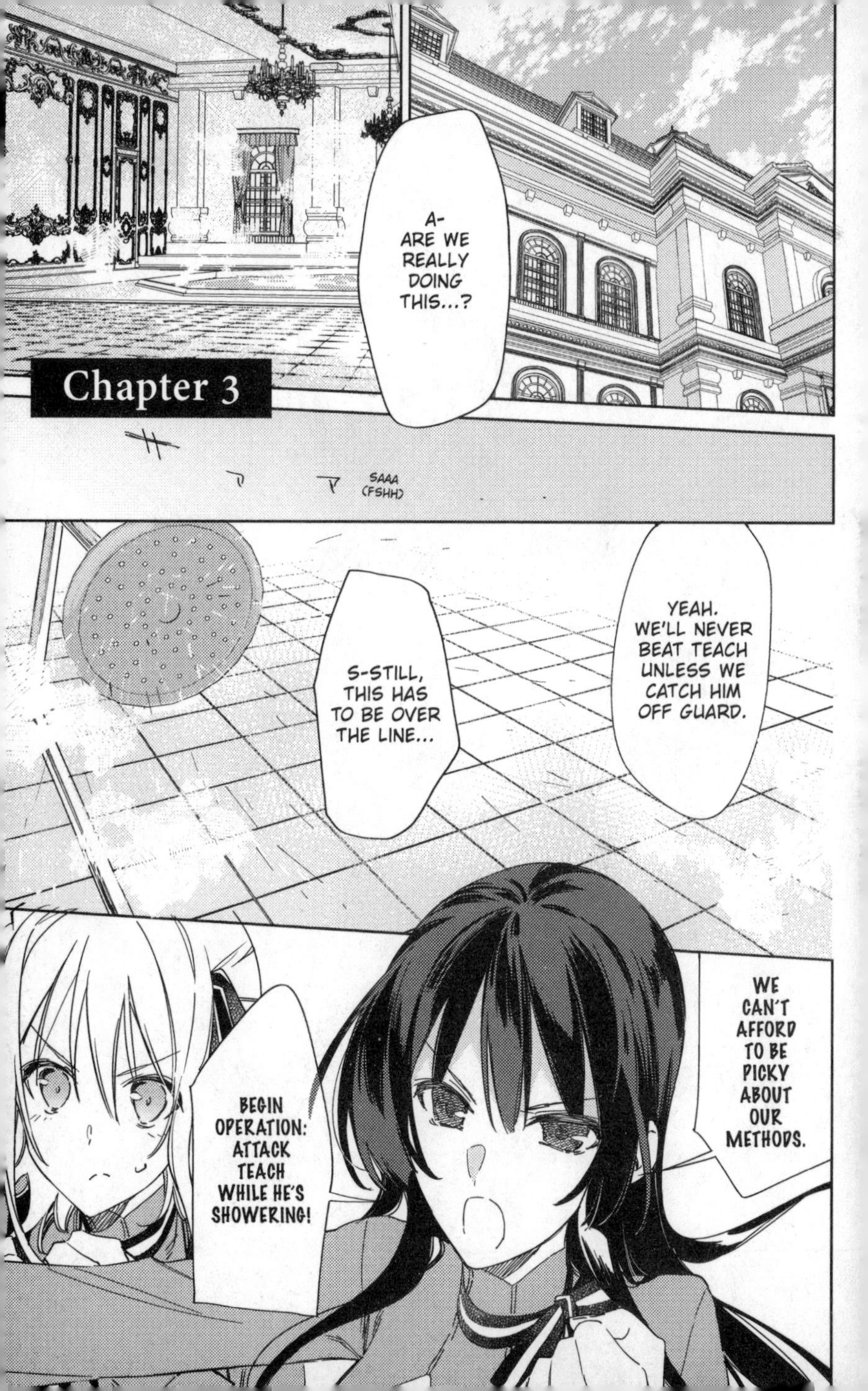
Chapter 3
A-ARE WE REALLY DOING THIS...?
SAAA (FSHH)
YEAH. WE'LL NEVER BEAT TEACH UNLESS WE CATCH HIM OFF GUARD.
S-STILL, THIS HAS TO BE OVER THE LINE...
WE CAN'T AFFORD TO BE PICKY ABOUT OUR METHODS.
BEGIN OPERATION: ATTACK TEACH WHILE HE'S SHOWERING!

# Chapter 3 — Theft

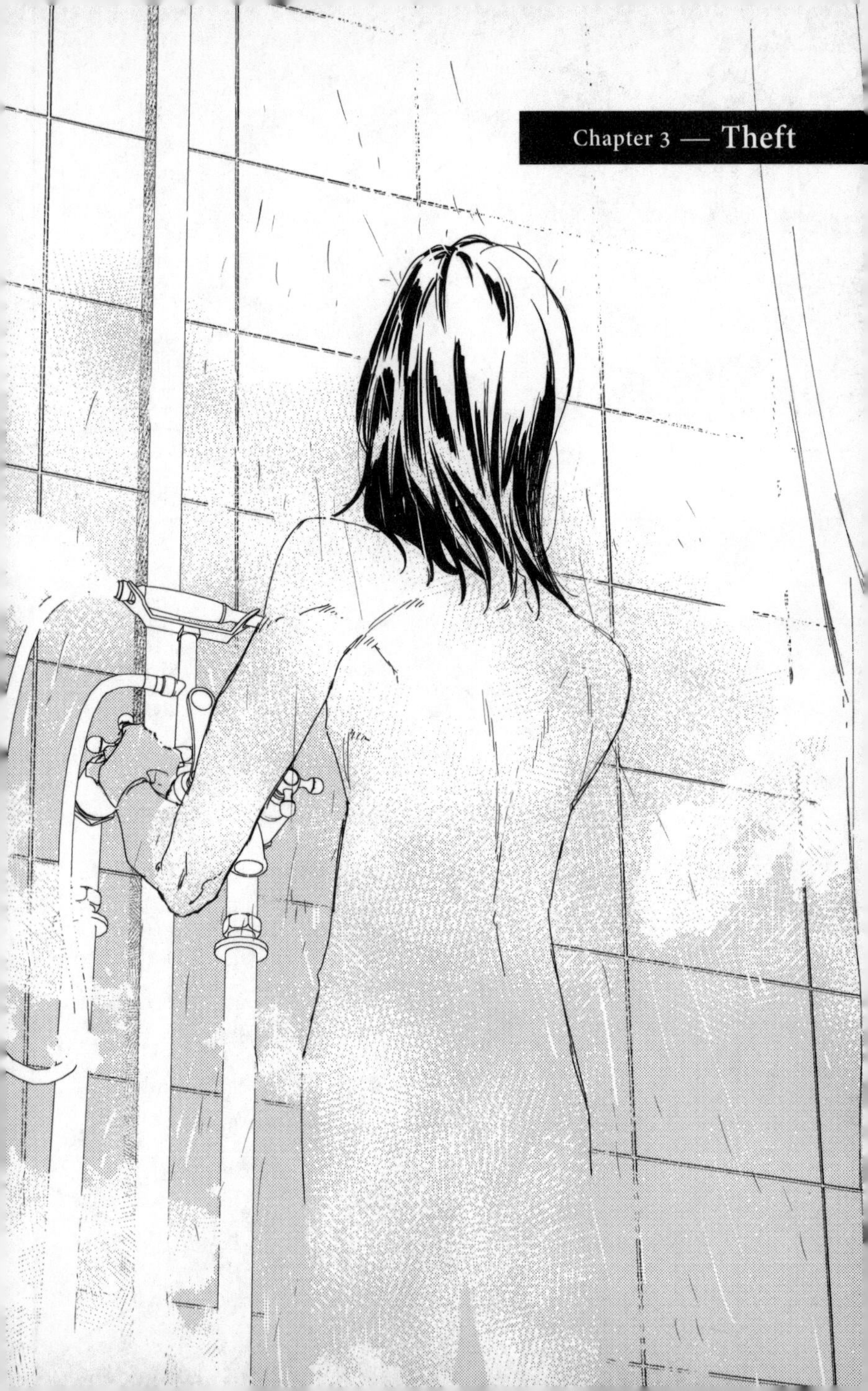

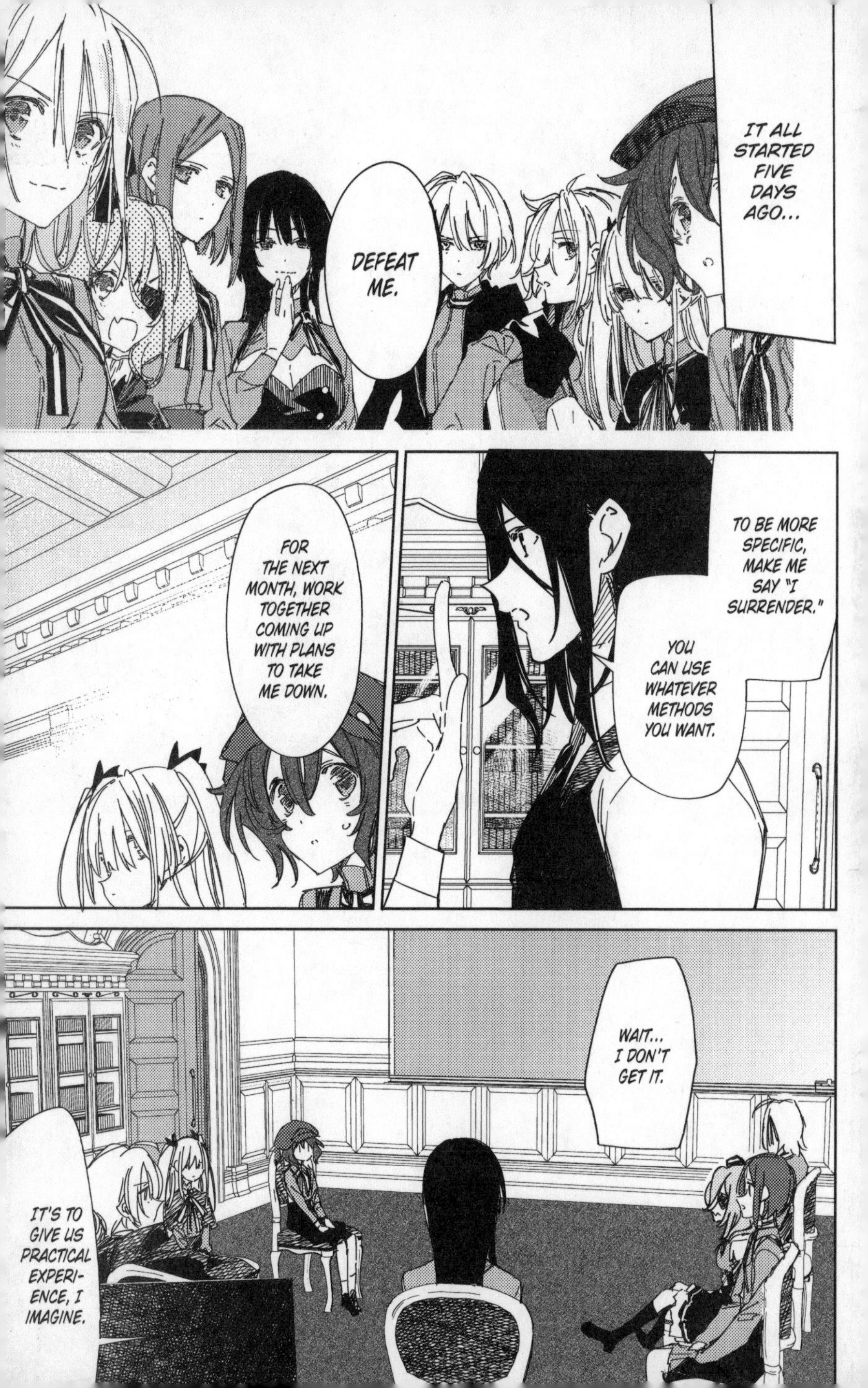
IT ALL STARTED FIVE DAYS AGO...
DEFEAT ME.
TO BE MORE SPECIFIC, MAKE ME SAY "I SURRENDER."
YOU CAN USE WHATEVER METHODS YOU WANT.
FOR THE NEXT MONTH, WORK TOGETHER COMING UP WITH PLANS TO TAKE ME DOWN.
WAIT... I DON'T GET IT.
IT'S TO GIVE US PRACTICAL EXPERIENCE, I IMAGINE.

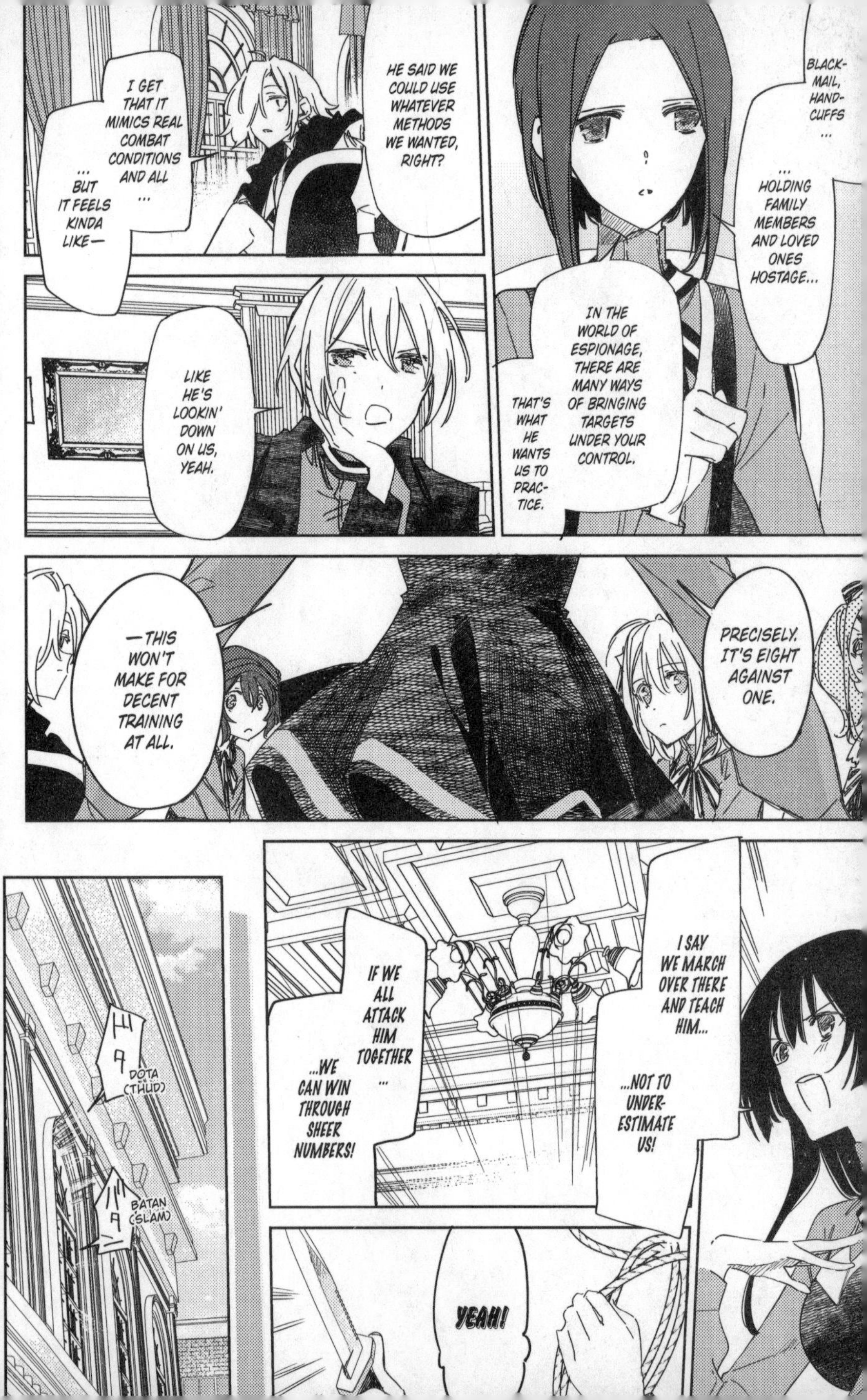
BLACK-MAIL, HAND-CUFFS...
...HOLDING FAMILY MEMBERS AND LOVED ONES HOSTAGE...
IN THE WORLD OF ESPIONAGE, THERE ARE MANY WAYS OF BRINGING TARGETS UNDER YOUR CONTROL.
THAT'S WHAT HE WANTS US TO PRAC-TICE.
HE SAID WE COULD USE WHATEVER METHODS WE WANTED, RIGHT?
I GET THAT IT MIMICS REAL COMBAT CONDITIONS AND ALL...
...BUT IT FEELS KINDA LIKE—
LIKE HE'S LOOKIN' DOWN ON US, YEAH.
PRECISELY. IT'S EIGHT AGAINST ONE.
—THIS WON'T MAKE FOR DECENT TRAINING AT ALL.
I SAY WE MARCH OVER THERE AND TEACH HIM...
...NOT TO UNDER-ESTIMATE US!
IF WE ALL ATTACK HIM TOGETHER...
...WE CAN WIN THROUGH SHEER NUMBERS!
YEAH!
DOTA (THUD)
BATAN (SLAM)

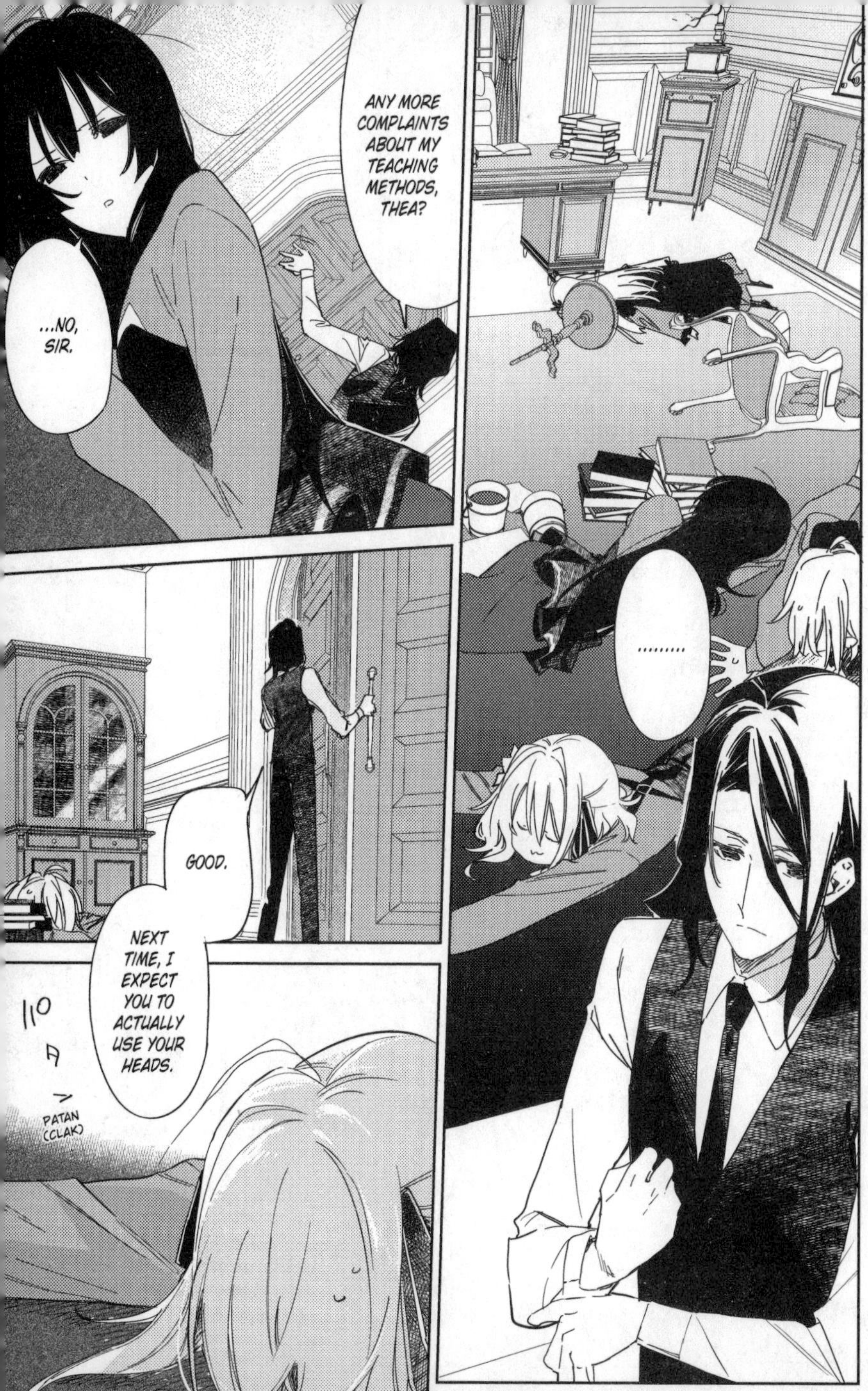
.........
ANY MORE COMPLAINTS ABOUT MY TEACHING METHODS, THEA?
...NO, SIR.
GOOD.
NEXT TIME, I EXPECT YOU TO ACTUALLY USE YOUR HEADS.
PATAN (CLAK)

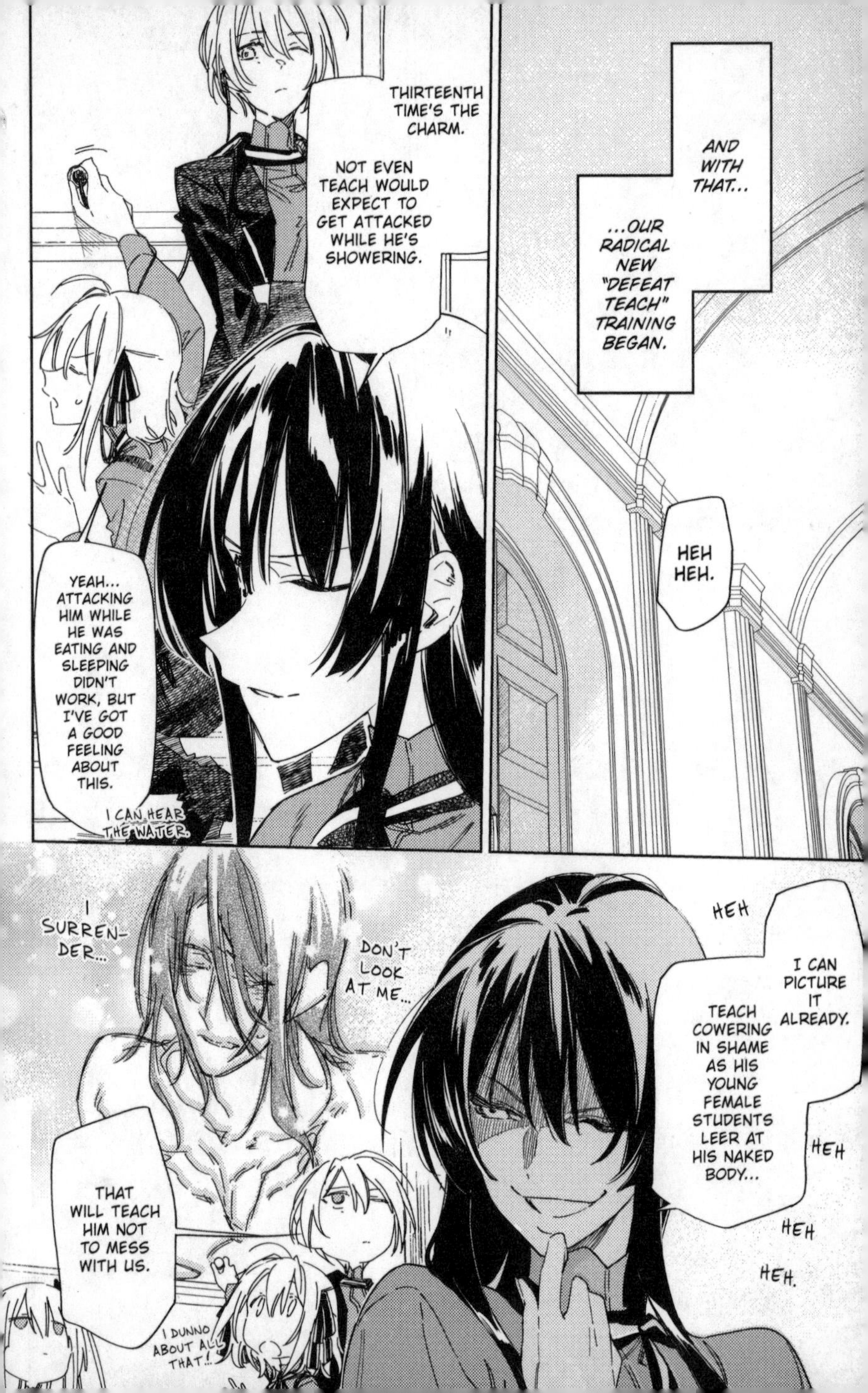
AND WITH THAT...
...OUR RADICAL NEW "DEFEAT TEACH" TRAINING BEGAN.
HEH HEH.
THIRTEENTH TIME'S THE CHARM.
NOT EVEN TEACH WOULD EXPECT TO GET ATTACKED WHILE HE'S SHOWERING.
YEAH... ATTACKING HIM WHILE HE WAS EATING AND SLEEPING DIDN'T WORK, BUT I'VE GOT A GOOD FEELING ABOUT THIS.
I CAN HEAR THE WATER.
HEH
I CAN PICTURE IT ALREADY.
TEACH COWERING IN SHAME AS HIS YOUNG FEMALE STUDENTS LEER AT HIS NAKED BODY...
HEH
HEH
HEH.
DON'T LOOK AT ME...
I SURREN-DER...
THAT WILL TEACH HIM NOT TO MESS WITH US.
I DUNNO ABOUT ALL THAT!

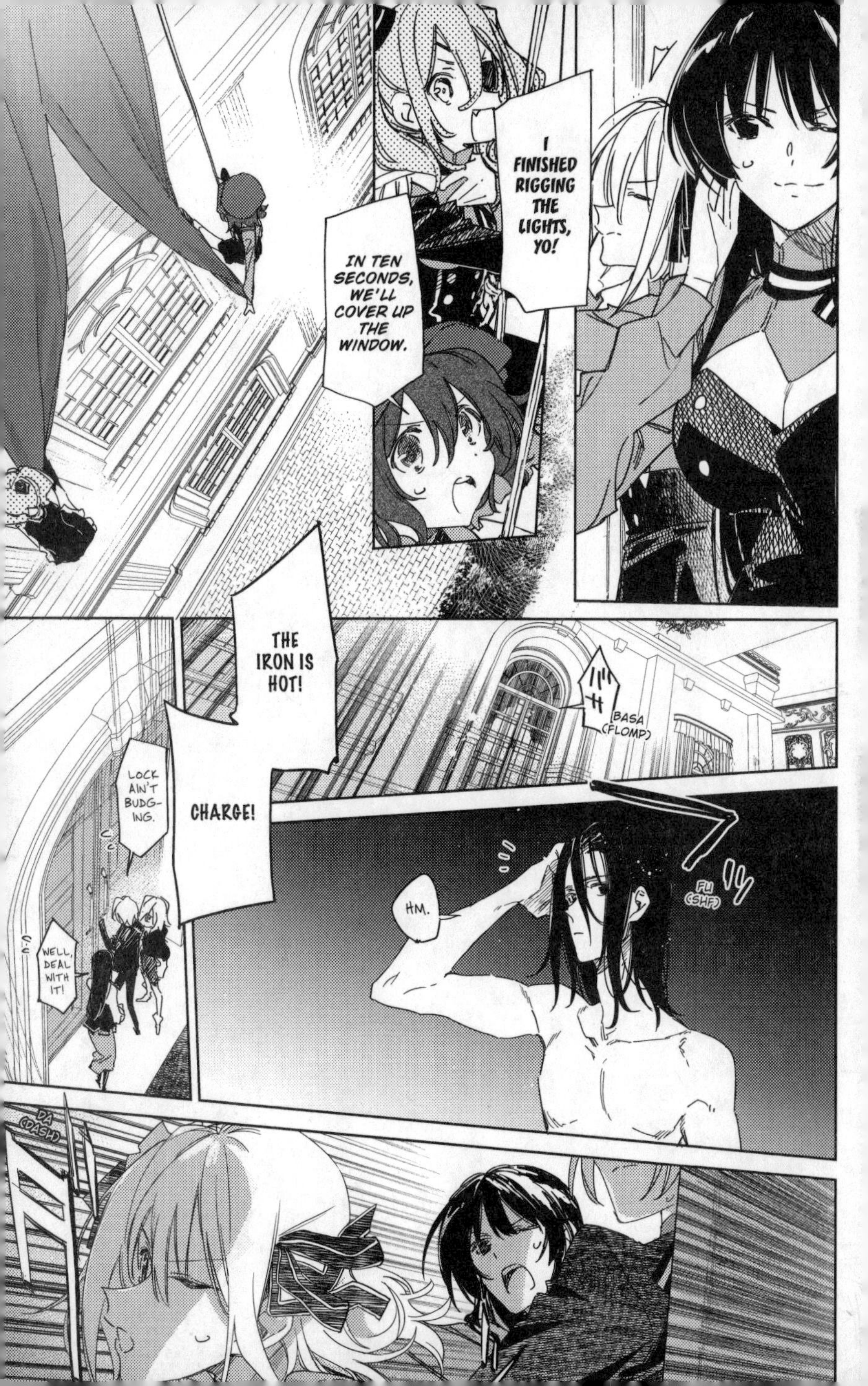
I FINISHED RIGGING THE LIGHTS, YO!
IN TEN SECONDS, WE'LL COVER UP THE WINDOW.
THE IRON IS HOT!
BASA (FLOMP)
FU (SHF)
HM.
CHARGE!
LOCK AIN'T BUDGING.
WELL, DEAL WITH IT!
DA (DASH)

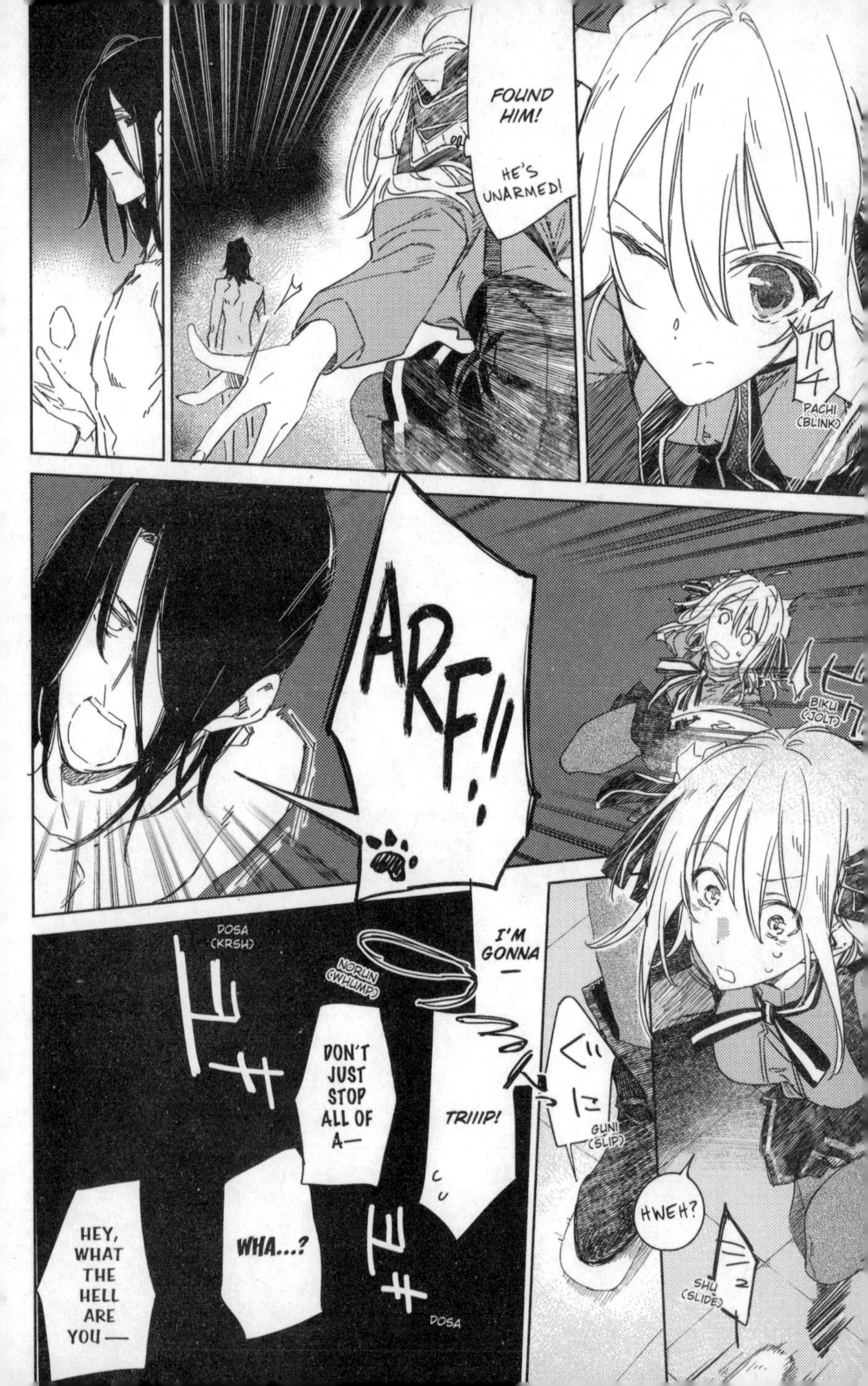
PACHI (BLINK)
FOUND HIM!
HE'S UNARMED!
BIKU (JOLT)
ARF!!
I'M GONNA—
GUNI (SLID)
HWEH?
SHU (SLIDE)
NORUN (WHUMP)
DON'T JUST STOP ALL OF A—
TRIIIP!
DOSA (KRSH)
WHA...?
HEY, WHAT THE HELL ARE YOU—
DOSA

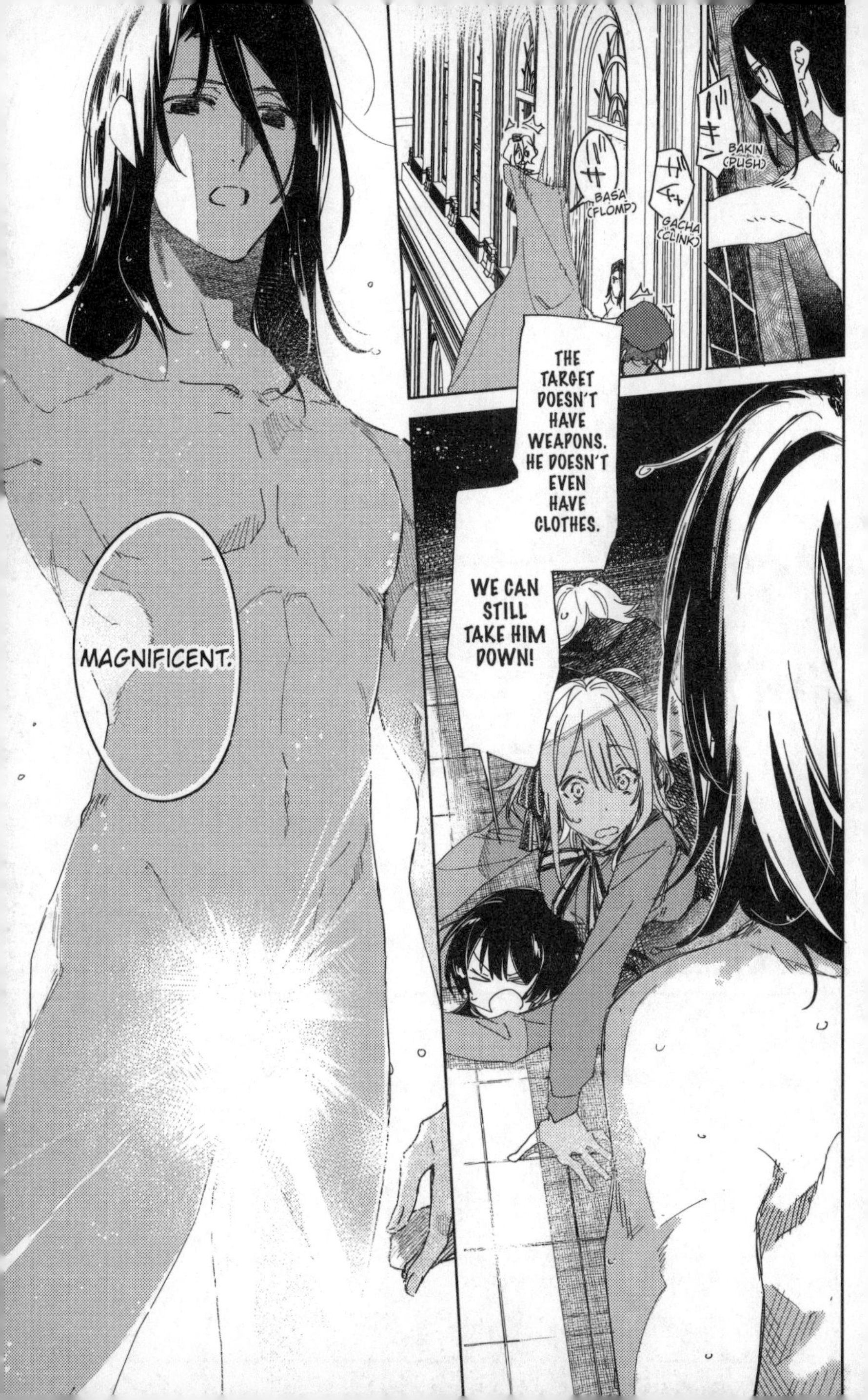
BAKIN (PUSH)
GACHA (CLINK)
BASA (FLOMP)
THE TARGET DOESN'T HAVE WEAPONS. HE DOESN'T EVEN HAVE CLOTHES.
WE CAN STILL TAKE HIM DOWN!
MAGNIFICENT.

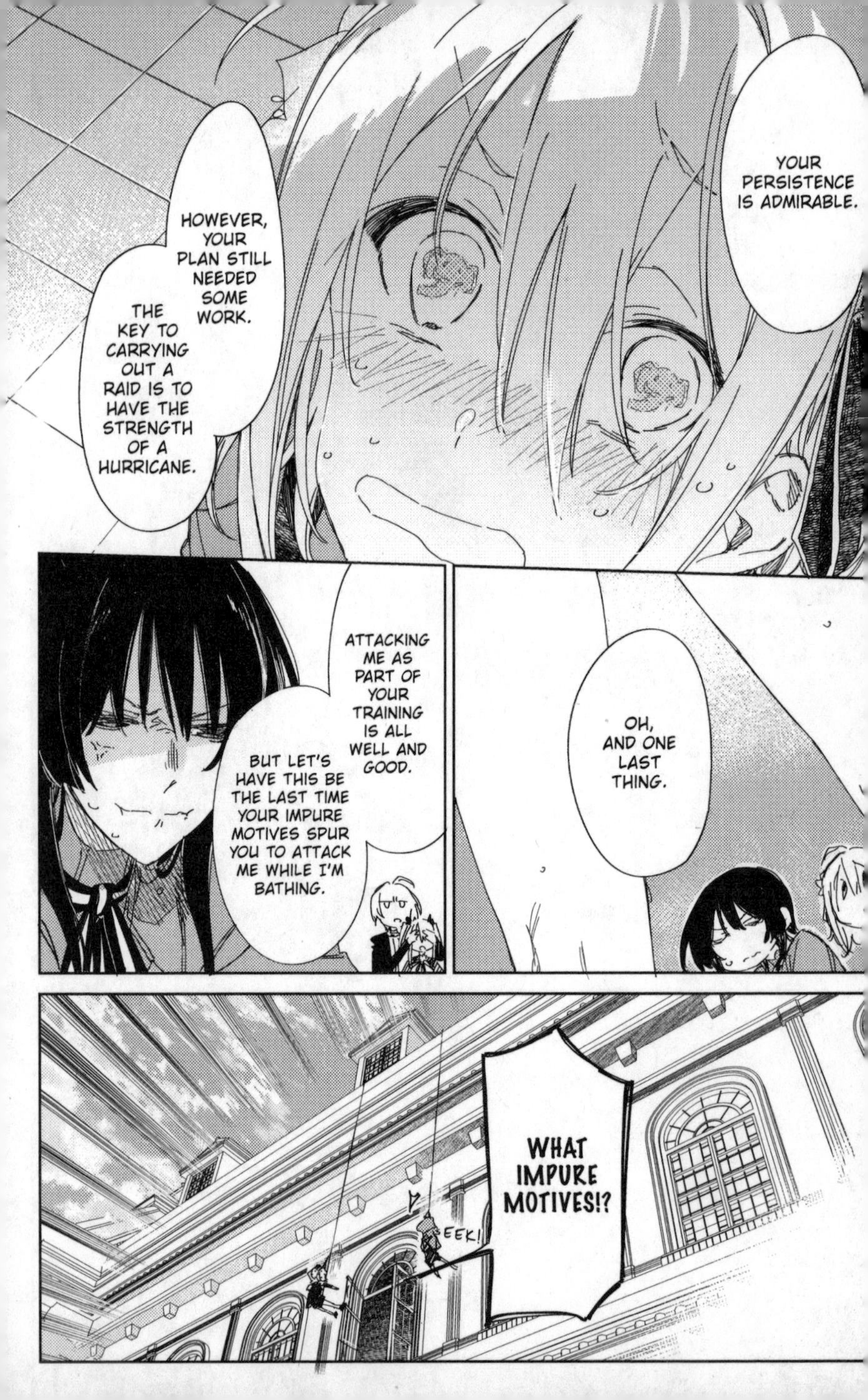
YOUR PERSISTENCE IS ADMIRABLE.
HOWEVER, YOUR PLAN STILL NEEDED SOME WORK.
THE KEY TO CARRYING OUT A RAID IS TO HAVE THE STRENGTH OF A HURRICANE.
OH, AND ONE LAST THING.
ATTACKING ME AS PART OF YOUR TRAINING IS ALL WELL AND GOOD.
BUT LET'S HAVE THIS BE THE LAST TIME YOUR IMPURE MOTIVES SPUR YOU TO ATTACK ME WHILE I'M BATHING.
WHAT IMPURE MOTIVES!?
EEK!

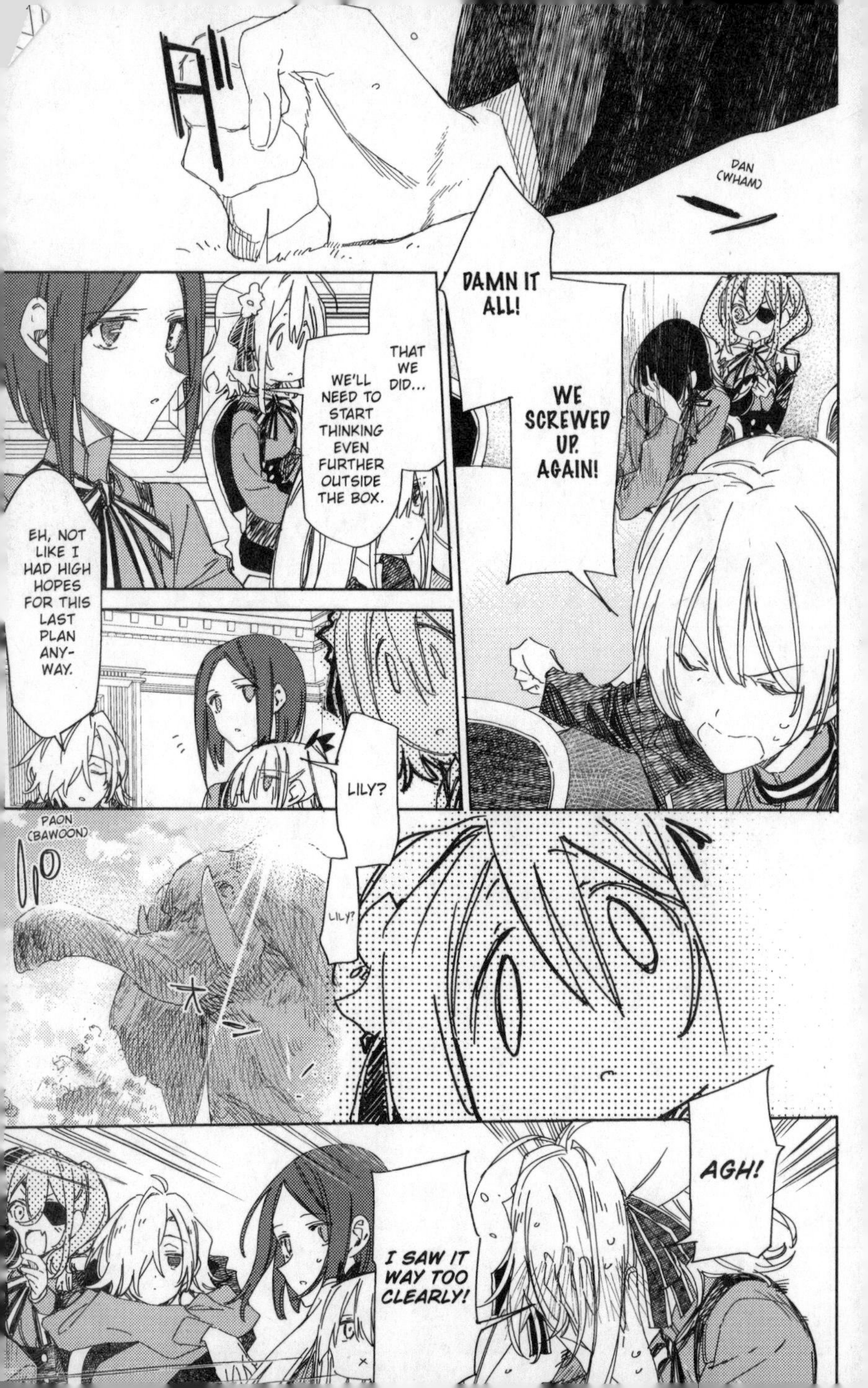
DAN (WHAM)
DAMN IT ALL!
WE SCREWED UP. AGAIN!
THAT WE DID...
WE'LL NEED TO START THINKING EVEN FURTHER OUTSIDE THE BOX.
EH, NOT LIKE I HAD HIGH HOPES FOR THIS LAST PLAN ANYWAY.
LILY?
LILY?
PAON (BAWOON)
AGH!
I SAW IT WAY TOO CLEARLY!

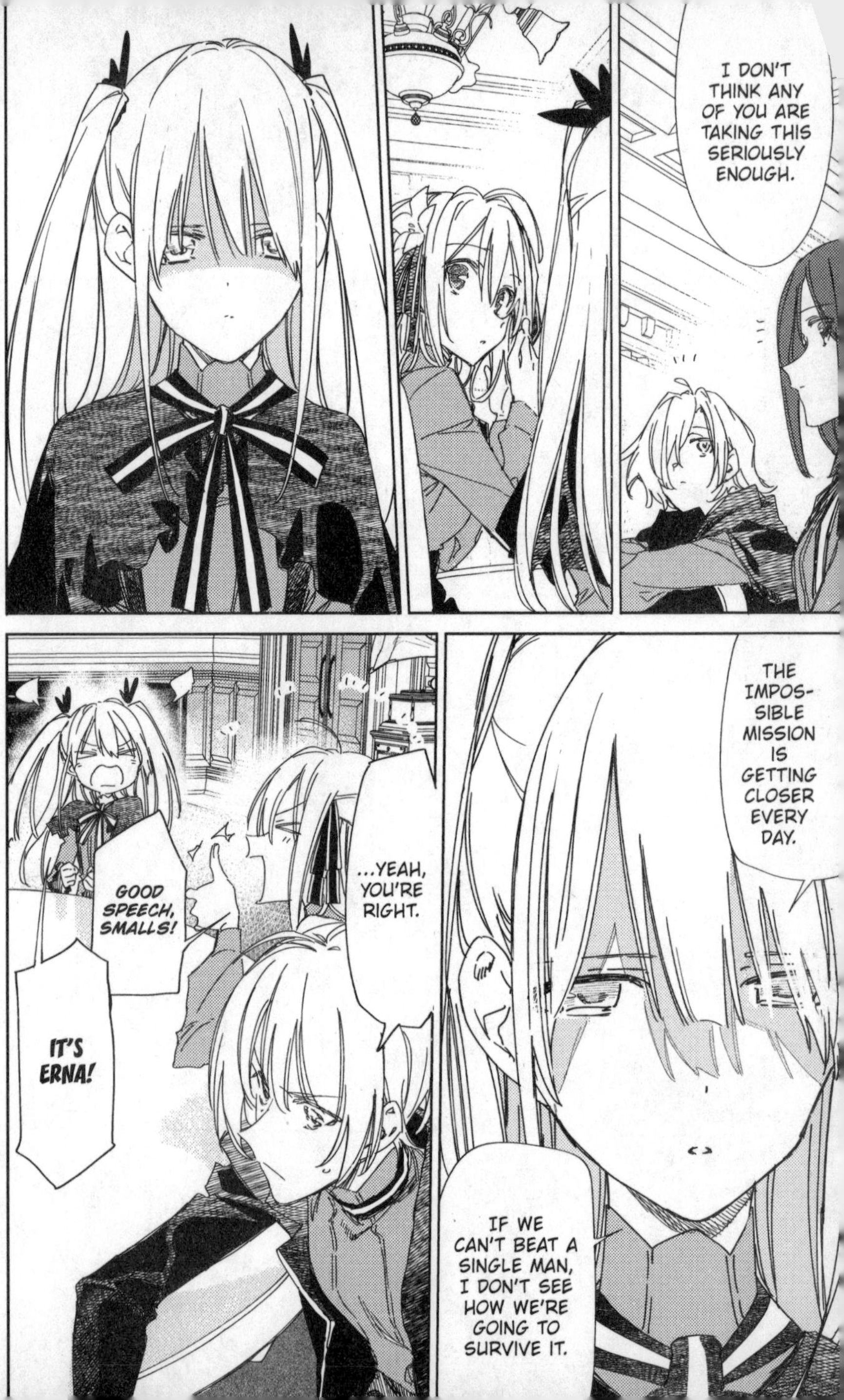
I DON'T THINK ANY OF YOU ARE TAKING THIS SERIOUSLY ENOUGH.
THE IMPOSSIBLE MISSION IS GETTING CLOSER EVERY DAY.
IF WE CAN'T BEAT A SINGLE MAN, I DON'T SEE HOW WE'RE GOING TO SURVIVE IT.
...YEAH, YOU'RE RIGHT.
GOOD SPEECH, SMALLS!
IT'S ERNA!

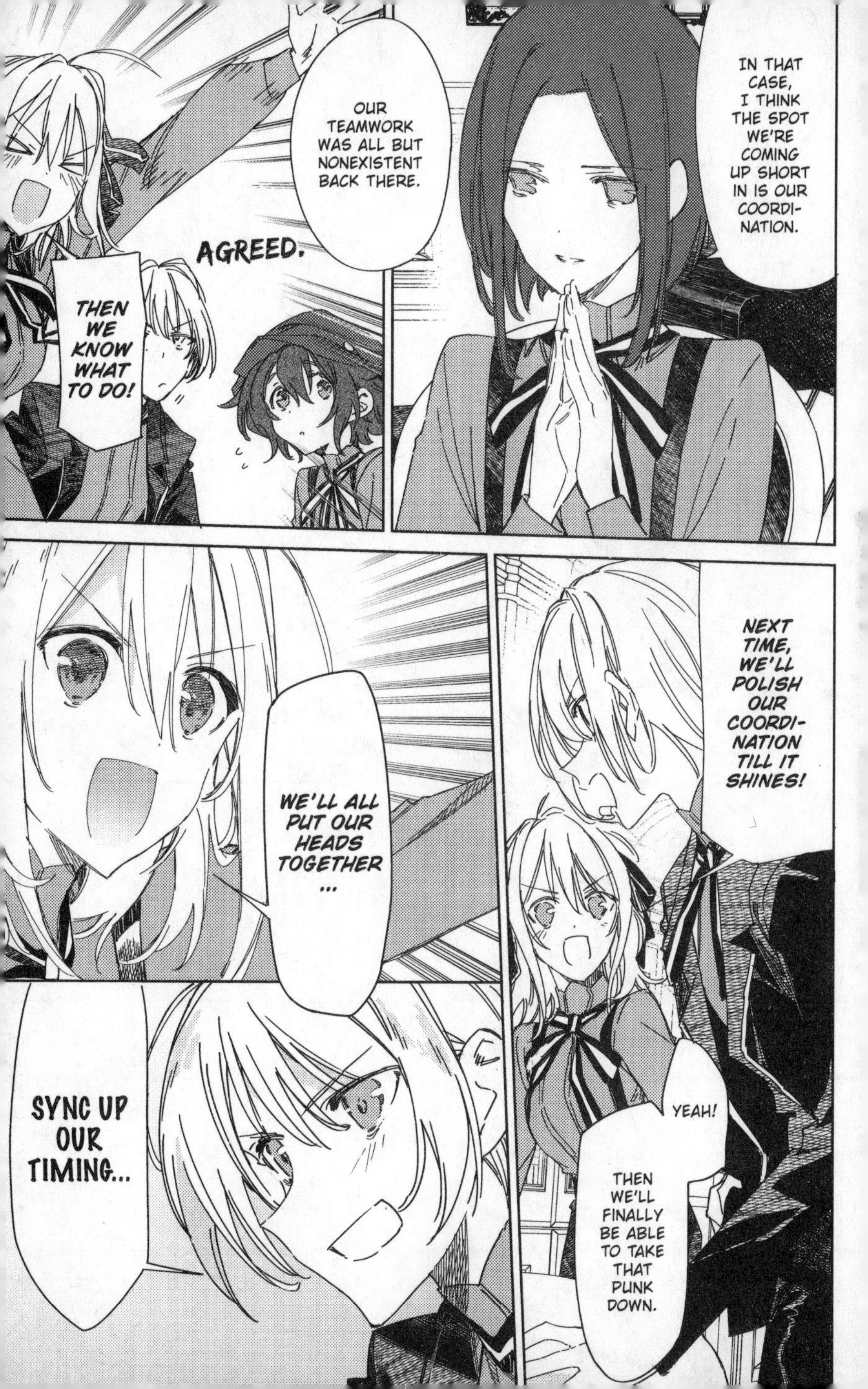
IN THAT CASE, I THINK THE SPOT WE'RE COMING UP SHORT IN IS OUR COORDINATION.
OUR TEAMWORK WAS ALL BUT NONEXISTENT BACK THERE.
AGREED.
THEN WE KNOW WHAT TO DO!
NEXT TIME, WE'LL POLISH OUR COORDINATION TILL IT SHINES!
YEAH!
THEN WE'LL FINALLY BE ABLE TO TAKE THAT PUNK DOWN.
WE'LL ALL PUT OUR HEADS TOGETHER...
SYNC UP OUR TIMING...

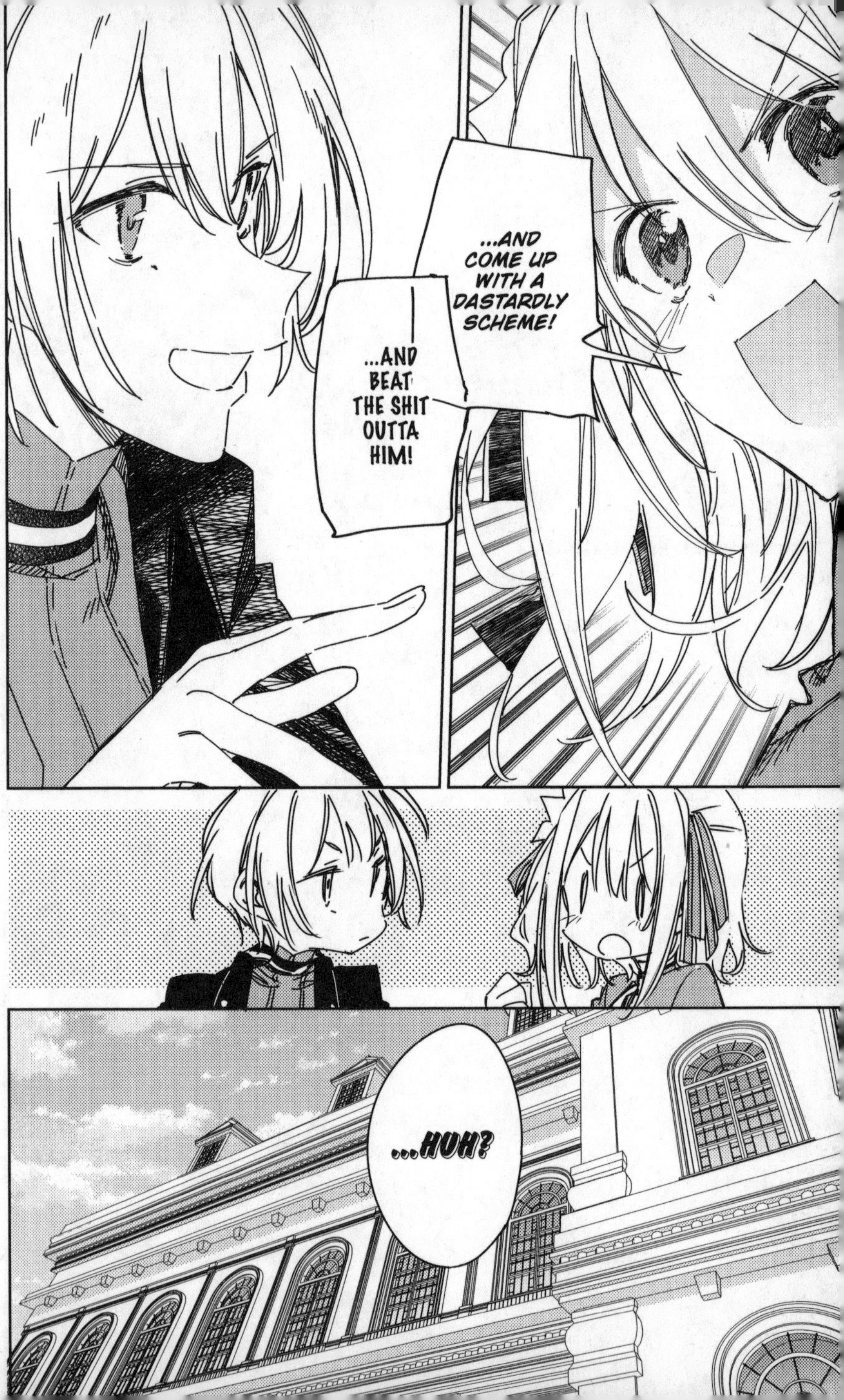
...AND COME UP WITH A DASTARDLY SCHEME!
...AND BEAT THE SHIT OUTTA HIM!
...HUH?

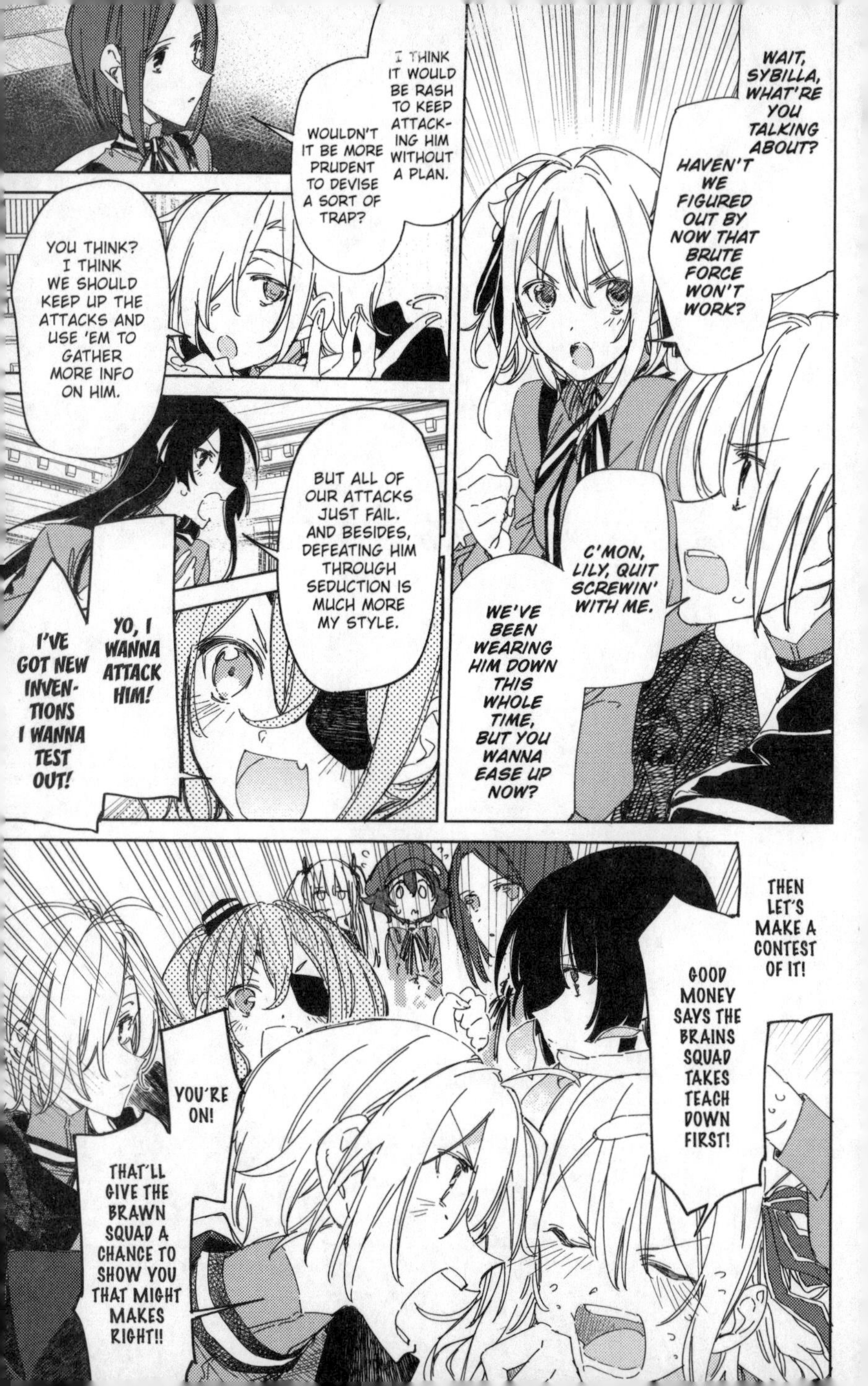
WAIT, SYBILLA, WHAT'RE YOU TALKING ABOUT?
HAVEN'T WE FIGURED OUT BY NOW THAT BRUTE FORCE WON'T WORK?
C'MON, LILY, QUIT SCREWIN' WITH ME.
WE'VE BEEN WEARING HIM DOWN THIS WHOLE TIME, BUT YOU WANNA EASE UP NOW?
I THINK IT WOULD BE RASH TO KEEP ATTACKING HIM WITHOUT A PLAN.
WOULDN'T IT BE MORE PRUDENT TO DEVISE A SORT OF TRAP?
YOU THINK? I THINK WE SHOULD KEEP UP THE ATTACKS AND USE 'EM TO GATHER MORE INFO ON HIM.
BUT ALL OF OUR ATTACKS JUST FAIL. AND BESIDES, DEFEATING HIM THROUGH SEDUCTION IS MUCH MORE MY STYLE.
YO, I WANNA ATTACK HIM!
I'VE GOT NEW INVENTIONS I WANNA TEST OUT!
THEN LET'S MAKE A CONTEST OF IT!
GOOD MONEY SAYS THE BRAINS SQUAD TAKES TEACH DOWN FIRST!
YOU'RE ON!
THAT'LL GIVE THE BRAWN SQUAD A CHANCE TO SHOW YOU THAT MIGHT MAKES RIGHT!!

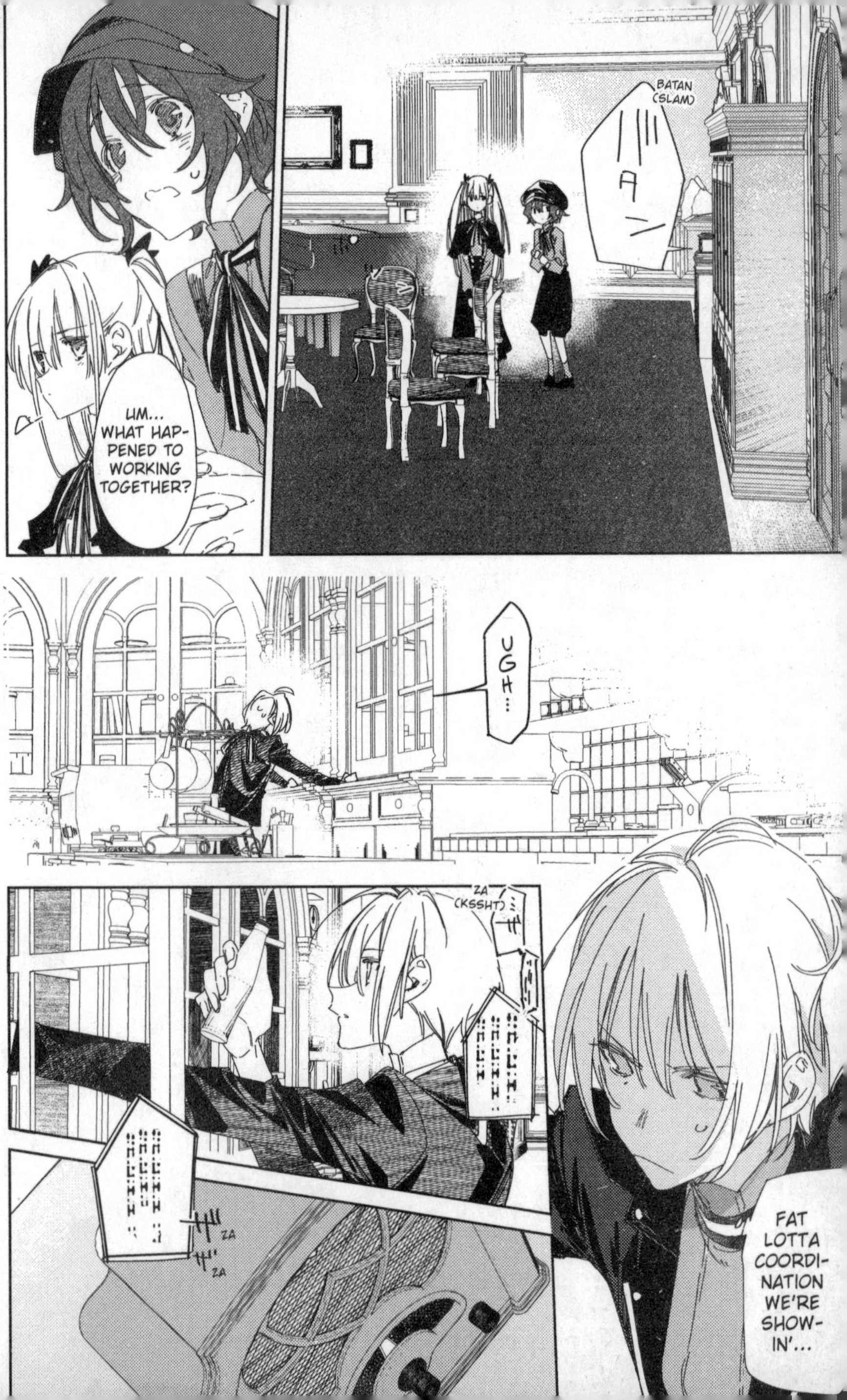
BATAN (SLAM)
UM... WHAT HAPPENED TO WORKING TOGETHER?
UGH...
FAT LOTTA COORDINATION WE'RE SHOWIN'...
ZA (KSSHT)
ZA
ZA

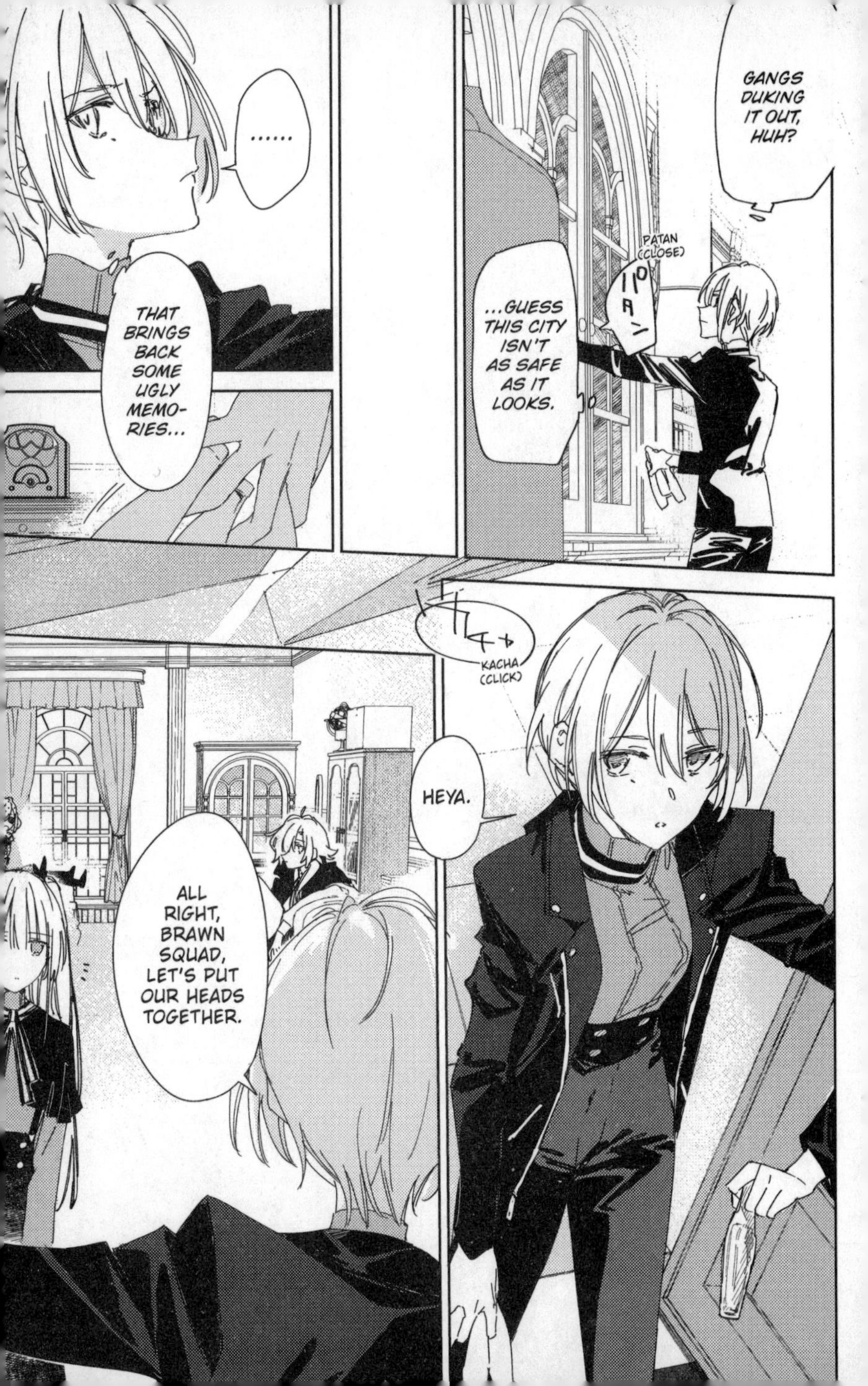
GANGS DUKING IT OUT, HUH?
PATAN (CLOSE)
...GUESS THIS CITY ISN'T AS SAFE AS IT LOOKS.
......
THAT BRINGS BACK SOME UGLY MEMO-RIES...
KACHA (CLICK)
HEYA.
ALL RIGHT, BRAWN SQUAD, LET'S PUT OUR HEADS TOGETHER.

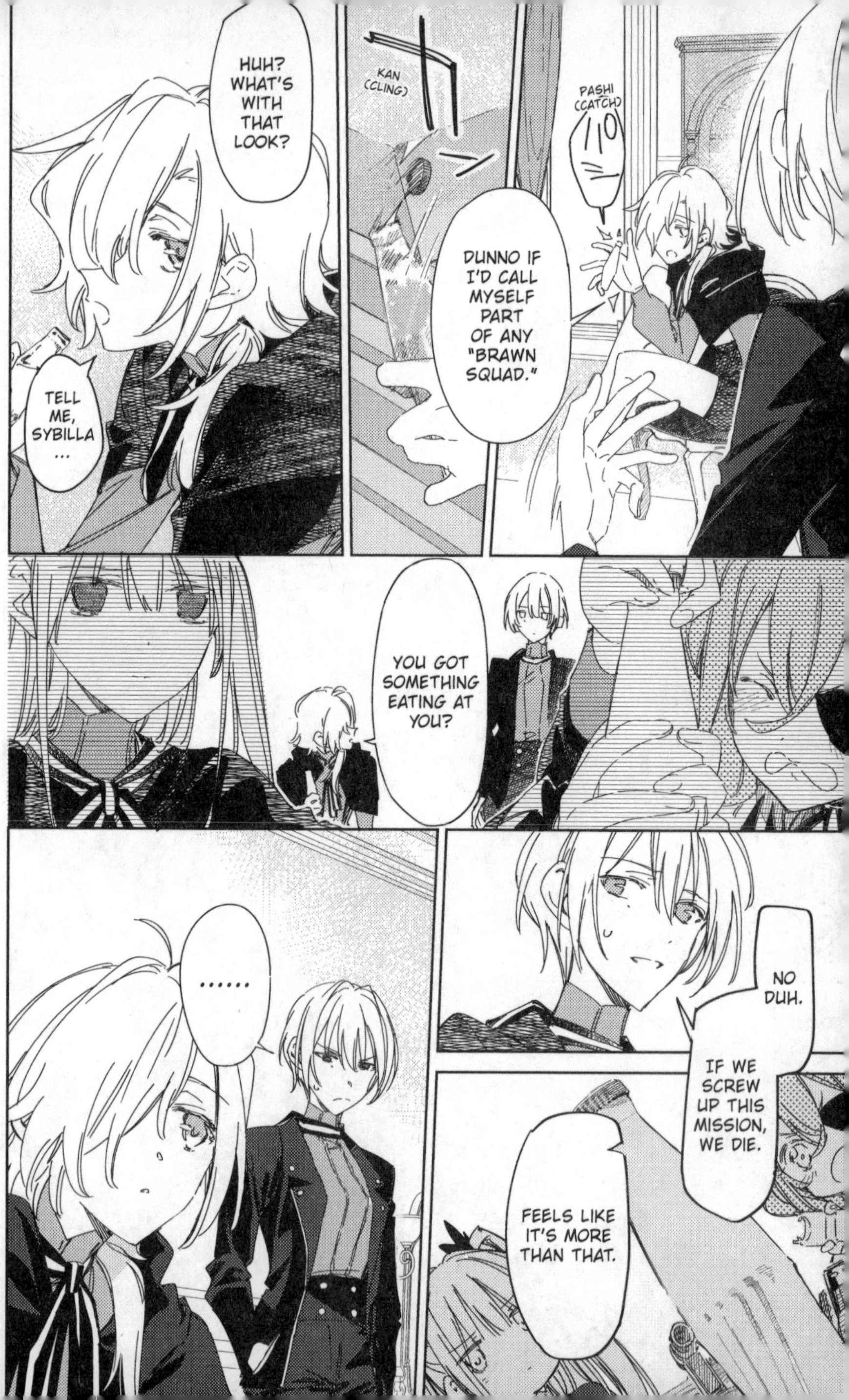
PASHI (CATCH)
DUNNO IF I'D CALL MYSELF PART OF ANY "BRAWN SQUAD."
KAN (CLING)
HUH? WHAT'S WITH THAT LOOK?
TELL ME, SYBILLA...
YOU GOT SOMETHING EATING AT YOU?
NO DUH.
IF WE SCREW UP THIS MISSION, WE DIE.
FEELS LIKE IT'S MORE THAN THAT.
......

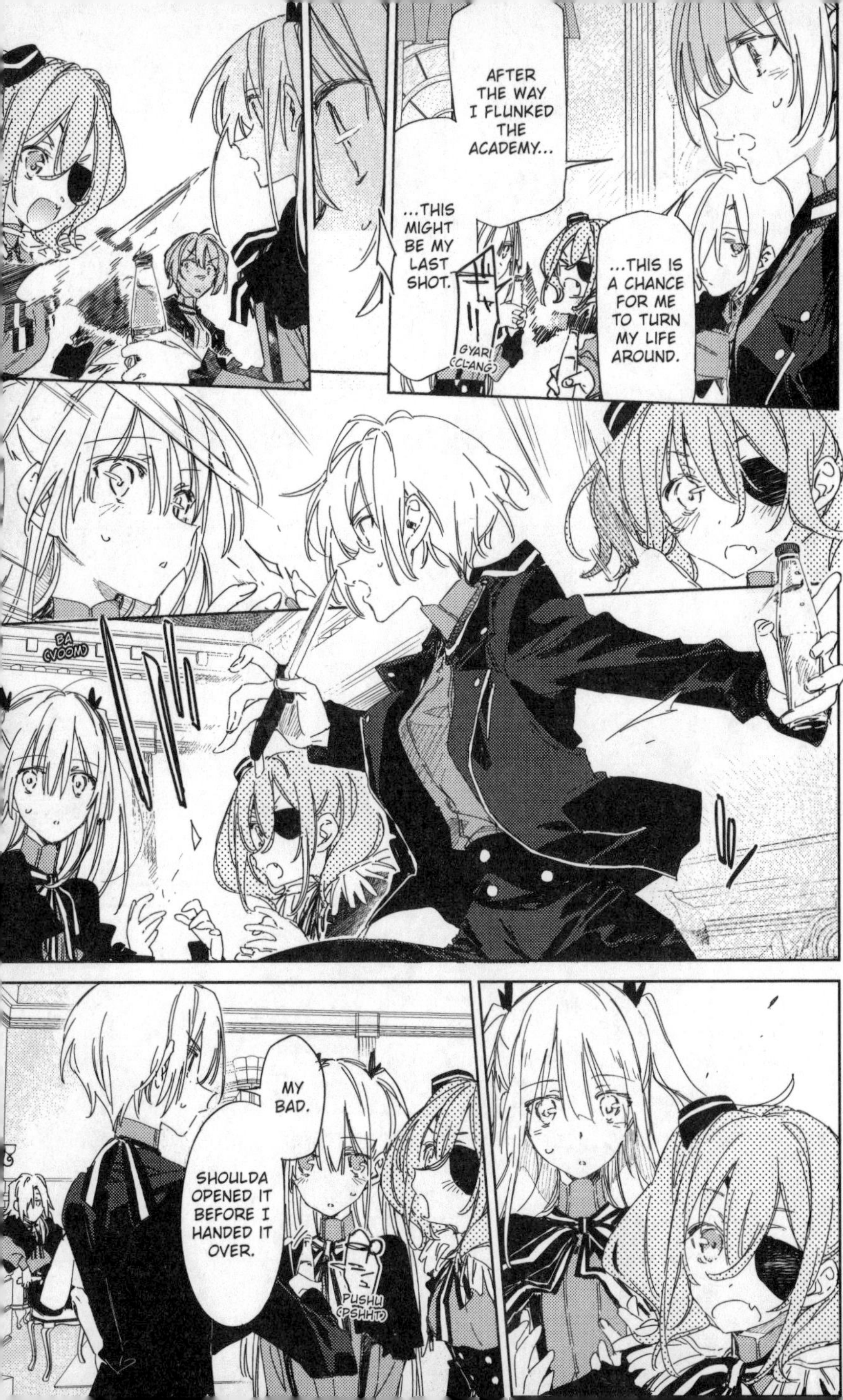
AFTER THE WAY I FLUNKED THE ACADEMY...
...THIS MIGHT BE MY LAST SHOT.
...THIS IS A CHANCE FOR ME TO TURN MY LIFE AROUND.
GYARI (CLANG)
BA (VOOM)
MY BAD.
SHOULDA OPENED IT BEFORE I HANDED IT OVER.
PUSHU (PSHHT)

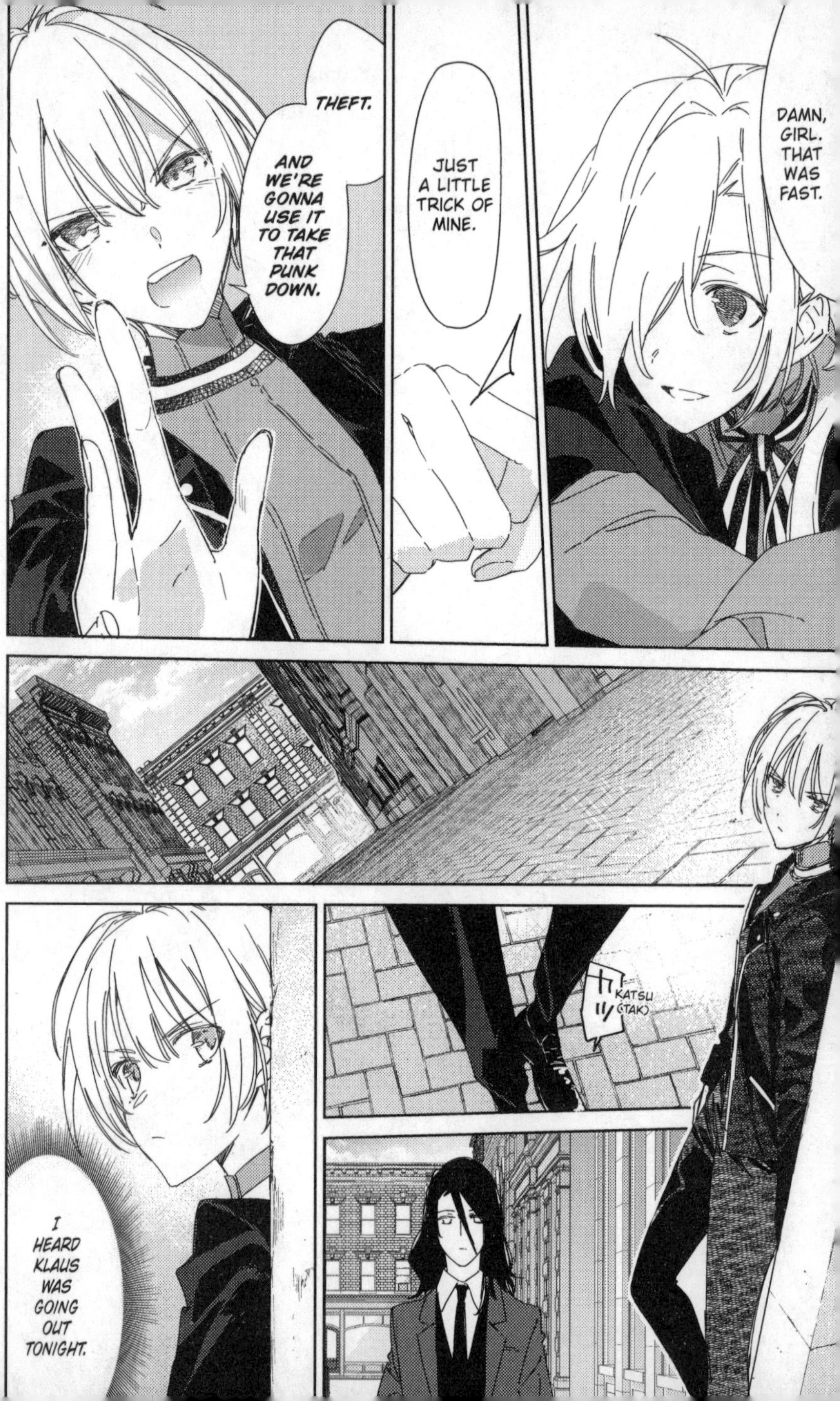
DAMN, GIRL. THAT WAS FAST.
JUST A LITTLE TRICK OF MINE.
THEFT.
AND WE'RE GONNA USE IT TO TAKE THAT PUNK DOWN.
KATSU (TAK)
I HEARD KLAUS WAS GOING OUT TONIGHT.

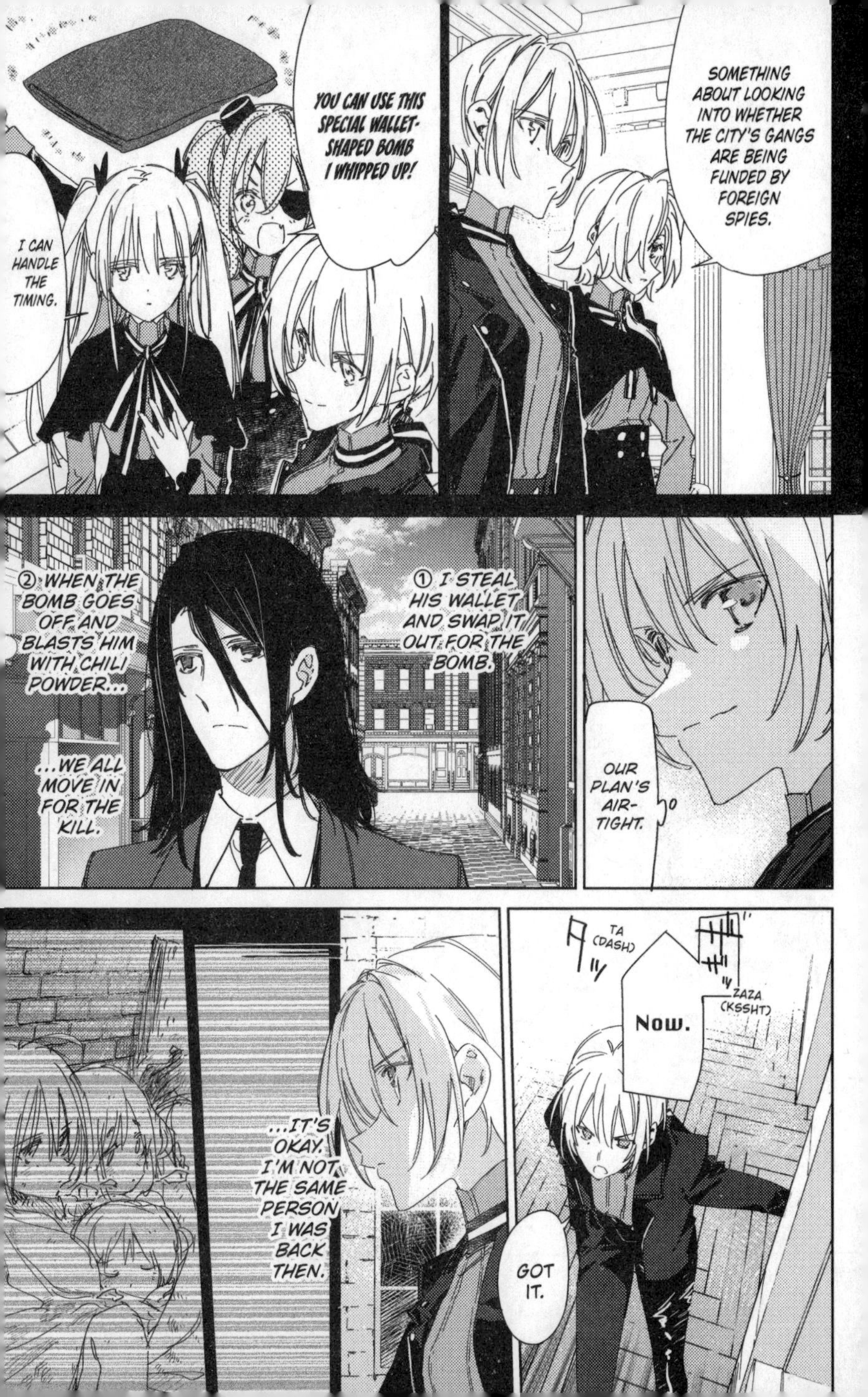
SOMETHING ABOUT LOOKING INTO WHETHER THE CITY'S GANGS ARE BEING FUNDED BY FOREIGN SPIES.
YOU CAN USE THIS SPECIAL WALLET-SHAPED BOMB I WHIPPED UP!
I CAN HANDLE THE TIMING.
OUR PLAN'S AIR-TIGHT.
① I STEAL HIS WALLET AND SWAP IT OUT FOR THE BOMB.
② WHEN THE BOMB GOES OFF AND BLASTS HIM WITH CHILI POWDER...
...WE ALL MOVE IN FOR THE KILL.
TA (DASH)
ZAZA (KSSHT)
Now.
GOT IT.
...IT'S OKAY. I'M NOT THE SAME PERSON I WAS BACK THEN.

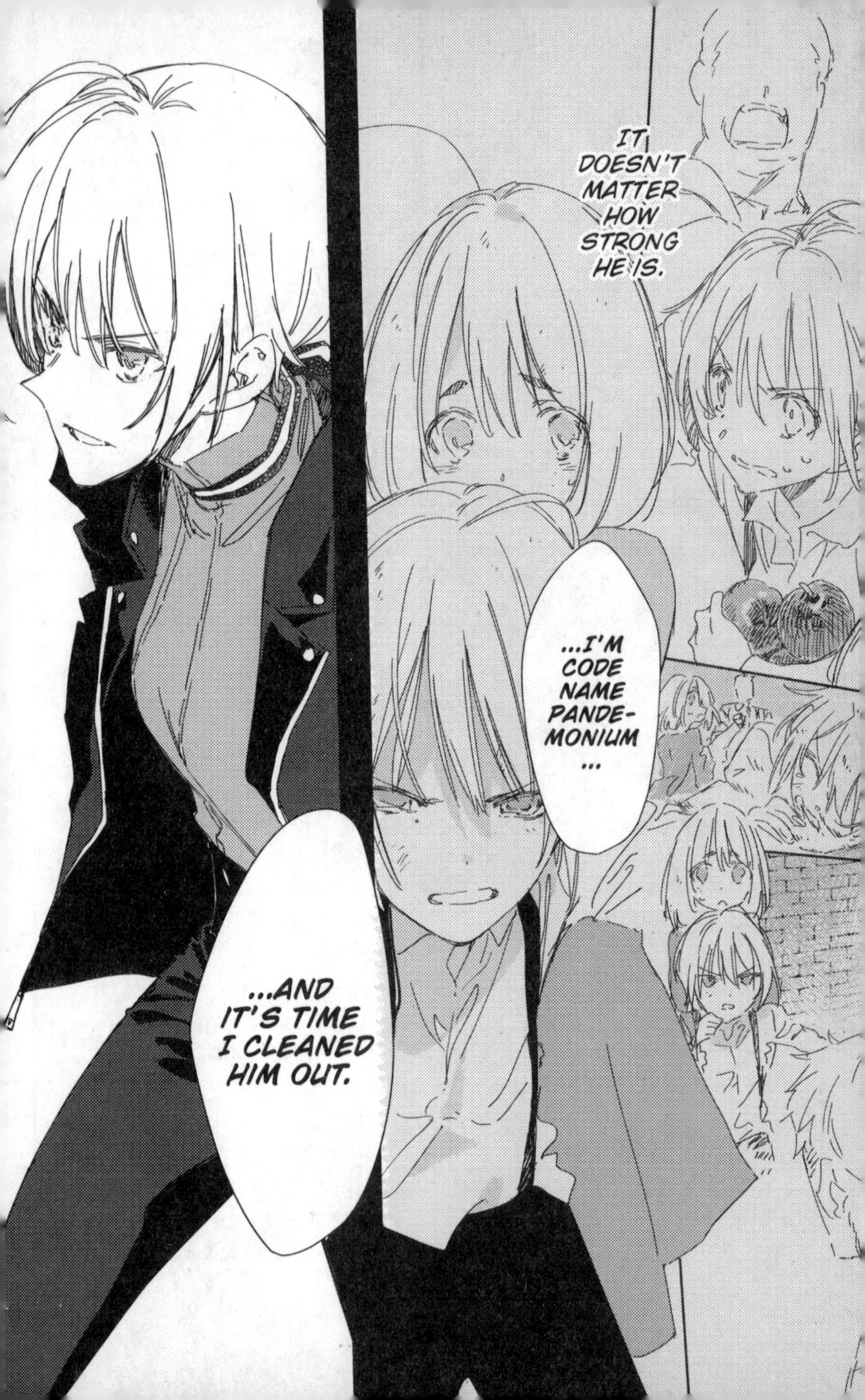
IT DOESN'T MATTER HOW STRONG HE IS.
...I'M CODE NAME PANDE-MONIUM...
...AND IT'S TIME I CLEANED HIM OUT.

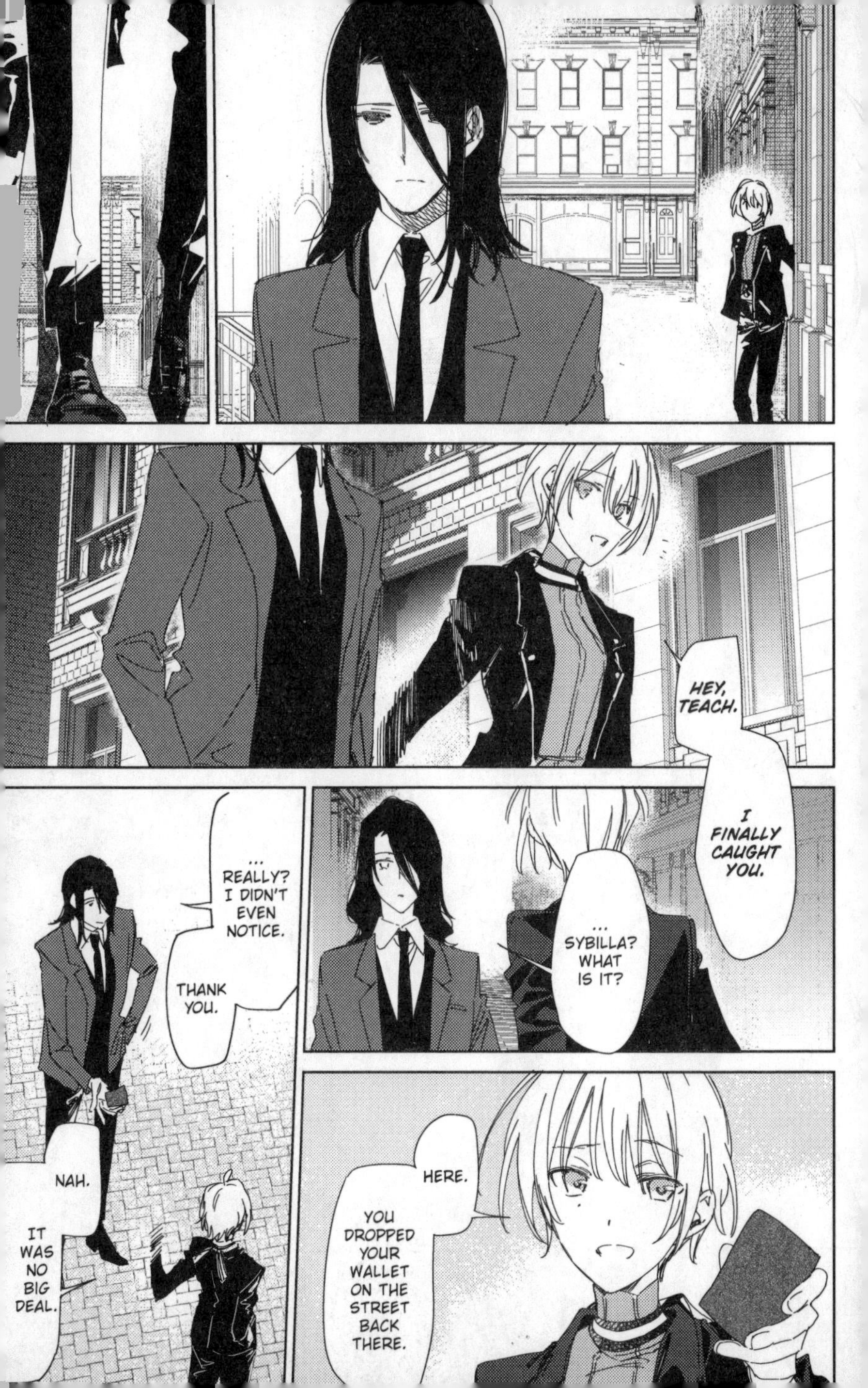
HEY, TEACH.
I FINALLY CAUGHT YOU.
... SYBILLA? WHAT IS IT?
HERE.
YOU DROPPED YOUR WALLET ON THE STREET BACK THERE.
... REALLY? I DIDN'T EVEN NOTICE.
THANK YOU.
NAH.
IT WAS NO BIG DEAL.

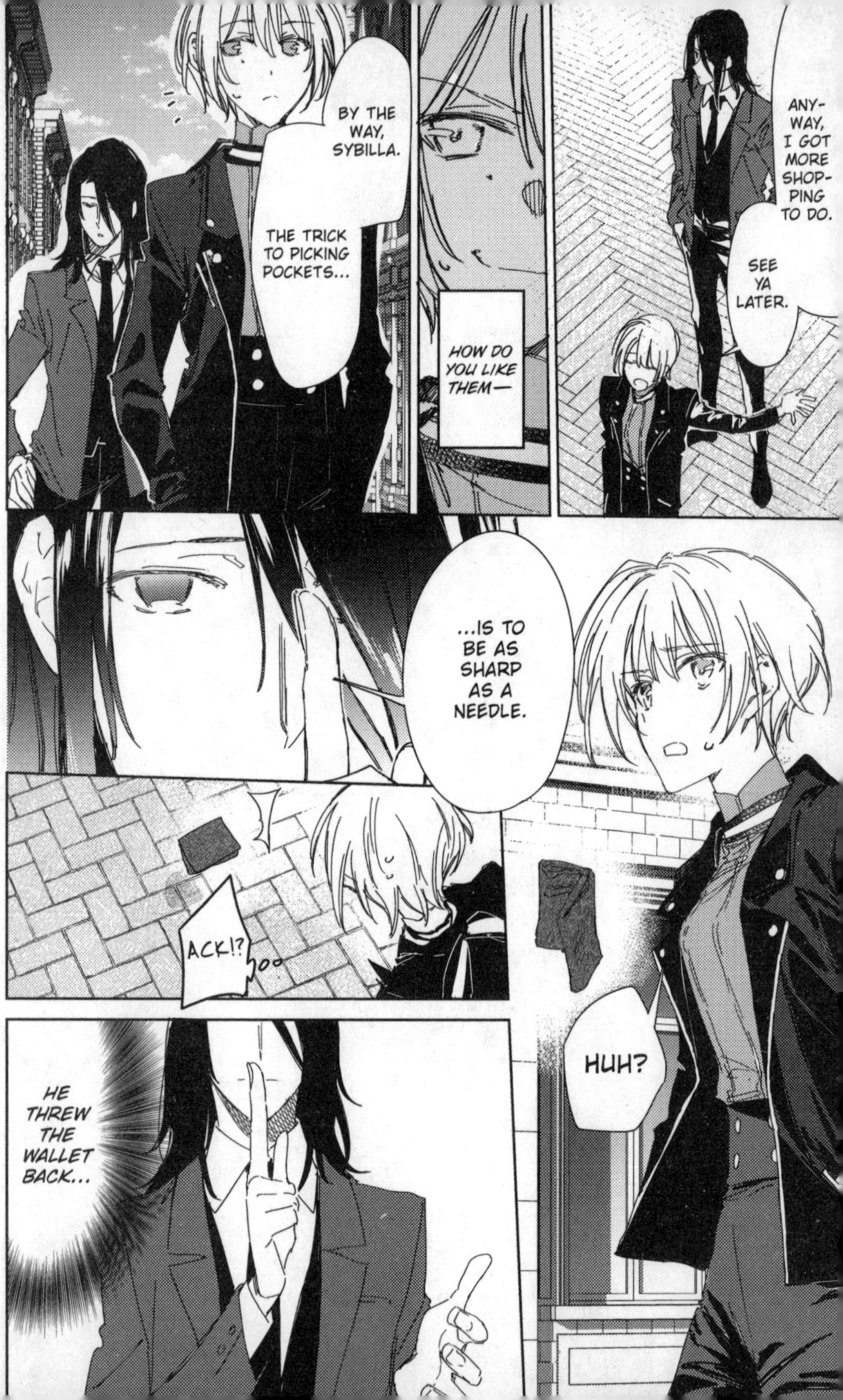

ANY-WAY, I GOT MORE SHOP-PING TO DO.
SEE YA LATER.
HOW DO YOU LIKE THEM—
BY THE WAY, SYBILLA.
THE TRICK TO PICKING POCKETS...
HUH?
...IS TO BE AS SHARP AS A NEEDLE.
ACK!?
HE THREW THE WALLET BACK...

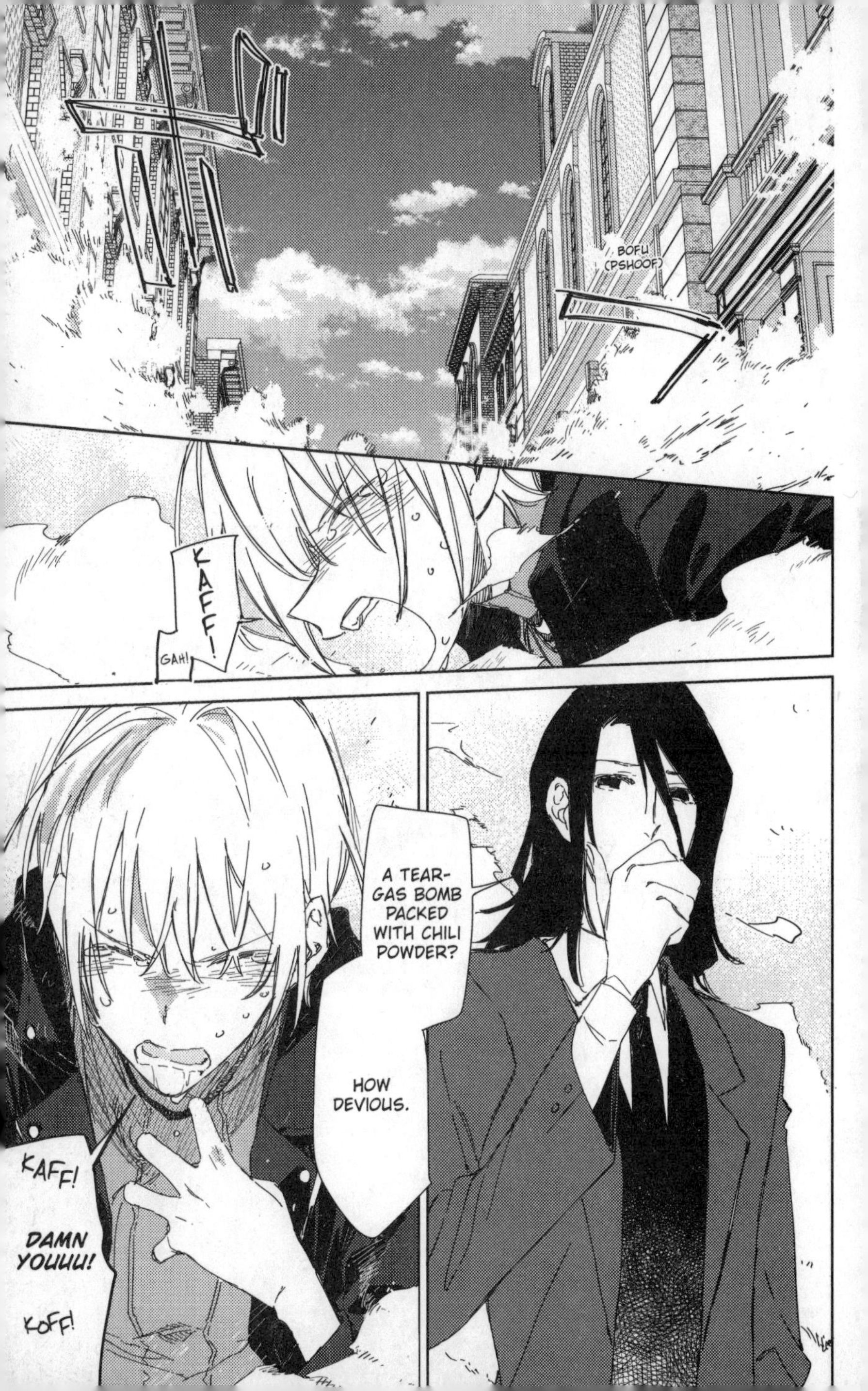
BOFU
(PSHOOF)
KAFF!
GAH!
A TEAR-GAS BOMB PACKED WITH CHILI POWDER?
HOW DEVIOUS.
KAFF!
DAMN YOUUU!
KOFF!

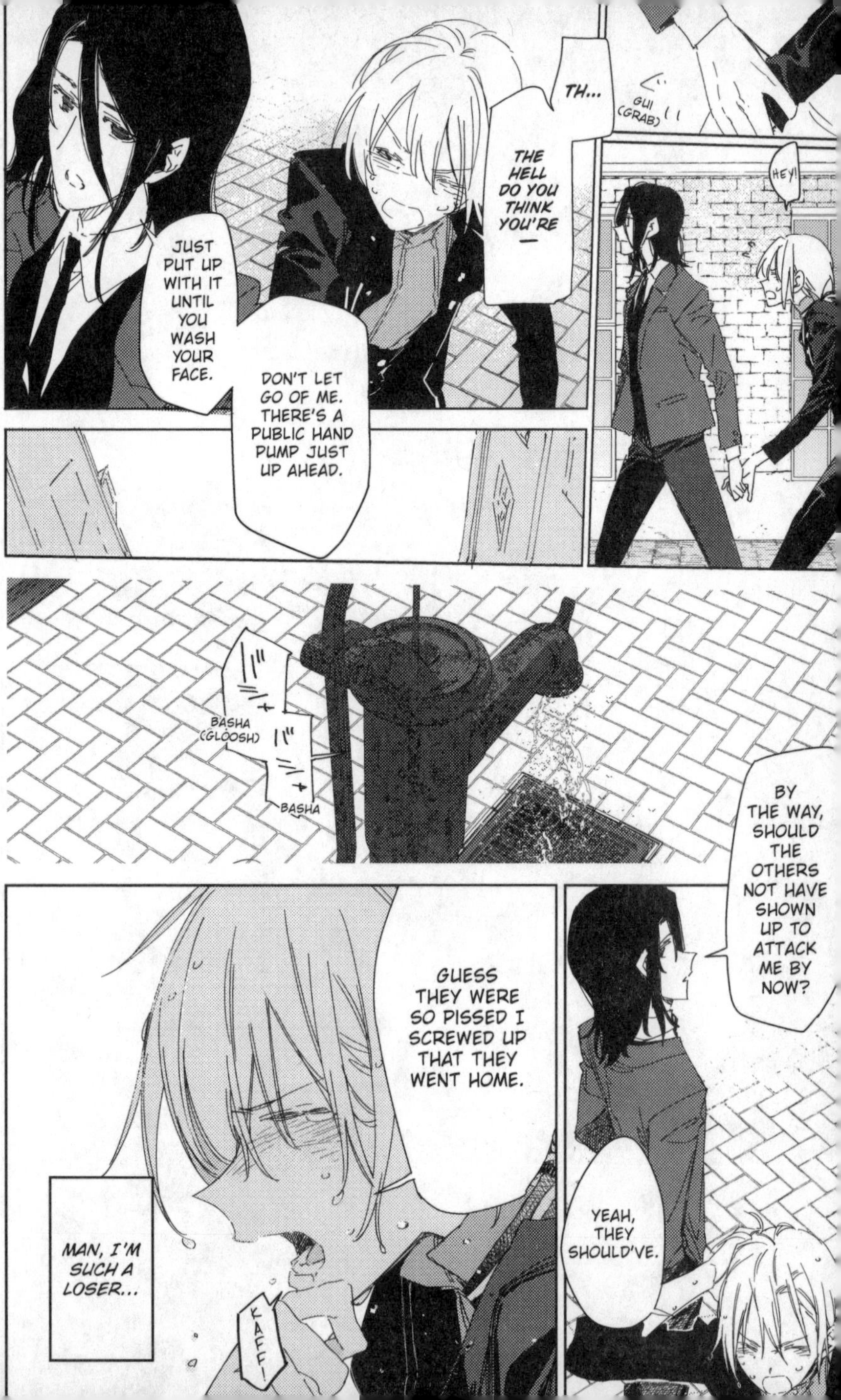
TH...
GUI (GRAB)
THE HELL DO YOU THINK YOU'RE—
JUST PUT UP WITH IT UNTIL YOU WASH YOUR FACE.
HEY!
DON'T LET GO OF ME. THERE'S A PUBLIC HAND PUMP JUST UP AHEAD.
BASHA (GLOOSH)
BASHA
BY THE WAY, SHOULD THE OTHERS NOT HAVE SHOWN UP TO ATTACK ME BY NOW?
YEAH, THEY SHOULD'VE.
GUESS THEY WERE SO PISSED I SCREWED UP THAT THEY WENT HOME.
MAN, I'M SUCH A LOSER...
KAFF!

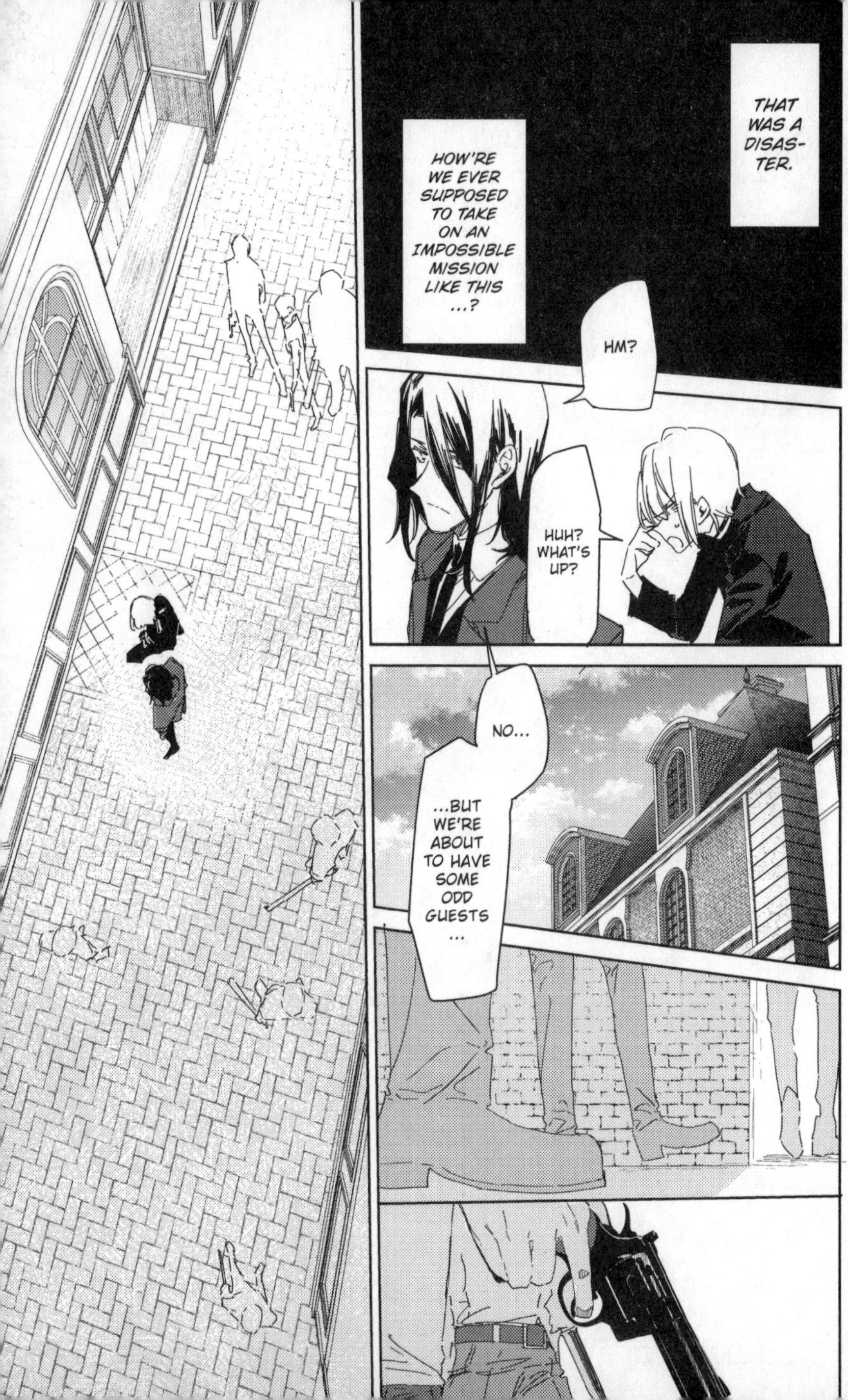
THAT WAS A DISASTER.
HOW'RE WE EVER SUPPOSED TO TAKE ON AN IMPOSSIBLE MISSION LIKE THIS ...?
HM?
HUH? WHAT'S UP?
NO...
...BUT WE'RE ABOUT TO HAVE SOME ODD GUESTS ...

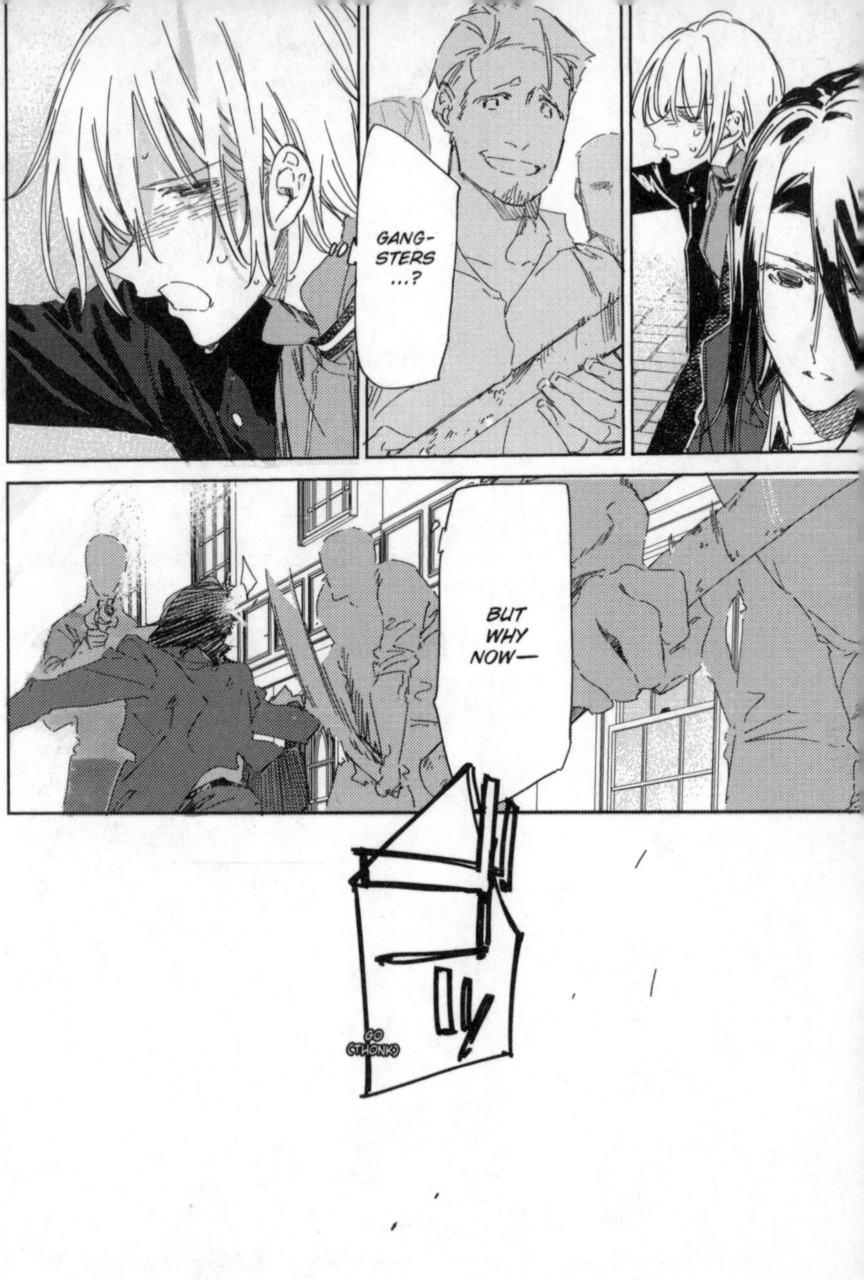
GANG-STERS ...?
BUT WHY NOW—
GO (THONK)

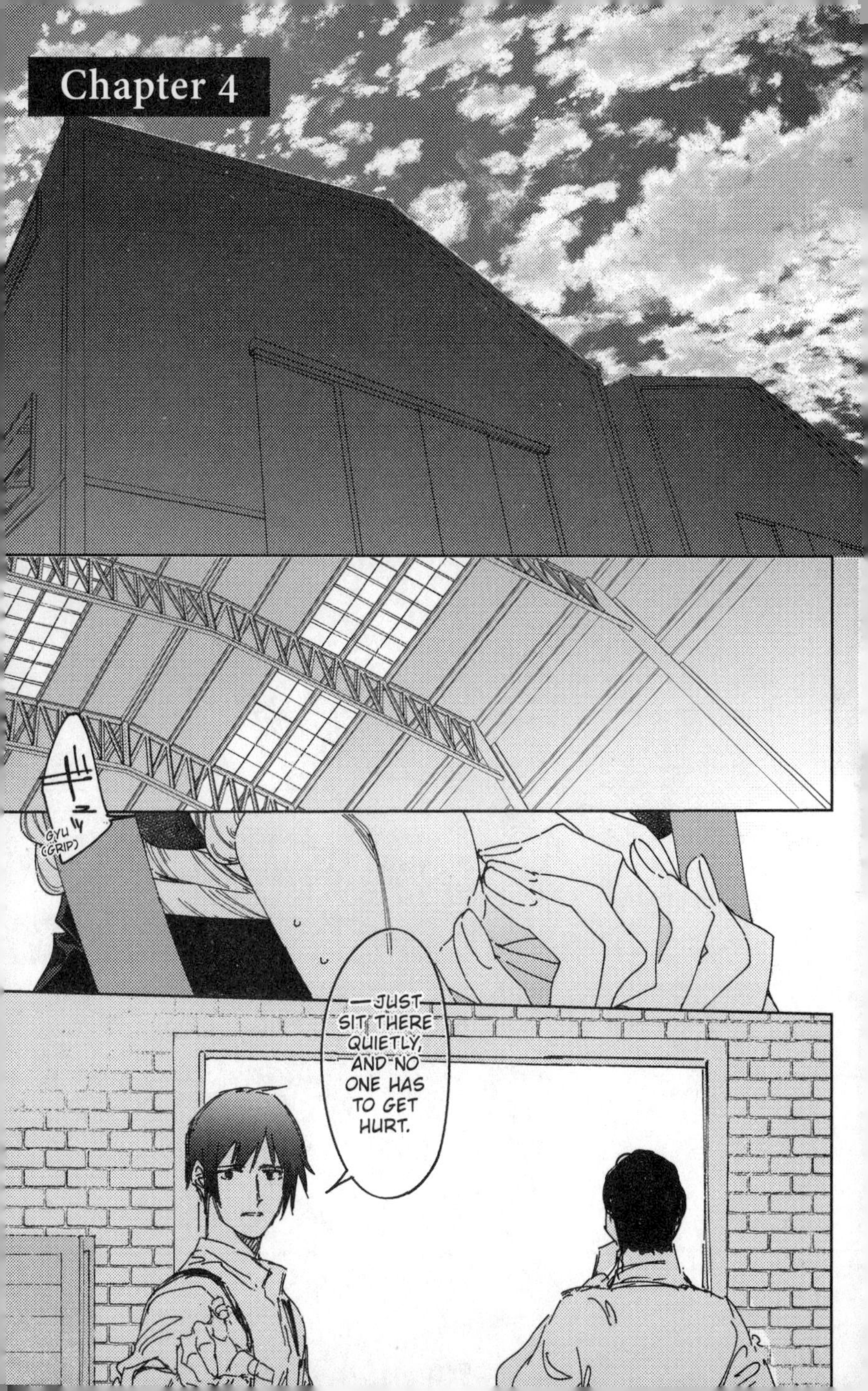
Chapter 4
GYU (GRIP)
—JUST SIT THERE QUIETLY, AND NO ONE HAS TO GET HURT.

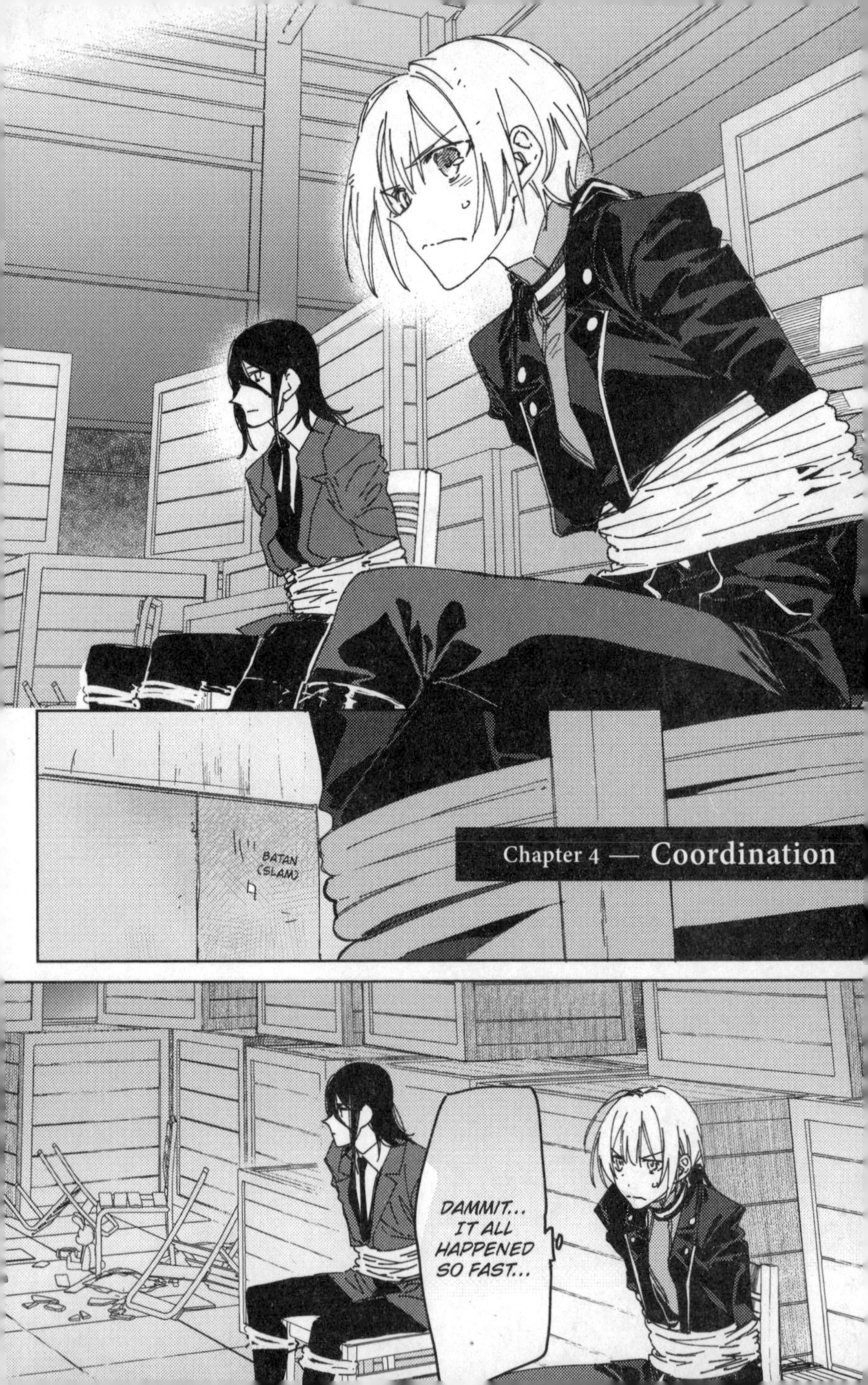
Chapter 4 — Coordination
BATAN (SLAM)
DAMMIT... IT ALL HAPPENED SO FAST...

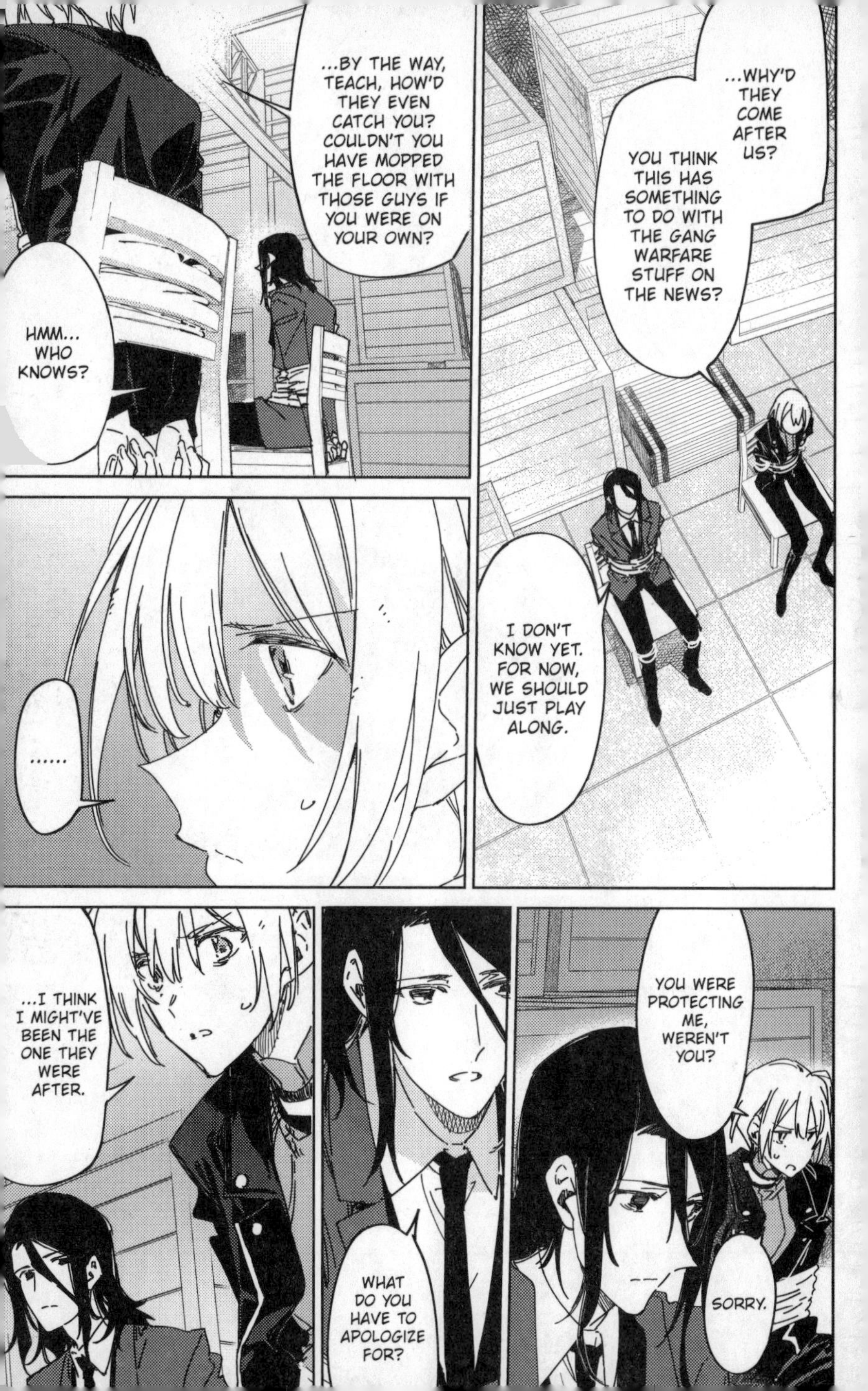
...WHY'D THEY COME AFTER US?
YOU THINK THIS HAS SOMETHING TO DO WITH THE GANG WARFARE STUFF ON THE NEWS?
I DON'T KNOW YET. FOR NOW, WE SHOULD JUST PLAY ALONG.
...BY THE WAY, TEACH, HOW'D THEY EVEN CATCH YOU? COULDN'T YOU HAVE MOPPED THE FLOOR WITH THOSE GUYS IF YOU WERE ON YOUR OWN?
HMM... WHO KNOWS?
......
YOU WERE PROTECTING ME, WEREN'T YOU?
SORRY.
WHAT DO YOU HAVE TO APOLOGIZE FOR?
...I THINK I MIGHT'VE BEEN THE ONE THEY WERE AFTER.

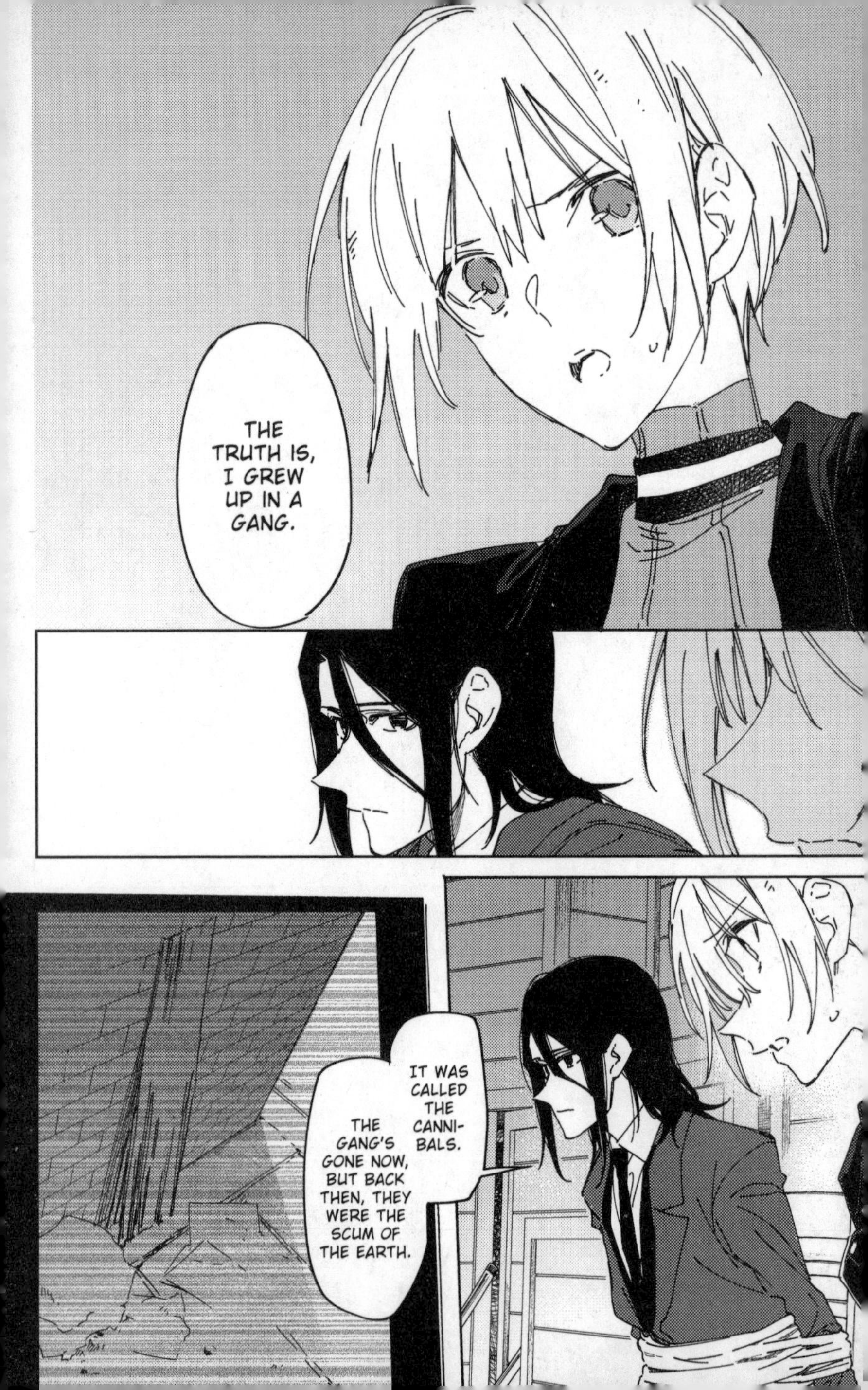
THE TRUTH IS, I GREW UP IN A GANG.
IT WAS CALLED THE CANNIBALS.
THE GANG'S GONE NOW, BUT BACK THEN, THEY WERE THE SCUM OF THE EARTH.

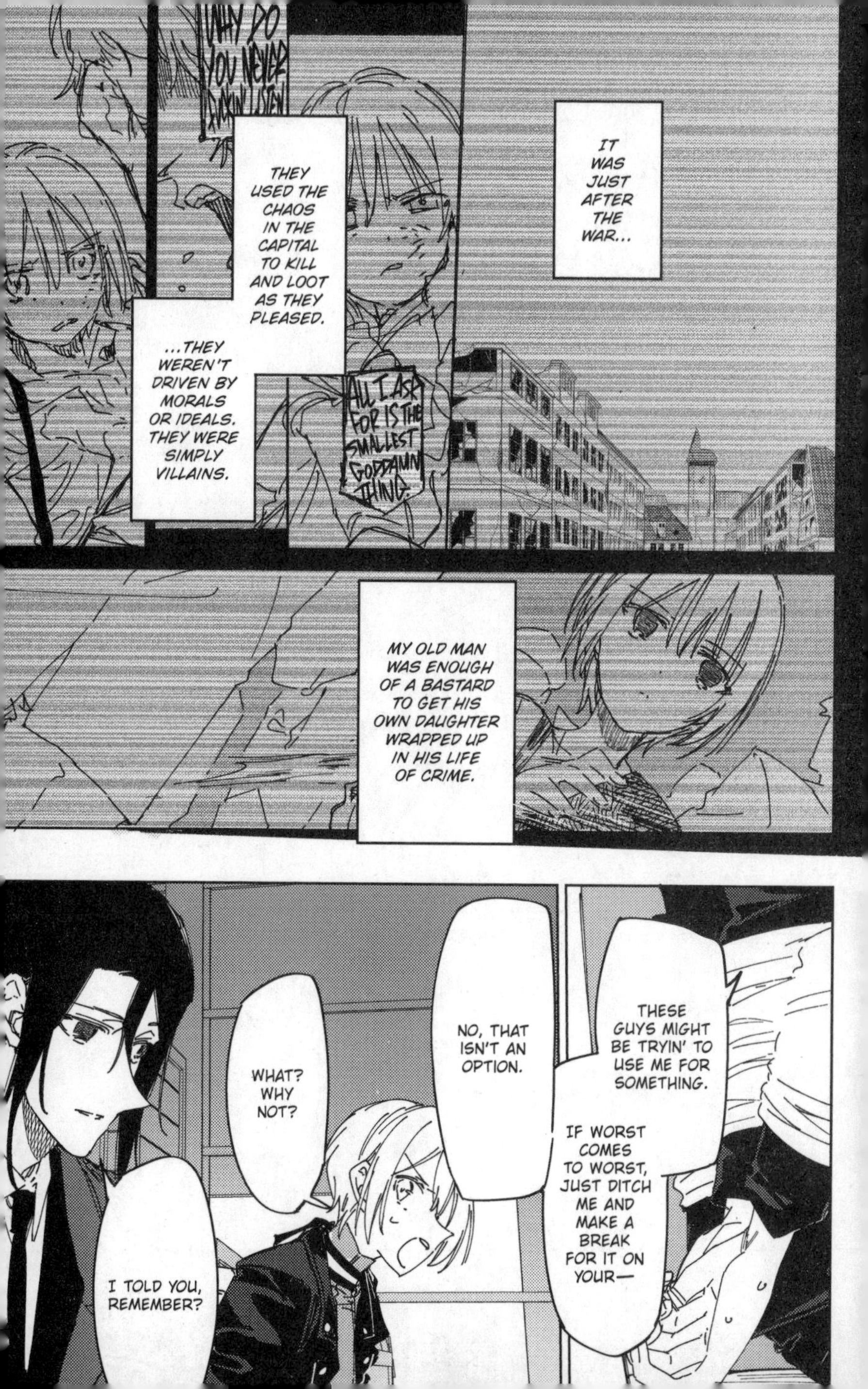
IT WAS JUST AFTER THE WAR...
THEY USED THE CHAOS IN THE CAPITAL TO KILL AND LOOT AS THEY PLEASED.
ALL I ASK FOR IS THE SMALLEST GODDAMN THING.
...THEY WEREN'T DRIVEN BY MORALS OR IDEALS. THEY WERE SIMPLY VILLAINS.
WHY DO YOU NEVER FUCKIN' LISTEN!
MY OLD MAN WAS ENOUGH OF A BASTARD TO GET HIS OWN DAUGHTER WRAPPED UP IN HIS LIFE OF CRIME.
THESE GUYS MIGHT BE TRYIN' TO USE ME FOR SOMETHING.
IF WORST COMES TO WORST, JUST DITCH ME AND MAKE A BREAK FOR IT ON YOUR—
NO, THAT ISN'T AN OPTION.
WHAT? WHY NOT?
I TOLD YOU, REMEMBER?

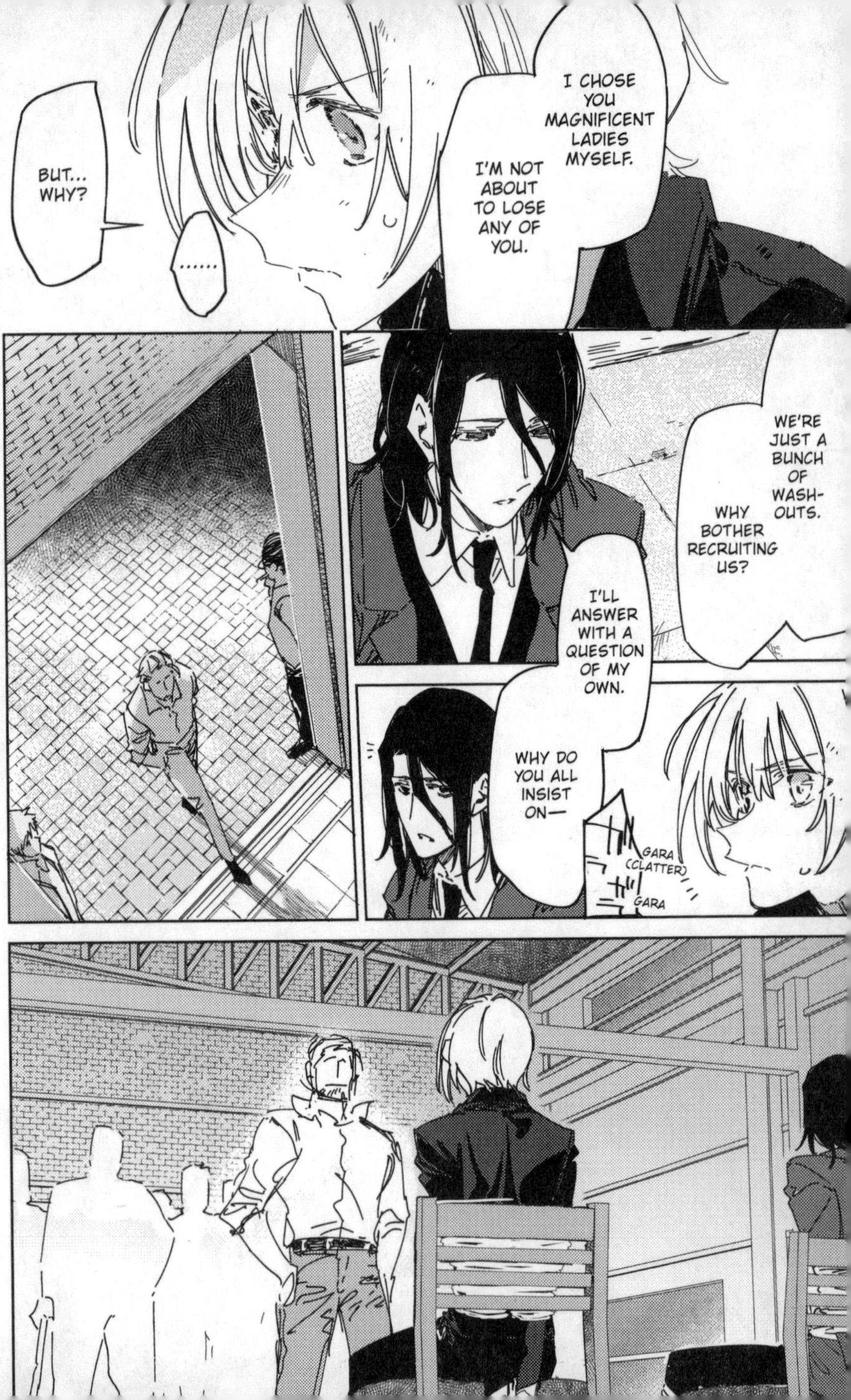
I CHOSE YOU MAGNIFICENT LADIES MYSELF.
I'M NOT ABOUT TO LOSE ANY OF YOU.
......
BUT... WHY?
WE'RE JUST A BUNCH OF WASH-OUTS.
WHY BOTHER RECRUITING US?
I'LL ANSWER WITH A QUESTION OF MY OWN.
WHY DO YOU ALL INSIST ON—
GARA (CLATTER)
GARA

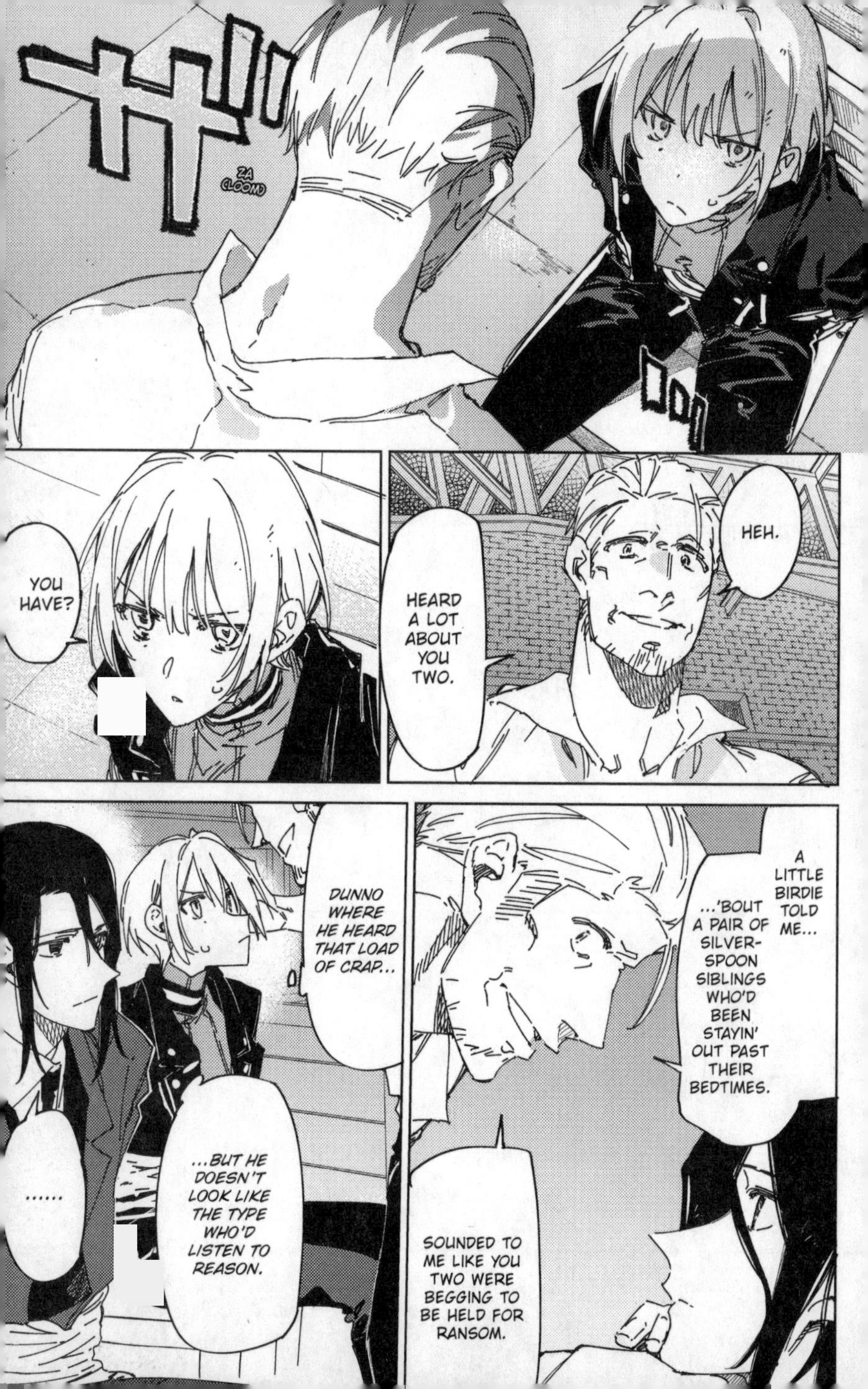
ZA CLOOM
HEH.
HEARD A LOT ABOUT YOU TWO.
YOU HAVE?
A LITTLE BIRDIE TOLD ME...
...'BOUT A PAIR OF SILVER-SPOON SIBLINGS WHO'D BEEN STAYIN' OUT PAST THEIR BEDTIMES.
SOUNDED TO ME LIKE YOU TWO WERE BEGGING TO BE HELD FOR RANSOM.
DUNNO WHERE HE HEARD THAT LOAD OF CRAP...
...BUT HE DOESN'T LOOK LIKE THE TYPE WHO'D LISTEN TO REASON.
......

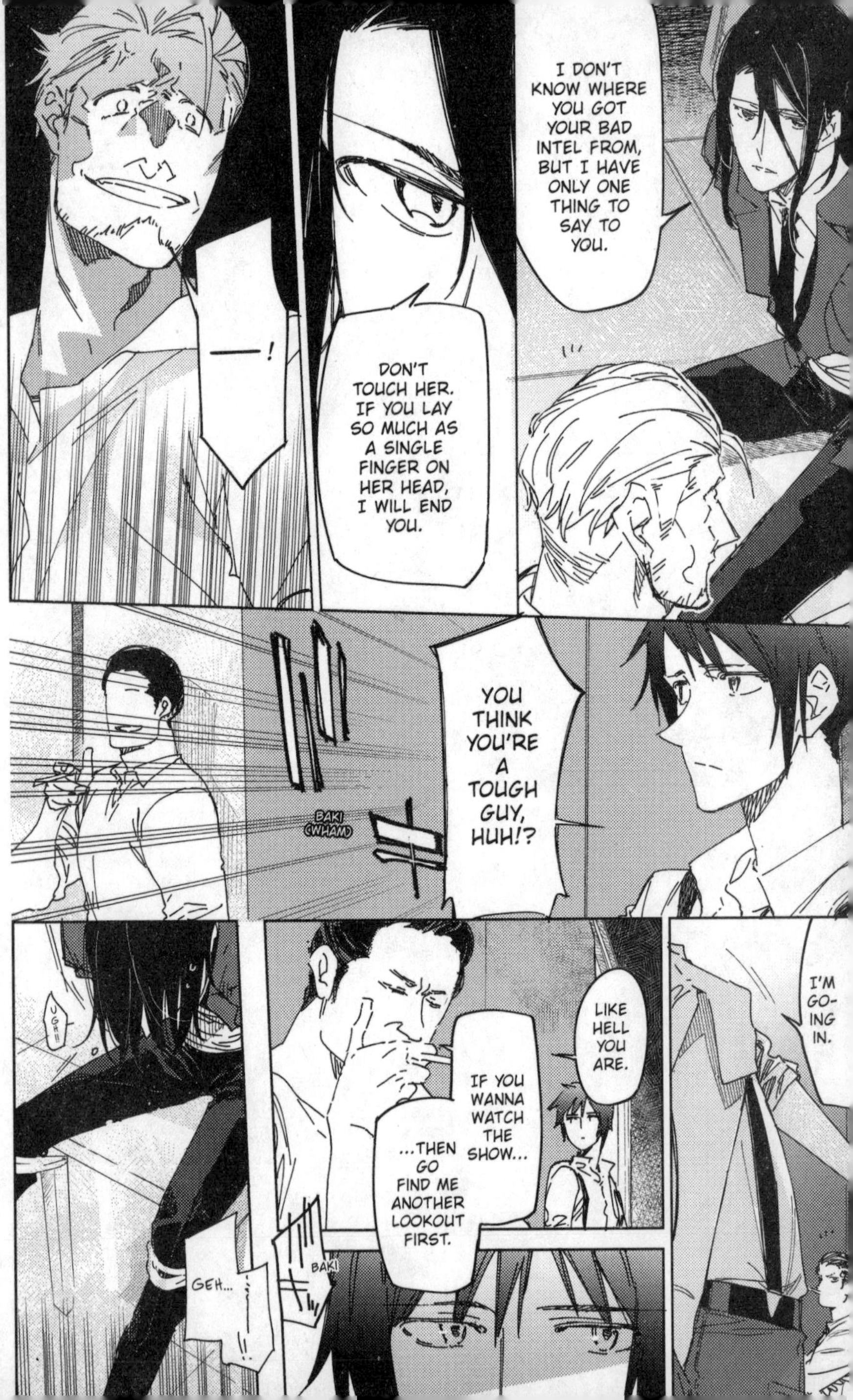
I DON'T KNOW WHERE YOU GOT YOUR BAD INTEL FROM, BUT I HAVE ONLY ONE THING TO SAY TO YOU.
DON'T TOUCH HER. IF YOU LAY SO MUCH AS A SINGLE FINGER ON HER HEAD, I WILL END YOU.
——!
YOU THINK YOU'RE A TOUGH GUY, HUH!?
BAKI (WHAM)
I'M GOING IN.
LIKE HELL YOU ARE.
IF YOU WANNA WATCH THE SHOW...
...THEN GO FIND ME ANOTHER LOOKOUT FIRST.
BAKI
UGH!!
GEH...
...!!

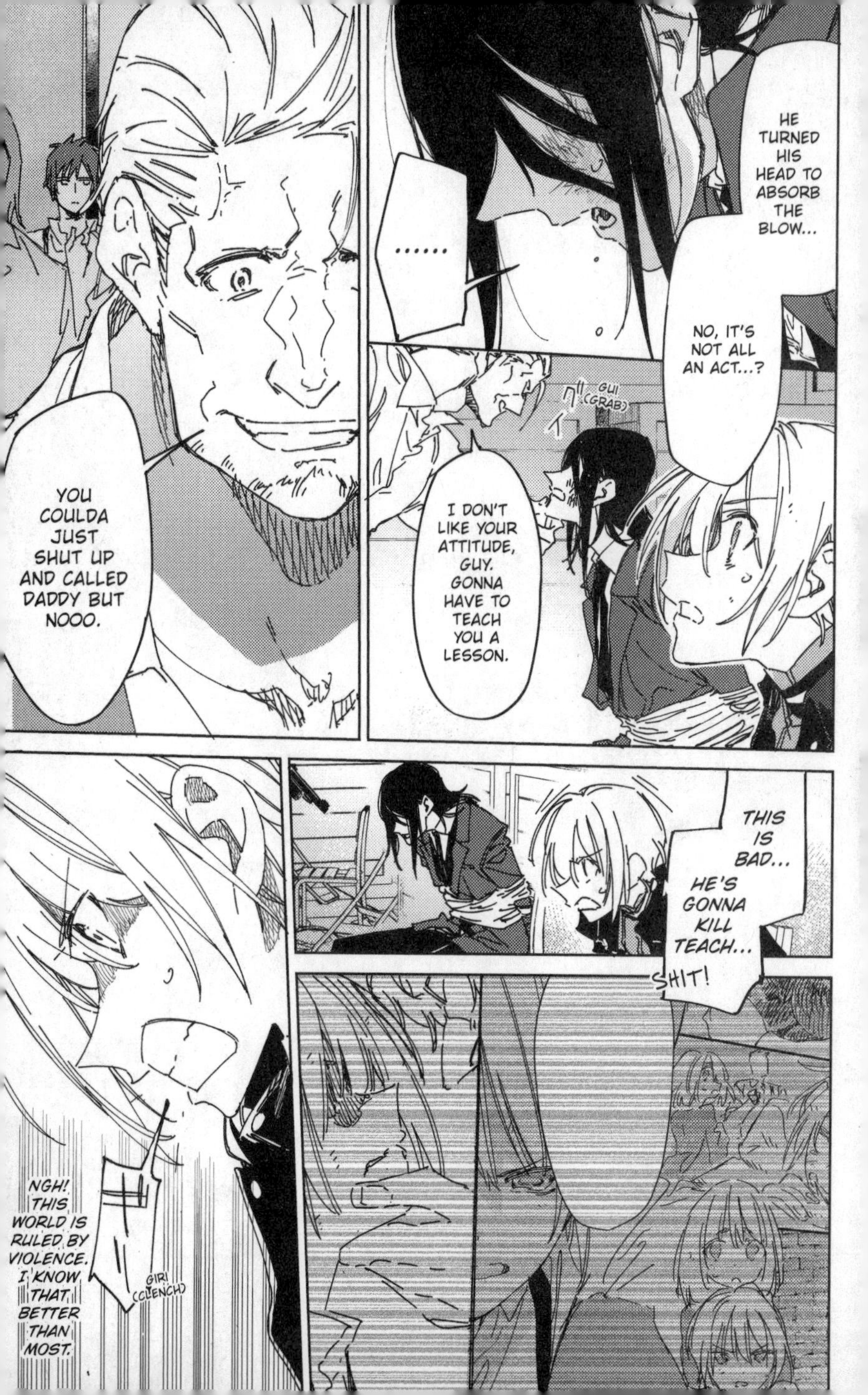

HE TURNED HIS HEAD TO ABSORB THE BLOW...
......
NO, IT'S NOT ALL AN ACT...?
GUI (GRAB)
I DON'T LIKE YOUR ATTITUDE, GUY. GONNA HAVE TO TEACH YOU A LESSON.
YOU COULDA JUST SHUT UP AND CALLED DADDY BUT NOOO.
THIS IS BAD...
HE'S GONNA KILL TEACH...
SHIT!
NGH! THIS WORLD IS RULED BY VIOLENCE. I KNOW THAT BETTER THAN MOST.
GIRI (CLENCH)

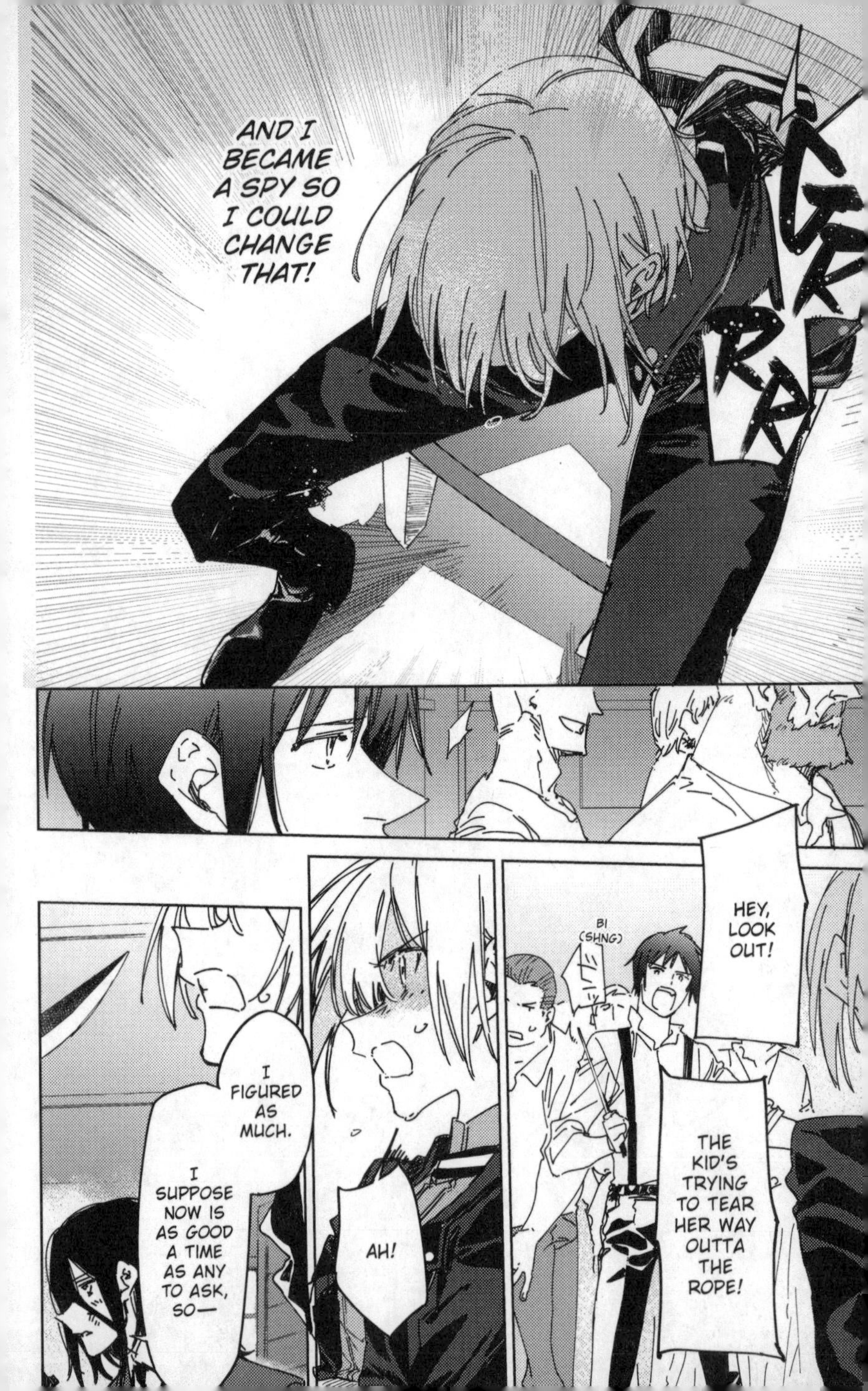
AND I BECAME A SPY SO I COULD CHANGE THAT!
HEY, LOOK OUT!
BI (SHNG)
THE KID'S TRYING TO TEAR HER WAY OUTTA THE ROPE!
AH!
I FIGURED AS MUCH.
I SUPPOSE NOW IS AS GOOD A TIME AS ANY TO ASK, SO—

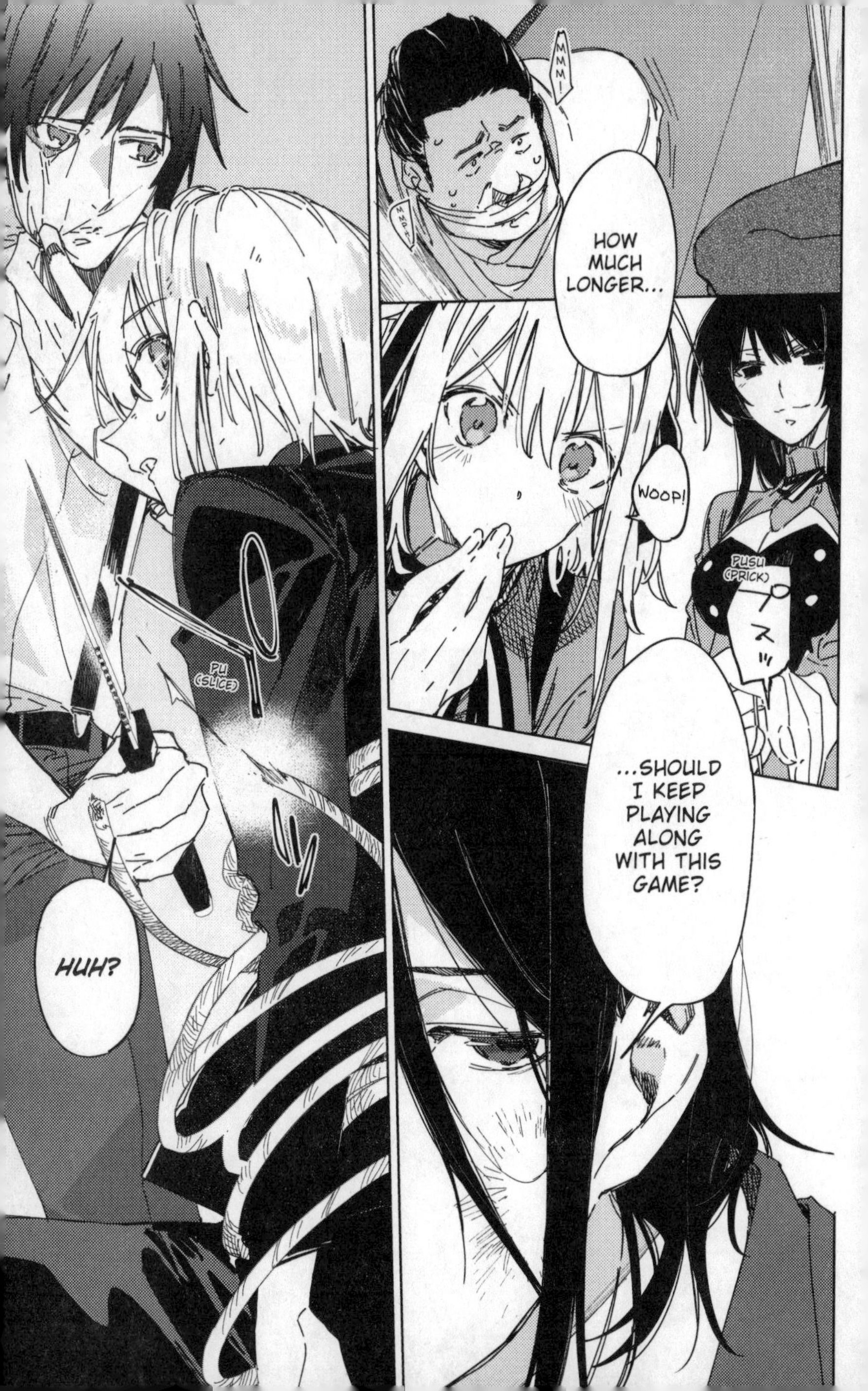
MMM!
MMPH
HOW MUCH LONGER...
WOOP!
PUSU (PRICK)
...SHOULD I KEEP PLAYING ALONG WITH THIS GAME?
PU (SLICE)
HUH?

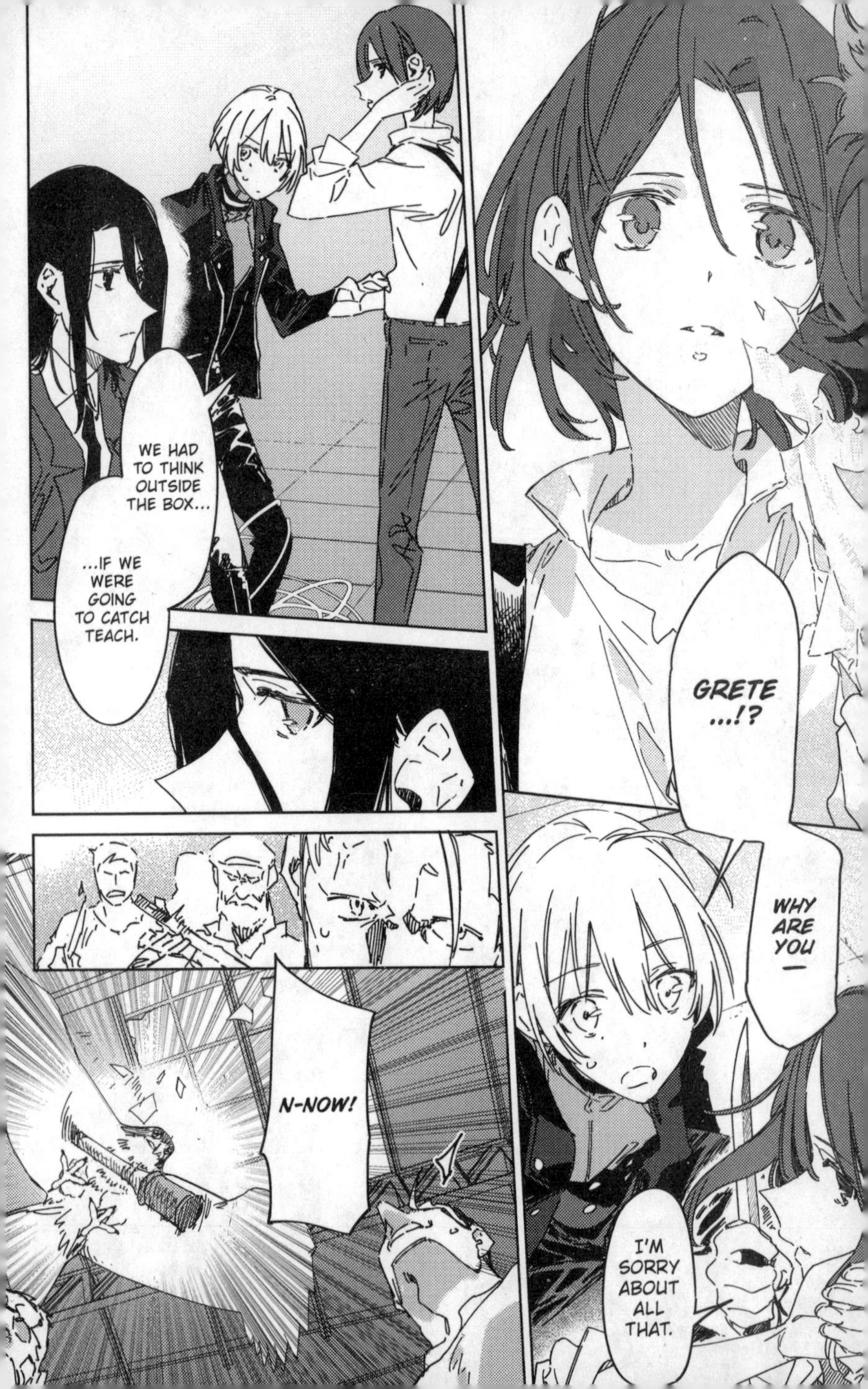
GRETE ...!?
WE HAD TO THINK OUTSIDE THE BOX...
...IF WE WERE GOING TO CATCH TEACH.
WHY ARE YOU —
I'M SORRY ABOUT ALL THAT.
N-NOW!

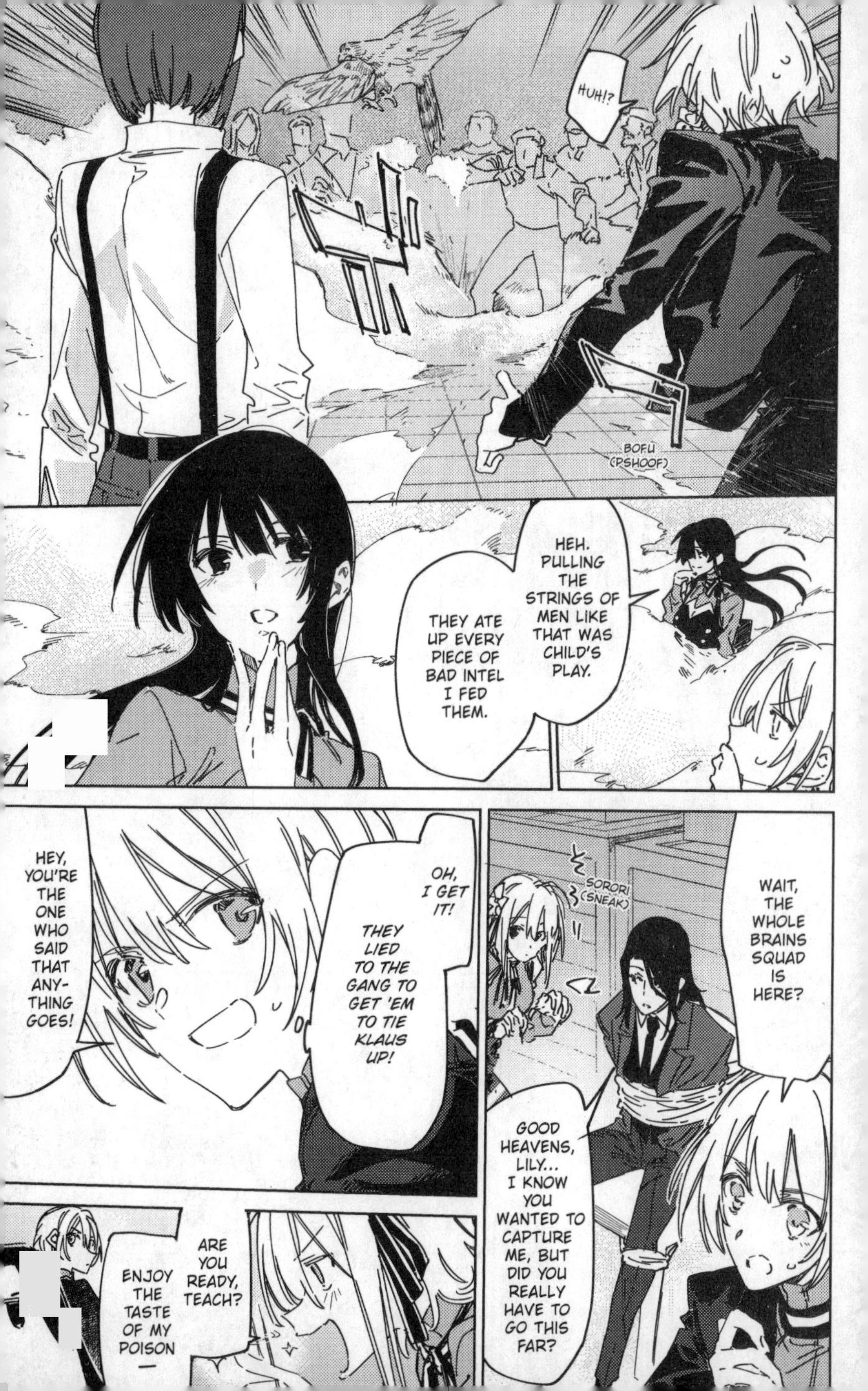
HUH!?
BOFU (PSHOOF)
HEH. PULLING THE STRINGS OF MEN LIKE THAT WAS CHILD'S PLAY.
THEY ATE UP EVERY PIECE OF BAD INTEL I FED THEM.
WAIT, THE WHOLE BRAINS SQUAD IS HERE?
SORORI (SNEAK)
GOOD HEAVENS, LILY... I KNOW YOU WANTED TO CAPTURE ME, BUT DID YOU REALLY HAVE TO GO THIS FAR?
OH, I GET IT!
THEY LIED TO THE GANG TO GET 'EM TO TIE KLAUS UP!
HEY, YOU'RE THE ONE WHO SAID THAT ANY-THING GOES!
ARE YOU READY, TEACH?
ENJOY THE TASTE OF MY POISON—

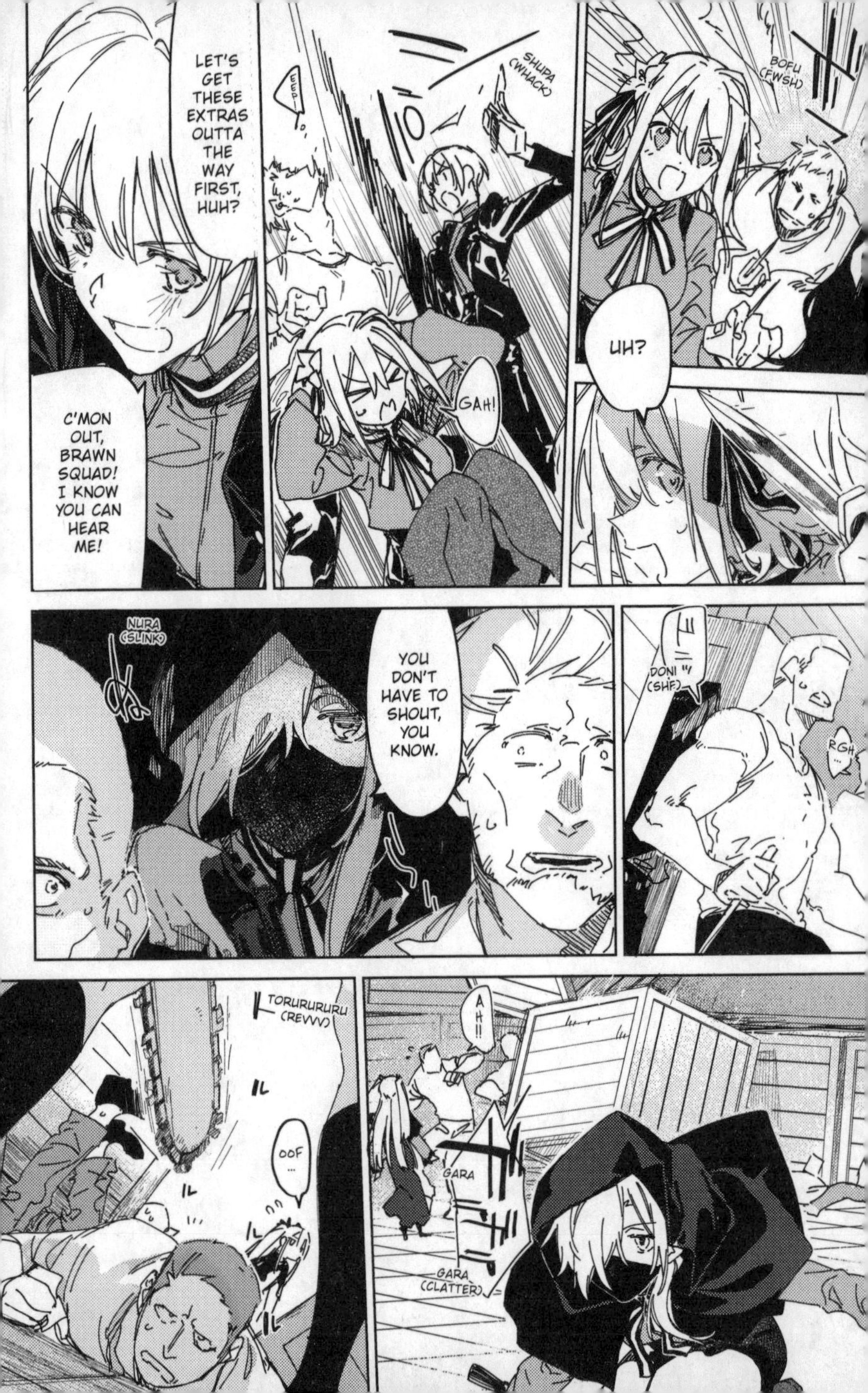
BOFU (FWSH)
UH?
SHUPA (WHACK)
EEP!
GAH!
LET'S GET THESE EXTRAS OUTTA THE WAY FIRST, HUH?
C'MON OUT, BRAWN SQUAD! I KNOW YOU CAN HEAR ME!
DONI (SHF)
RGH...
YOU DON'T HAVE TO SHOUT, YOU KNOW.
NURA (SLINK)
AH!!
GARA
GARA (CLATTER)
TORURURURU (REVVV)
OOF...

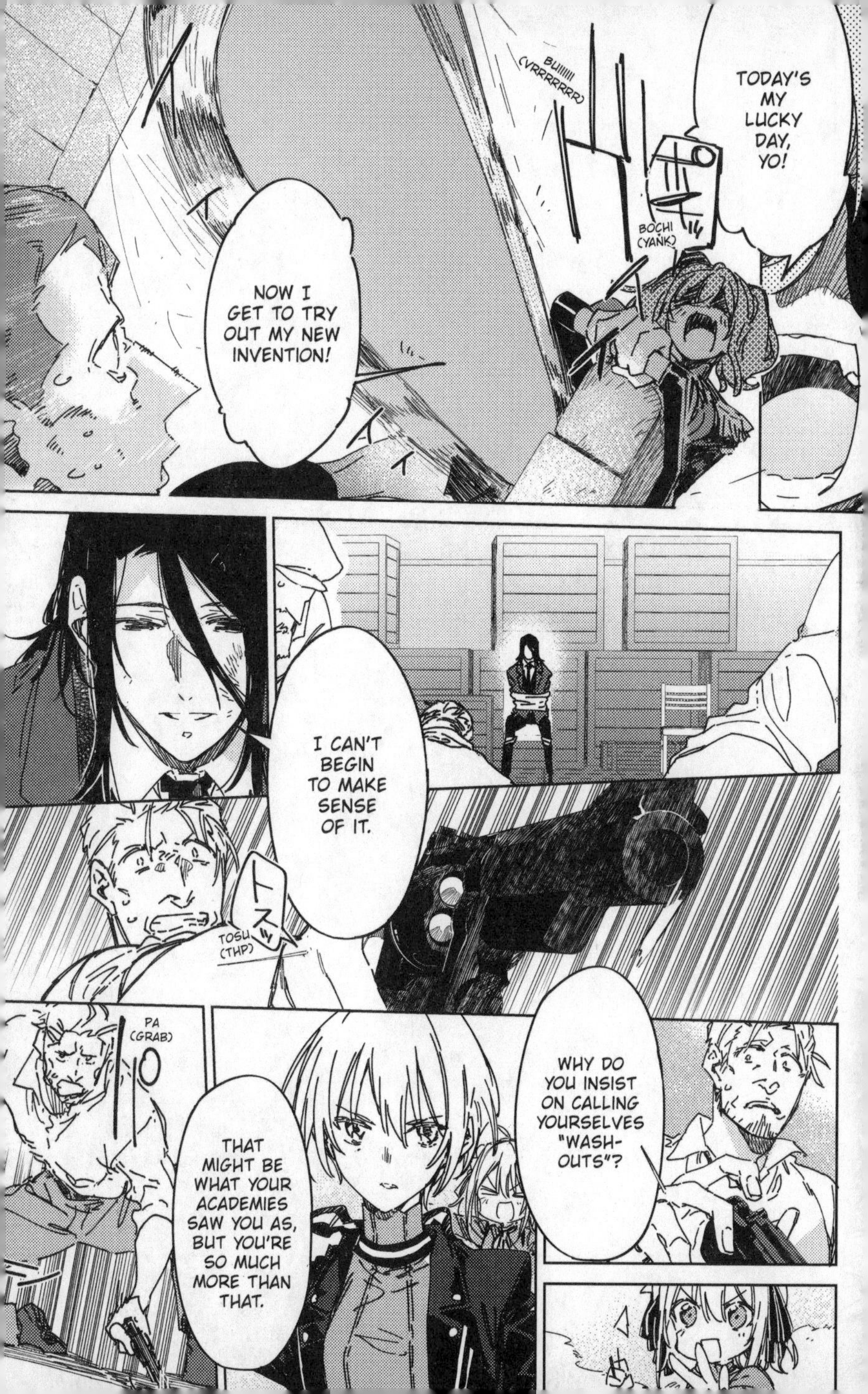
TODAY'S MY LUCKY DAY, YO!
BUIIIII (VRRRRRRR)
BOCHI (YANK)
NOW I GET TO TRY OUT MY NEW INVENTION!
I CAN'T BEGIN TO MAKE SENSE OF IT.
TOSU (THP)
WHY DO YOU INSIST ON CALLING YOURSELVES "WASH-OUTS"?
THAT MIGHT BE WHAT YOUR ACADEMIES SAW YOU AS, BUT YOU'RE SO MUCH MORE THAN THAT.
PA (GRAB)

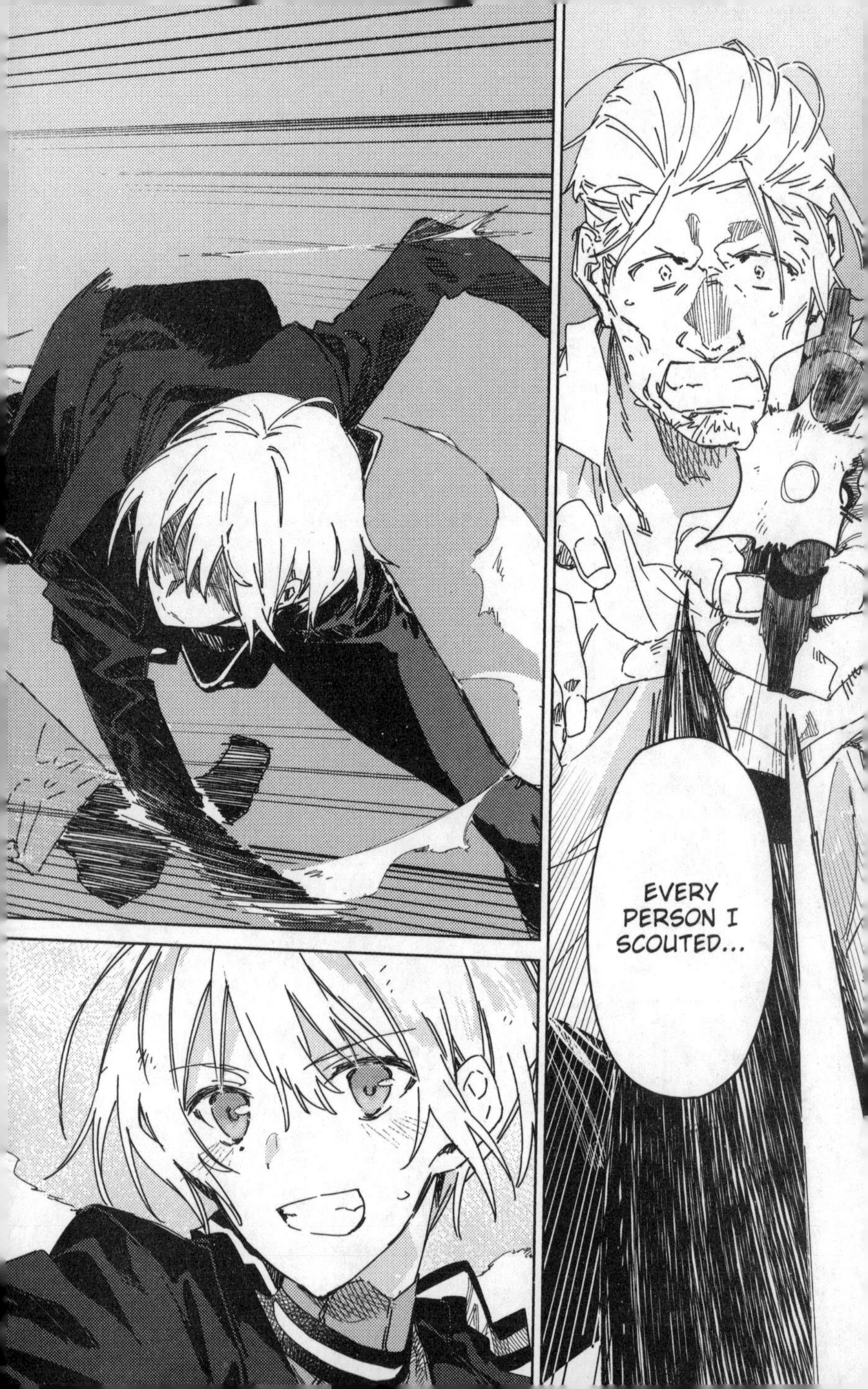
EVERY PERSON I SCOUTED...

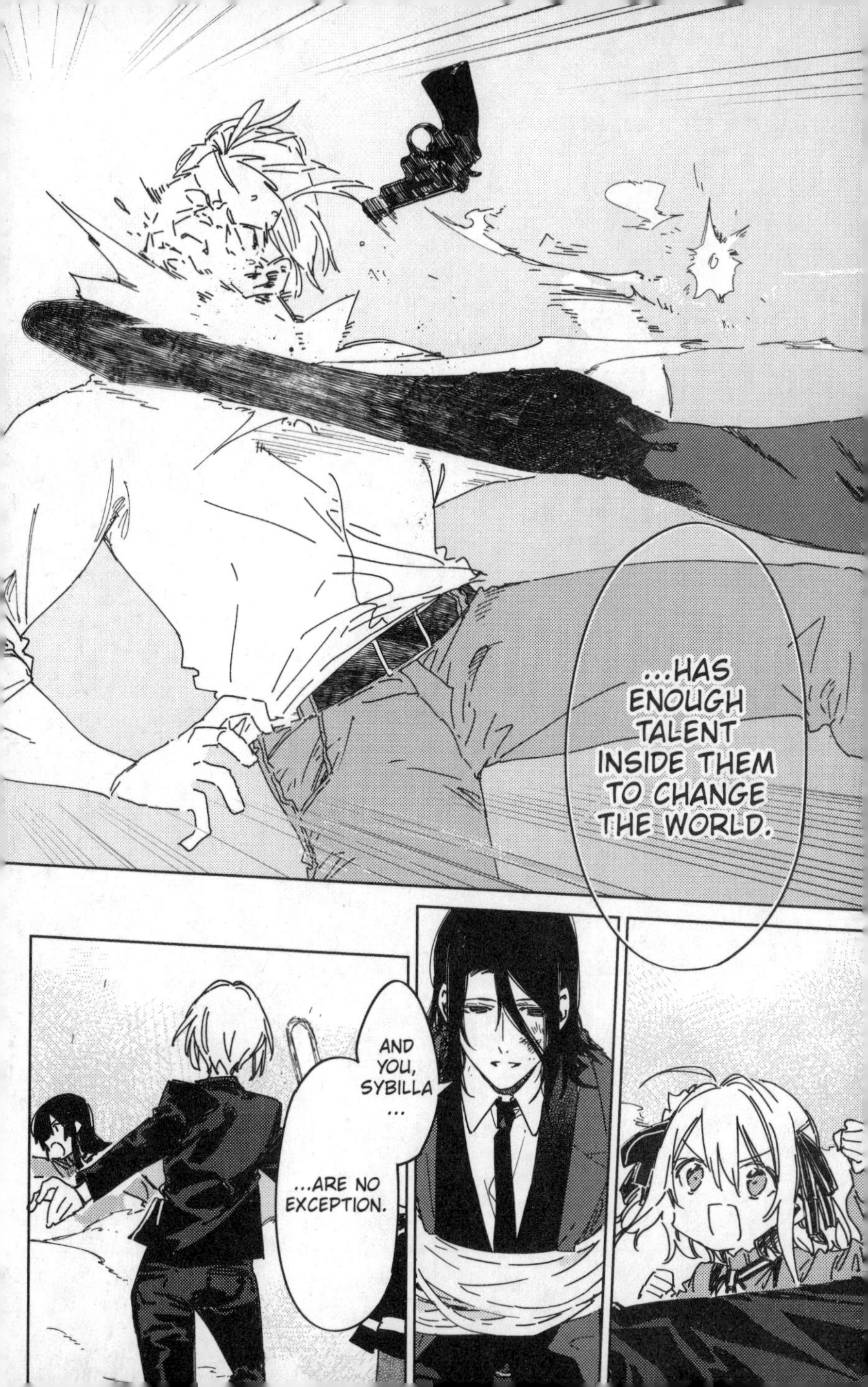
...HAS ENOUGH TALENT INSIDE THEM TO CHANGE THE WORLD.
AND YOU, SYBILLA ...
...ARE NO EXCEPTION.

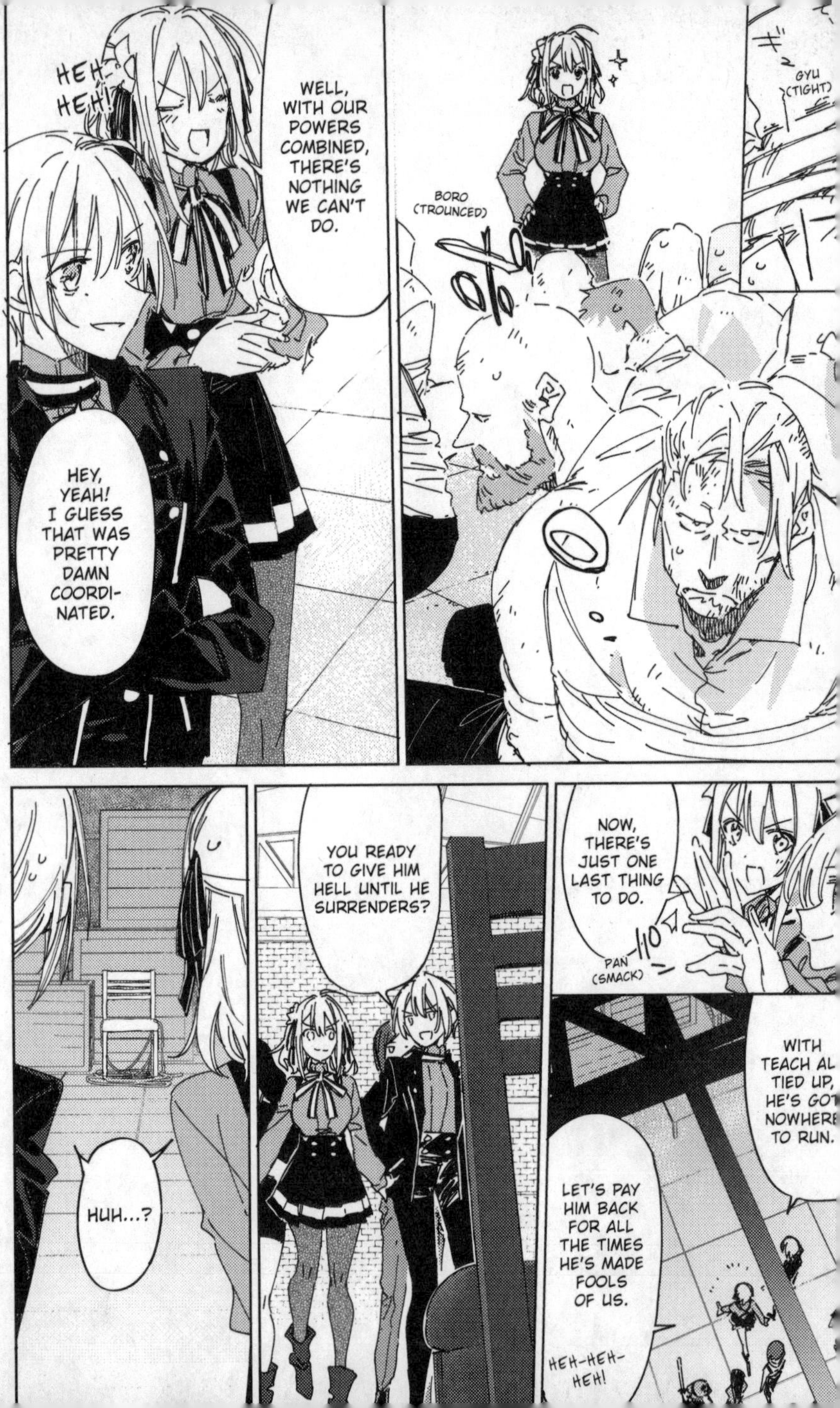
GYU (TIGHT)
BORO (TROUNCED)
HEH-HEH!
WELL, WITH OUR POWERS COMBINED, THERE'S NOTHING WE CAN'T DO.
HEY, YEAH! I GUESS THAT WAS PRETTY DAMN COORDINATED.
NOW, THERE'S JUST ONE LAST THING TO DO.
PAN (SMACK)
WITH TEACH AL TIED UP, HE'S GOT NOWHERE TO RUN.
LET'S PAY HIM BACK FOR ALL THE TIMES HE'S MADE FOOLS OF US.
HEH-HEH-HEH!
YOU READY TO GIVE HIM HELL UNTIL HE SURRENDERS?
HUH...?

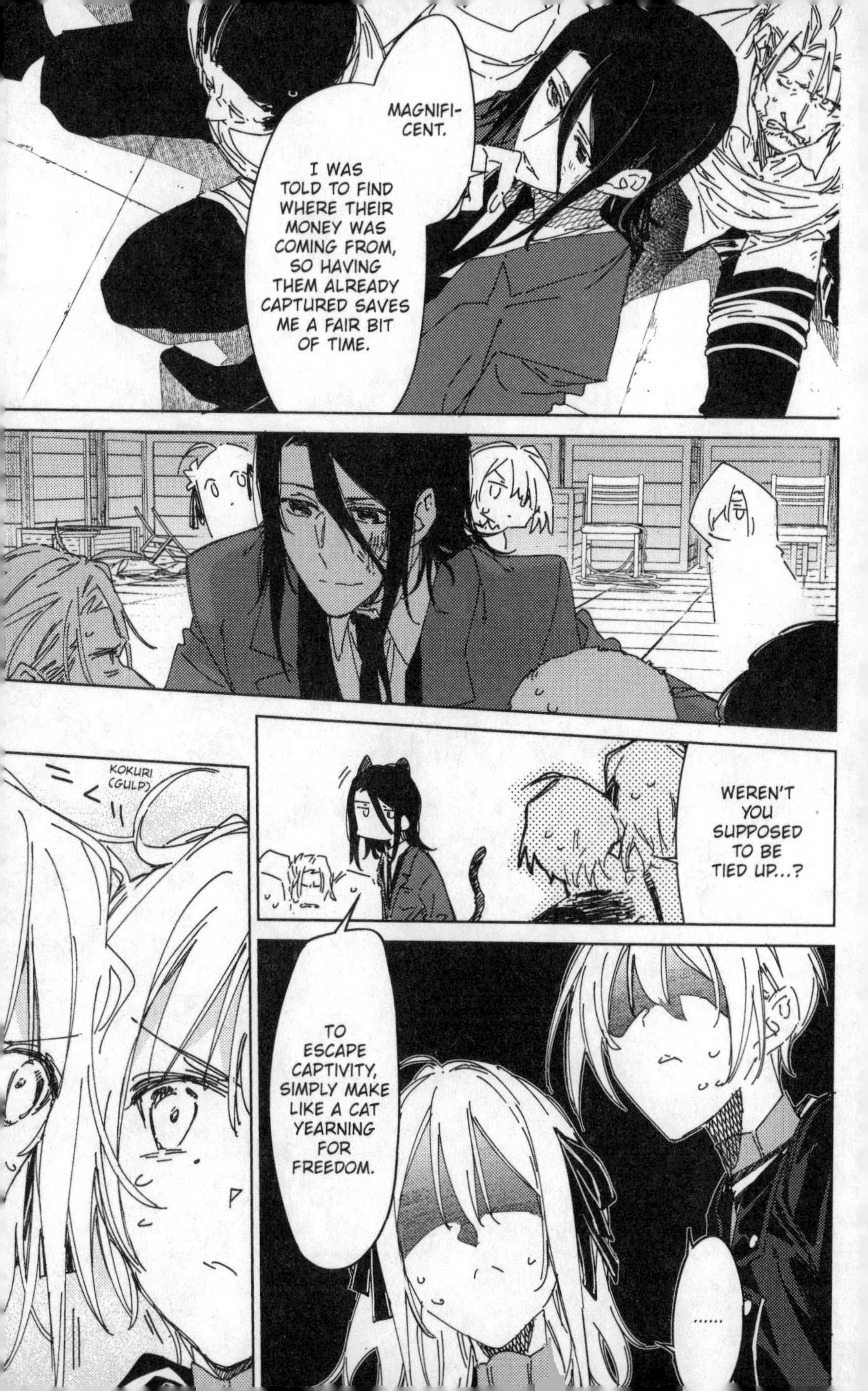
MAGNIFI-CENT.
I WAS TOLD TO FIND WHERE THEIR MONEY WAS COMING FROM, SO HAVING THEM ALREADY CAPTURED SAVES ME A FAIR BIT OF TIME.
WEREN'T YOU SUPPOSED TO BE TIED UP...?
TO ESCAPE CAPTIVITY, SIMPLY MAKE LIKE A CAT YEARNING FOR FREEDOM.
......
KOKURI (GULP)

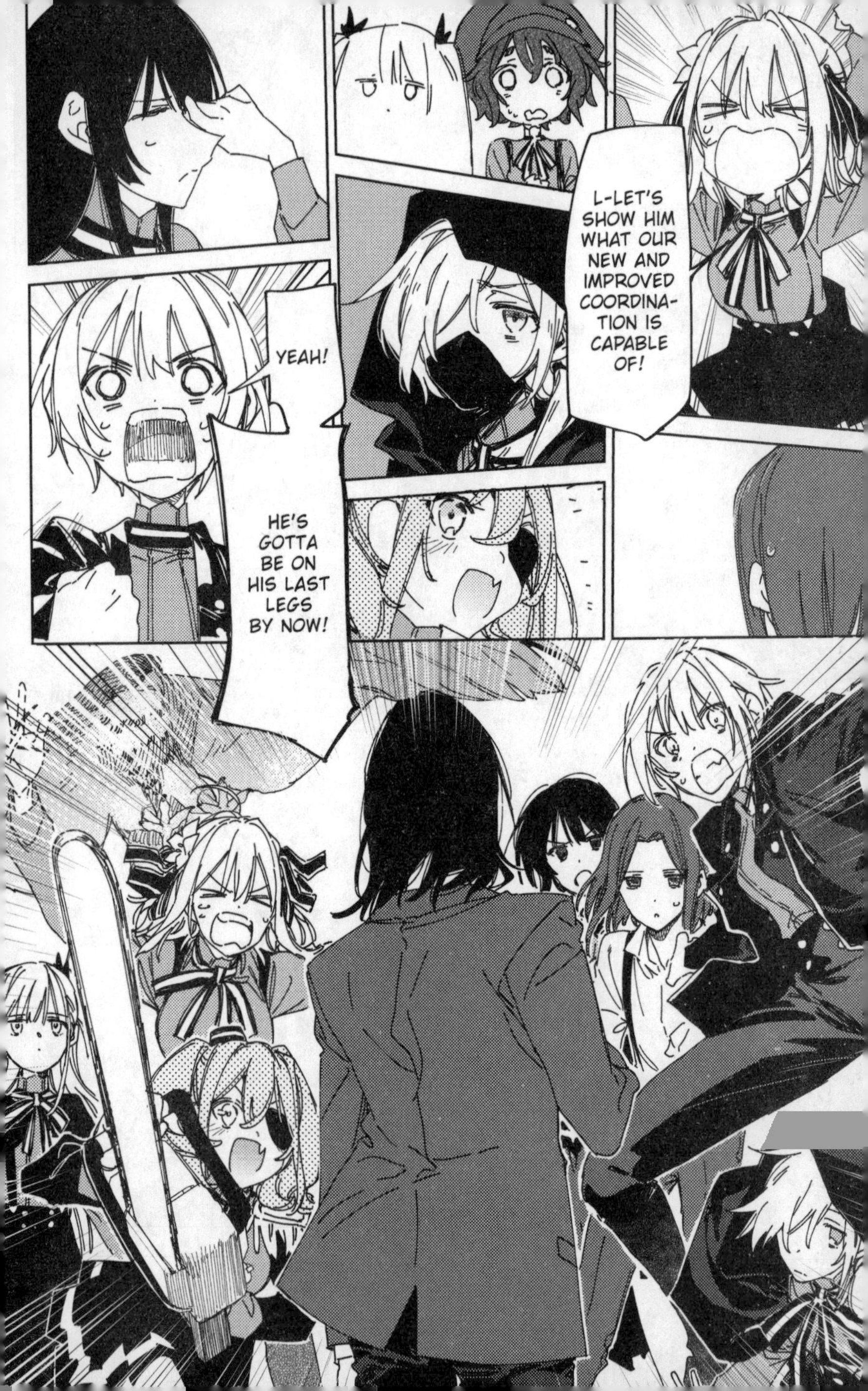
L-LET'S SHOW HIM WHAT OUR NEW AND IMPROVED COORDINA-TION IS CAPABLE OF!
YEAH!
HE'S GOTTA BE ON HIS LAST LEGS BY NOW!

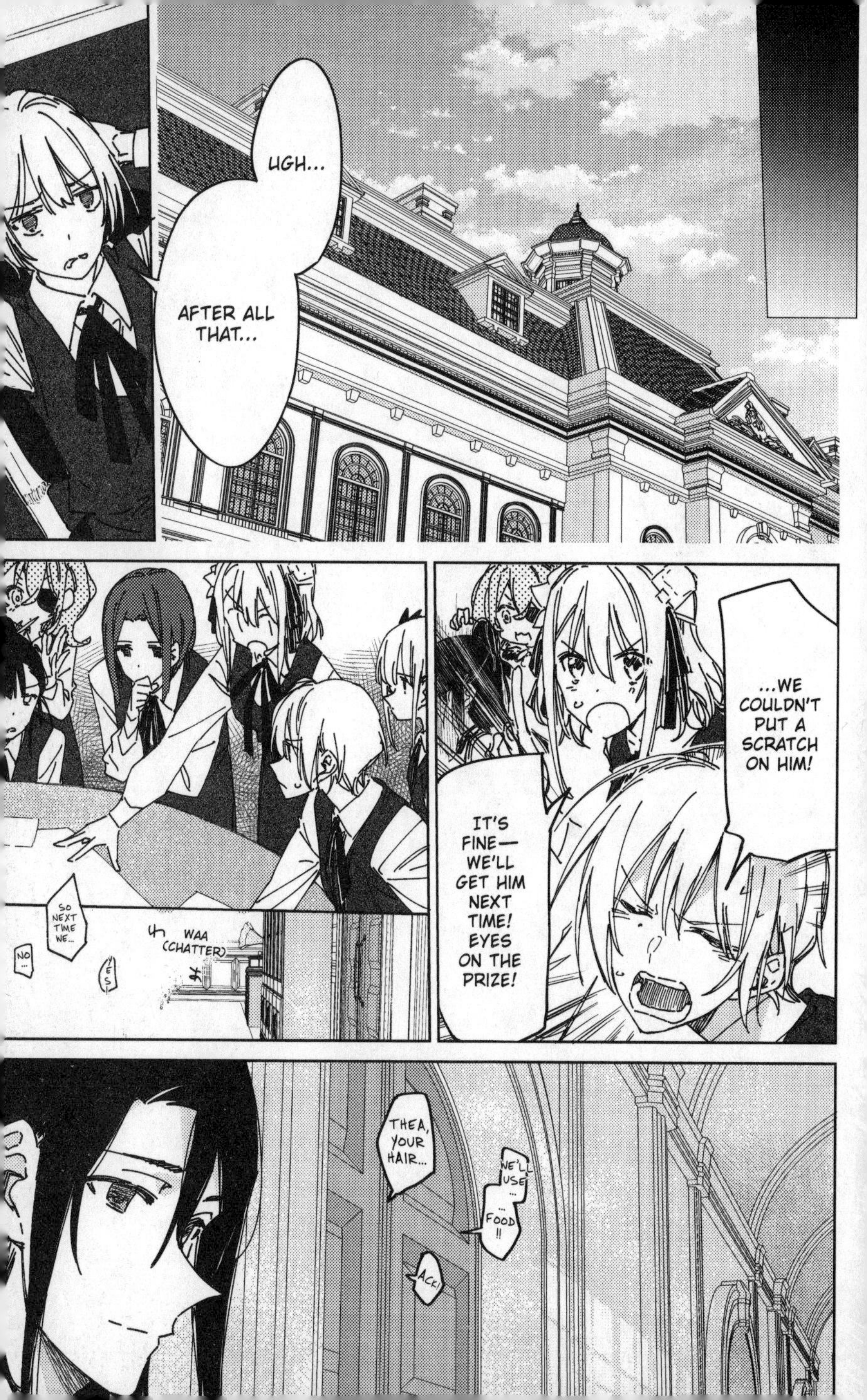
UGH...
AFTER ALL THAT...
...WE COULDN'T PUT A SCRATCH ON HIM!
IT'S FINE—WE'LL GET HIM NEXT TIME! EYES ON THE PRIZE!
SO NEXT TIME WE...
WAA (CHATTER)
YES
NO...
THEA, YOUR HAIR...
WE'LL USE... ...FOOD!!
ACK!

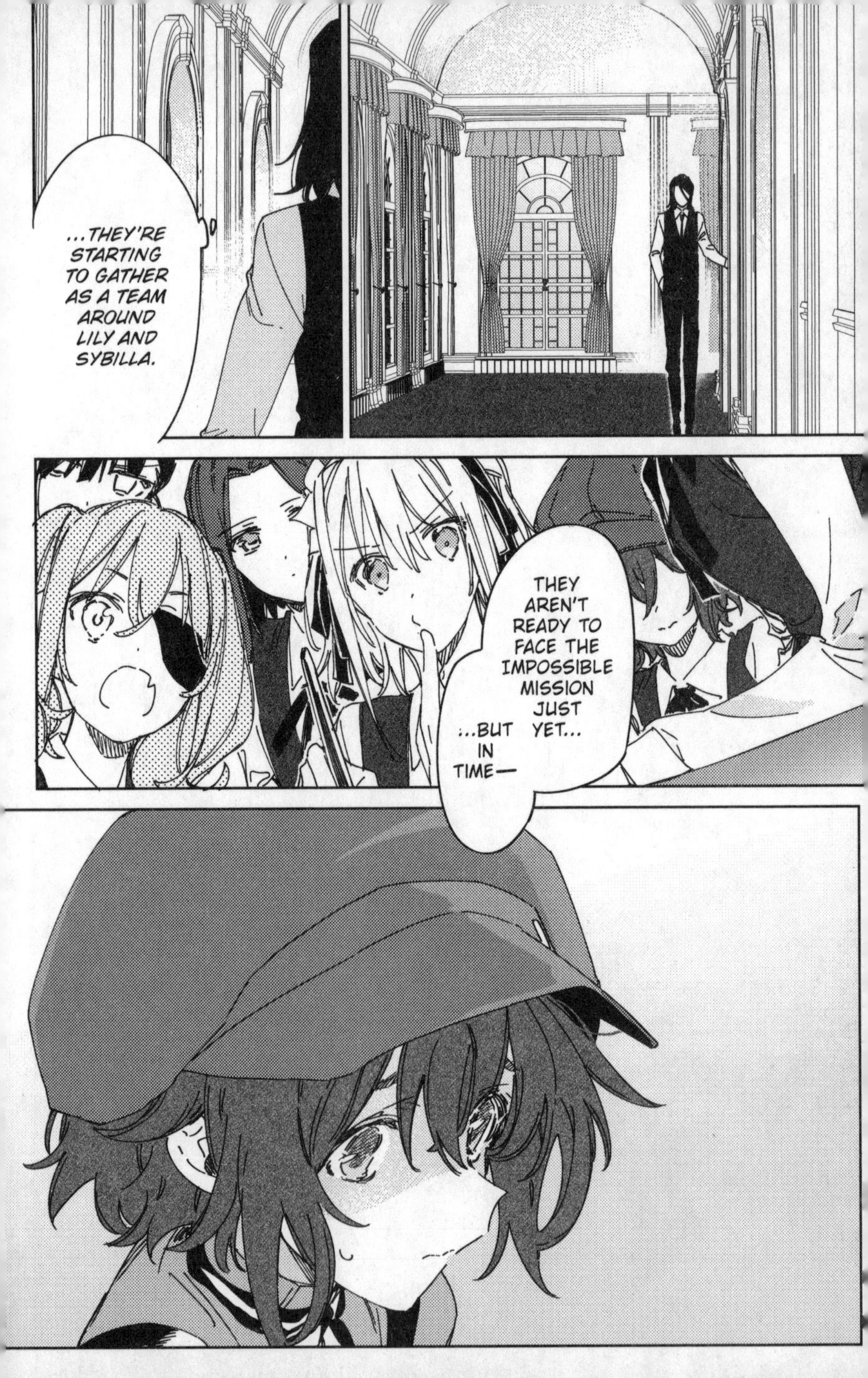
...THEY'RE STARTING TO GATHER AS A TEAM AROUND LILY AND SYBILLA.
THEY AREN'T READY TO FACE THE IMPOSSIBLE MISSION JUST YET...
...BUT IN TIME—

# Chapter 5

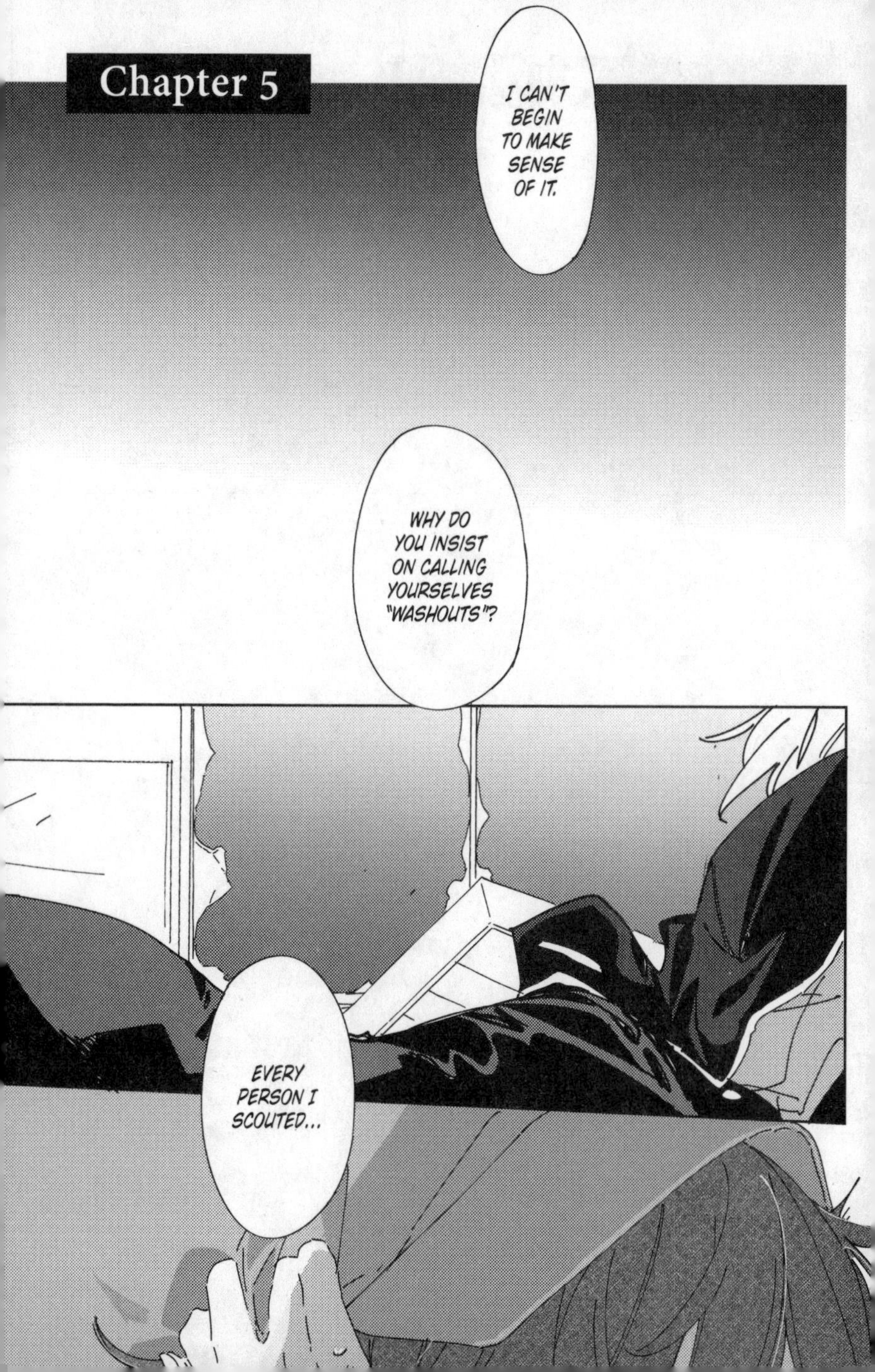
I CAN'T BEGIN TO MAKE SENSE OF IT.
WHY DO YOU INSIST ON CALLING YOURSELVES "WASHOUTS"?
EVERY PERSON I SCOUTED...

# Chapter 5 — Discovery

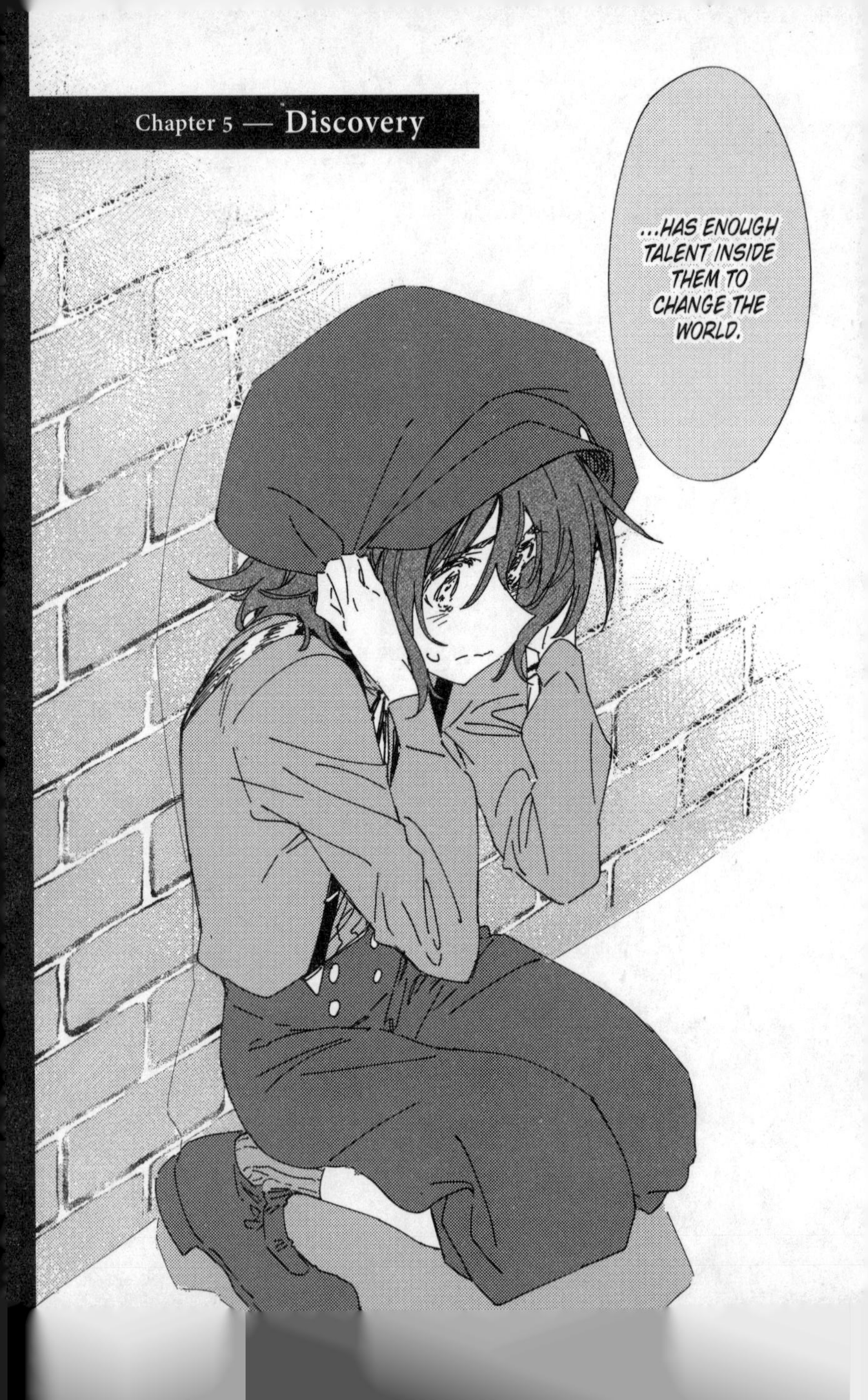
...HAS ENOUGH TALENT INSIDE THEM TO CHANGE THE WORLD.

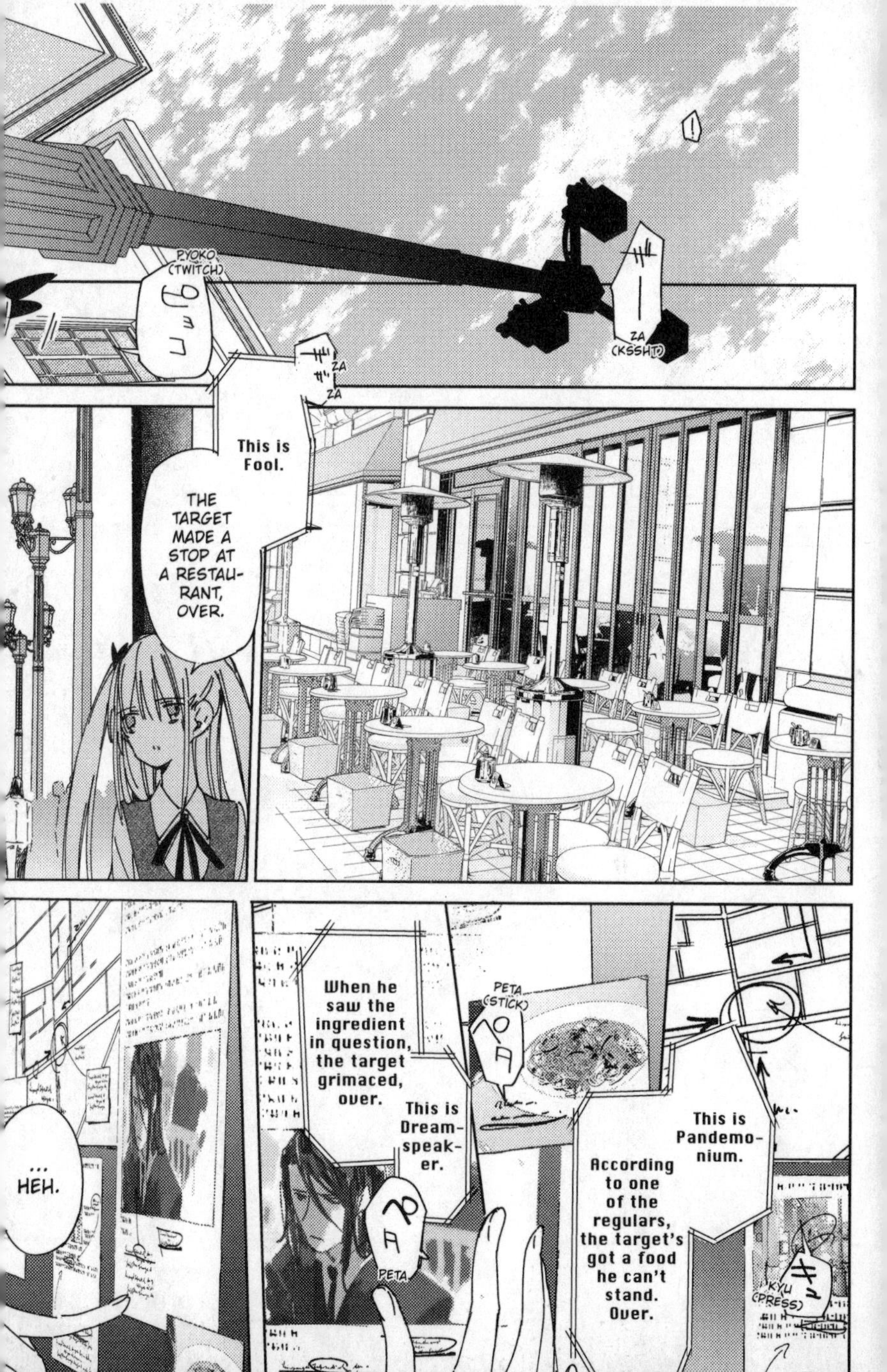
!
ZA (KSSHT)
ZA ZA
PYOKO (TWITCH)
This is Fool.
THE TARGET MADE A STOP AT A RESTAURANT, OVER.
KYU (PRESS)
This is Pandemonium.
According to one of the regulars, the target's got a food he can't stand. Over.
PETA (STICK)
When he saw the ingredient in question, the target grimaced, over.
This is Dream-speaker.
PETA
... HEH.

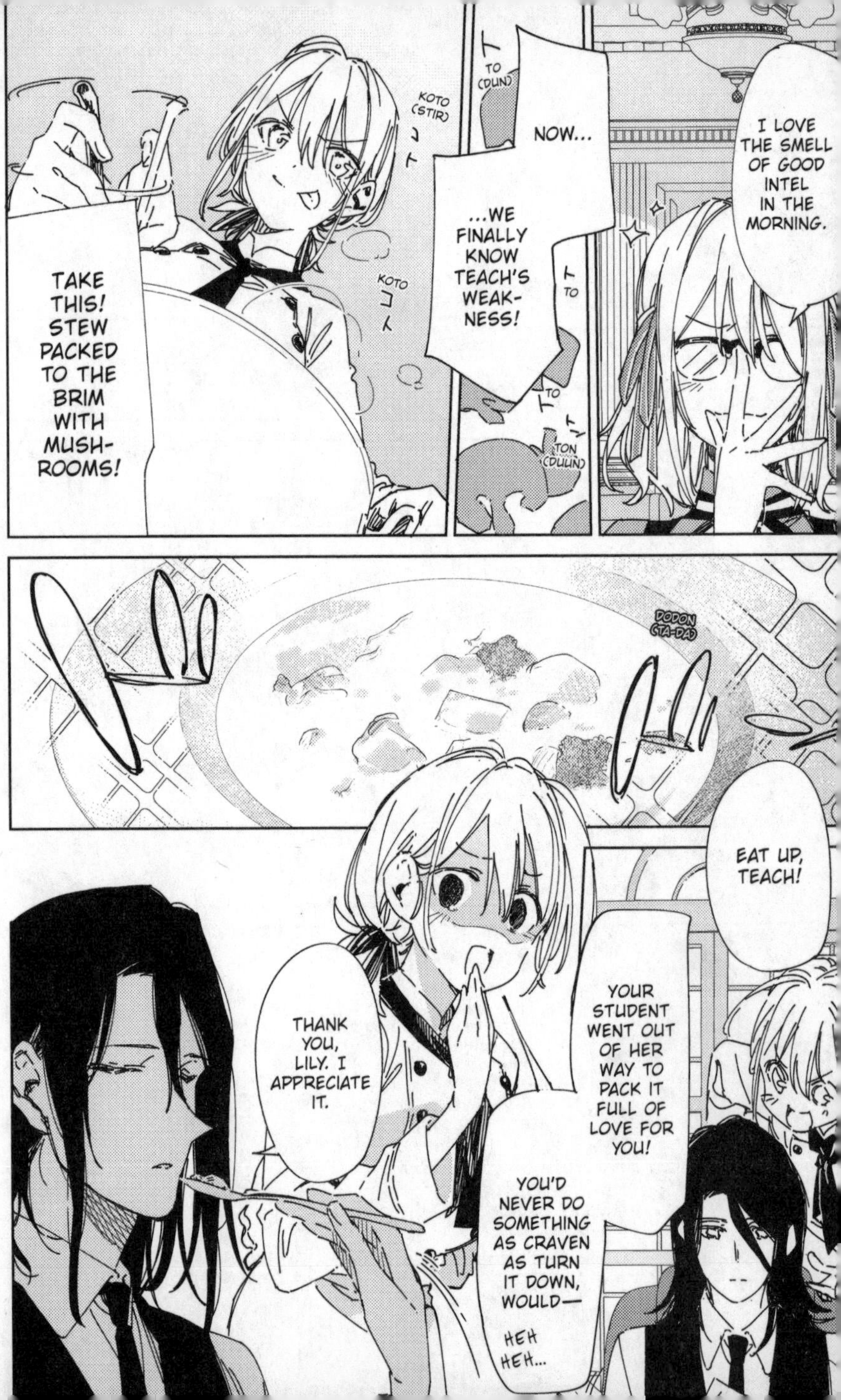
I LOVE THE SMELL OF GOOD INTEL IN THE MORNING.
TO (DUN)
NOW...
...WE FINALLY KNOW TEACH'S WEAKNESS!
TO
TO
TON (DUUN)
KOTO (STIR)
KOTO
TAKE THIS! STEW PACKED TO THE BRIM WITH MUSH-ROOMS!
DODON (TA-DA)
EAT UP, TEACH!
YOUR STUDENT WENT OUT OF HER WAY TO PACK IT FULL OF LOVE FOR YOU!
YOU'D NEVER DO SOMETHING AS CRAVEN AS TURN IT DOWN, WOULD—
HEH HEH...
THANK YOU, LILY. I APPRECIATE IT.

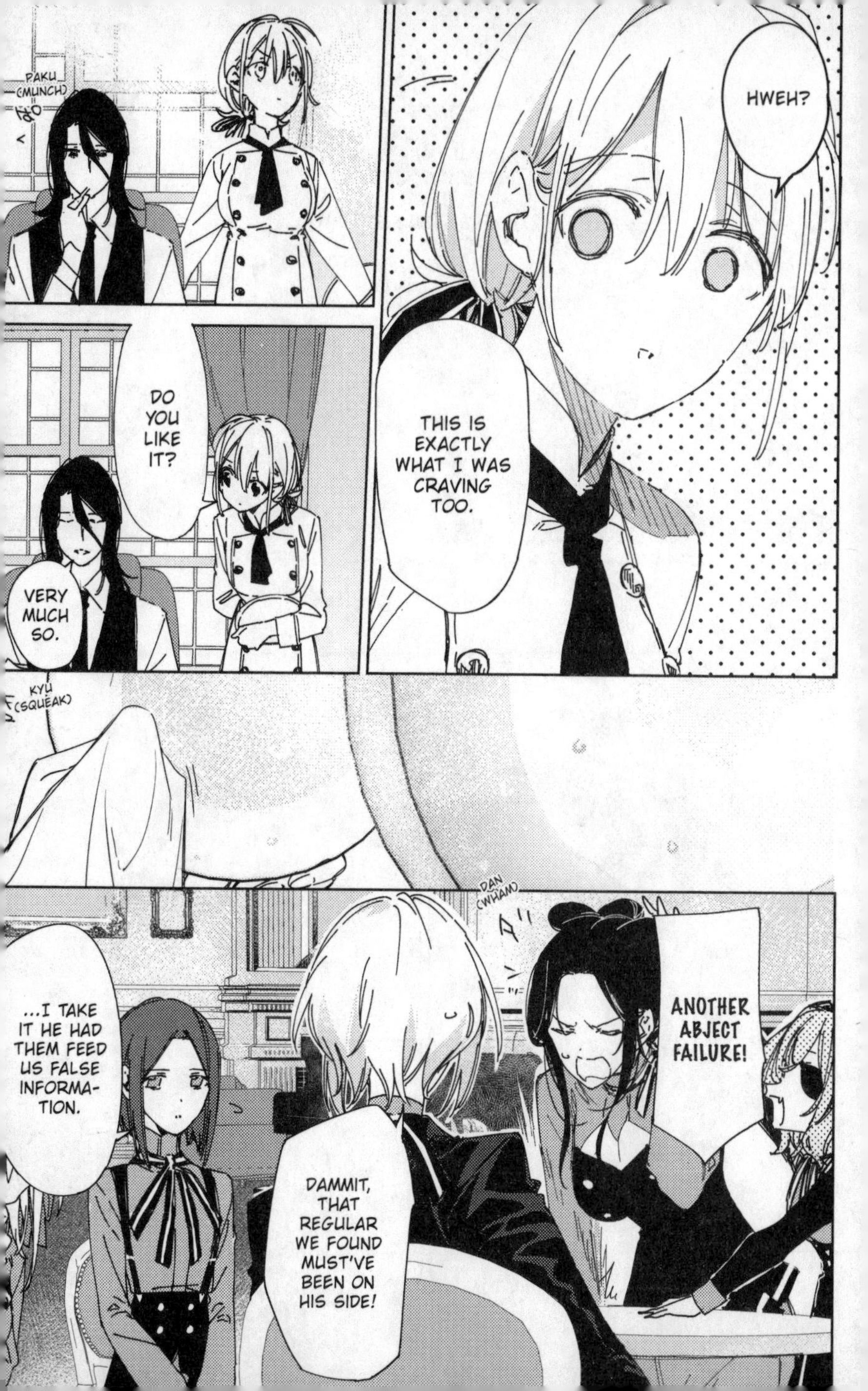
HWEH?
THIS IS EXACTLY WHAT I WAS CRAVING TOO.
PAKU (MUNCH)
DO YOU LIKE IT?
VERY MUCH SO.
KYU (SQUEAK)
DAN (WHAM)
ANOTHER ABJECT FAILURE!
DAMMIT, THAT REGULAR WE FOUND MUST'VE BEEN ON HIS SIDE!
...I TAKE IT HE HAD THEM FEED US FALSE INFORMATION.

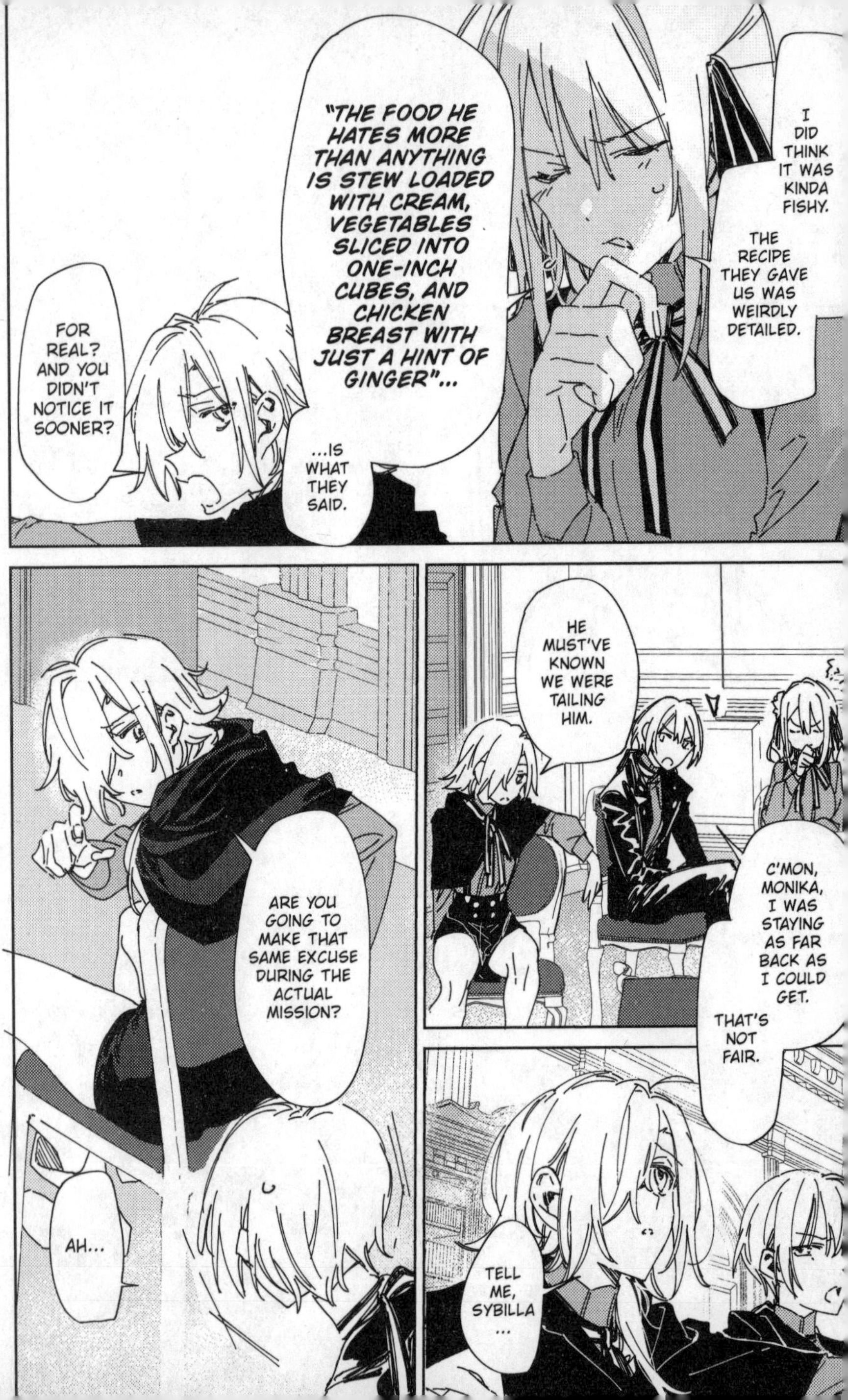
I DID THINK IT WAS KINDA FISHY.
THE RECIPE THEY GAVE US WAS WEIRDLY DETAILED.
"THE FOOD HE HATES MORE THAN ANYTHING IS STEW LOADED WITH CREAM, VEGETABLES SLICED INTO ONE-INCH CUBES, AND CHICKEN BREAST WITH JUST A HINT OF GINGER"...
...IS WHAT THEY SAID.
FOR REAL? AND YOU DIDN'T NOTICE IT SOONER?
HE MUST'VE KNOWN WE WERE TAILING HIM.
C'MON, MONIKA, I WAS STAYING AS FAR BACK AS I COULD GET.
THAT'S NOT FAIR.
TELL ME, SYBILLA ...
ARE YOU GOING TO MAKE THAT SAME EXCUSE DURING THE ACTUAL MISSION?
AH...

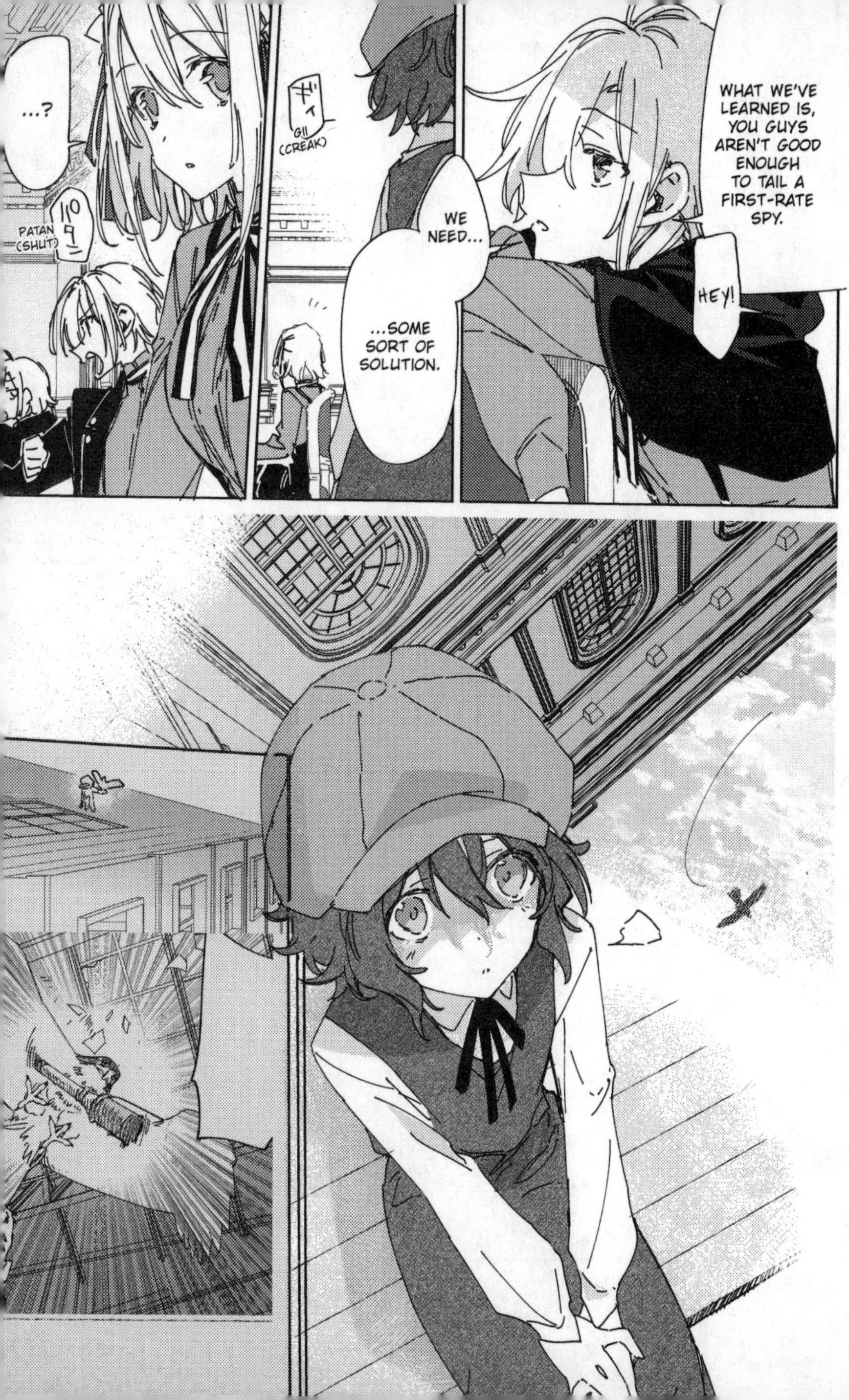
WHAT WE'VE LEARNED IS, YOU GUYS AREN'T GOOD ENOUGH TO TAIL A FIRST-RATE SPY.
HEY!
WE NEED...
...SOME SORT OF SOLUTION.
ギィ
GII (CREAK)
...?
パタン
PATAN (SHUT)

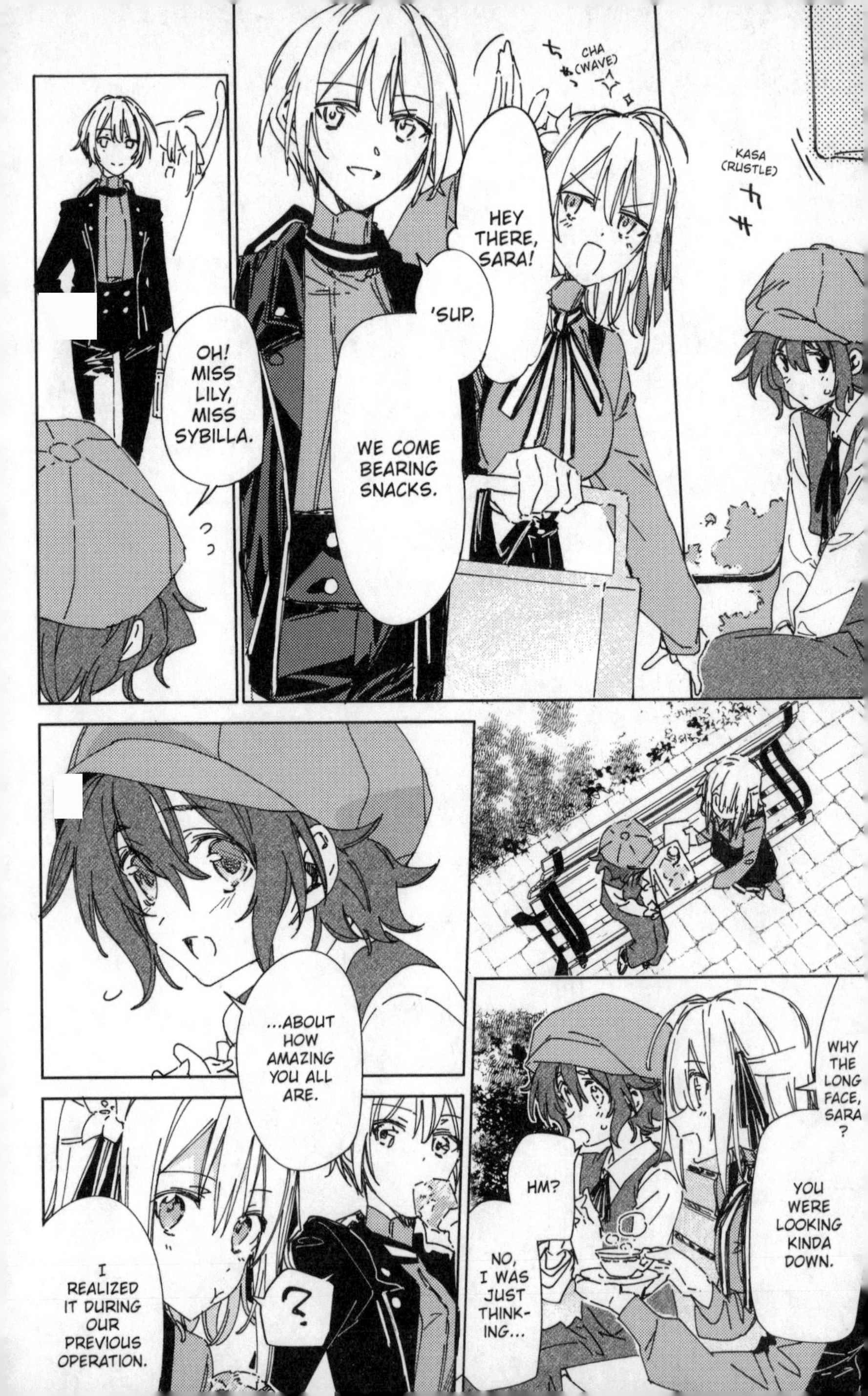
KASA (RUSTLE)
CHA (WAVE)
HEY THERE, SARA!
'SUP.
WE COME BEARING SNACKS.
OH! MISS LILY, MISS SYBILLA.
WHY THE LONG FACE, SARA?
YOU WERE LOOKING KINDA DOWN.
HM?
NO, I WAS JUST THINKING...
...ABOUT HOW AMAZING YOU ALL ARE.
I REALIZED IT DURING OUR PREVIOUS OPERATION.

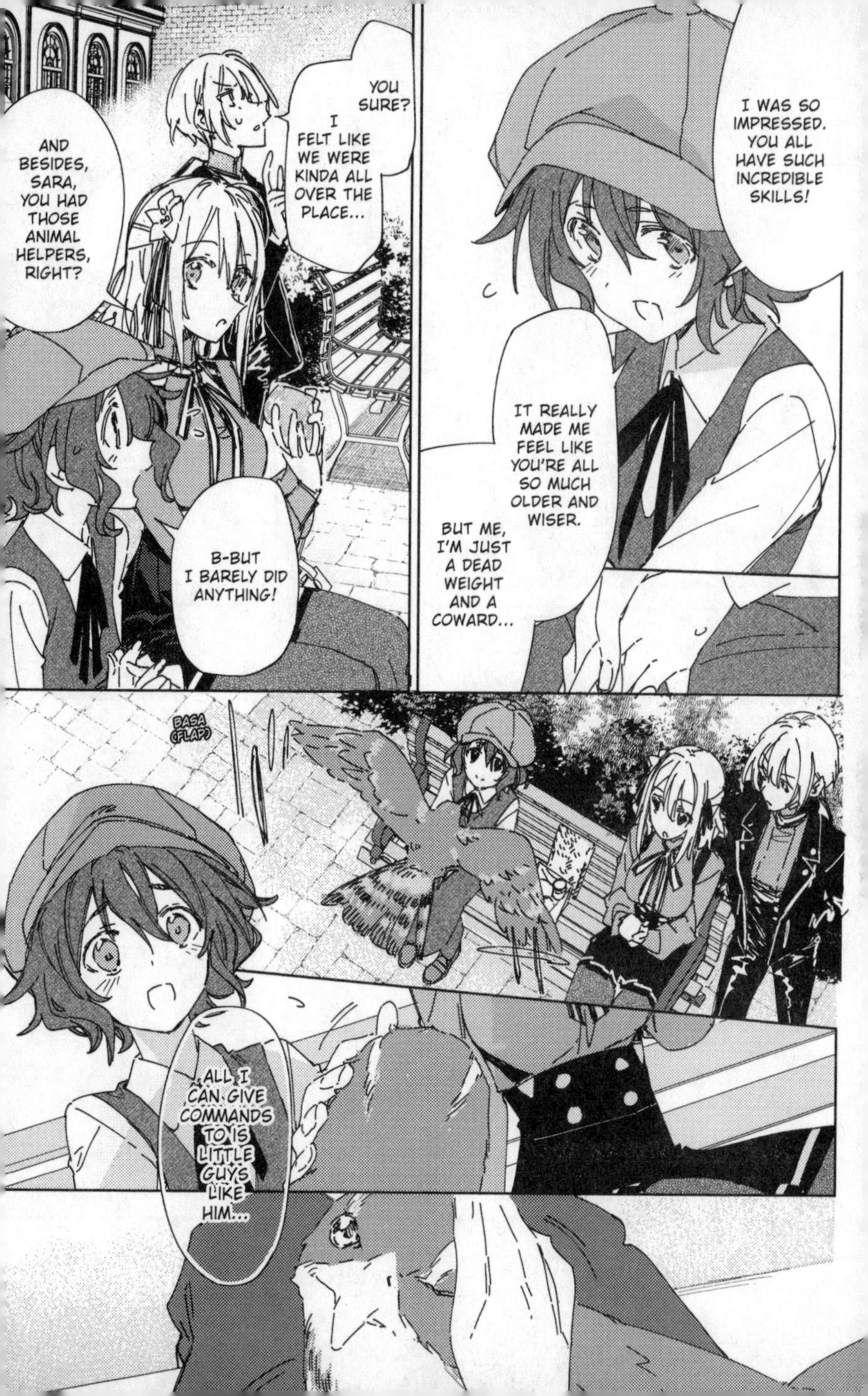
I WAS SO IMPRESSED. YOU ALL HAVE SUCH INCREDIBLE SKILLS!
IT REALLY MADE ME FEEL LIKE YOU'RE ALL SO MUCH OLDER AND WISER.
BUT ME, I'M JUST A DEAD WEIGHT AND A COWARD...
YOU SURE?
I FELT LIKE WE WERE KINDA ALL OVER THE PLACE...
AND BESIDES, SARA, YOU HAD THOSE ANIMAL HELPERS, RIGHT?
B-BUT I BARELY DID ANYTHING!
BASA (FLAP)
ALL I CAN GIVE COMMANDS TO IS LITTLE GUYS LIKE HIM...

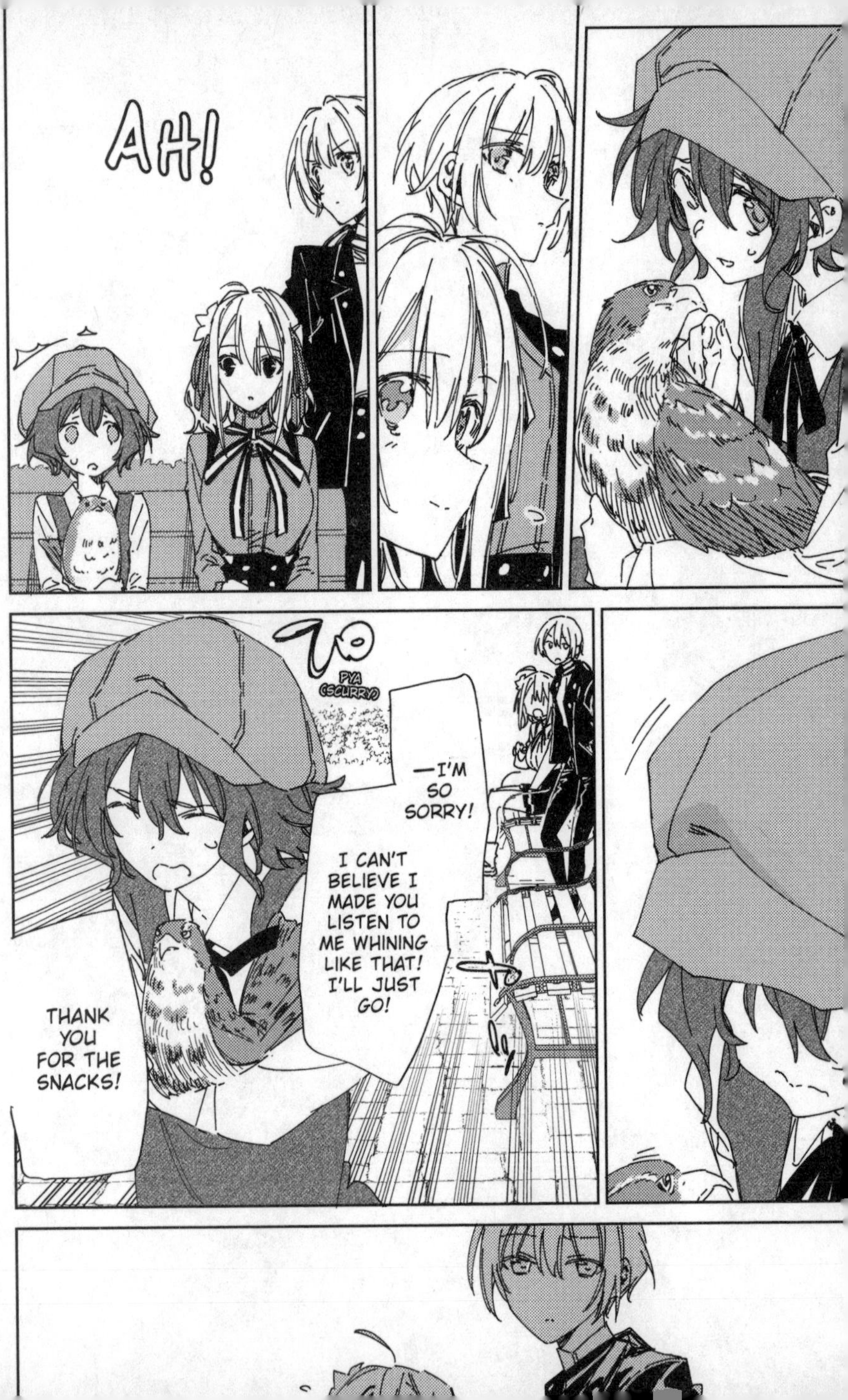
AH!
PYA (SCURRY)
—I'M SO SORRY!
I CAN'T BELIEVE I MADE YOU LISTEN TO ME WHINING LIKE THAT! I'LL JUST GO!
THANK YOU FOR THE SNACKS!

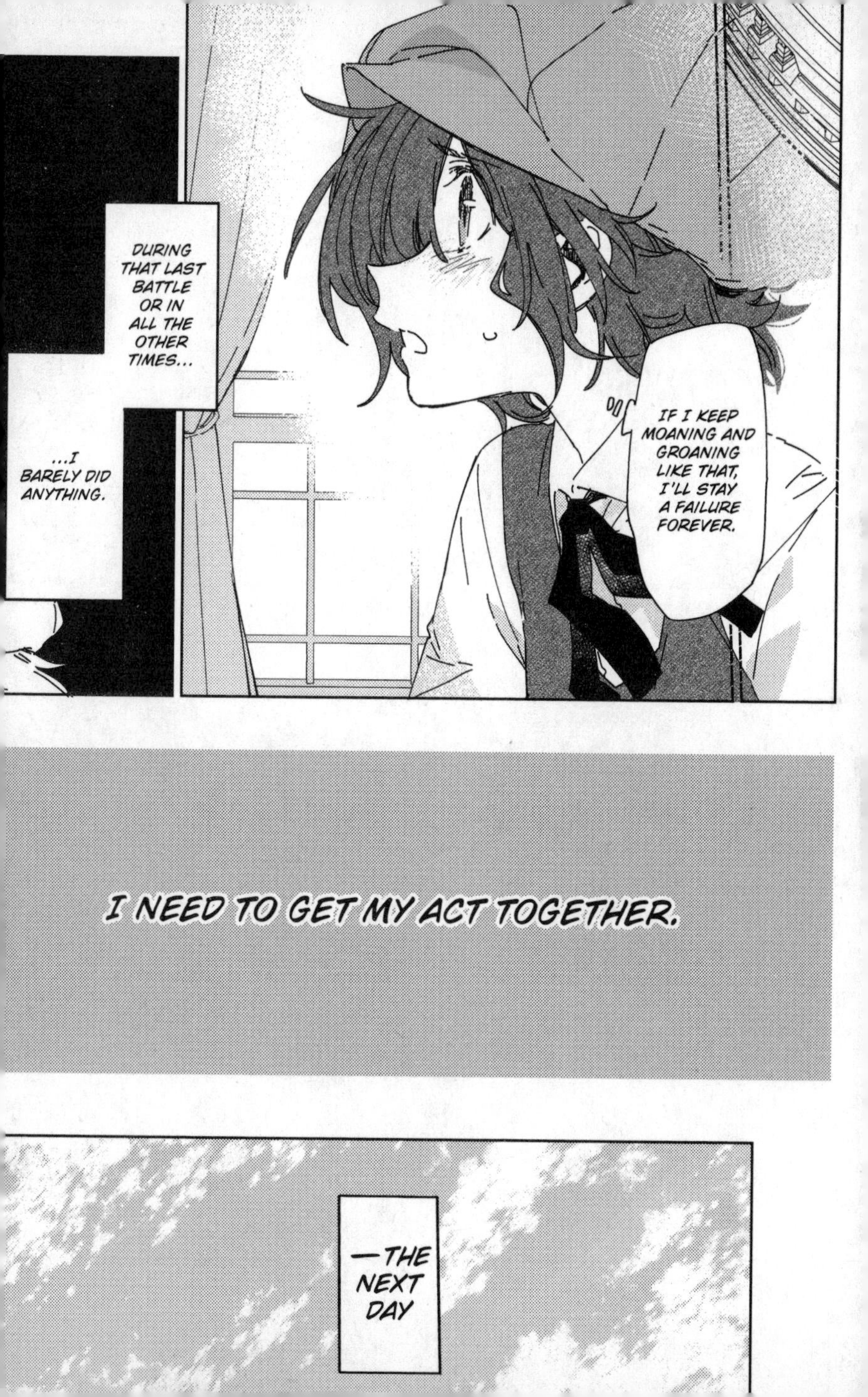
DURING THAT LAST BATTLE OR IN ALL THE OTHER TIMES...
...I BARELY DID ANYTHING.
IF I KEEP MOANING AND GROANING LIKE THAT, I'LL STAY A FAILURE FOREVER.
I NEED TO GET MY ACT TOGETHER.
—THE NEXT DAY

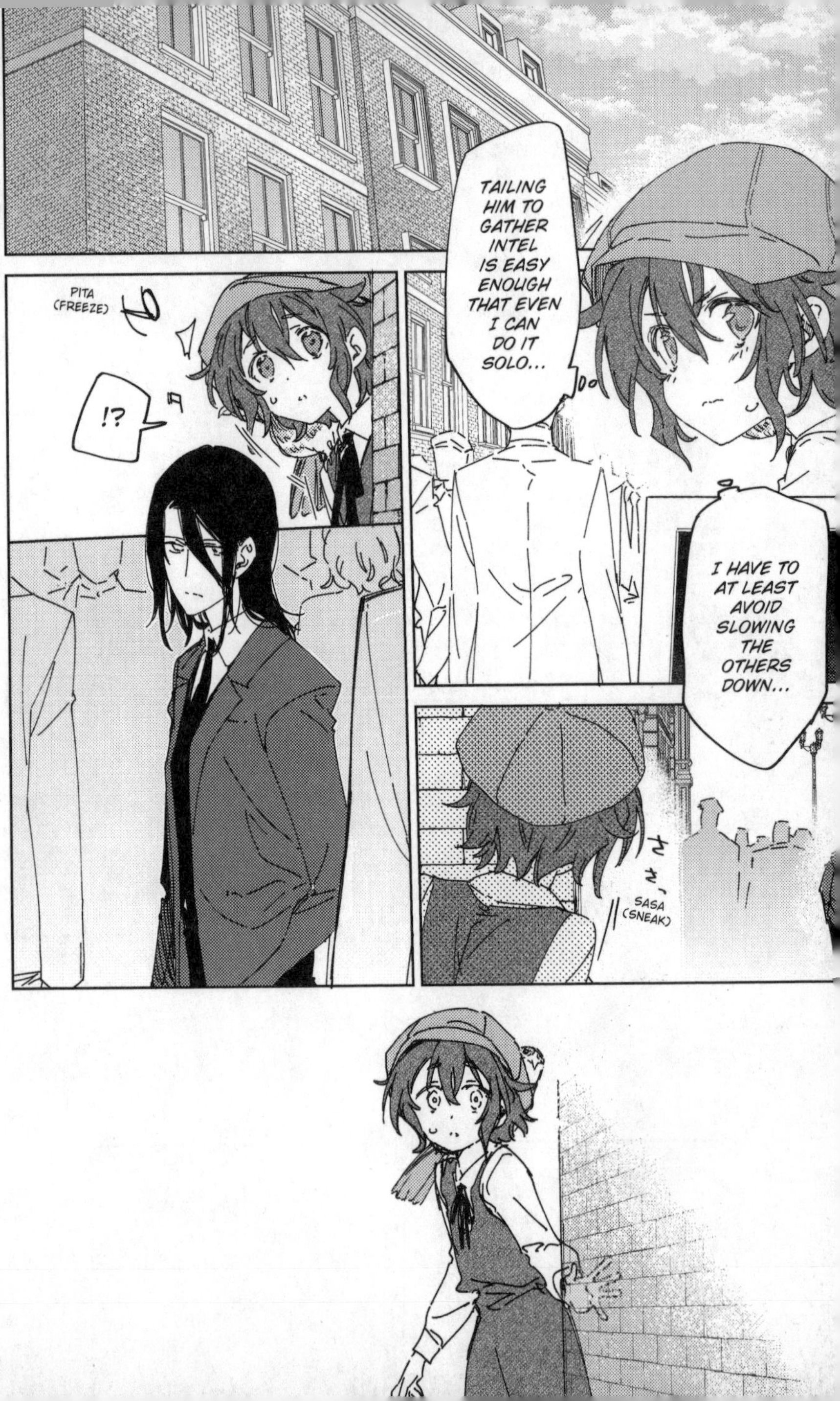
TAILING HIM TO GATHER INTEL IS EASY ENOUGH THAT EVEN I CAN DO IT SOLO...
I HAVE TO AT LEAST AVOID SLOWING THE OTHERS DOWN...
SASA (SNEAK)
PITA (FREEZE)
!?

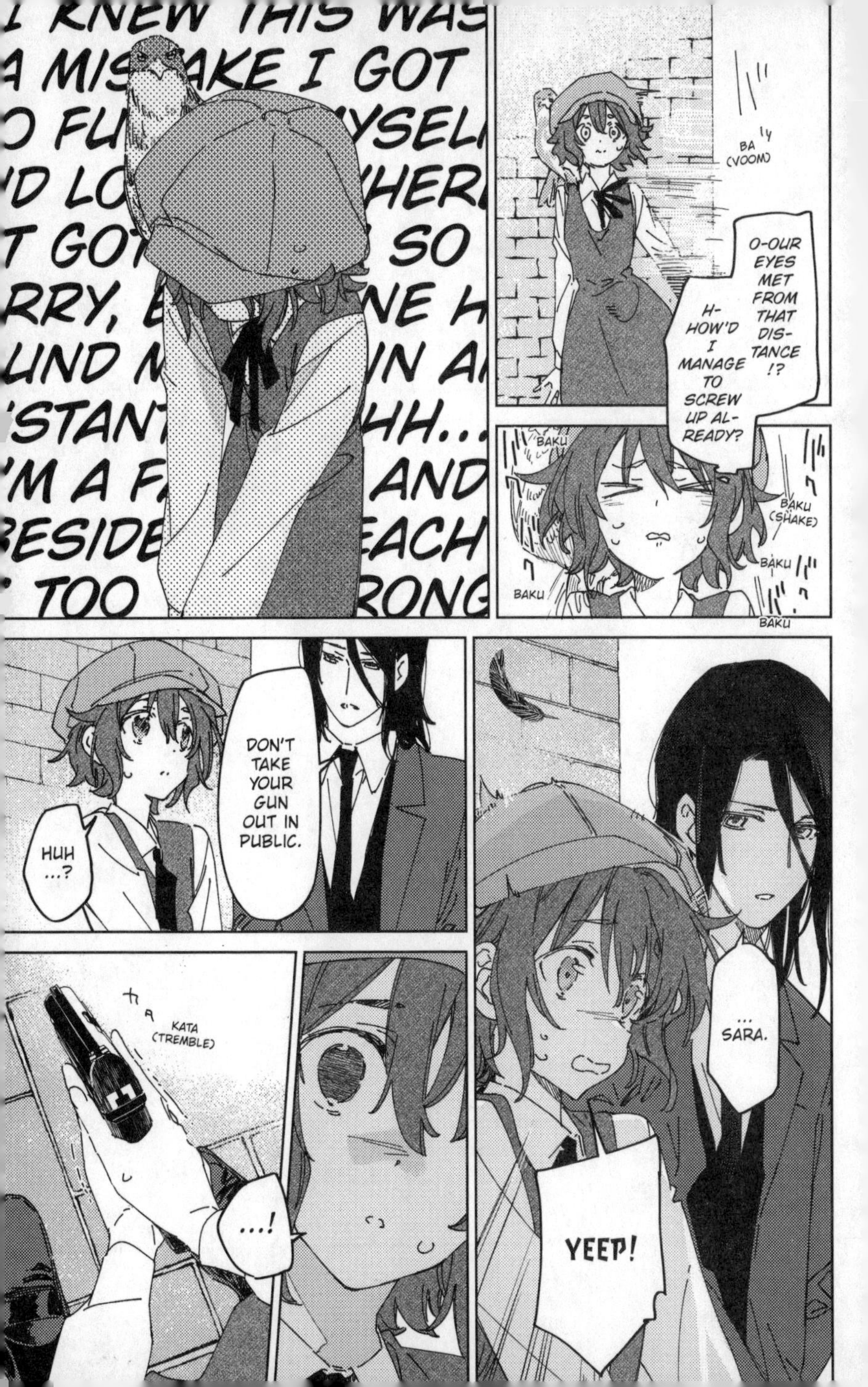
BA
(VOOM)
O-OUR EYES MET FROM THAT DIS-TANCE !?
BAKU
BAKU
(SHAKE)
BAKU
BAKU
BAKU
H-HOW'D I MANAGE TO SCREW UP AL-READY?
...SARA.
YEEP!
DON'T TAKE YOUR GUN OUT IN PUBLIC.
HUH ...?
...!
KATA
(TREMBLE)

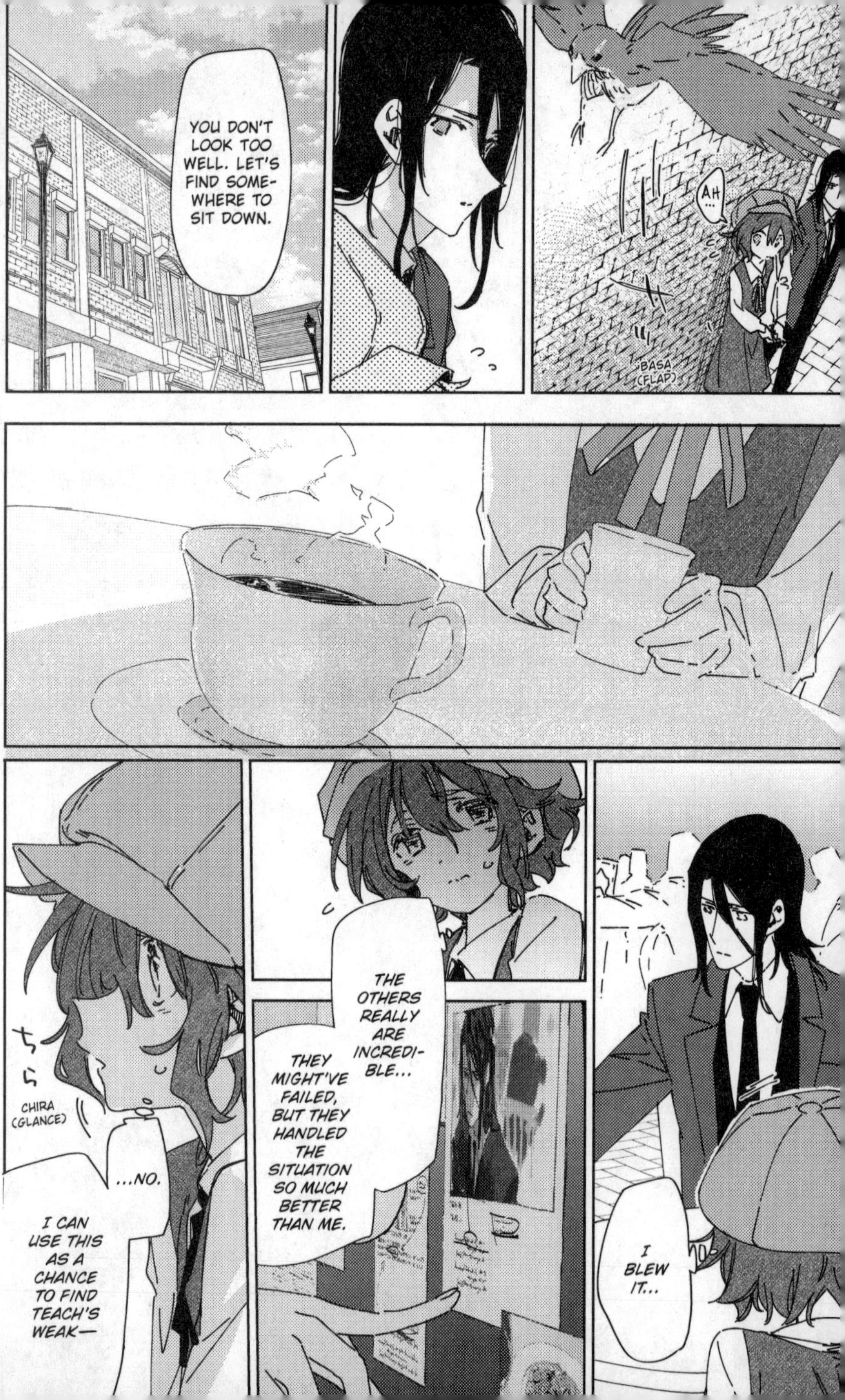
AH...
BASA (FLAP)
YOU DON'T LOOK TOO WELL. LET'S FIND SOME-WHERE TO SIT DOWN.
I BLEW IT...
THE OTHERS REALLY ARE INCREDI-BLE...
THEY MIGHT'VE FAILED, BUT THEY HANDLED THE SITUATION SO MUCH BETTER THAN ME.
CHIRA (GLANCE)
...NO.
I CAN USE THIS AS A CHANCE TO FIND TEACH'S WEAK—

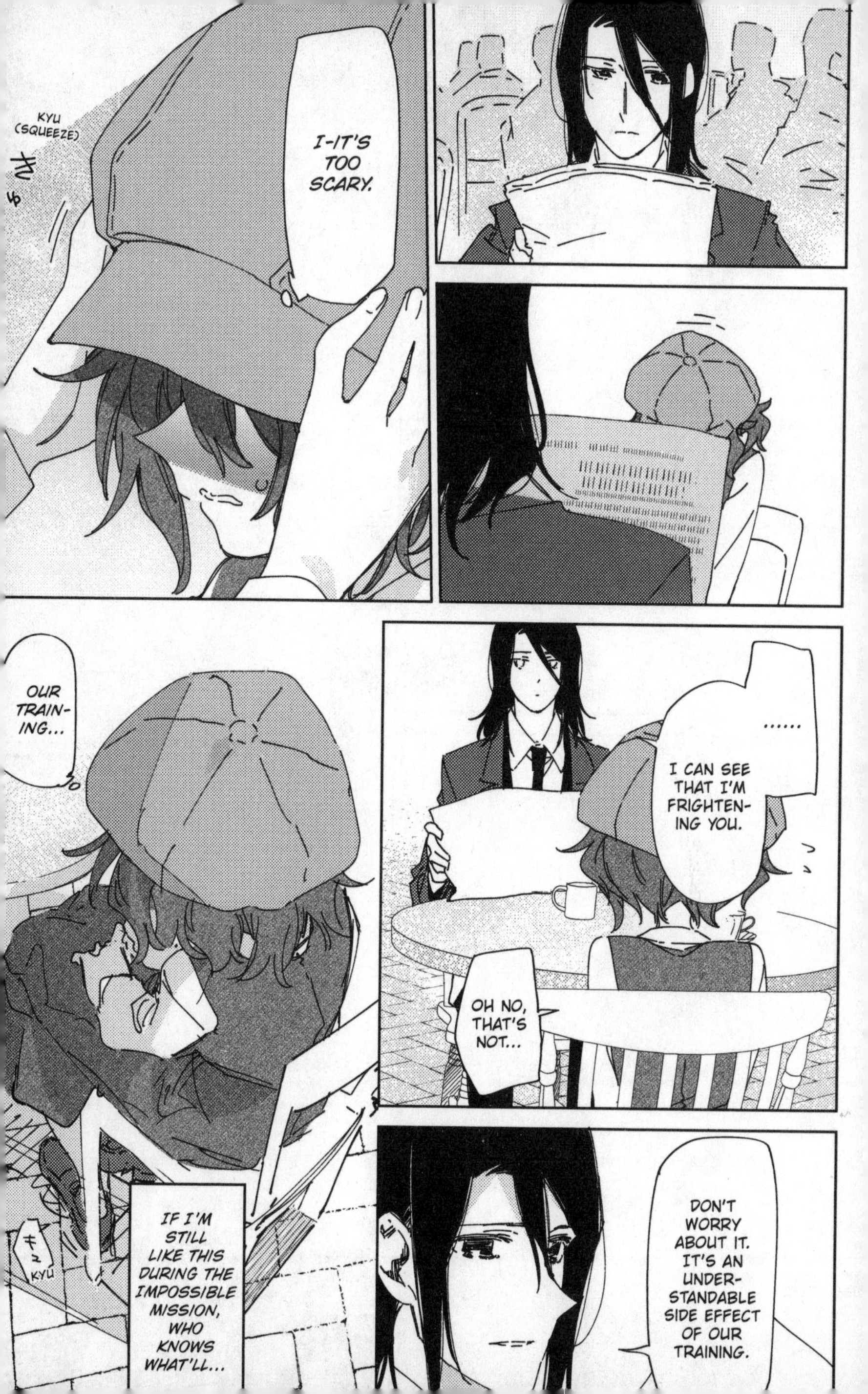
KYU (SQUEEZE)
I-IT'S TOO SCARY.
......
I CAN SEE THAT I'M FRIGHTENING YOU.
OH NO, THAT'S NOT...
DON'T WORRY ABOUT IT. IT'S AN UNDERSTANDABLE SIDE EFFECT OF OUR TRAINING.
OUR TRAINING...
IF I'M STILL LIKE THIS DURING THE IMPOSSIBLE MISSION, WHO KNOWS WHAT'LL...
KYU

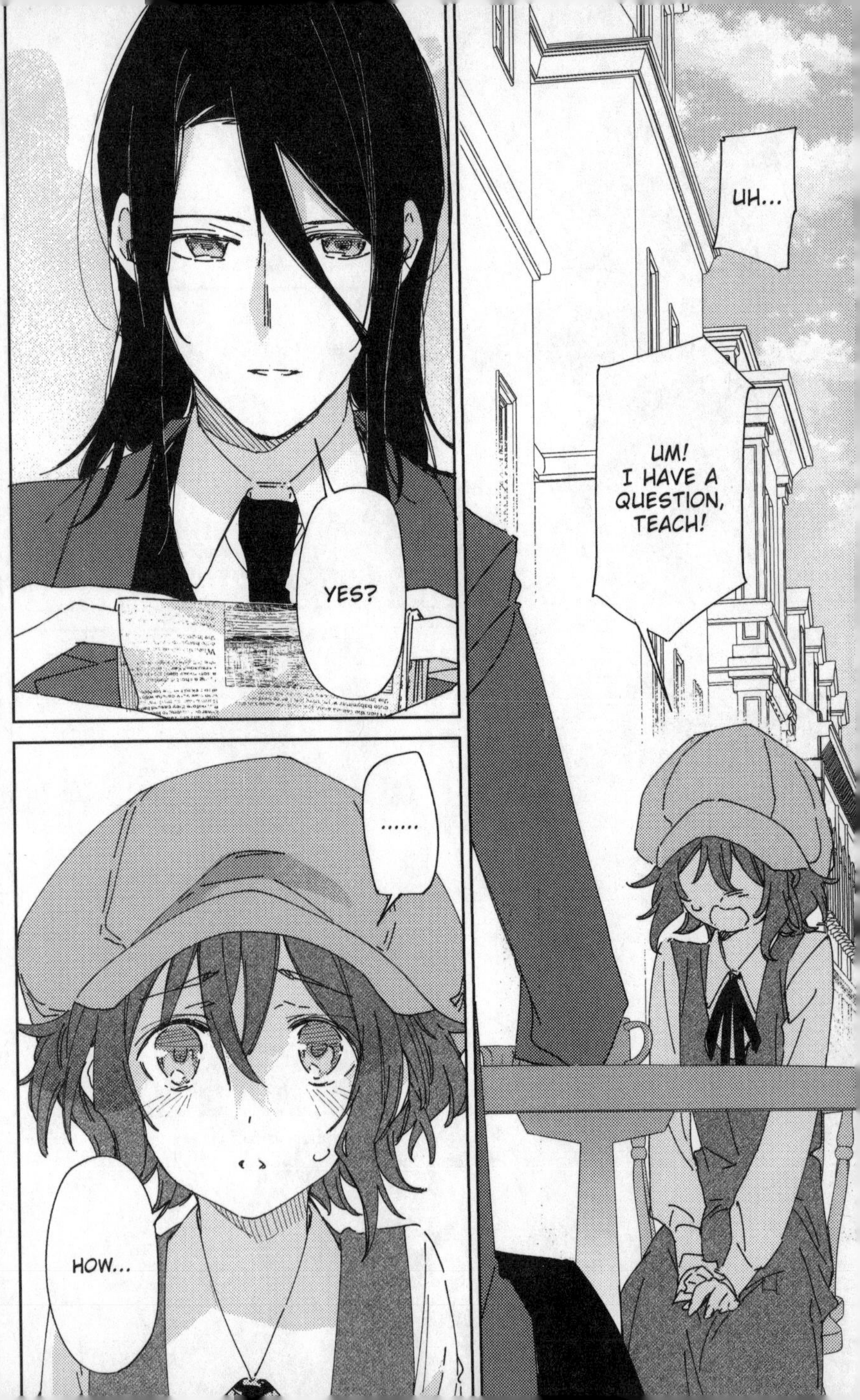
UH...
UM! I HAVE A QUESTION, TEACH!
YES?
......
HOW...

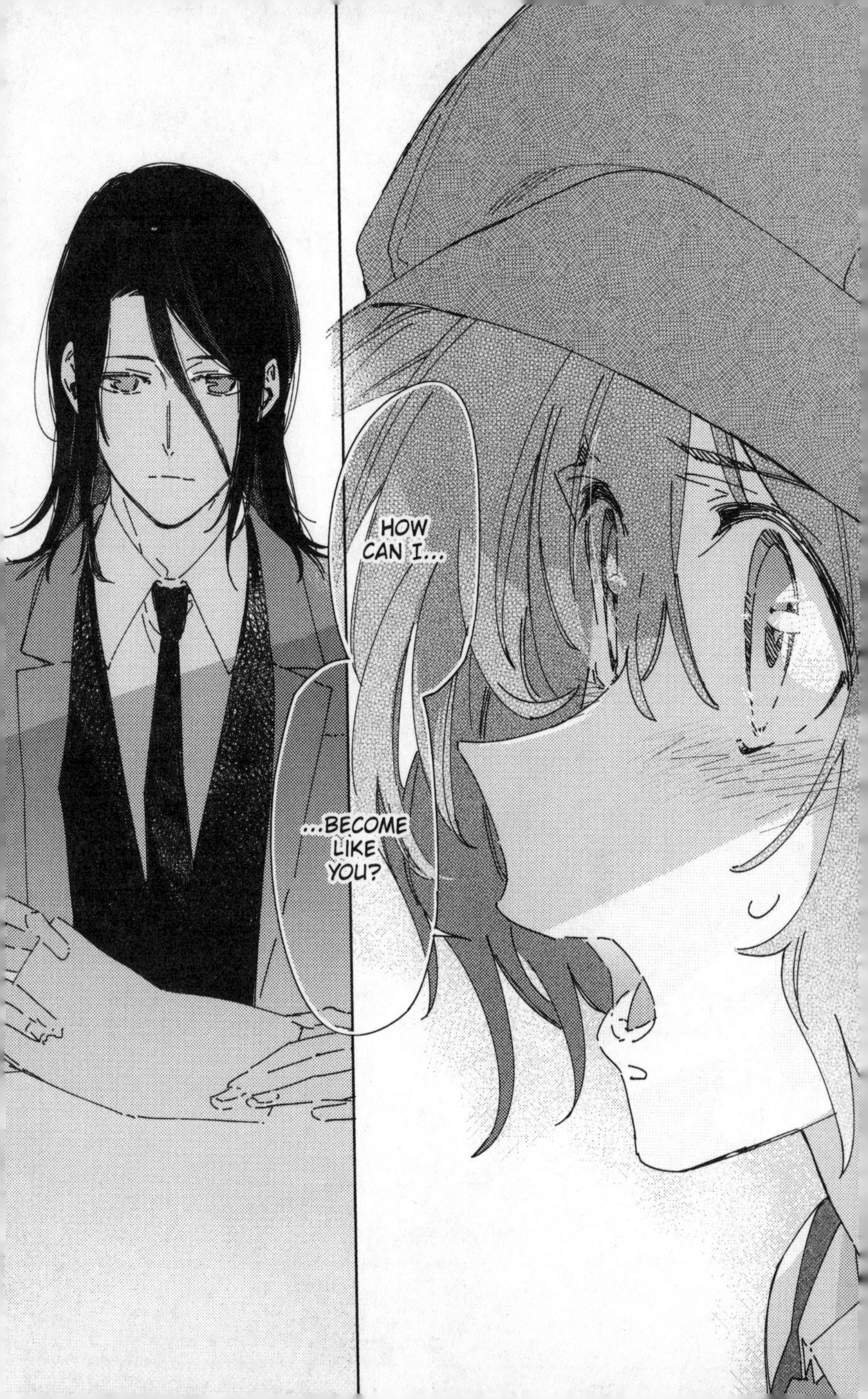
HOW CAN I...
...BECOME LIKE YOU?

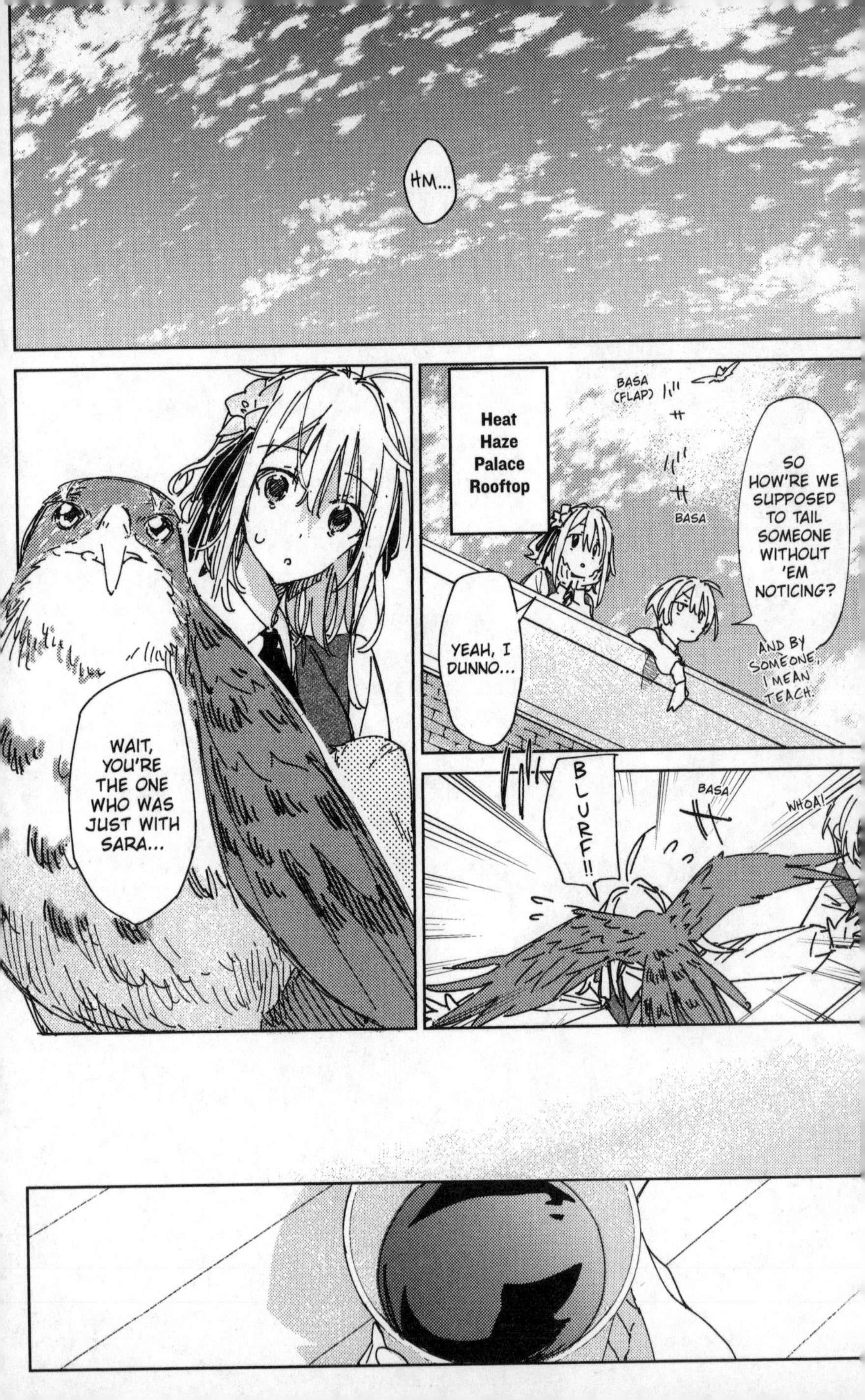
HM...
Heat Haze Palace Rooftop
BASA (FLAP)
BASA
SO HOW'RE WE SUPPOSED TO TAIL SOMEONE WITHOUT 'EM NOTICING?
AND BY SOMEONE, I MEAN TEACH.
YEAH, I DUNNO...
BASA
WHOA!
BLURF!!
WAIT, YOU'RE THE ONE WHO WAS JUST WITH SARA...

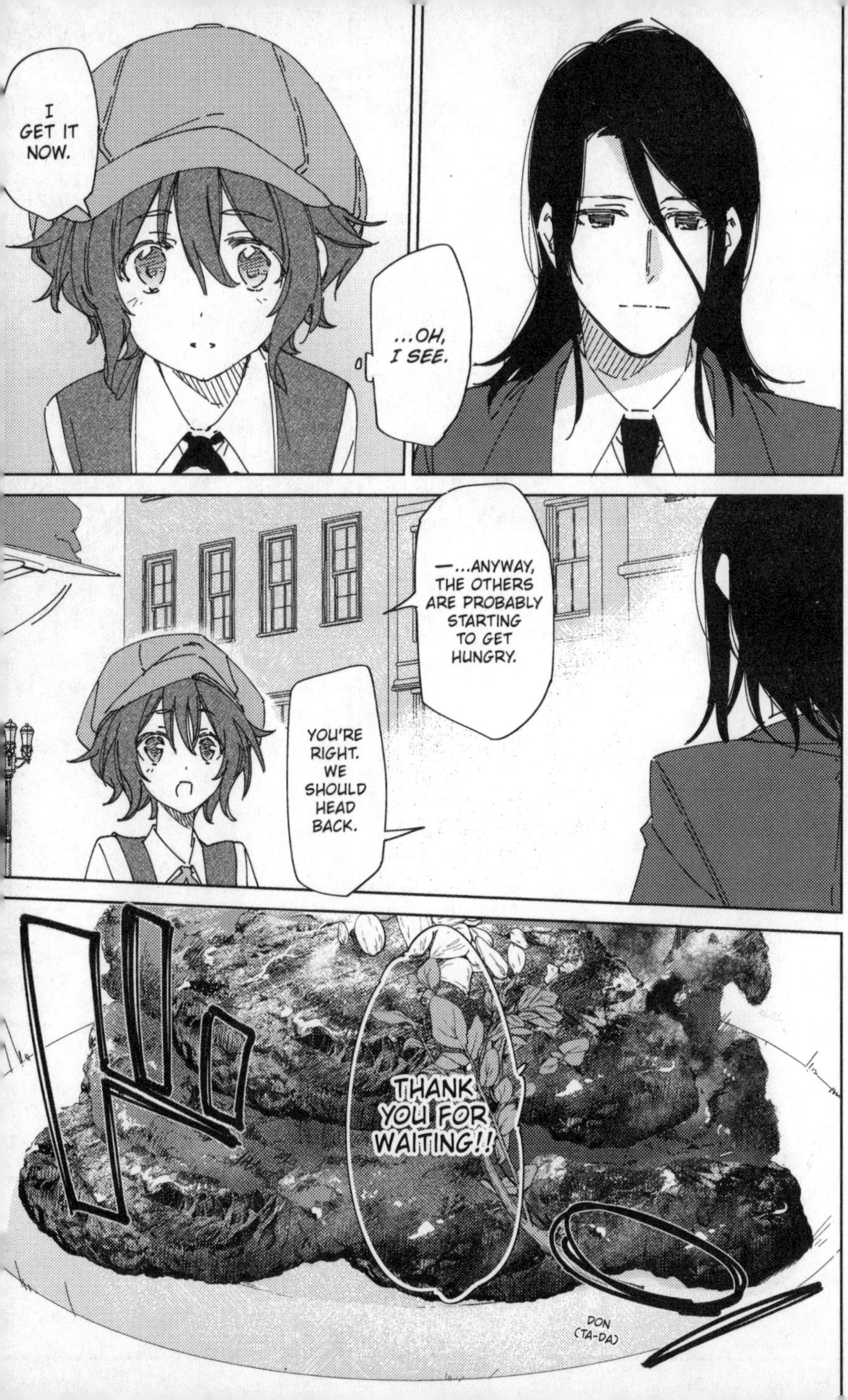
...OH, I SEE.
I GET IT NOW.
—...ANYWAY, THE OTHERS ARE PROBABLY STARTING TO GET HUNGRY.
YOU'RE RIGHT. WE SHOULD HEAD BACK.
THANK YOU FOR WAITING!!
DON (TA-DA)

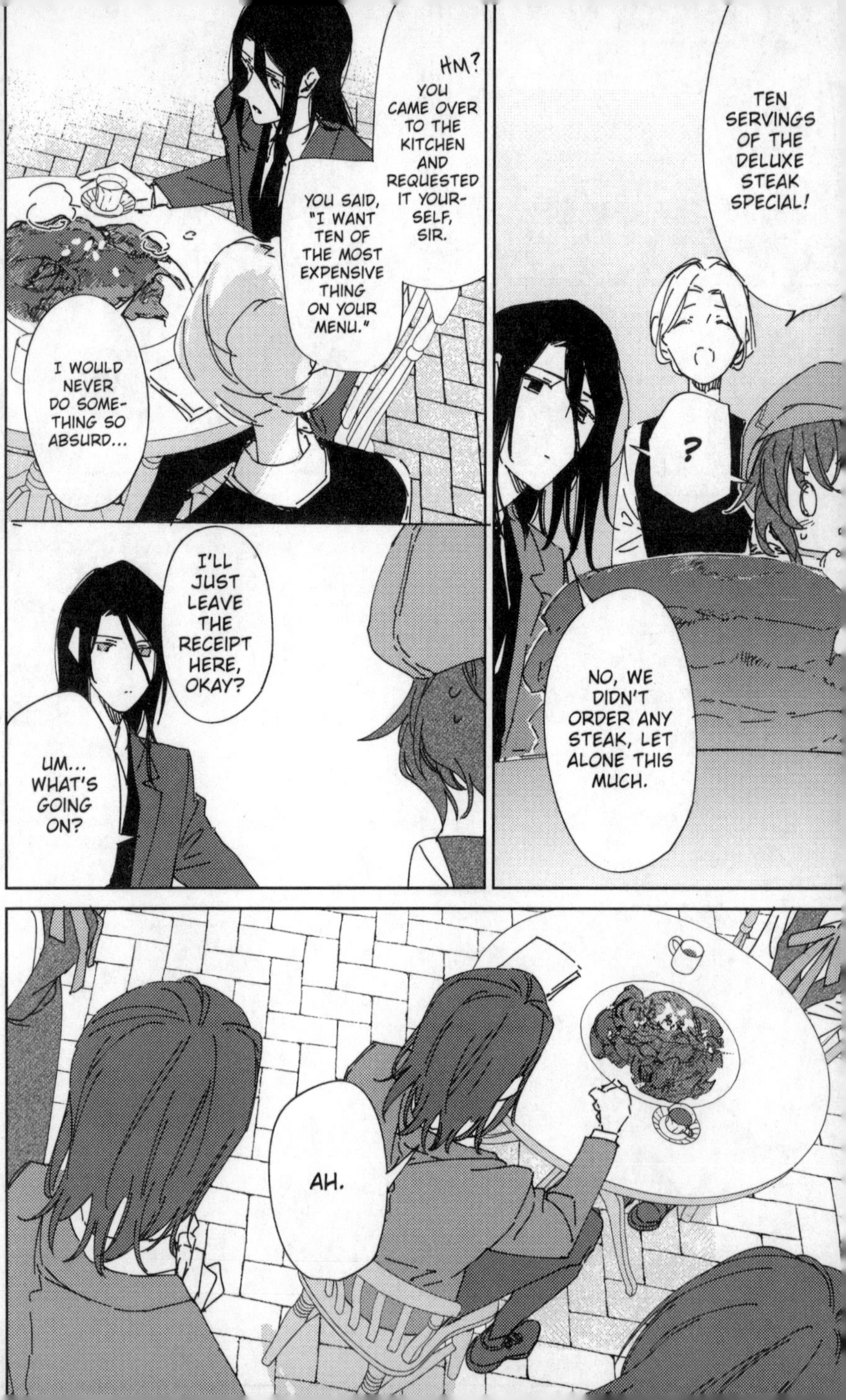
TEN SERVINGS OF THE DELUXE STEAK SPECIAL!
?
NO, WE DIDN'T ORDER ANY STEAK, LET ALONE THIS MUCH.
HM?
YOU CAME OVER TO THE KITCHEN AND REQUESTED IT YOURSELF, SIR.
YOU SAID, "I WANT TEN OF THE MOST EXPENSIVE THING ON YOUR MENU."
I WOULD NEVER DO SOMETHING SO ABSURD...
I'LL JUST LEAVE THE RECEIPT HERE, OKAY?
UM... WHAT'S GOING ON?
AH.

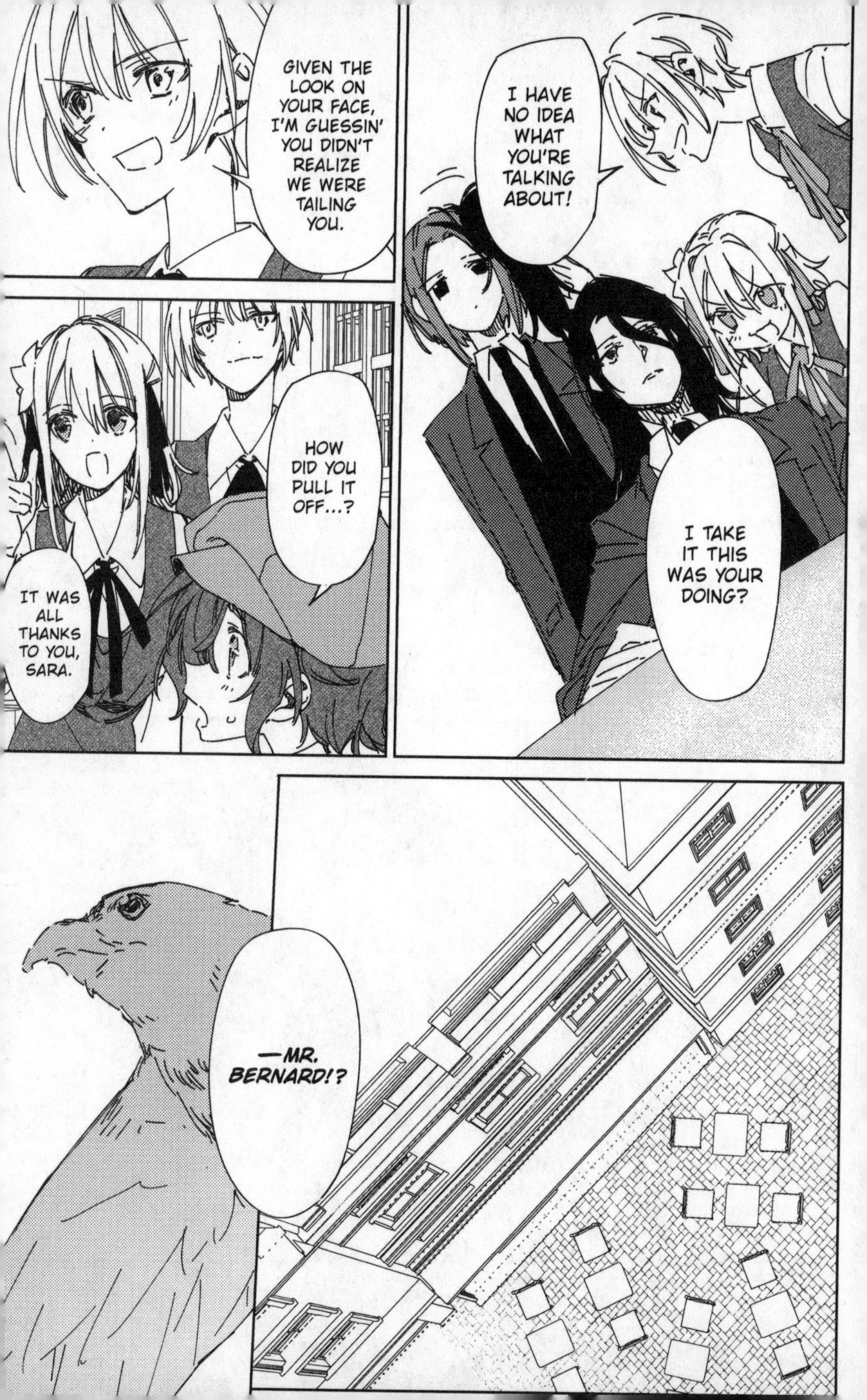
I HAVE NO IDEA WHAT YOU'RE TALKING ABOUT!
I TAKE IT THIS WAS YOUR DOING?
GIVEN THE LOOK ON YOUR FACE, I'M GUESSIN' YOU DIDN'T REALIZE WE WERE TAILING YOU.
HOW DID YOU PULL IT OFF...?
IT WAS ALL THANKS TO YOU, SARA.
—MR. BERNARD!?

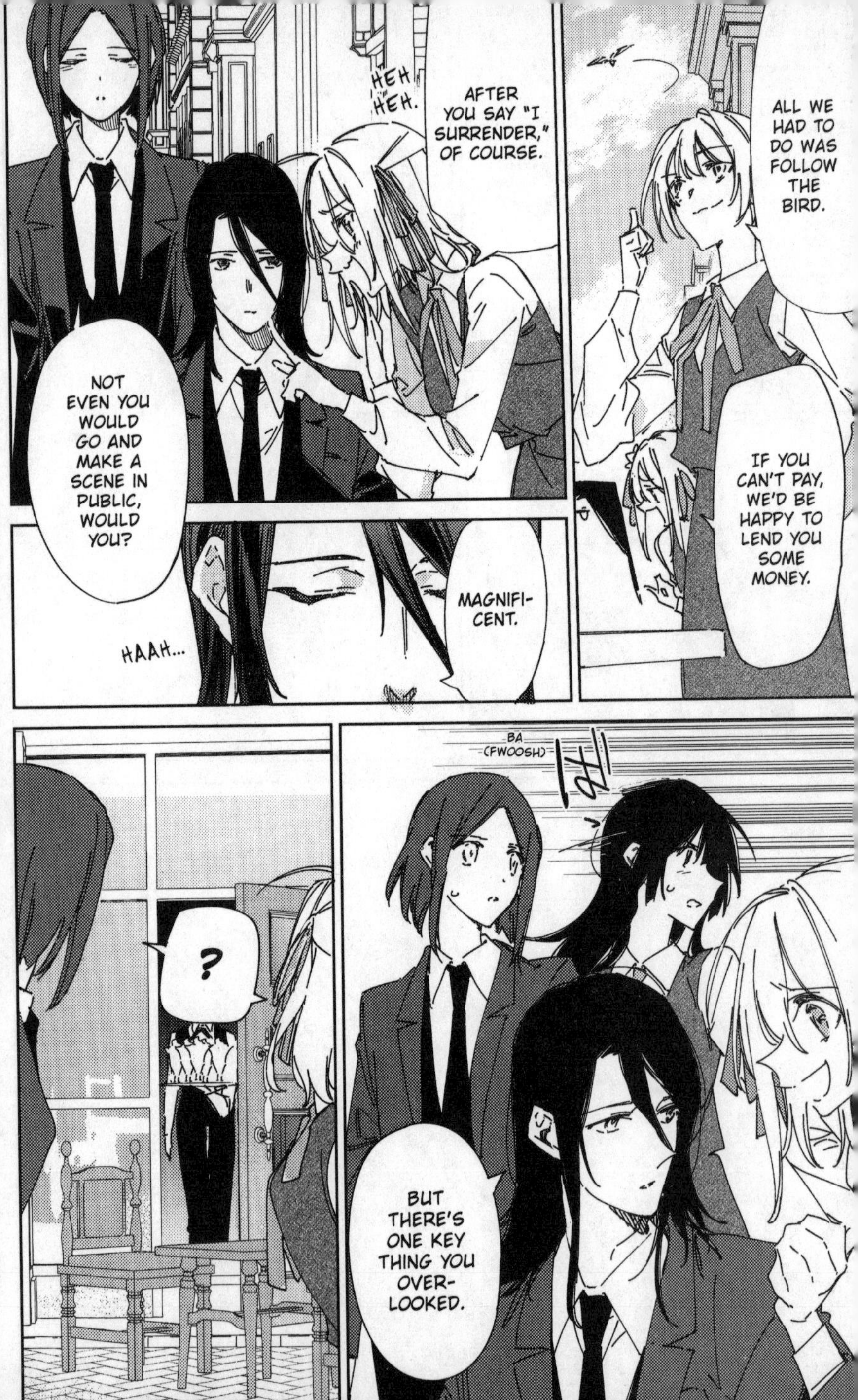
ALL WE HAD TO DO WAS FOLLOW THE BIRD.
IF YOU CAN'T PAY, WE'D BE HAPPY TO LEND YOU SOME MONEY.
HEH HEH.
AFTER YOU SAY "I SURRENDER," OF COURSE.
NOT EVEN YOU WOULD GO AND MAKE A SCENE IN PUBLIC, WOULD YOU?
MAGNIFI-CENT.
HAAH...
BA (FWOOSH)
!?
BUT THERE'S ONE KEY THING YOU OVER-LOOKED.
?

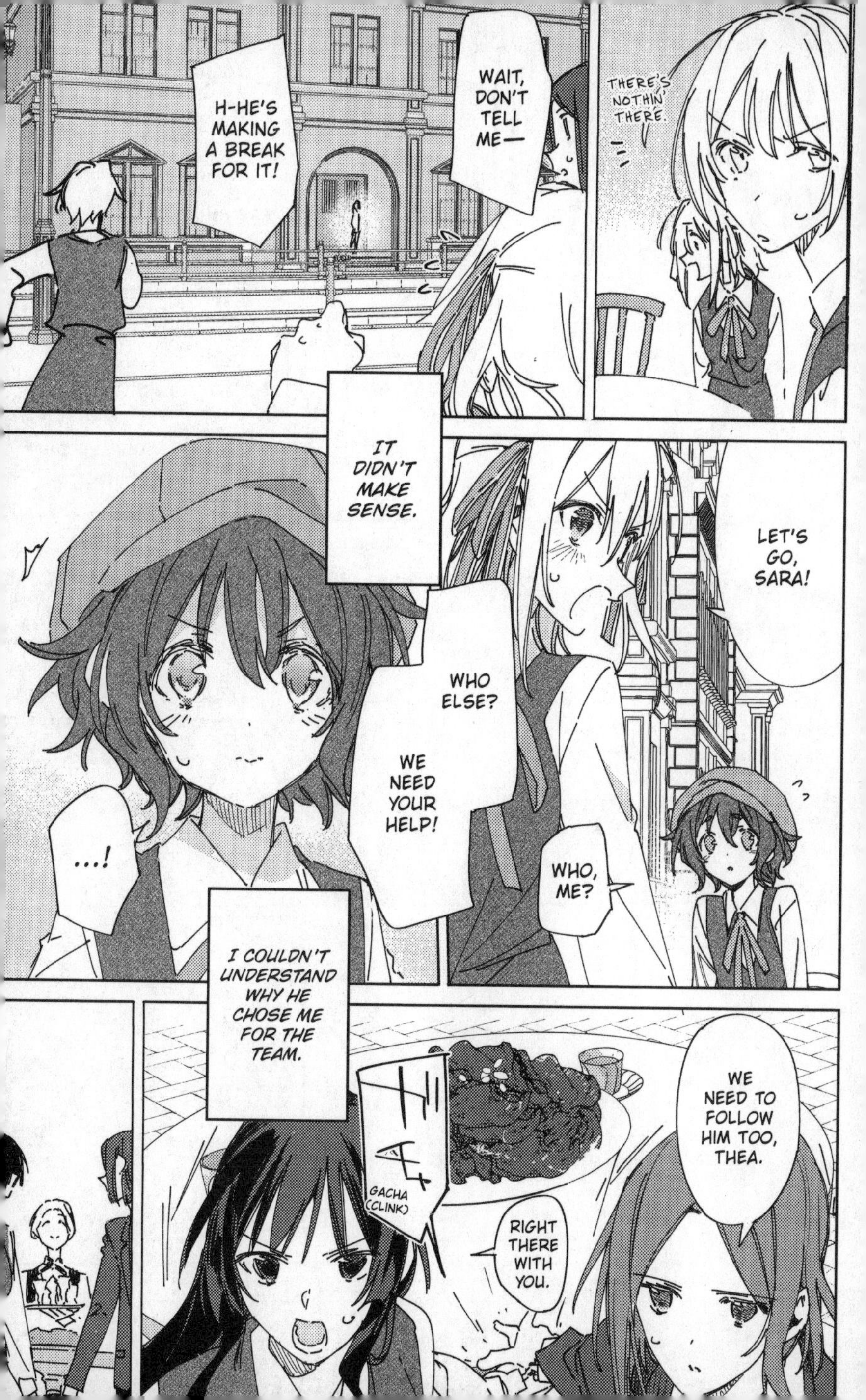
THERE'S NOTHIN' THERE.
WAIT, DON'T TELL ME—
H-HE'S MAKING A BREAK FOR IT!
LET'S GO, SARA!
IT DIDN'T MAKE SENSE.
WHO, ME?
WHO ELSE?
WE NEED YOUR HELP!
...!
I COULDN'T UNDERSTAND WHY HE CHOSE ME FOR THE TEAM.
WE NEED TO FOLLOW HIM TOO, THEA.
GACHA (CLINK)
RIGHT THERE WITH YOU.

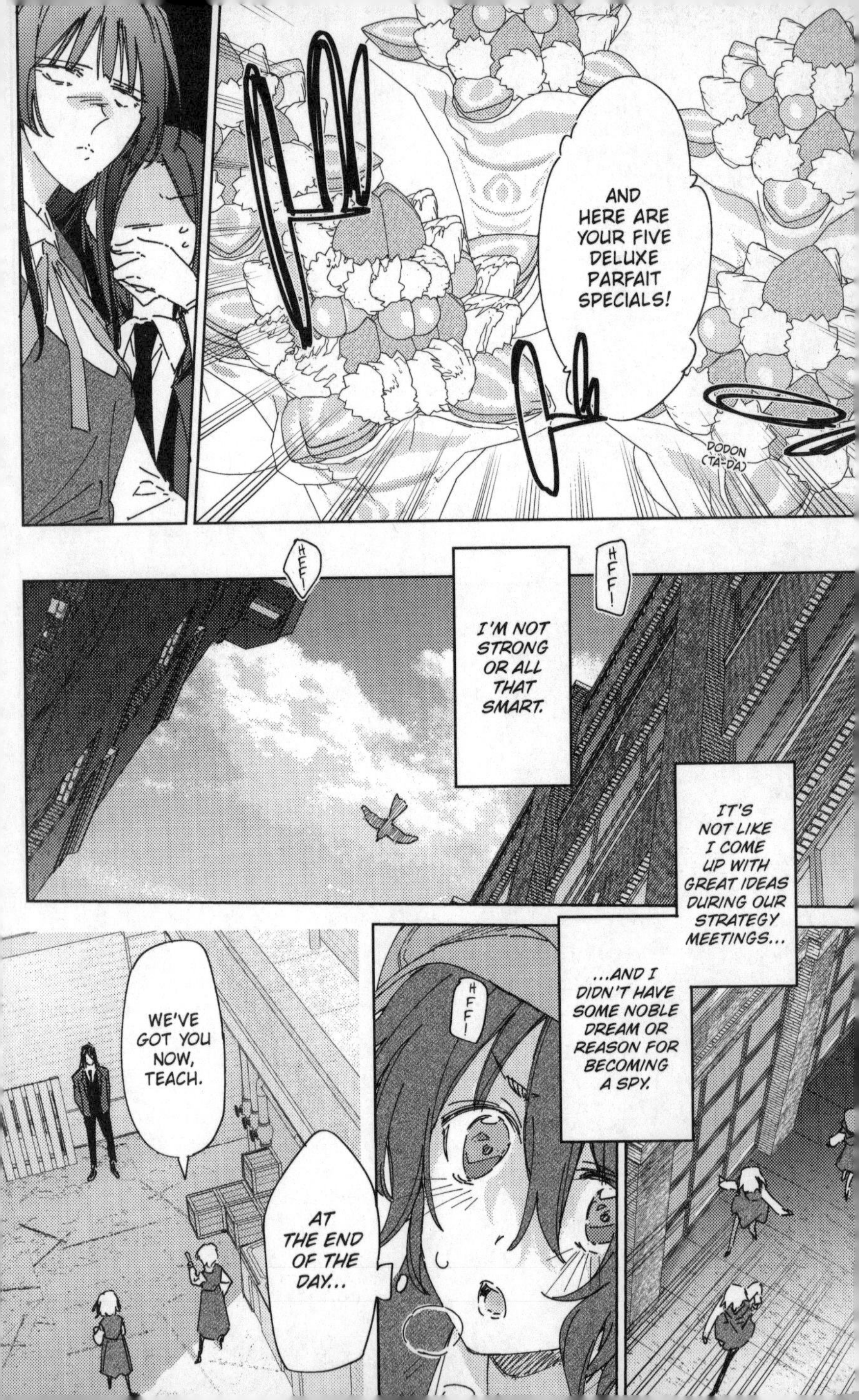
AND HERE ARE YOUR FIVE DELUXE PARFAIT SPECIALS!
DODON (TA-DA)
HFF!
I'M NOT STRONG OR ALL THAT SMART.
HFF!
IT'S NOT LIKE I COME UP WITH GREAT IDEAS DURING OUR STRATEGY MEETINGS...
...AND I DIDN'T HAVE SOME NOBLE DREAM OR REASON FOR BECOMING A SPY.
HFF!
AT THE END OF THE DAY...
WE'VE GOT YOU NOW, TEACH.

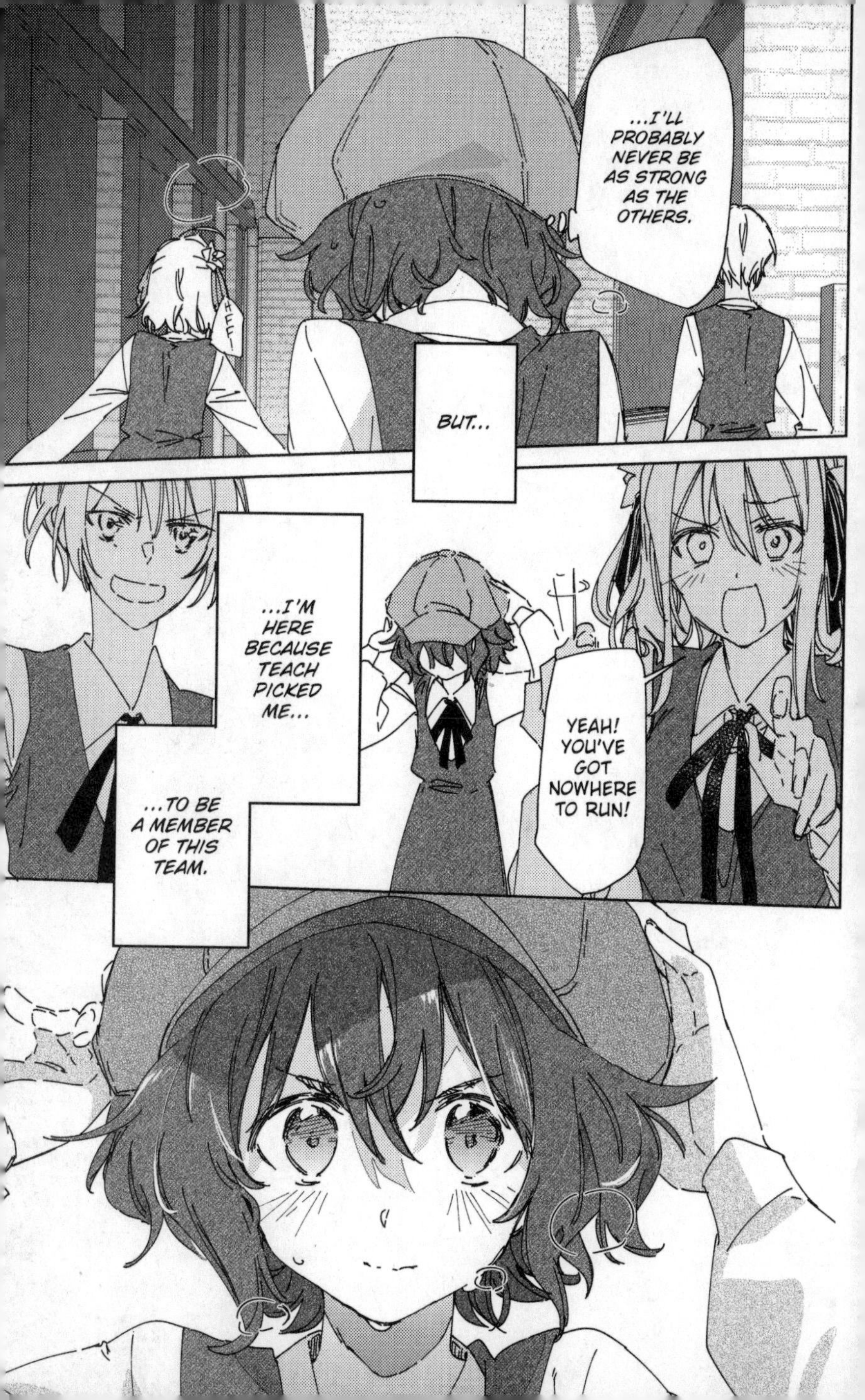
...I'LL PROBABLY NEVER BE AS STRONG AS THE OTHERS.
HFF!
BUT...
YEAH! YOU'VE GOT NOWHERE TO RUN!
...I'M HERE BECAUSE TEACH PICKED ME...
...TO BE A MEMBER OF THIS TEAM.

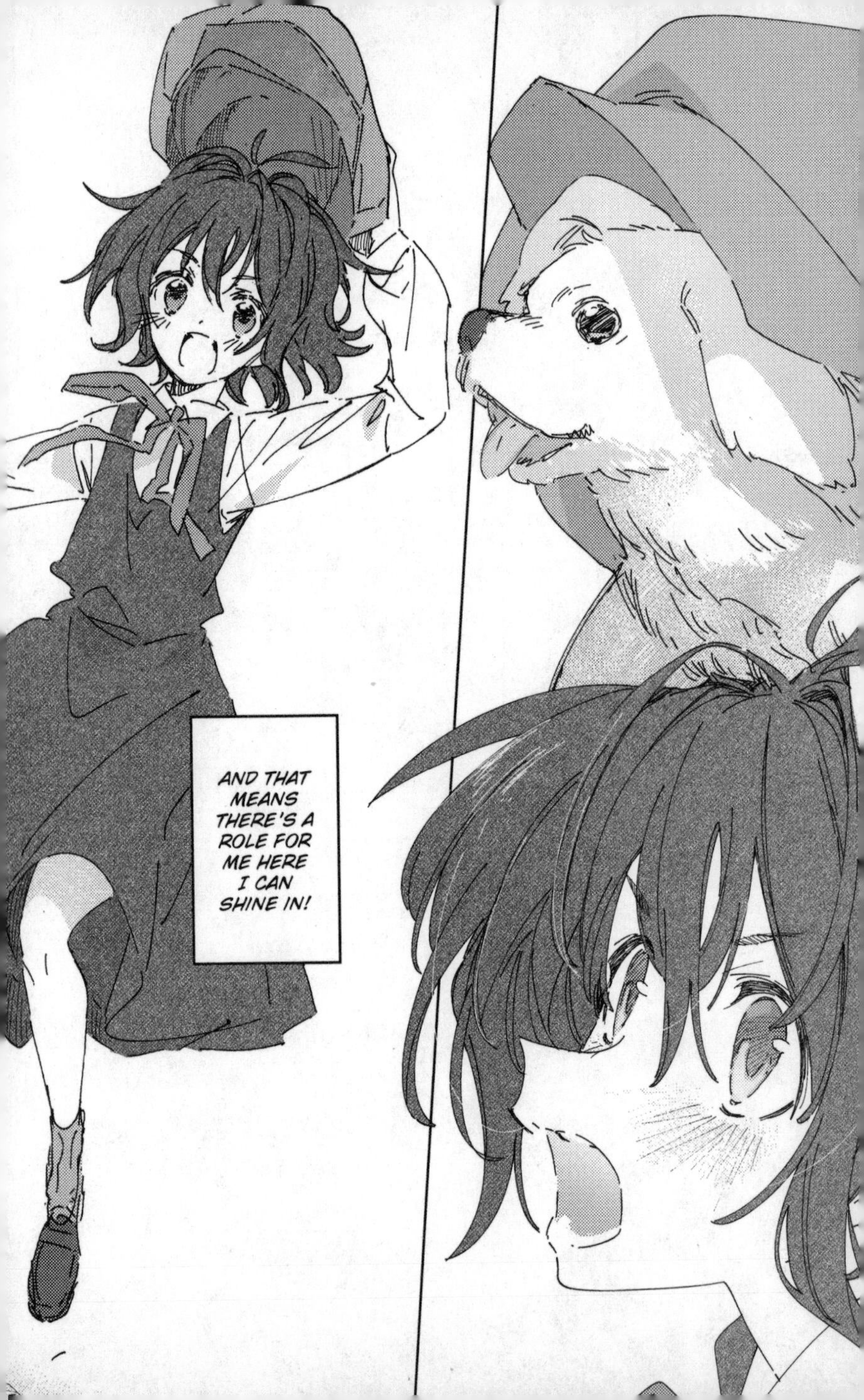
AND THAT MEANS THERE'S A ROLE FOR ME HERE I CAN SHINE IN!

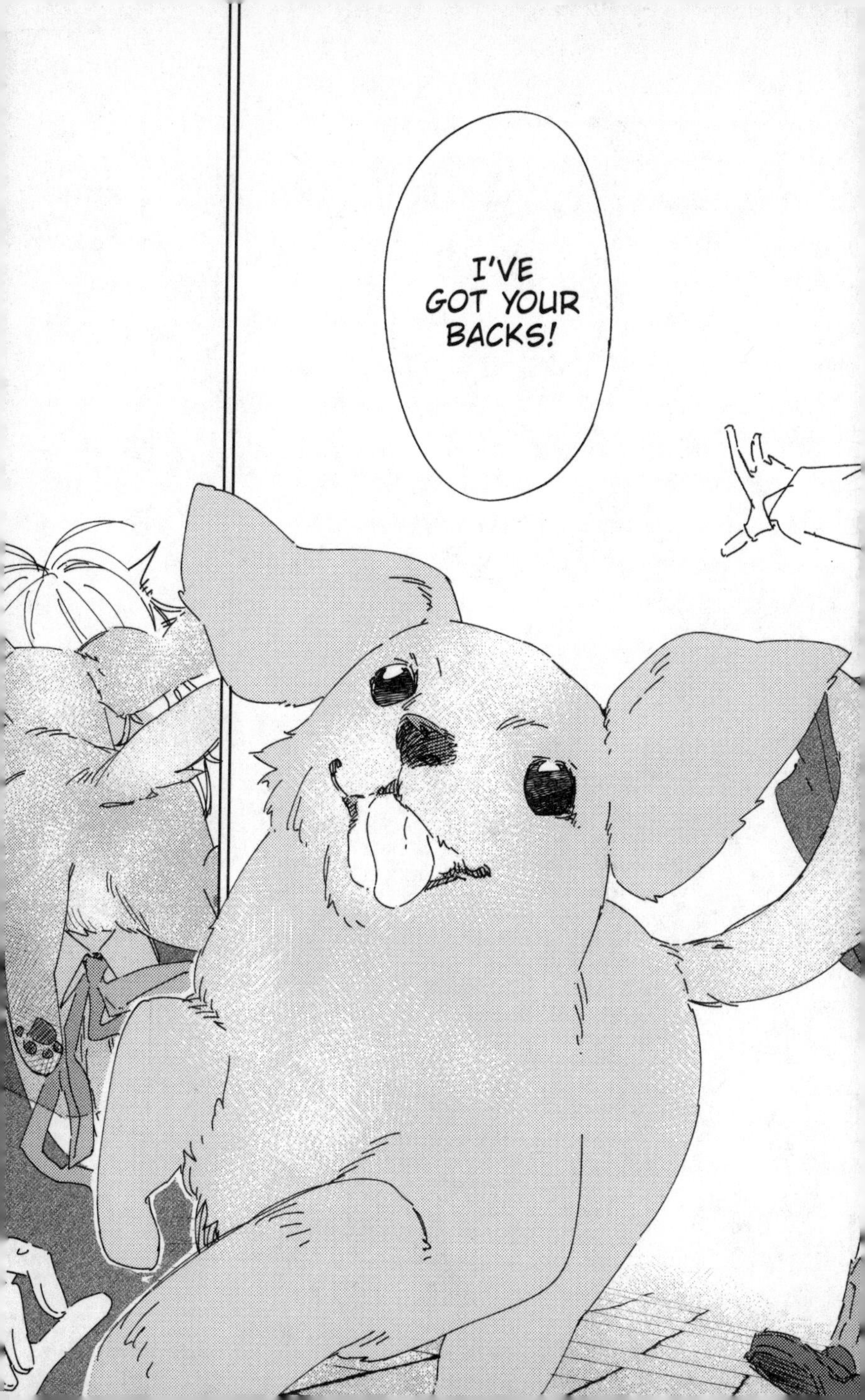
I'VE GOT YOUR BACKS!

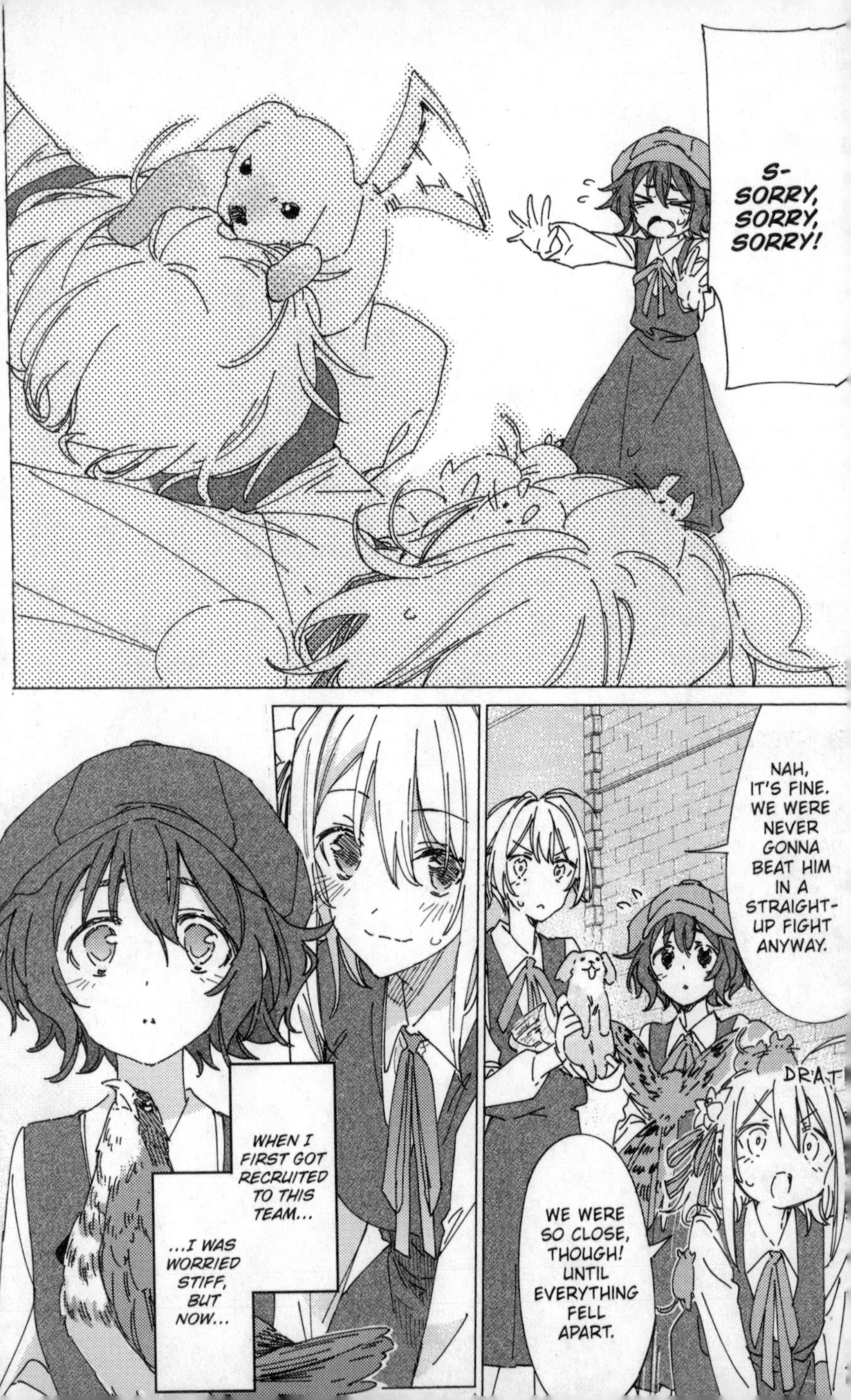
S- SORRY, SORRY, SORRY!
NAH, IT'S FINE. WE WERE NEVER GONNA BEAT HIM IN A STRAIGHT-UP FIGHT ANYWAY.
DRAT
WE WERE SO CLOSE, THOUGH! UNTIL EVERYTHING FELL APART.
WHEN I FIRST GOT RECRUITED TO THIS TEAM...
...I WAS WORRIED STIFF, BUT NOW...

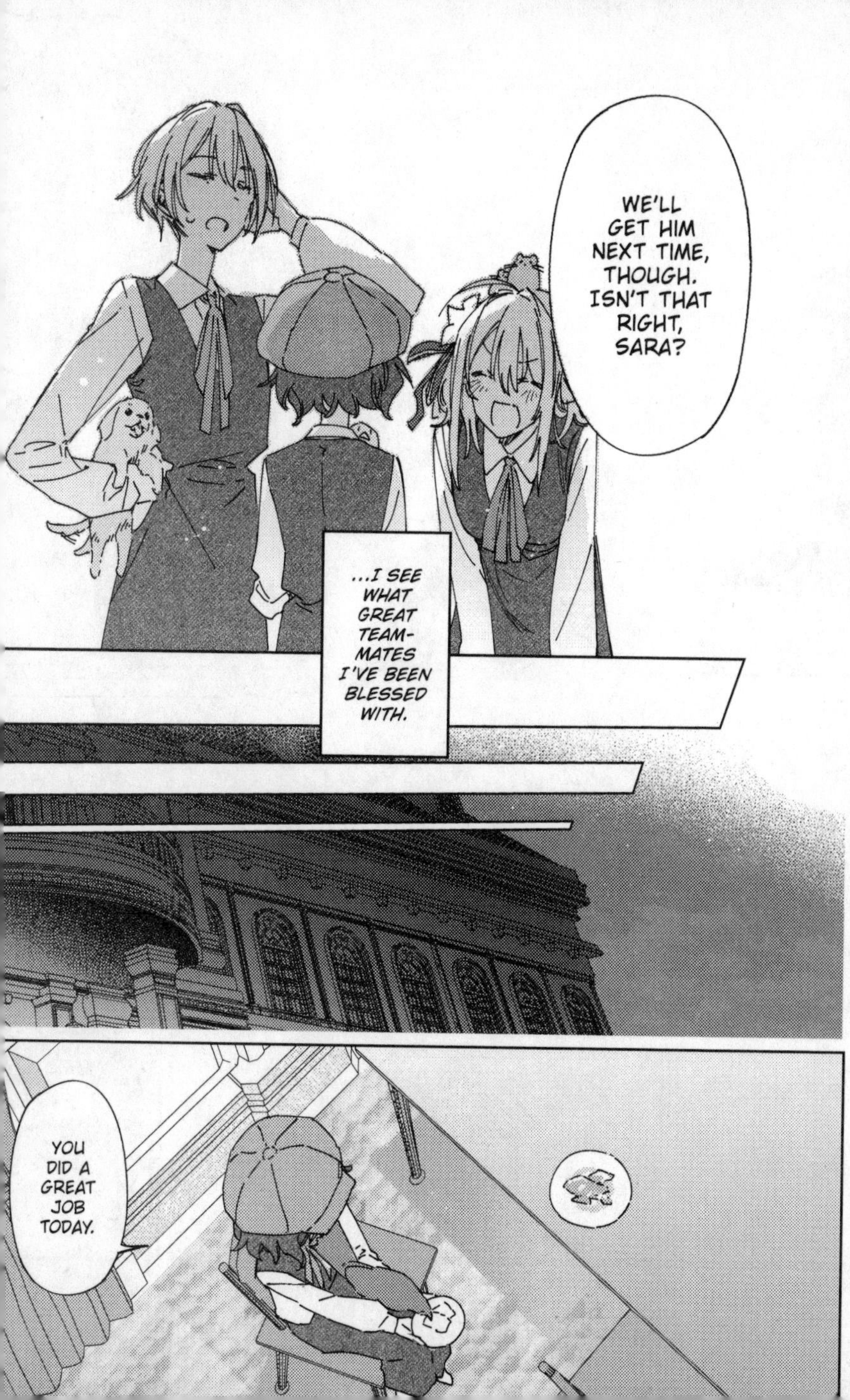
WE'LL GET HIM NEXT TIME, THOUGH. ISN'T THAT RIGHT, SARA?
...I SEE WHAT GREAT TEAM-MATES I'VE BEEN BLESSED WITH.
YOU DID A GREAT JOB TODAY.

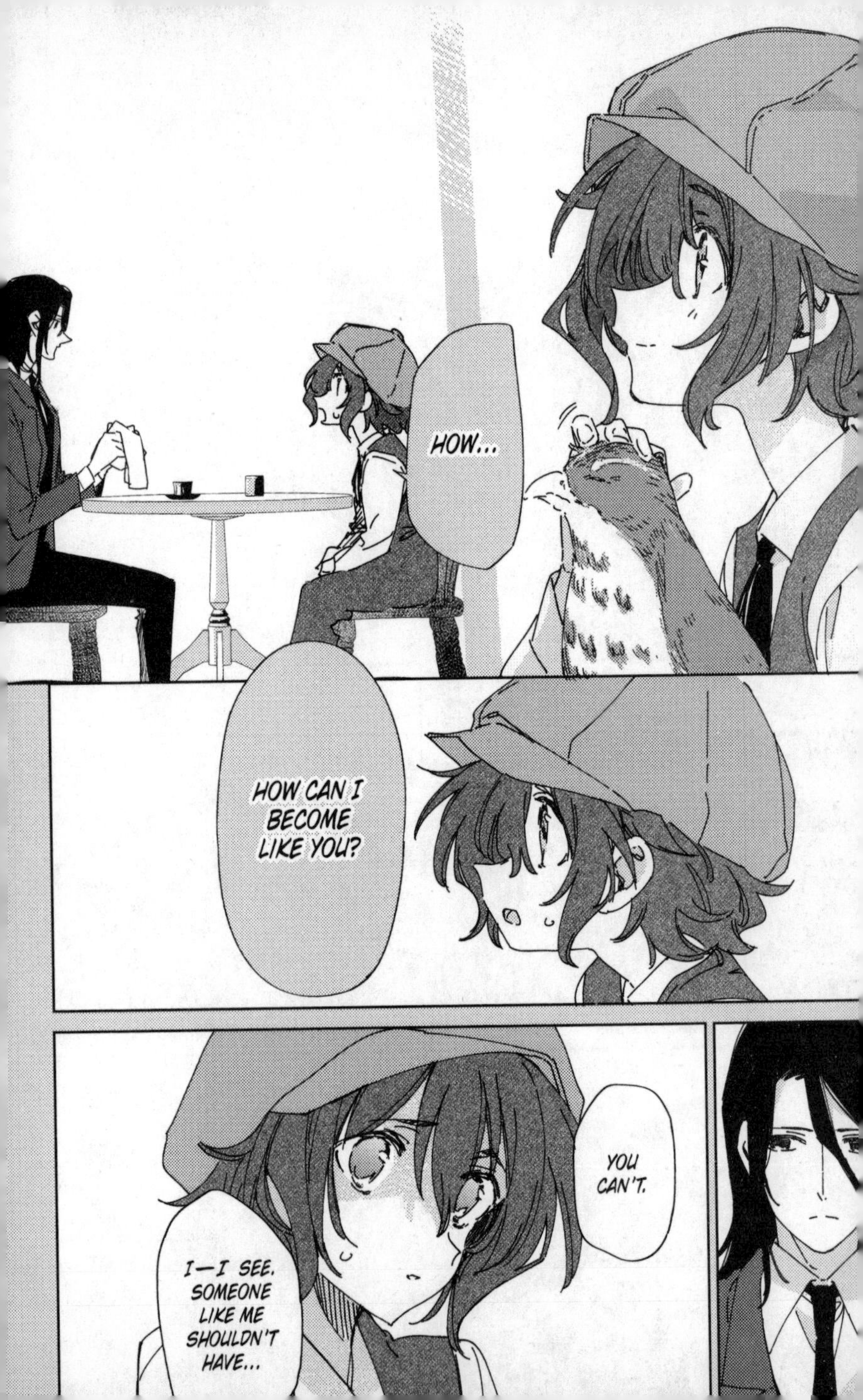
HOW...
HOW CAN I BECOME LIKE YOU?
YOU CAN'T.
I—I SEE. SOMEONE LIKE ME SHOULDN'T HAVE...

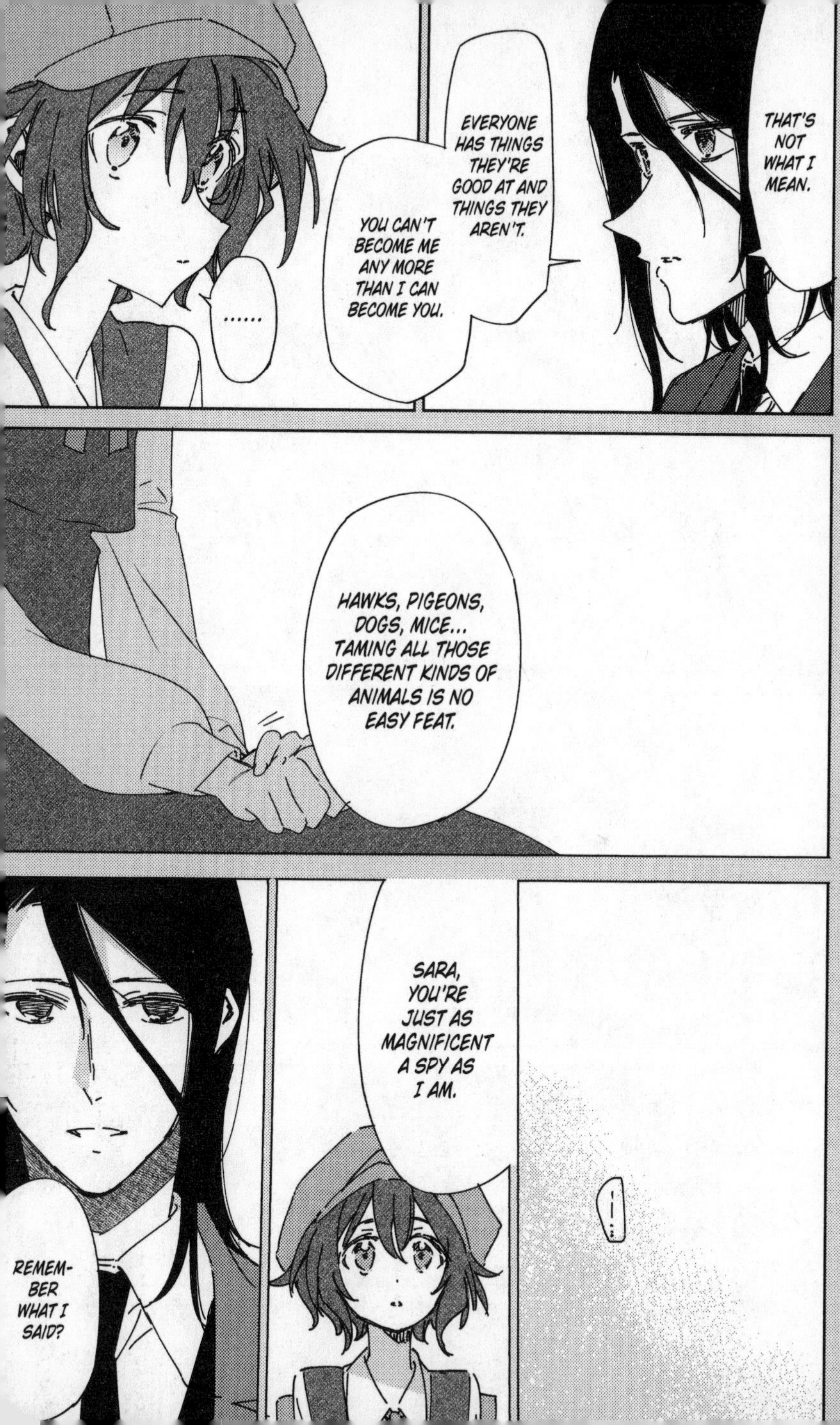
THAT'S NOT WHAT I MEAN.
EVERYONE HAS THINGS THEY'RE GOOD AT AND THINGS THEY AREN'T.
YOU CAN'T BECOME ME ANY MORE THAN I CAN BECOME YOU.
......
HAWKS, PIGEONS, DOGS, MICE... TAMING ALL THOSE DIFFERENT KINDS OF ANIMALS IS NO EASY FEAT.
!
SARA, YOU'RE JUST AS MAGNIFICENT A SPY AS I AM.
REMEM-BER WHAT I SAID?

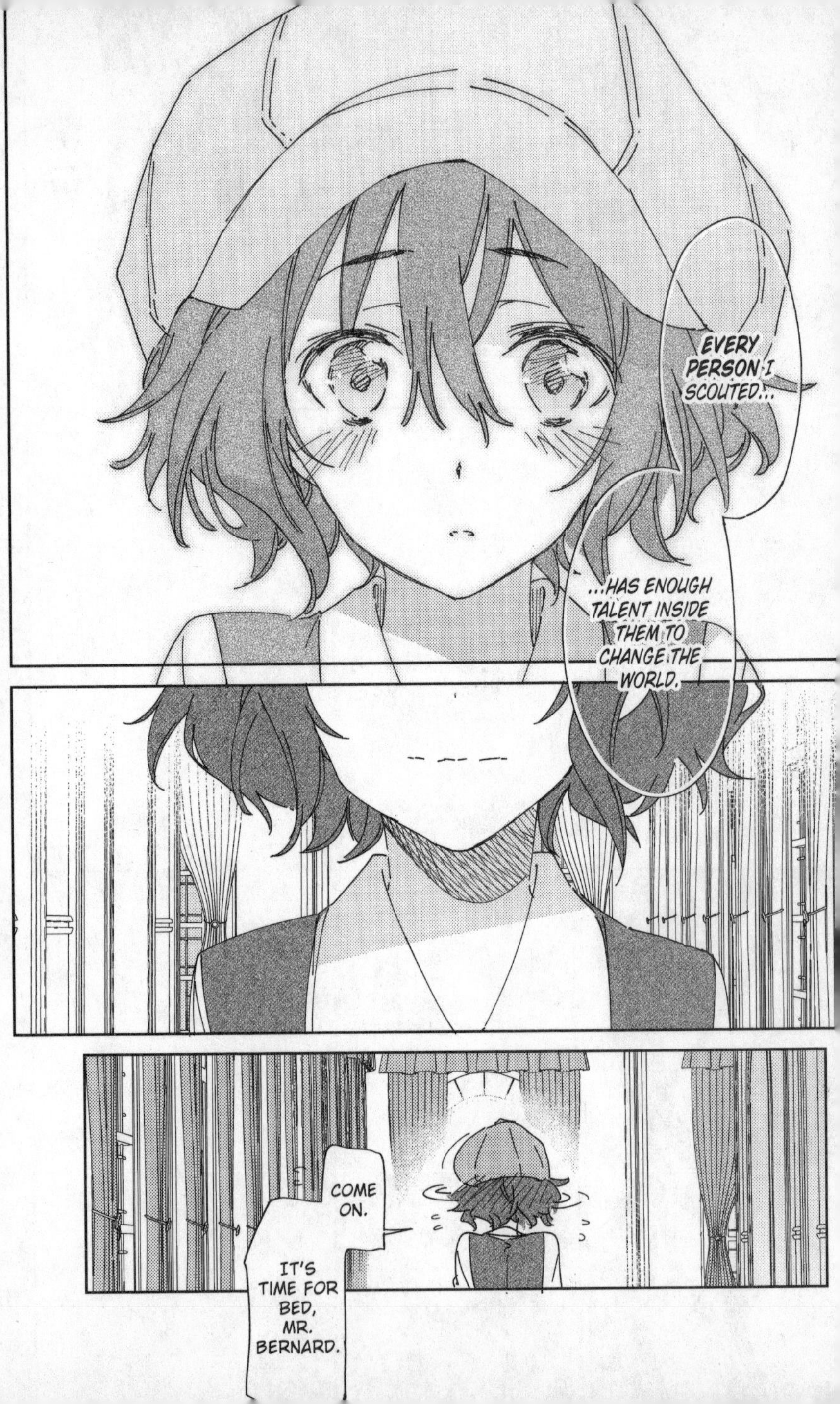
EVERY PERSON I SCOUTED...
...HAS ENOUGH TALENT INSIDE THEM TO CHANGE THE WORLD.
COME ON.
IT'S TIME FOR BED, MR. BERNARD.

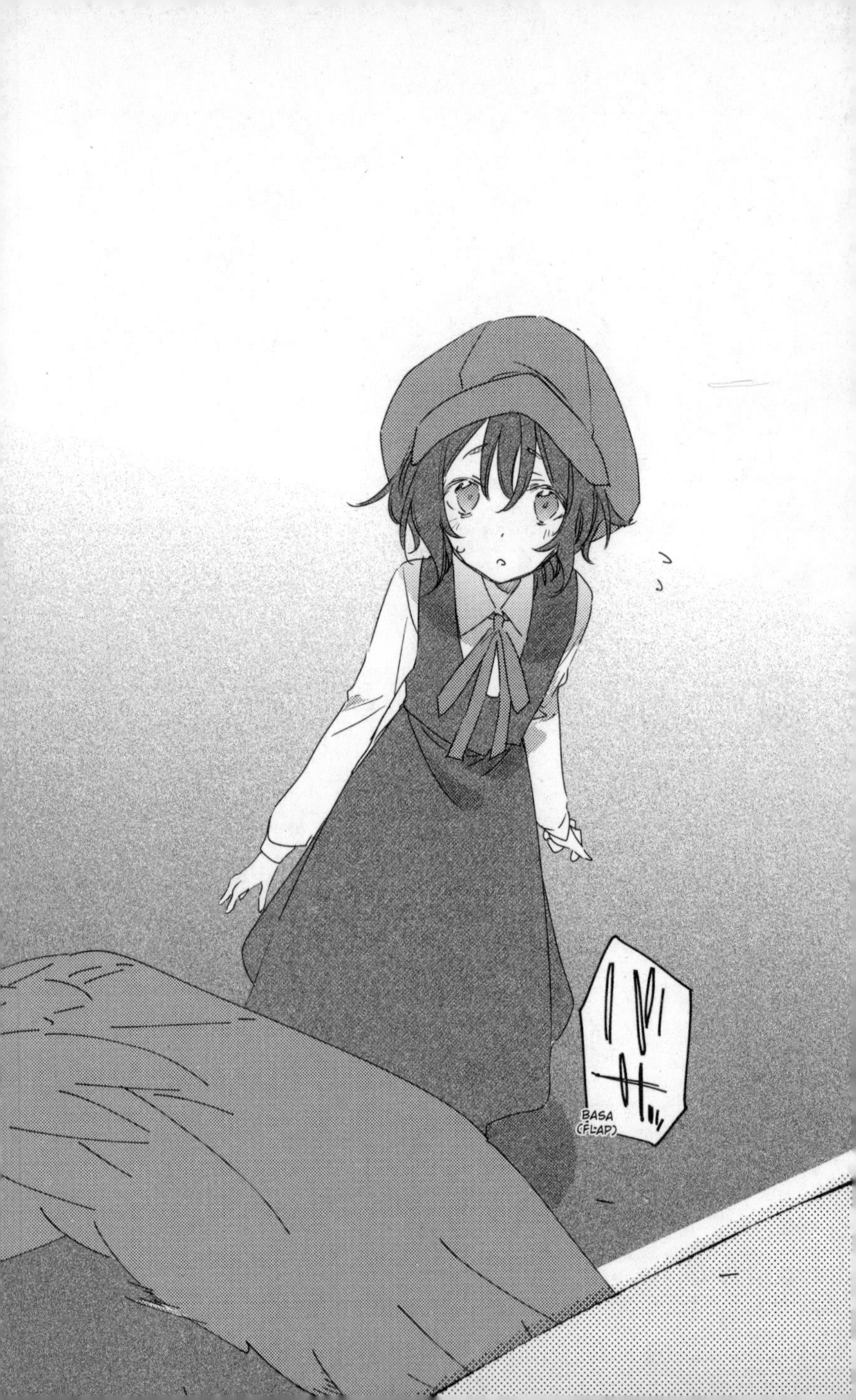
BASA
(FLAP)

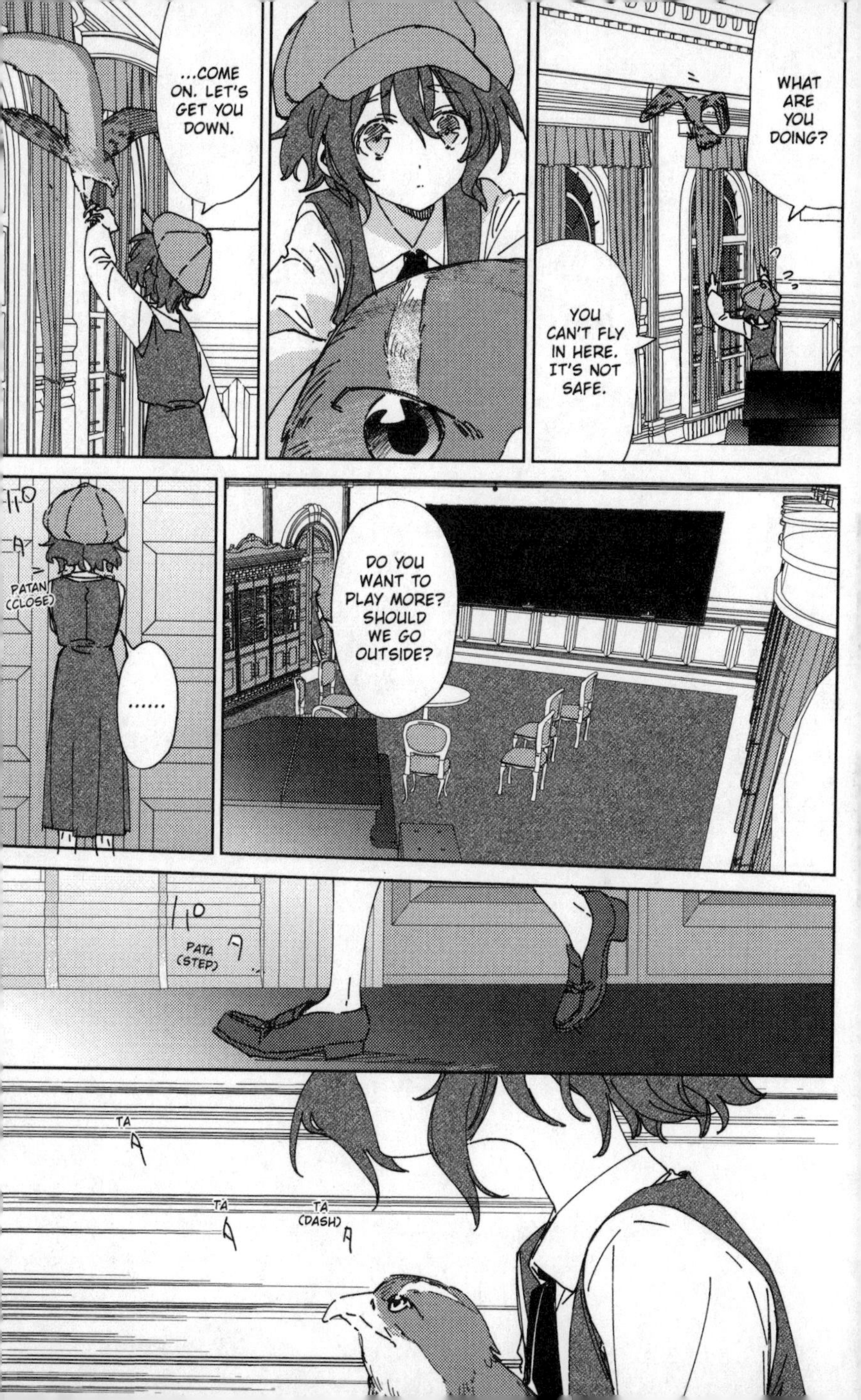
WHAT ARE YOU DOING?
YOU CAN'T FLY IN HERE. IT'S NOT SAFE.
...COME ON. LET'S GET YOU DOWN.
DO YOU WANT TO PLAY MORE? SHOULD WE GO OUTSIDE?
PATAN (CLOSE)
......
PATA (STEP)
TA
TA
TA (DASH)

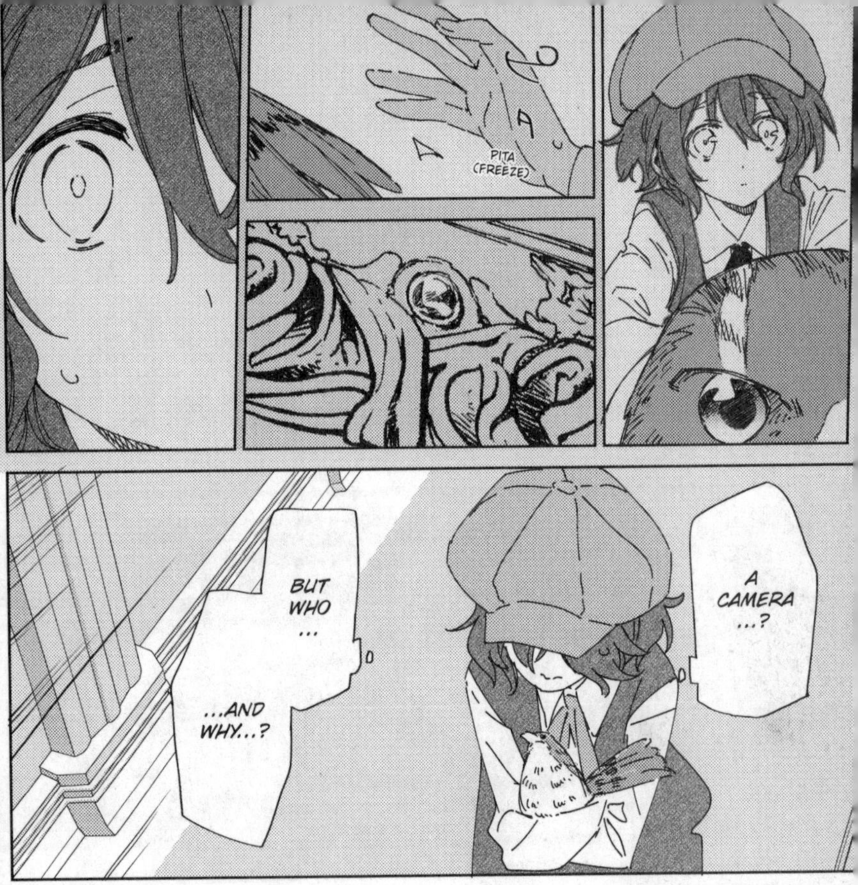
PITA (FREEZE)
A CAMERA ...?
BUT WHO ...
...AND WHY...?

WHAT'S REALLY GOING ON HERE AT LAMPLIGHT —?

To be continued...

SPY
CLASSROOM

# AFTERWORD

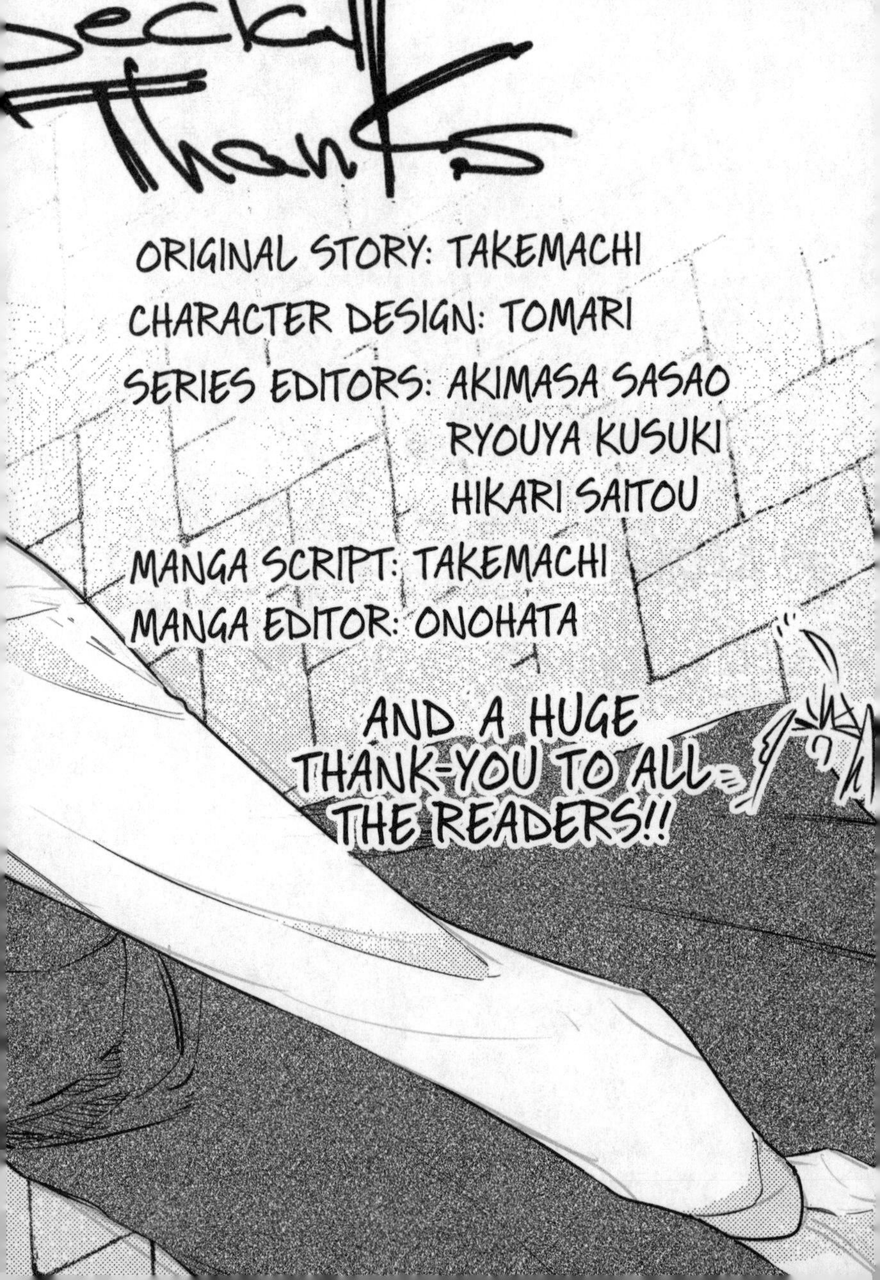
pecial Thanks
ORIGINAL STORY: TAKEMACHI
CHARACTER DESIGN: TOMARI
SERIES EDITORS: AKIMASA SASAO
RYOUYA KUSUKI
HIKARI SAITOU
MANGA SCRIPT: TAKEMACHI
MANGA EDITOR: ONOHATA
AND A HUGE THANK-YOU TO ALL THE READERS!!

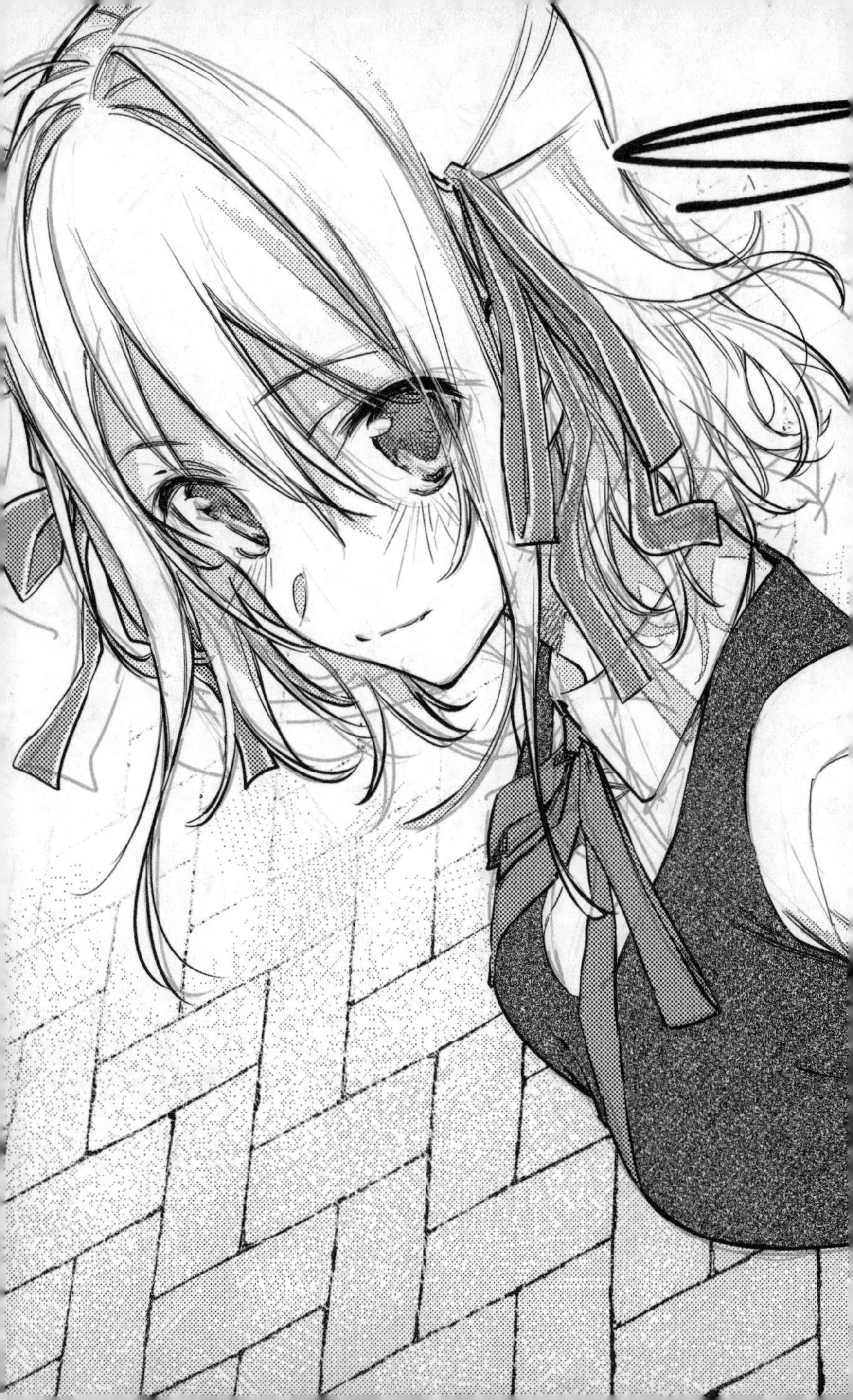

WHY WERE THE GIRLS RECRUITED?
LOOK AT ME...
WILL THEY BE ABLE TO BEAT KLAUS, THE GREATEST SPY IN THE WORLD?

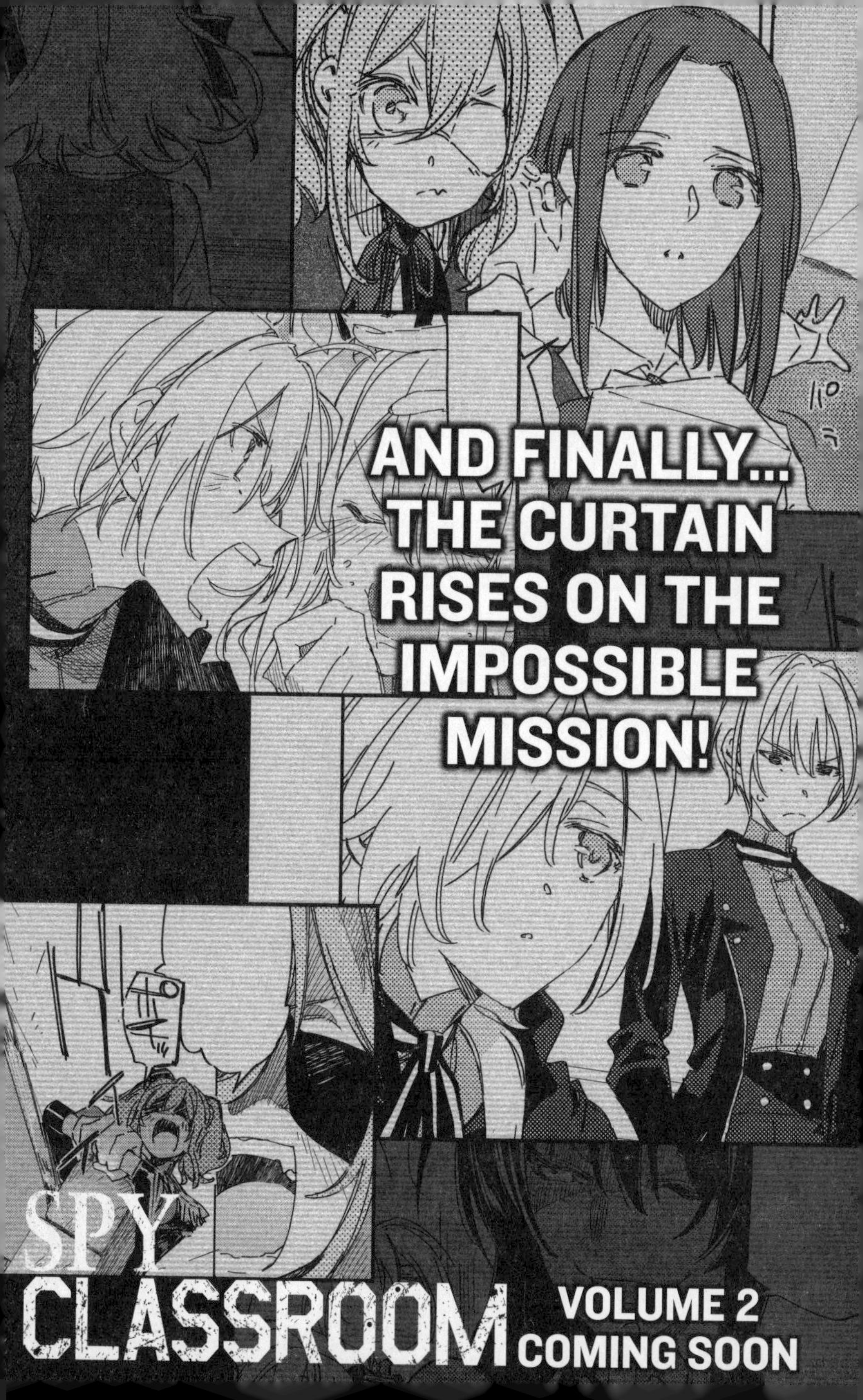
AND FINALLY... THE CURTAIN RISES ON THE IMPOSSIBLE MISSION!
SPY CLASSROOM
VOLUME 2 COMING SOON

# The Detective Is Already Dead

## When the story begins without its hero

Kimihiko Kimizuka has always been a magnet for trouble and intrigue. For as long as he can remember, he's been stumbling across murder scenes or receiving mysterious attaché cases to transport. When he met Siesta, a brilliant detective fighting a secret war against an organization of pseudohumans, he couldn't resist the call to become her assistant and join her on an epic journey across the world.

...Until a year ago, that is. Now he's returned to a relatively normal and tepid life, knowing the adventure must be over. After all, the detective is already dead.

**Volume 1 available wherever books are sold!**

# COMBATANTS WILL BE DISPATCHED!

# BUNGO STRAY DOGS

Volumes 1–20
available now

Yen Press

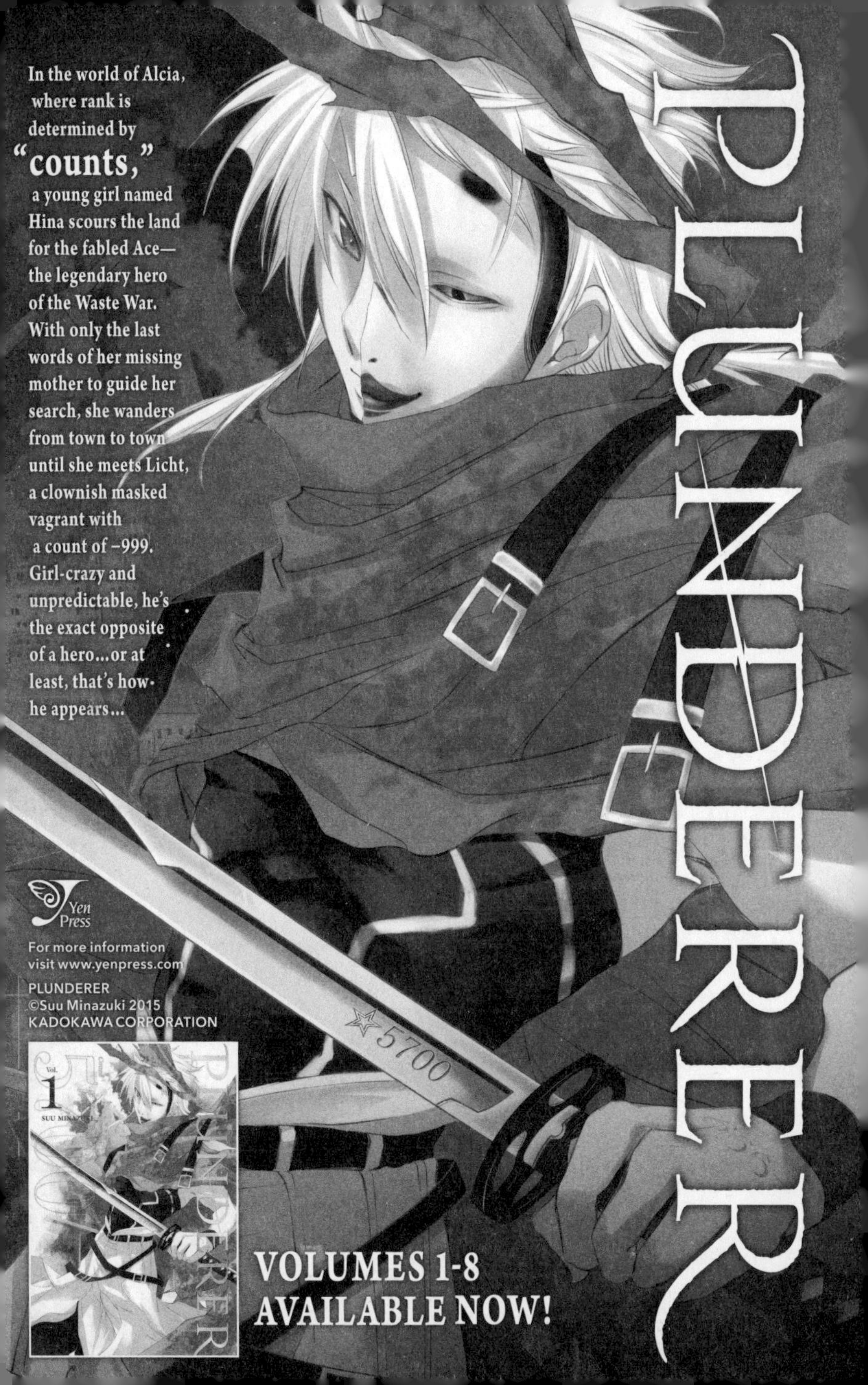

In the world of Alcia, where rank is determined by **"counts,"** a young girl named Hina scours the land for the fabled Ace—the legendary hero of the Waste War. With only the last words of her missing mother to guide her search, she wanders from town to town until she meets Licht, a clownish masked vagrant with a count of −999. Girl-crazy and unpredictable, he's the exact opposite of a hero...or at least, that's how he appears...

# PLUNDERER

## VOLUMES 1-8 AVAILABLE NOW!

# SPY CLASSROOM 01

**SeuKaname**

■ ORIGINAL STORY
**Takemachi**

■ CHARACTER DESIGN
**Tomari**

■ TRANSLATION **Nathaniel Hiroshi Thrasher**    ■ LETTERING **Arbash Mughal**

SPY KYOSHITSU Vol. 1
© SeuKaname 2020
© Takemachi, Tomari 2020
First published in Japan in 2020 by KADOKAWA CORPORATION, Tokyo.
English translation rights arranged with KADOKAWA CORPORATION, Tokyo
and Yen Press, LLC through Tuttle-Mori Agency, Inc.

English translation © 2022 by Yen Press, LLC

Yen Press
150 West 30th Street, 19th Floor
New York, NY 10001

Visit us at yenpress.com
facebook.com/yenpress
twitter.com/yenpress
yenpress.tumblr.com
instagram.com/yenpress

First Yen Press Edition: January 2022

Yen Press is an imprint of Yen Press, LLC.
The Yen Press name and logo are trademarks of Yen Press, LLC.

Library of Congress Control Number: 2021948867

ISBNs: 978-1-9753-3888-6 (paperback)
978-1-9753-3889-3 (ebook)

10 9 8 7 6 5 4 3 2 1

WOR

Printed in the United States of America